Urban Problems and
Public Policy Choices

edited by
Joel Bergsman
Howard L. Wiener

Published in cooperation with the
Washington Operations Research Council

The Praeger Special Studies program—utilizing the most modern and efficient book production techniques and a selective worldwide distribution network—makes available to the academic, government, and business communities significant, timely research in U.S. and international economic, social, and political development.

Urban Problems and Public Policy Choices

PRAEGER SPECIAL STUDIES IN U.S. ECONOMIC, SOCIAL, AND POLITICAL ISSUES

Praeger Publishers　　New York　Washington　London

Library of Congress Cataloging in Publication Data
Main entry under title:

Urban problems and public policy choices.

(Praeger special studies in U. S. economic, social, and political issues)
   1. Cities and towns—United States—Congresses.
I. Bergsman, Joel.   II. Wiener, Howard L.
HT123.U755   1975   301.36'3'0973   75-8400
ISBN   0-275-05860-3

PRAEGER PUBLISHERS
111 Fourth Avenue, New York, N.Y. 10003, U.S.A.

Published in the United States of America in 1975
by Praeger Publishers, Inc.

Printed in the United States of America

The urban crisis was ended, by presidential proclamation, several years ago. But poverty persists, much urban housing is still inadequate, pollution and congestion increase, and a whole gamut of services ranging from care for the aged to collection of garbage don't always get done very well.

Governments try to do something about these problems, with mixed results. Solutions—the word itself carries within it the seeds of failures—usually cost money, and they also may encounter political constraints at the polls and bureaucratic and institutional constraints within the agencies that are supposed to implement them. The nation needs programs designed to do the jobs for less money and in ways that can reduce political obstacles and change bureaucratic inertia into enthusiasm.

The chapters in this volume describe some of these problems and show part of the cutting edge of progress in the design, operation, and evaluation of urban social programs. The subjects range from highly abstract theoretical models of residential segregation and political bargaining within city governments, through analyses of the supply and demand for key urban services such as care for the aged, housing, and transportation, through the design of programs to improve the provision of these services, to descriptions of nitty-gritty experimental programs in education and drug addiction treatment. Evaluation, the equally crucial process of providing feedback after the programs are in operation, is also treated in several chapters. This range mirrors the process of program design—from basic study of underlying processes, through analysis of market behavior, design of the first experimental or pilot programs, to implementation and evaluation.

Taken as a whole, then, the chapters presented here describe by example the continuing process of designing public programs. They highlight the issues facing policy makers, the knowledge and analysis needed to support choices among alternative program designs, and the difficulties at the frontier of the state of this art. The analysts who contributed to this volume, and all their colleagues, are working now to make these studies obsolete. We only regret that the process doesn't go faster.

This volume originated as the proceedings of a symposium on urban growth and development, sponsored by the Washington Operations Research Council and The Urban Institute, held in Washington,

D.C., on April 16 and 17, 1973. The administrative and logistic aspects were the responsibility of the Symposium Committee, which included Paul Hughes, Frank Dahlhaus, Peyton Wynns, Misha Kadick, William Lindsay, and Donald Rosene. The success of the symposium was due in no small part to their diligence and efficiency and it is a pleasure to acknowledge with thanks their efforts. We also wish to thank Ellison Burton and Armand Weiss, WORC presidents during 1972-73 and 1973-74, respectively, and William Gorham, president of The Urban Institute, for their support.

Joel Bergsman
Program Chairman
Howard Wiener
WORC Symposium Chairman

LIST OF TABLES

LIST OF FIGURES

INTRODUCTION:
URBAN RESEARCH
AND POLICY MAKING

1

HOW POLICY
MAKERS LOOK AT
OPERATIONS RESEARCH
Clifford W. Graves

The rising interest in developing a national growth policy should be no surprise to most readers. The accepted conventional wisdom is that present growth patterns may be undesirable and that economic development and population growth are too unevenly distributed among regions of the country between urban and rural areas. This, in turn, is believed to increase the environmental and social problems of the cities, sap the strength of rural regions, and fail to correspond to the styles of living desired by many people. At the same time the growth patterns of the large urban areas continue to be physically distorted, wasteful of resources and urban infrastructure, governmentally fragmented, and socially divisive.

This "conventional wisdom" is being increasingly supported by census and other data that can be subjected to rigorous analysis. For instance:

- The biggest cities are growing bigger and the smallest are eroding further, making life more difficult and expensive in both.
- Metropolitan areas are growing, but almost two-thirds of all counties lost population between 1960 and 1970.
- Public opinion polls consistently show that people would prefer to live somewhere outside a big city if adequate public services were available. The easiest option is apparently suburbia—and both the small towns and major center cities are losing out as a result.
- Social and environmental indicators show that the poor are bearing an unfair share of the costs of these patterns.

These and many similar concerns are being reflected in a major effort to develop a national policy with two objectives: achieving balanced and orderly growth. And many of the policy issues would seem to be made to order for the kinds of analyses that are produced by operations research.

Why haven't all levels of government taken advantage of these skills to improve their decision making? The answers probably are the imponderables and our inability to measure properly the data available.

Unfortunately, the imponderables include most of the really crucial factors in national growth. For example, in population estimates, the difference of an average of one child per woman (between the ages of 15 and 44 today) would mean a population difference of 50 million by the end of the century. Demographers' lack of success in predicting fertility rates is really not very surprising, given that 80 percent of the next ten years' babies will be born to women who aren't now married. And the choices made by these young women and their partners may produce a second peak effect in the 1990s when the babies of the 1970s are having their children. Even if all families who will have children during the rest of the century were to average out at the "replacement" level (2.1 children) and there were no further immigration, it will still take a century for the U.S. to reach a balance between births and deaths and thus have zero population growth.

Some of the other imponderables are just as difficult to predict. The location of jobs, for instance, is a basic factor in any population distribution strategy, but probably 90 percent of these kinds of decisions—such as where to build a new industrial plant—are probably made outside of any public policy or planning framework. And many are still on personal preferences of the executives—not on economic or market analysis.

I'm still sure all of us make our own moving decisions more on myths than on facts or logic. It would be interesting, for instance, to know how each of us at this meeting made the career and moving decisions that resulted in our being here today. I doubt if anyone would agree to use our collective decisions to construct a valid mobility model for operations researchers. But I'm afraid that a number of policy makers have been given models that look impressive but are based on just such shaky foundations.

I am reminded of an extensive study of fire station location that clearly showed that most of them were in the "wrong" place. Unfortunately, from the mayors' point of view, the model did not incorporate the most critical factor—the resistance and political strength of the neighborhoods who didn't want "their" fire station moved away.

Even if we choose problems where the political imponderables aren't as significant, the policy-making level of government can't be confident until operations researchers can clearly demonstrate they have adequate and accurate data to work with. Data on growth and environmental quality are particularly deficient in both quantity and quality.

Too many management researchers have been unable to satisfactorily explain that the evaluation of the important variables is extremely difficult. One reason is that most of us are linear thinkers. We still count, 1, 2, 3, 4, when we should all be working harder to count exponentially. Too few people realize that growth and environmental relations are rarely linear—a little air pollution is harmless, more is an annoyance, but a great deal is lethal. Jay Forrester has done a fine job in awakening awareness of exponential growth, but it is hard for us to place much reliance on forecasts that we don't really understand when we have little confidence in the inputs and when we are beginning to realize the difficulty of putting the proper weight on interacting forces.

Perhaps the biggest single conceptual difficulty that policy makers have with models is that any model has to be simplified so much to be handled mathematically that it is hard to imagine that models will ever be truly representative of the real world of urban growth.

As an example I might use Switzerland, a country about one-tenth the size of California. For five years the Swiss have conducted an extensive study of national growth policy models. Their conclusion is: "Don't depend on models for policy making—you just have to assume away too many significant differences in life-style."

The "Limits of Growth" model, for instance, looks at only five factors: population growth, natural resources, industrial output, pollution generation, and food production. Anyone can add a dozen or more factors that are of equal importance—for instance, individual and national social goals or personal desires that turn into major political forces. In fact the whole umbrella of factors that add up to "Quality of Life" is only partly reflected. Some of the alternative futures that have been projected, like one square foot of land per person, make "Doomsday" quite attractive by comparison.

We are, of course, in no way trying to diminish the importance of research in this area. The federal government's role in policy research and evaluation will become increasingly important as we turn over program operations to state and local governments under the administration's revenue-sharing philosophy. As the states assume more management responsibilities, they too will be putting more reliance on operations research in many of the areas discussed in this volume. The increasing emphasis we are putting on "management" in our state and local planning and management assistance programs is designed to accelerate this trend.

This trend toward more emphasis on national growth research, incidentally, is a worldwide phenomenon.

The typical experience of all national governments is that the moment they have to deal with problems of national urban growth they begin to realize how difficult and complex the problem is. After some pragmatic actions (usually programs to slow down the growth of their major city) that have no significant impact—even massive efforts in the USSR to slow down the growth of Moscow haven't worked—government turns to research. Like planning, it seems like an alternative that may do some good and is not very controversial.

But this approach doesn't work too well either. There never seems to be enough time for policy makers to wait for the results of profound research. And often the predictions from models are politically embarassing. The political process just does not seem to work in a rational way. Nor does the usual research process—good science and good politics seem incompatible. Perhaps one reason is that too many researchers are trying the impossible—deciding what "the public interest" should be—when the policy maker knows there really is no such thing.

He realizes though, that there are "public interests" and that they are made up of the interests of different subsets of the "public" that sooner or later will force him to action.

Another reason is that researchers tend to drop hints that, given more time and money, they can answer all the questions and solve all the problems. But policy makers have learned that their best (and maybe only) hope is that some research has been done or a model developed somewhere that will shed at least a little light on their problem. By now they know they won't find the complete, solid, scientifically justified answer or the perfect master plan lying in some dark corner.

What are some of the dark corners that we would like to see illuminated by operations research? This volume is making a good start by focusing on the critical problem areas of urban growth—public services, social and political processes, land use, and the environment. Some other questions come to mind, such as: What are the real consequences to metropolitan areas and states of the spreading movement to adapt "no-growth" policies by local government? How can operations research techniques be used in actually developing and implementing local or state growth plans? Can we refine our projections by looking at past federal investments and completed public works projects to see what the real growth impacts were? Or whether the original forecasts and cost/benefit analyses were valid? How can we begin to evaluate the imponderables?

There are many other questions that could be discussed, but I want to leave you with a word of warning. Regardless of the progress we are making in research, policy decisions have to be made. As much as we would like to be able to stop the world occasionally or postpone a crisis until we are more confident of our decision, we know that our system just doesn't work this way. For any researcher to be useful he has to accept this hard fact of life.

This is one of the hardest steps in the transition from the academic world to government. No one really teaches how to come from the cloistered tower of learning to the firing line where the researher's role is to have the right ammunition available when a target of opportunity appears. Books like this are a most effective way of filling this gap.

In conclusion, I doubt if there is any policy maker who isn't anxious (and maybe desperate) for whatever light can be thrown on his problems. He is probably suspicious because he has been over-sold on models in the past but he realizes how hard it is to understand the complex network of interrelationships in urban growth. And most realize that there is more merit than we care to admit in the hypothesis stated by Brian Berry at a White House meeting on urban growth policy: "Complex urban systems are frequently counter-intuitive, resistant to policy changes, and moreover, show opposite short-term and long-term responses so that politically expedient programs seeking short-term payoffs invariably set the stage for longer-term degeneration." In other words, policy makers are learning enough to know that models should carry a warning label: "May be hazardous to the health of traditional urban decision making."

**URBAN RESEARCH:
ONE PERSPECTIVE**
Frederick O'R. Hayes

Research is a pretentious word. If you happen to have a Ph.D
and are gainfully employed by a university, a "think tank," or a
laboratory, the word has that good, solid, substantial, comfortable
feeling to it—like prime rib, roaring fire, graduate education, or
sound management. And if you say scientific research, with all those
visions of test tubes popping in our heads, most people will agree it's
a good thing.

But urban research, government research, or program analysis
are fish in a different bowl. All those visions of test tubes and atom
smashers vanish and the operative word becomes "studies," a word
used most frequently in the phrase "studies on the shelf," which in
turn is a roommate of "plans on the shelf." The popular connotations
are all bad. We place "studies" in opposition to "action"—and action,
we all know, is good. Scholars and analysts may know better, but in
the colder world outside, all those congressmen, senators, state
legislators, city councilmen, politicians, and practical men say "No,
we've had enough studies. It's time to do something."

Perhaps I exaggerate and perhaps things have improved a bit
since that time a congressman had the House in stitches and the research program in tatters as he read titles from a catalog of housing
research, most of it not government financed. Funds are being appropriated and used for program and urban research—and in some areas
program failure has created a demand among some for study and
research. But the overall atmosphere is not positive. Maybe we who
advocate program research are not telling them what we really want
and why we need it.

For the first thing we need, I go along with Sergeant Friday of
"Dragnet" fame: "All we want is the facts, ma'am, just the facts,
ma'am." The answer to that one, if you're interested, is: "We've

got all kinds of data lying around, more data than we can ever use." And if you measure data by the bushel, that's probably right. But we don't want data, we want the facts—and that's a different story. Kurt Vonnegut in <u>Cat's Cradle</u> has one of his characters say, "Render nothing unto Caesar because Caesar doesn't know what's really going on." He's right.

At the top of any large, complex organization what is "known" usually includes some conventional wisdom, hearsay, misinformation, and many blanks. Sometimes things are "known" but not in specific terms. Or they are "known" at some level deep in the organization but not to top management. Or the facts are buried in different operating reports, separate and unintegrated and rarely focused.

When the researcher or analyst talks about models, or analysis of whatever fancy ilk, half or more of the money for the project usually goes for the collection and organization of the facts. And often three-fourths of the benefits come from these facts.

It costs money to find out that detective investigation only solves a small percentage of serious crimes and only a minute percentage of some crimes, like burglary. It costs money because no one asked the question before. Or, after all the talk of welfare tenements all over New York City, it costs money to find out that only 4 percent of welfare recipients live in buildings that are 70 percent or more occupied by welfare recipients. Or to find out how much it should take to do a decent job of maintaining an apartment in New York and how much tenants can afford to pay. Or even to discover that some sanitation districts are more efficient than others and why. Or to determine where welfare recipients are coming from. Or to know how well open admissions students are doing at City University.

The need sometimes seems endless. In a world of large organizations, programs, and related social and economic phenomena an accurate and valid picture of the underlying reality is extraordinarily difficult to obtain and, in a rapidly changing world, to maintain. The chief of a rural volunteer fire department can experience it all directly. The chief of a department like New York's, with 14,000 men in some 400 companies answering nearly 300,000 alarms annually, must get most of it from abstractions (numbers, reports) organized to give him a basic picture that may be ultimately a matter of as much art as science.

With all of this it is difficult to convince anyone who has not wrestled with the problem how ignorant we are of the programs we operate, the results they produce, and the phenomena with which they are concerned. And there are many who are directing agencies and programs who are no more aware of their own ignorance of what goes on under their aegis. Our biggest single problem is to get the answer to that fundamental question: "What's up, Doc—specifically, I mean, " or "What is really going on?" and a related question: "What are the effects of what we are doing?" and the yardstick question: "Is anyone else doing any better?"

I don't want to dismiss analytical models, but most of the best of them are really an extension of the job of collecting and organizing the facts. We simulate because we cannot otherwise see reality clearly. We use Markov chains to see the outcomes we are actually getting from the chains of sequential events that characterize many of our public systems, especially criminal justice and education.

But the contributions of the researcher and analyst to fact-gathering are curcial. Getting the facts sounds easy, but in fact it is rare that an adequate information system can be built without a preliminary stab at program analysis that identifies the data needed.

The process of finding out what's going on can be a very complicated one. In the federal government, especially, it is uncommon to have a direct, nonstop connection between the actions of the federal program authority and the results the program is expected to serve. There are three reasons for this.

First, ours is a federal system. Despite the vast range of differences among our modern presidents, each has elected to follow a federal style, eschewing direct operations in favor of grants-in-aid to the states, cities, school districts, and other local governments. Virtually all of the programs focused on our major urban and domestic problems are so carried out. This inserts into the process a new agent independent of the federal agency—capable of resisting federal requirements, sometimes incapable of competent performance, and with varying degrees of readiness to do the job.

This poses first the simple problem of probabilities. With new grant in Program X, what is the likelihood of effective performance? How many of the states are likely to perform at superior levels? How many at substandard levels? This can be done systematically where something is known about past state performance in other programs and current state staffing in the relevant areas of performance. But only rarely is this kind of organized knowledge available, and, moreover, at the program design stage, no one wants to get it—policy determiners don't want to be told that in 15 of the 50 states program results are likely to be abysmal.

Once programs are operative the grant-in-aid system makes it difficult to secure relevant data on program operation. The difficulty increases with the degree of state or local discretion, with the number of discrete and different activities or projects conducted under the program, and with the number of grantees. Programs providing funds through the states to local governments or nonprofit organizations have another degree of complexity. In a large and diverse program, such as the Title I program of the Elementary and Secondary Education Act, it is almost impossible for the federal administrators to acquire accurate and current knowledge of what is being done under the program or the results it is achieving. Yet it is possible to achieve that objective. It means a major investment in better information systems—if you'll excuse that overused phrase—and also in program evaluation and analysis, for the new data from a uniform reporting system has limited value in itself.

But the more serious problem is how we improve things. How do we increase the capacity and, sometimes, the interest in the states to do an effective job with the program. We know that it has not been solved by the established practice of throwing language, whether legislative or administrative, at the problem.

The second reason why federal programs seldom have direct responsibility for achieving their objectives is the strong American taste for handling problems through marginal government intervention. This means we are not creating systems, but, rather, that we are sticking our finger into existing systems and often it is not one finger but several, frequently without demonstrating that degree of coordination that would indicate that the fingers belonged to a single pair of hands.

In its simplest form this is a market situation. Say we finance a new health clinic or a neighborhood center and no one comes. The customers have rejected us—not unlike Ford's Edsel caper—and we say next time we will do an analysis of potential demand. But it gets more complicated quickly. People do come to the neighborhood center, but they demand a different service than the one offered. Or we require appointments and a family doctor system in the health clinic, but the clients don't keep appointments and continue to appear without one.

The real cases are legion. The Federal Housing Administration had on its books throughout the 1950s a complex program of "yield insurance" designed to stimulate new investment in housing; not a single application was ever processed. Our manpower programs of the last decade are not without their successes, but the high dropout rates and placement failures suggest that the programs were not based upon an accurate understanding of either the job market or the psychology of the client group. The huge amounts expended for compensatory and remedial education have resulted in failure so widespread as to raise serious doubts as to our underlying comprehension of the problem. Our expectations for the community action program were less specific but it is fair to say that its results deviated wildly from expectations. The Medicaid-Medicare programs have resulted in costs that have exceeded every initial estimate.

Nowhere is the problem more complex than in the case of urban development. Let's start with a simple case: a medium sized housing development. The builder depends upon successful completion of a series of interrelated deals or arrangements: (1) to secure control of the land; (2) to obtain construction and mortgage financing; (3) to obtain FHA mortgage insurance; (4) to secure local government approvals through the land-use regulation process (he must satisfy zoning requirements, obtain building permits, and often secure variations from existing zoning restrictions); (5) to market the houses or apartments at a price covering his costs and returning a profit. Now that's what's going on back on the ranch. Meanwhile, in Washington we've decided we want more and better housing, integrated employment opportunities, higher development and land planning standards, 20 percent of the units for middle- and low-income families, assurance of racial integration, assurance of no adverse environmental impact, and minimum infrastructure requirements.

These are implemented through a series of different programs, some purely regulatory, some carrying subsidies such as 235 and 236 grants to reduce interest rates, some operating directly on the developer, some through state and local governments.

Sometimes (surprisingly?) we do not get what we want—or perhaps discover a few unanticipated adverse side effects. The reason is clear. We are intervening in a complex behavioral system where the results depend upon our understanding of a large group of different actors in terms of motivations, options, and perceptions and the effect of their interactions on final results.

We need to know more about (1) developer economics; (2) the socio-politico-bureaucratic factors in local land-use regulation; (3) the cost effects of all regulatory approaches—federal as well as state and local; (4) the demand for housing and the operation of housing markets; and (5) the politics and economics of infrastructure development. We could add a few more but the list makes my point. As soon as we reject the direct approach—that is to go out and build the housing under federal sponsorship—in favor of marginal intervention, we need to know a lot more about how people behave and how they are likely to react to intervention. As we build more marginal programs and add more federal objectives on top of the existing system, our need for behavioral research increases.

A third factor is the strong tendency to introduce conflicting objectives into federal programs, without any clear notion as to how they will be resolved. The housing case above obviously involves such conflicts. The environmentalists have introduced a new and proper concern with what the economists call externalities. But that concern, as enacted into federal legislation, does not provide any means for distinguishing between facilities that are optional or even frivolous and those that are important or perhaps essential. As a result, we see Congress overriding its own legislation to assure construction of the Alaskan pipeline and to establish mechanisms for power plant siting. In other cases we find equity considerations fighting with program objectives. Oil depletion allowances have for years been attacked as a giveaway and perhaps they are, but no one seems to know the extent to which they are a needed incentive to oil discovery and production.

In the best of worlds we are not going to be able to predict the outcomes resulting from all federal programs and policies. We can, however, greatly improve our performance above present levels.

We need urban and government research and program analysis, and we need much more than we've been getting. Most important, we need just to know what is happening now. We need to give special attention to the often complex behavioral response of individuals, families, businesses, and state and local governments to the inducement opportunities and constraints of federal programs, because it is these responses that determine the results ultimately obtained.

3

PLANNING AND EVALUATION: THE VIEWPOINT FROM A NEIGHBORHOOD SETTLEMENT HOUSE
Donald G. Murray, Jr.

The question of whether or not poverty programs do plan and do evaluate their successes or failures is the subject of much controversy and debate. Poverty program critics cite inadequate data collection and research systems and faulty planning and evaluative structures as basic reasons for poverty program failure. They argue for the elimination of poverty programs because they have no criteria for measuring and validating their performance and no method for properly assessing the information they do collect. Their perspective places total responsibility for planning and evaluation on each individual poverty program and assumes that resources exist within each program to handle these dual tasks. It is my contention that community-based poverty programs such as Friendship House in Washington, D. C., recognized the need for and the importance of the planning and evaluative processes but applied these two tools in a random manner or when immediate, identifiable, and clear-cut needs presented themselves.

An examination of the programs offered by Friendship House directly reflects a planned response by this one agency to meet the needs of its community. The Child Development Center was established to provide working and welfare mothers with quality child care; the Martin Luther King Co-Op Store developed as a result of public housing residents deciding that a need existed in their area for a food store; the Project Link-Outreach Senior Citizen Program addressed itself to meeting the total needs of the neglected elderly; the Kuumba Cultural Arts Center provided black youths with the creative vehicle for their natural talents and abilities; and the Advocacy program developed community leadership and fought side by side with area citizens and groups to improve the quality of their lives in housing, health, education, and employment. Friendship House has opted for meeting people's needs over satisfying program processes; as a result of this choice, long-range planning and evaluation have been relegated to a secondary role within the agency.

Local poverty programs found themselves faced with other realities that retarded their assessment capabilities. Friendship House had to implement objectives that were unrealistic and for which no objective measurements had been developed. The program was provided with a totally inadequate budget in terms of the problems it had to resolve. Its staff was composed primarily of unskilled or semiskilled community residents and at no time did Friendship House have assigned to it a specific staff person whose primary responsibilities were research, program monitoring, and planning and evaluation. These tasks were assumed by the existing administrative personnel along with their other duties. The need for persons to assume this function was recognized by Friendship House and included in its proposals, but never did the Office of Economic Opportunity (OEO) provide funds for this specific purpose.

Constantly changing OEO program guidelines presented real problems to community-based poverty programs. An illustration of how shifting guidelines can affect a program's service delivery capacity can be seen in the area of economic development. Under OEO's original mandate, Friendship House operated as an advocacy agency utilizing a mixture of social service and community organization. Staff were hired from the community and master degree social workers administered the poverty programs. The skills required were oriented toward human service and the basic thrust was organizing residents to improve conditions within their environment. Then in 1970 the OEO unilaterally decreed that economic development should be a main goal of poverty programs. The problems that poverty programs had originally been set up to resolve were still there and the basic staff structures had remained unchanged. Yet now these bodies were being asked to implement a new goal that required a different set of skills, a different kind of staff, and a different orientation. The move into economic development was not accompanied by in-depth staff training, funds to hire the needed consultants, or by a rearrangement of community priorities. Local poverty programs were informed of the guideline change and to receive continued funding adjusted their program priorities. The abrupt shift to economic development by the OEO resulted in local poverty programs taking on a new objective with no real preparation, real understanding, and real skills to put this concept into operation.

Competitiveness among community-based poverty programs seriously weakened their ability to maximize the impact of their joint resources on common citywide problems. From the inception of the "War On Poverty" this attitude was fostered by the automatic division of the poor into poverty program "target areas" and reinforced by the deep sense of funding insecurity that permeated the whole poverty program structure. The establishment of individual "turfs" by community-based poverty programs resulted in their working to resolve problems from a narrow and isolated context. Each local poverty program felt strong pressure to justify its being. This individualistic orientation to survival effectively hindered the development of a permanent coalition of organizations around common problems and issues.

The coordination breakdown between local government agencies and community-based poverty programs hindered the service delivery capacity of both sectors. Duplication of services, gaps in service, and short-circuited communication and coordination channels were the natural consequences of vacuum planning. Recognition that community residents would be the real beneficiaries of a strong cooperative partnership between local government agencies and nongovernment agencies was overshadowed by the mutual suspicion and distrust that the two groups had for one another.

The reluctance of private and government funding sources to make grants to local-based poverty programs for new and innovative program ideas hindered these programs' ability to meet their community's real needs. Community-based poverty programs were penalized because they did not have a long track record of obtaining grants or of handling funds. This conservative attitude on the part of major funding sources prevented local poverty programs from testing out new approaches they had developed to combat basic community problems. The growth potential of poverty programs and of the communities they served was severely limited by funding sources' unwillingness to assume a major role in promoting social change in poverty communities.

A final limitation on program processes within local poverty programs is that community residents' priorities tended to reflect services that they were familiar with rather than the service that might be most needed. Surveys conducted by Friendship House show that area residents asked consistently for tutoring services, day care centers, or programs of a recreational nature. Yet nowhere in its service area is there an alcoholic treatment facility, a mental health facility, or a public assistance satellite office. Poverty programs must take a more aggressive educational role in terms of community program education or they will find themselves constantly at odds with their service community over priorities.

The problems faced by poverty programs in developing systematic planning and evaluative mechanisms can be overcome. The importance of these program processes is established and what now is needed is the manpower commitment to implement such a system.

Coordination among the other key components in the human service areas must be initiated at all levels, and meeting the needs of people must become the common goal. The question of whether these two tools will be properly utilized by poverty programs remains an unanswered one, but the potential is there.

INTRODUCTION
TO PART II
Dennis R. Young

The theme of Part II is "the delivery of public services." But what exactly do we mean by that? According to Webster, the word "delivery" means, among other definitions, "a giving out or distributing; as of goods or mail." For our purposes we might add to goods and mail public services such as education, health care, police and fire protection, care of the elderly, sanitation services, drug rehabilitation and crime prevention services, and manpower training services.

But what about delivery, that is, giving out or distributing these services? Our interest here obviously lies in developing ways of improving the efficiency, quality, reliability, or equity with which services are provided. However, these objectives can be pursued from a number of different approaches.

For example, operations research techniques can help to route and schedule garbage trucks, street sweepers, locate fire stations, and, in deference to Mr. Webster, design routes and schedules for mail delivery.

In a different approach, information systems can be designed to provide and analyze data to allow the managers of service supply agencies to make better decisions in allocating resources, designing operations, and hence improving the delivery of their services.

The chapters in this section emphasize a third approach: improving the economic and institutional arrangements through which the delivery of services is organized. Here we deal with the incentive structures to which producers, consumers, and others involved in the supply and demand for services respond and the institutional factors that encourage or constrain innovation and adaption to changes in external conditions and to changes in levels of performance.

These chapters address the institutional issues of service delivery from several different perspectives. William Pollak analyzes the merits and disadvantages of a spectrum of economic/organizational alternatives ranging from straight income supplements to enhance elderly consumers' purchasing power in the marketplace, to arrangements under which the elderly person is assisted by a "coordinating agent" to help with acquisition of needed services. In contrast, Stanley Altman and his colleagues are concerned with a service—sanitation—provided directly by government; the question they confront is how to develop and institutionalize a system of evaluation that will effectively motivate and enhance the capability of public servants to improve performance.

By a fortuitous coincidence, and not through foresight in planning, I regret to say, the demonstration project that Altman et al. describe in connection with evaluation of sanitation—Project Scorecard—utilizes manpower provided under the supported work experiment that Lee Friedman describes in the final chapter. This program, developed by the Vera Institute of Justice, provides ex-addicts with jobs in a variety of local services; it is simultaneously a rehabilitation, crime-prevention, and manpower development service that is provided under a unique and innovative institutional framework.

ORGANIZATIONAL ISSUES IN THE PROVISION OF COMMUNITY CARE TO THE IMPAIRED ELDERLY
William Pollak

Many elderly persons have chronic physical or mental functional impairments that prevent them from carrying out tasks that are essential to the maintenance of independent living. For example, strokes, severe arthritis, hip injuries, and other impairments make it impossible for many older persons to do their own shopping, laundering, housecleaning, bathing, meal preparation, and other tasks. In many instances these conditions are stabilized: Although intensive medical attention is not required, the condition cannot be reversed through rehabilitation. Persons suffering from these impairments may be unable to manage alone, although they may be able to live in the community indefinitely if the tasks that are beyond their physical or mental capacities are performed for them on a continuing basis.

THE PRESENT POLICY CONTEXT

Financing

Both of the two major federal medical-finance programs, Medicare and Medicaid, will finance home health care including personal and maintenance care. They will do so, however, only under restrictive conditions that effectively deny the financing of home-care services for persons with stabilized chronic (rather than acute) conditions. Consequently, under present arrangements care services for chronically impaired persons in the community are financed on a hit-or-miss basis by several federal and federal/state programs— most of them administered by the Department of Health, Education, and Welfare—and by private contributions.

Government grant programs include those of the Administration on Aging and the Health Services and Mental Health Administration. These fund state and local planning and the provision of nutrition, transportation, counselling, information, and other services by social-service agencies. The Social Services program under the public assistance titles of the Social Security Act provides services directly or pays profit and nonprofit agencies (as well as individuals) for services provided to eligible impaired elderly persons. Financing through the block-grant programs is spotty and is distributed among communities in response to their varying propensities and abilities to tap federal grant programs. The Social Services program, though more complete in coverage, is a joint federal/state program that permits great variation among states in the types of services provided and in the income levels used to define eligibility. [1]

Federal grant programs, the Social Services program, and private contributors together are generally believed to finance an inadequate quantity of community services. Brahna Trager, for example, evaluates the adequacy of home care by comparing the availability of home helps (homemaker-home health aides) in the United States with availability in Western European nations.

> The range in population ratio in the Western European countries is from approximately one home help per 760 in Denmark to one home help to 2,000 population in France. The ratio in France is considered inadequate— most of the countries which participate in the International Association consider that a ratio of more than one to 1,500 population constitutes inadequate services. The ratio in the United States at present time is less than one to 7,000 population, with the cluster mostly in urban areas of the Eastern seaboard. [2]

She also considers the quality of service and notes that

> home health services, where they do exist are under-financed, limited in their capacity to cover the population in need, frequently lacking in essential components which might make them an effective resource. [3]

Organization

Service provision is not organized in any single way. To some degree, however, the organization of service is a function of client income. If low-income elderly impaired persons know about and have access to the program (and many do not), * and if their state and county programs meet the potential attainable under federal law, the Old Age Assistance and Social Services programs can provide information and placement services, can manage community care, and can finance needed care services produced by the agency or purchased for clients from private profit and nonprofit suppliers. In many localities, however, the Social Services program does not finance or provide many of the services needed by the impaired elderly. Eligible low-income clients then are served in the same way as old persons with incomes above but not far above Old Age Assistance eligibility. If they are in the community they generally will not be provided with referral assistance, financial assistance, or services by the Welfare or Social Services program. Instead, if they require community care they are likely, if served at all by formal programs, to be served by philanthropic service and referral agencies. The services they receive are likely to be subsidized by private contributions or by government grants that finance services generally rather than purchase services for particular clients.

For poor and near-poor elderly persons who seek assistance through a public or private agency, the service obtained will depend on the skill and determination of the worker handling the case. Part of that worker's task is to select a package of services suited to the client's condition and family situation. Much of the effort and skill in "coordinating" services on behalf of the client under existing programs is employed, however, not in selecting appropriate services but in locating agencies that will provide service on favorable terms and in extracting services or service-funding from government or private agencies whose regulations, eligibility requirements, and red tape greatly complicate and sometimes dominate the coordinative task. These obstacles, of course, are not accidental but are the inevitable concomitants of a delivery system with several sources of funding, each of which are incapable of satisfying all service demands, and which provide subsidies to producers (rather than consumers) who ration scarce services administratively. In other words, many of the problems now experienced in assembling service packages for low-income clients derive not from the technical difficulty of

---

*This is evidenced by the success of programs such as the S.O.S. project of the Office of Economic Opportunity that attempted to locate individuals eligible for assistance who were not receiving it.

matching services with the family setting and impairment condition of the client, but from the scarcity of resources and the manner in which these resources are rationed. *

Persons in the higher-income brackets are, again, served differently. Although middle- and upper-income persons may use services produced by philanthropic agencies, they may also purchase services in private markets. They may rent special housing, have groceries delivered, and purchase restaurant meals in order to compensate for functional impairments. Since in most cases these services may be purchased—albeit at high cost—it would not be surprising to find that their higher incomes enable such persons to remain in the community at levels of functioning (particularly physical levels of functioning) that would result in institutionalization for persons with lower incomes.

ORGANIZATIONAL MODELS

The manner in which service delivery is organized affects performance in many ways: allocative efficiency (the mesh of the quantity, quality, and mix of services that are produced with the quantity, quality, and mix of service that clients want or need), production efficiency, service quality, the degree of consumer independence, and equity in the distribution of service. This does not mean, however, that only organizational considerations are important. Indeed, if resources are insufficient that deficit will be the primary constraint on performance and no amount of organizational change, coordination, and planning will eliminate problems caused by inadequacy of resources. Organizational change may enhance the impact of expanded resources, but it cannot fill a resource void. Although this chapter does not discuss funding sources, its analysis is relevant whether funding is provided through an expanded home-care program under Medicare, through a home-care component of a national health insurance program, or through some other finance mechanism.

---

*Good workers excel not only in the skill with which they match services to client needs but also in their ability to secure services for their clients. Since the supply of subsidized services is limited, these latter efforts merely bring to the fortunate clients of good workers services that otherwise would go to others.

Impairment-Payment Program

The most basic aspects of organizing service for impaired persons include (1) the way in which subsidies are initially routed—to consumers, to producers, or to a "service coordinator"; (2) the form of subsidies—cash, vouchers limited to one or several services, or block grants; and (3) the sector that produces services. Other dimensions of service organization frequently are related to these and will be considered below.

The first organizational form, termed an impairment-payment program, is very rudimentary—indeed it is really not a service system in the conventional sense. It contains three elements. First, elderly persons with severe functional impairments would be assessed on the degree of their impairments in order to identify the resource cost these impairments impose (difficulties that arise in assessing "impairment cost" should not exceed those that arise in normal service programs when services—rather than the cost of services—must be prescribed). Second, clients would be granted an impairment payment. For Old Age Assistance recipients whose regular payment is intended to cover normal financial need this payment would equal impairment costs. For those whose normal needs are self-financed the impairment payment could be equal to impairment costs, or could be made to represent a declining share of impairment cost with increasing income if it were desired that those with an ability to pay bear some or all of the cost of their impairments. Impairment payments could also reflect variations in the availability of nonfinancial family resources. Finally, recipients would use their cash payments to purchase the mix of services and goods most appropriate to their needs—in each instance buying services or goods from the supplier whose price-quality combination is most satisfactory to the individual consumer.

Severely impaired persons or families responsible for them, regardless of their financial situation, often are unaware of the range of available supportive services and of how these services might assist in coping with particular situations. Therefore, it would be wise to establish concurrently with this (or any other) organizational form a centralized and well-publicized service to provide information about available services and the quality of alternative suppliers and to assess client needs where clients or their families desire information or assistance.

There is much to be said for centralized provision of this service. Most importantly it would increase the likelihood that people will know of at least one source of assistance. This would help ensure that when aid is needed people will not founder because they don't know where to go. Second, since the cost of obtaining information and monitoring the quality of services does not vary with the number of people to whom information is provided, there are economies of scale that can be captured by a single agency. Centralization also might increase the likelihood that some kind of meaningful monitoring of service providers would occur since, with information centralized, all of the returns to a service monitoring program would flow through one agency. If, on the other hand, information were dispensed by many agencies it is probable that none would have enough users to justify the expense of a service monitoring effort. If the service evaluations were based on objective information or client survey responses, the procedure might dampen inevitable political opposition to the explicit addition of evaluation to the information function by a public or nonprofit agency.

Advantages

Before considering problems of the impairment-payment program as a means of providing services for elderly persons in the community, it is worth recognizing the virtues of such a program. First, the payment program would facilitate the fitting of services to felt disabilities and a meshing of services with the individual's particular life setting and style. Second, it would make the distribution of resources according to uniform criteria easier than it is under systems that rely on grants to service providers. Third, if consumers receive subsidies directly, they would be free to reject unsatisfactory service since rejection of one supplier's service on quality grounds would not result in termination of assistance. This would, perhaps, change the relationship between clients and suppliers from the dependent one prevailing when subsidies are provided to a producer, who is then in the position of "giving charity" rather than "selling services." This freedom of choice is the most apparent virtue of an organizational form relying heavily on the market: Clients who are dissatisfied with the cost of a particular service, or the manner in which it is provided, can shift their purchases to other suppliers of the same service or to other services that may be more satisfactory.

The freedom of choice within the constraint of the impairment payment thus benefits individual clients using services at a given moment in time. In addition it promotes effective operation of the service system over time. The purchase decisions of the group of clients constitutes a form of evaluation of service mix, efficiency, and quality in which the results are fed back to service providers. The market then forces systemic response to the content of the evaluations, since rejected suppliers must either enhance the desirability

of their services or go out of business, while accepted suppliers tend
to expand. This organizational mode thus embodies a mechanism that
compels service output to respond to evaluations.

Problems

The advantages of an impairment-payment approach, however,
may well be dominated by major flaws. These are present on both the
consumer (demand) side and on the producer (supply) side.

On the demand side many of the potential beneficiaries of community care programs are mentally impaired and incapable of selecting
a satisfactory service mix or of policing service quality. The impairment-payment scheme is obviously inappropriate for these individuals, although the objection applies neither to mentally alert but
physically impaired individuals nor to mentally impaired individuals
with relatives who can serve as their proxy consumers.

The effective operation of markets, however, requires not only
that buyers be alert but that they have the energy to "shop around":
that is, markets cannot be relied upon to provide an appropriate mix
and quality of service unless buyers have the energy and ability to
obtain information, to compare prices, to judge quality in relation to
prices, and to switch suppliers when prices or quality are unsatisfactory. The prevalence of concern over victimization of elderly consumers reflects doubt about their consumer competence. The available
evidence, though it reveals problems, does not demonstrate either
that consumer problems plague the elderly more than other groups
or that mentally competent but physically impaired persons cannot
effectively select services and monitor the quality of service provided
to them.

The competence of the elderly to consume services is also
affected by three characteristics of services targeted toward the
maintenance of independent living. First, many services can be
delivered to the user. This eliminates the transportation problem,
which is one of the major obstacles to the effective use of markets
by the elderly. Second the services are temporally divisible. This
reduces the risks associated with the selection of unsatisfactory suppliers since consumption can be shifted at low cost to alternative
producers. It is no coincidence that the most severe problems of
consumer victimization arise in the provision of high-cost and indi-
visible goods or services where one-shot consumption decisions are
large and irreversible (furnace and other household repairs, surgical
operations, etc.). Third, the characteristics of the service (as well
as the ability of the individual) influence the individual's capacity to
judge quality. Even laymen with no mental impairment are not com-

petent to judge many of the technical aspects of a doctor's work—to know, for example, whether diagnoses are accurate. This would not, however, seem to be a major problem with home-care services, which generally are not technical and are accessible to normal consumer evaluation.

Limited mental competence and limited consumer knowledge are genuine obstacles to the effective operation of the impairment-payment program for those clients who are living alone or living with someone who is also limited.

Aside from their inability to police the market, it is often implied that even mentally competent elderly impaired consumers do not know their own needs and consequently are likely to spend their impairment payment on services and commodities that will benefit them less than those that would be used if, instead, services were directly provided. When applied to mentally competent individuals consuming services with no consumption "externalities" (discussed below), this argument is basically a philosophical one. It alleges that other persons (those designing a services program) know better than the individual how resources destined for his or her use are best employed.

Discussion here is clouded by the inevitable difficulty of establishing a mental competence threshold below which elderly individuals should have service consumption decisions made for them. Even if a relatively low level of mental functioning defines competence, the preemption of consumption decisions should not be undertaken lightly and should be undertaken with the understanding that the denial of choice and the prescription of services may themselves foster a dependency whose minimization should be an objective of any program.

In some cases the way an individual's impairment resources are allocated will have effects beyond the individual. For example, an individual might devote a smaller share of his impairment payment to nutrition than would a service program with the same total allocation. If this results in premature and costly hospitalization, then others in addition to the individual bear the cost of that person's consumption choices. To the degree that such "externalities" exist an economic (nonphilosophical) case may be made for restricting or guiding the individual. It should be mentioned, however, that almost no evidence exists concerning the relative effectiveness in maintaining independence of resources allocated in response to personal choices and resources allocated through a direct services program.

What evidence there is in this area is fragmentary and conflicting. It is true that the probability of institutionalization declines as incomes rise—suggesting that higher incomes may be partially employed to purchase services and goods that enable continued living in the community. The relationship, however, may also be attributable to a positive association between health and income or to the impoverishment that may result from institutionalization. A study conducted at the Benjamin Rose Institute[4] suggests that some direct service programs may increase dependence: Aged individuals who received additional social services and were visited frequently by a social worker were more likely to be institutionalized (a form of high dependence) than were clients who received normal services. It was hypothesized that this occurred because "even with an ancillary home service program, social workers have a tendency to move people into protective settings when they become involved with them in an intensive, individualized fashion."[5] The findings of this study must be regarded as tentative because of the small sample size and shortcomings in the research design. Another Benjamin Rose Institute study, which limited the direct participation of social workers, indicated that among a group of elderly persons released from a rehabilitation hospital the provision of home-health aides significantly reduced reentry to institutions.[6]

Three problems seem to dominate discussions of the market's supply-side failures in meeting the service needs of the elderly: Private producers do not respond to needs; when private producers do respond, the prices charged are "too high"; and the quality of service is low because private producers are concerned with profits first and with clients second, if at all.

The observation that markets may not respond to needs is correct: Markets will respond only to those consumer needs that are backed by a willingness and ability to pay—that is, only to those "needs" that are also "demands." The failure of a market to respond to a need can often be explained by one of two phenomena. First, there may be a discrepancy between the demands of a consumer and the demands imputed to him by an observer who notes the market's failure to respond to the need that he, but not the consumer, perceives. For example, after entering the dust-filled, cluttered home of a 72-year-old man, a social worker may criticize the market's neglect of the consumer's need for homemaker services. The problem may not be market nonresponse; rather, it may be consumer ignorance of the available homemaker services, or a difference in the value placed upon a clean home by the old man and the social worker. The second possibility is that the consumer, though feeling the need for service, does not have sufficient income to convert felt need into market demand. Neither explanation dictates the rejection of market supply.

The inadequacy of the incomes of impaired elderly persons undoubtedly explains many of their observed unmet needs. This would be alleviated by the impairment-payment program. However, it is often suggested that private producers do not respond even to economic demands. * For example, middle-income persons who are willing and able to pay a profitable price are alleged to be unable to purchase homemaker and other needed services from private suppliers. This is difficult to understand because most of the services considered here—chore, transportation, meal, homemaker, and other care services—are not technical products requiring highly trained personnel or unusually scarce inputs that call for supply-side intervention. Rather, they are similar to services regularly supplied in the market. If services thought to be demanded are not supplied, it is either because private producers are insensitive to latent demands or because there is not actually a demand. †

The general responsiveness of private suppliers to exotic, expensive, and once-latent tastes suggests circumspection in asserting supplier negligence in sensing and responding to economic demands for fairly prosaic services needed by impaired elderly persons. Stair elevators and mechanical devices that assist in bathing are produced and sold; it seems improbable that markets that are sensitive to demands for those items would be insensitive to economic demands for delivered meals, transportation, and other services.

This general conclusion notwithstanding, there clearly are instances when the market does not respond to economic demands for service (at levels that would cover costs). Analyses of these must have reference to the particular and possibly unique market circumstances in which they occur. For example, the alleged failure of the market to supply homemaker services to cost-remunerating demands may be the result of several factors. ‡ It is possible that people place

---

*Economic demands are backed by a willingness to pay a price sufficient to cover (efficient) production costs plus normal profit.

†Evidence in this area is elusive. It is virtually impossible to tell which cause operates without experimentally marketing the service in question.

‡This lack of response to the demand for homemaker and related services by those able to pay is not universal as is often implied. In Washington, D. C., for example, several private-for-profit organizations will provide homemakers (often referred to as "companions" or "nurse's aides") for a price lower than that charged by the nonprofit homemaker agency to clients whose incomes exceed the maxi-

insufficient trust in proprietary suppliers to purchase such a sensitive product from them and therefore will express demands only to trusted nonprofit suppliers. The supply activity of nonprofit agencies may also act to limit private market responses to economic demands. Philanthropic suppliers tend to provide subsidized service. However, a given level of subsidy funds will support only a constrained supply of subsidized service. Philanthropic providers may not realize that with unsatisfied economic demands they can expand service beyond the constraint level at no net cost to the agency by charging a remunerative price, or they may choose not to expand supply because they fear that doing so would sacrifice quality. If either phenomenon constrains the philanthropic suppliers' price and quantity below their market-clearing levels, the effect may be a persistent excess demand that proprietary firms do not supply because they are discouraged by a subsidized quality or price with which they cannot compete. Finally, it is possible that the market fails to supply some particular services because latent demands are not perceived by potential proprietary suppliers. *

Although the preceding discussion indicates that there are exceptions, in most cases the private market will respond to economic demands. The prevalence of assertions to the contrary is probably explained by the frequent inclusion of the qualifier "at reasonable cost." Thus "persons are unable to purchase homemaker services" becomes "persons are unable to purchase homemaker services at reasonable cost." With this modification the issue of nonresponse is merged with the issue of cost (and price) efficiency and becomes more tractable and relevant to policy discussion.

It must be noted that a service cost that is subjectively high is unreasonable only if it is high relative to the cost of efficiently producing the service. Several factors, however, may make a cost that is reasonable by this standard appear unreasonable or excessive. First, the cost of producing a service may inherently be much higher than people expect or think is "right" in some normative sense.

---

mum on their sliding scale. However, the private-for-profit agencies do not specifically train their homemakers and provide only minimal supervision. These observations, furthermore, are made in a major metropolitan area and are unlikely to be duplicated in small towns and rural areas.

*In the case of homemaker services it also is possible that supply is artificially constrained because homemaker employment is regarded as unprofessional and servile.

Second, the cost of service may be unusually (though not unreasonably) high if a service whose production is subject to economies of scale is demanded and produced on too small a scale to capture the scale economies. Third, the cost of producing a service in the private sector may appear unreasonable because a private sector price (for example, a restaurant) is compared with the price charged by a non-profit agency that subsidizes services, or uses volunteers or other inputs (school or church dining facilities) unavailable to proprietary suppliers. The lower real costs attainable with volunteers or other contributed inputs should nonetheless be captured in programs. Since it is difficult or impossible to integrate them into profit enterprises, this would argue against proprietary production of services where volunteer labor or contributed inputs are important. These reduced costs might still be obtainable under an impairment-payment program, since nonprofit agencies can sell services that are produced or de-livered partly by volunteers.

The preceding discussion examines the common observations that the private sector will not respond or will respond only at ex-cessive cost to demands for home-care service. Such observations, it has been argued here, often perceive excessive cost where costs will inevitably be high because of input-price, production, and scale realities. This does not mean, however, that prices charged by firms supplying existing service demands or demands created by an impair-ment-payment program will be reasonable. Private suppliers will not keep profits low voluntarily and can be counted upon to be efficient only when forced—that is, only when there is competition. This re-quires not only competent consumers but also a scale of demand sufficient to support several suppliers.* Because insufficient demand will exist in some geographic areas for some services, few generali-zations about the feasibility of market supply are likely to be valid. Demand for transportation services for the elderly, for example, may well exist on a scale that would support competition in one city while other services in that same city, and transportation services in other cities or in a rural area, might be demanded on an insufficient scale to support competing suppliers.

---

*A scale of demand that is too small to support suppliers com-peting for individual units of business (for example, individual meals) might support competition among suppliers who compete for an annual contract to supply a group of buyers whose demands are aggregated in a formal program. This point will arise in discussing other organization models.

The scale of demand required to support price competition among suppliers of a service to impaired elderly persons is affected by two other matters. First, because there are nonelderly consumers for many home-care services, total demands may suffice to support competition even though the demands of impaired elderly persons will not. Second, pressures that constrain prices, profits, and costs may come from potential as well as existing competitors. This is particularly relevant to those service markets where entry is free, and its importance increases if, as often occurs, the service is a close substitute in production for services produced for the general market. Thus if producers of general transportation and food services can easily shift production to services for the impaired elderly the possibility that they may shift will influence and constrain prices in the elderly services market even if the shift does not occur.

These comments have identified conditions that determine whether the impairment-payment mode would be likely to yield reasonably or unreasonably priced services. The discussion would apply as well in identifying the conditions under which markets are likely to produce services of satisfactory quality. Thus private suppliers may produce high-quality services that mesh with the needs and interests of clients. However, because proprietary suppliers will not have the interests of clients as a primary objective, suppliers can be relied upon to serve those interests effectively only if forced by market circumstances to do so. The degree to which the regulation of quality can be left to the market therefore depends again on matters just discussed: whether the scale of demand is sufficiently large to support competing suppliers, whether the service demands of the impaired elderly are independent or part of a larger total demand for services, whether services are close substitutes in production for generally produced services, and finally whether clients are sufficiently competent as consumers to enforce the provision of quality.

Discussion

Of the deficiencies attributed to an impairment-payment program, it has been argued that some are common to all programs of services for the impaired elderly—for example, high costs because of the small scale of demands. Other deficiencies, where present, might be solved within the context of such a program through service-specific solutions. For example, market nonresponse to latent service demands is generally unlikely, but where nonresponse to normal and impairment-payment financed demands is suspected, "infant industry" or start-up subsidies might be granted to stimulate production and demonstrate the existence of demands that ultimately would make production remunerative.

Other deficiencies are more fundamental. First, the impairment-payment scheme may be effective only in large communities. Even with subsidies the impaired elderly in towns and rural areas may be too few to generate service demands that will support competition or even to yield a market response. In those instances an organizational form that more directly regulates or manages supply may be required. Second, some undetermined proportion of those to be served by such a program both live alone and would be universally judged incapable of selecting a service package; others would be judged unable to operate satisfactorily in the market mode. These deficiencies, though not universal, might severly limit the applicability of the impairment-payment scheme. Third, equity is one potential virtue claimed for the impairment-payment form of organization. Equity could be attained, however, given present scarce financial resources, only by spreading resources so thin that few, if any, would derive significant benefit. Direct services programs, whatever their failings, do concentrate resources on those selected for care and, at the expense of client sovereignty, guarantee that minimal standards of nutrition, safety, socialization, and hygiene are maintained. Finally, political acceptance for a program directed at the chronically impaired elderly is likely to be based on a social concern with the particular problems created by impairments. Politicians, therefore, may be reluctant to support a cash program that permits neglect of those problems—even if the program is, in some sense, better for the persons to whom it is directed. The remainder of this chapter therefore examines other organizational prototypes that would correct these primarily demand-side deficiencies while retaining, to varying degrees, the advantages of the impairment-payment scheme.

Voucher Payment Program

A program of cash payments proportioned to the needs of individual impaired elderly may be prevented by pressure to provide particular services to meet specific identified needs. This problem could be circumvented with a minimal sacrifice of the impairment-payment program's advantages if, instead of cash, vouchers to purchase a limited range of services were provided to elderly persons with specific assessed functional impairments. Thus, for example, the use of vouchers might be limited to the purchase of transportation services, homemakers, personal-care services, delivered meals, housecleaning, shopping services, laundering, and so on. Sellers providing one or more services could then convert voucher receipts into cash. Vouchers could also be restricted to a few services or to a single service if the external benefits of that service justified the restriction.

Although voucher recipients would be constrained from purchasing many goods and services with their vouchers, they would have freedom to fit the mix of eligible services to their individual needs and tastes. They also would retain an independent, rather than dependent, position with respect to suppliers. The total supply of different services, the suppliers of particular services, and the quality of different services would be determined by the aggregated decisions of individual consumers rather than by administrators. If demands are sufficient to support competing suppliers and if consumers are capable of policing the cost and quality of services, then efficiency and service quality will be maintained by market forces. By restricting utilization of impairment payments to a limited set of services the voucher system would also assure the existence of demand for them, would advertise the existence of that demand, and would thereby stimulate the production of services needed by impaired elderly that might otherwise be available.

While avoiding one major drawback of the cash payment form of organization, vouchers introduce some problems of their own. First, they would introduce the administrative complication and expense of accrediting suppliers to assure that their services are among the set of approved services—a problem that is compounded for organizations that supply unapproved as well as approved services. These difficulties and the complication of converting voucher receipts into cash might deter some suppliers from providing service and reduce the level of competition available to assure efficiency and responsiveness. Second, vouchers might be further complicated by conditions and regulations required to limit the sale of vouchers and other client abuses whose effect is to circumvent the constraints meant to differentiate vouchers from cash. Third, the intended breadth of the constraints on vouchers might be, on the other side, thwarted by administrators anxious to limit the application of vouchers to a very narrow range of services considered "good" for recipients. Finally, the voucher scheme shares with a cash transfer program a dependence on consumer ability.

It might be thought that this last problem could be mitigated by limiting vouchers to purchases from nonprofit agencies. Such organizations, it is sometimes argued, have a direct rather than profit-derived interest in client welfare and can, therefore, be trusted to serve persons who are unable to protect their own interests. These contentions deserve more attention than can be given to them in the scope of this chapter. It should be noted, however, that nonprofit social service organizations evolved in an environment where success was achieved by appealing to philanthropic and public contributors and to social service professionals. Changing the rules—as would occur under vouchers—so that success and growth are achieved through appeal to different groups seeking different ends might well blur the traditional distinctions between proprietary and nonprofit suppliers of social services.

The problems posed by limited mental competence and consumer ability could, alternatively, be dealt with by employing a "public-coordinator/private-producer" or "private-coordinator/private-producer" mode for persons unable independently to consume effectively. These organizational modes could be used for all clients or could be used together with a voucher or cash program for a selected subset of the eligible population. The two modes are discussed in the following sections.

Public-Coordinator/Private-Supply

In the two preceding organizational forms production is private (profit and nonprofit) and subsidies are routed through consumers who (partly or completely) determine the mix of services and insure efficient production and quality service through their market behavior. The mental impairments of some clientele, however, limit the validity of this reasoning and the applicability of those organizational modes to persons who can consume effectively with at most the assistance of an information service. Consequently, a public-coordinator/private-supply mode might be employed for all clientele or for mentally impaired clientele in a system where the mentally able were provided with vouchers or cash.

Under a public-coordinator/private-supply arrangement clients' impairment-created needs would be assessed and a subsidy proportioned to client needs would be routed not to the individual but to a worker designated to make consumption decisions on his behalf and in his interest. This mode differs from current arrangements (for example, the Social Services program in many states) in which the worker selecting needed services simultaneously determines the level of resources allocated to the individual client. It thereby restricts workers to making the best of given resources and does not enable skilled workers to benefit clients by expanding their impairment resources—a strategy that benefits some individual clients only at the expense of other impaired elderly persons if the total program budget is not open ended.

Counseling (as distinguished from the selection of services and the provision of maintenance and personal-care services) could be included among the services purchased for clients by coordinators. Counseling, however, is probably more appropriately provided by the coordinator or someone in the same organization since it is integrally bound up with the selection of services. That is, when required by dependent persons, counseling should be considered a part of the centralizing force of coordination rather than as one of the several services assembled by that force.

This point and the need for coordination is repeatedly stressed in the literature on services for the impaired elderly. In the view of Eric Pfeiffer and his colleagues, for example,

> the most important clinical service offered by an agency . . . is not a specific therapeutic intervention but rather the coordination effort of all the services required by an individual while continuing contact is maintained with the individual. In fact, in terms of our list of services we have placed this at the highest level, even though the idea of coordination of services before any services have been named may superficially seem to be absurd. [7]

Coordination is probably facilitated by the channeling of funds through coordinators for individual clients. Then workers are not asking favors of a service-providing agency; rather, they are purchasing service. This is a lever to use in obtaining service and shaping the quality and character of service that is provided. Allocational efficiency furthermore is more likely to be attained by workers selecting services fitted to the needs and wishes of individual clients than by service-mix decisions made at a higher level as occurs with block grants to individual service providers. This is true at least partly because coordinators, like clients under the cash payment scheme, could use the impairment payment to purchase normally marketed services and goods where those more satisfactorily met needs than services provided by "social service" agencies.

Market pressures for production efficiency and high-quality personal-care and maintenance services could be exerted through the supplier choices made by the service worker in attempting to maximize the effectiveness of a limited impairment payment. As in the preceding methods of organizing service, clients could object to poor quality without endangering their receipt of service and might have a different relationship with suppliers than if service were provided as a gift. The quality of competing providers could be monitored to give workers better information with which to make service decisions. This evaluative monitoring would confront little opposition since the resulting information would be for internal use and would not have to be promulgated publicly. In those instances where the scale of demand is too small to support competition among suppliers at a moment in time, this form of organization would permit the public agency to make contractual arrangements (with payments related to the quantity of service used) of fixed duration that would permit competition over time.

In this system ultimate service providers are made accountable to workers by the market. A major problem is, in turn, creating a method for making workers effective and accountable, and establishing to whom they are accountable when clients are truly mentally incompetent. The Vocational Rehabilitation program employs an organizational model that resembles the form suggested here. Workers in that program, however, receive a total allotment to cover all of their cases rather than individual allotments tied to the assessed needs of particular clients. Workers then must use those resources as effectively as possible on the set of all clients assigned to them. They are encouraged to be effective since advancement is partly tied to the number of persons successfully rehabilitated. This system has problems but even its incentive virtue is not transferable to the maintenance of chronically impaired elderly persons since for them there frequently is no dominant and clear-cut single goal analogous to successful job placement. Reliance, therefore, would probably have to be placed on the selection of workers who have concern for the well being of clients and on the supervision of their efforts—although this conclusion should not impede attempts to develop some form of incentive mechanism.

If universally applied the public-coordinator/private-supply form of organization denies choice and independence to people who are capable of managing their own affairs if assisted with money or vouchers and with information when it is required. It therefore might be implemented side-by-side with one of the preceding organizational forms, sharing a common assessment procedure, and channeling individuals to the more and less dependent programs depending on their preference and competencies, and on the availability of responsible and willing relatives.

Private Coordinator/Private Supply

Several of the preceding organizational modes, by placing the coordinating and market-policing functions on clients or their families, neglect the dependent condition of many impaired elderly persons who have no family. Although the problem can be handled by establishing a public coordinator role, it also can be handled in other ways. For example, organizations might be created to provide, instead of individual services, complete care for the impaired individual in the home, including the selection and coordination of a service mix and the provision of services.[8] The organizations presumably would operate analagously to building contractors—coordinating all services, producing some (or all) services directly, and subcontracting for the production of services where appropriate.

Impaired elderly persons would be assigned an impairment cost. Those capable of picking among suppliers could be provided vouchers valued at that level and usable only to purchase complete care from among suppliers. Others could have a supplier selected by a public worker who in this instance would have a much narrower task than the public coordinators operating in the preceding organizational model. In both cases the individual making the agency choice would presumably select an organization that was both adept at coordinating services matched to client preferences and needs and was efficient in producing services so that the individual's fixed payment could finance a large volume of services.

This organizational mode thus resembles the voucher and public-coordinator/private-supply modes in relying on market incentives to maintain production efficiency and quality. It differs from them, however, in relying further on market forces to maintain allocative efficiency—that is, the coordinating and selecting of services—since supplier competence in that function would be required to attract business. The system might be easier for individuals to negotiate than one in which services were selected individually—but this would possibly be at the expense of independence. If such an organization is effective it might well evolve under a broader voucher program since there is nothing to prevent agencies, in that arrangement, from providing a cluster of coordinated services rather than individual services if that is what buyers seek.

The scale of demand required to support meaningfully different efficient organizations of this type is probably greater than the scale required to support providers of individual services. Consequently, competition for individual clients could be relied upon to regulate efficiency and quality only in densely populated areas with large numbers of impaired elderly (and other impaired persons). However, contracts for the care of all clients in an area might be made within single-care organizations—with the threat of contract loss used to maintain competitive pressure on the organization holding the contract at a moment in time.

CONCLUSIONS

The onset of severe impairments creates a need for supportive services and raises the cost of maintaining a minimum or given standard of living. Society could respond to these needs by making cash payments to functionally impaired persons. These could be proportioned to impairment levels and scaled to income, and would enable the impaired older person to select and purchase services of his own choosing.

Such a "system" of services would be questioned since markets are often alleged not to respond to service demands. An examination of the relevant arguments, however, finds them unconvincing. Markets, that is, are likely to supply homemaker, transportation, nutrition, and other supportive services where demands exist—and at reasonable cost where competition prevails. An impairment-payment program, however, would be less satisfactory as a means of organizing demand. Some functionally impaired persons live alone and are mentally incapable of managing their own affairs and selecting appropriate services, while other persons will be ineffective enforcers of cost and quality competition in the market. Furthermore, a program that singles out the impaired elderly for special treatment yet leaves them free to neglect impairment-created needs may be politically unacceptable.

This suggests other organizational modes that differ essentially in the way that they organize service demands: vouchers that restrict impairment payments to the purchase of selected services; a system of public coordinators purchasing privately produced services on behalf of clients; and a system of competing agencies each of which coordinates and provides services. Other organizational modes obviously can be created but the discussion restricts attention to the influence that these modes will have on service performance: efficiency, quality, equity, and the dependency position of clients. Speculative discussion obviously cannot reveal which organizational mode is most appropriate. However, by exploring the organization-performance relation the analysis suggests that future demonstrations be structured to evaluate not just the impact of different services but also the significance of organizing their delivery in different ways.

NOTES

1. See the discussion and tables in U.S. Senate, Committee on Finance, Social Services Regulations, Part 1 of 2 Parts, Hearings Before the Committee on Finance (Washington, D.C., May 1973).

2. Brahna Trager, Home Health Services in the United States, a report to the Special Committee on Aging, U.S. Senate, April 1972, p. 42.

3. Ibid., p. 9.

4. Margaret Blenker, Martin Bloom, and Margaret Nielson, "A Research and Demonstration Project of Protective Services," Social Casework 52, no. 8 (October 1971): 483-93.

5. Margaret Blenker, "Environmental Change and the Aging Individual," The Gerontologist 7 (1967): 104.

6. Margaret Nielson, Margaret Blenker, Martin Bloom, Thomas Downs, and Helen Beggs, "Older Persons After Hospitalization: A Controlled Study of Home Aide Service," American Journal of Public Health 62, no. 8 (August 1972): 1094-1101.

7. Eric Pfeiffer, Designing a System of Care—The Clinical Perspective, Presented at the National Conference on Alternatives to Institutional Care for Older Americans, Practice and Planning, at Duke University, Durham, N.C., June 1-3, 1972, p. 9.

8. These are the same as the "Personal Care Organizations" proposed by Morris and others at the Levinson Gerontological Policy Institute at Brandeis University. Helen Kistin, Elizabeth Harris, and Robert Morris, An Alternative to Institutional Care for the Elderly and the Disabled: A Proposal for a New Policy, Levinson Gerontological Policy Institues, Brandeis University (Waltham, Mass., April 1971).

5

INSTITUTIONAL FRAMEWORK FOR EVALUATING MUNICIPAL SERVICES

Stanley M. Altman,
Paul M. Nawrocki, and
Francis J. Potter

From 1971 to 1973 the Program for Urban and Policy Sciences of the State University of New York at Stony Brook served as a technical advisory group to New York City's Environmental Protection Administration. During this time the program collaborated with the Department of Sanitation on a wide range of studies aimed at understanding and changing operational procedures of the department. Because of the timeliness and relevance of the problems addressed and the commitment of Commissioner Herbert Elish to improving the operation of his department, most recommendations were implemented.

To date, the primary focus of the collaborative research has been improving the internal operations of the Sanitation Department.

This work was supported in part by the National Science Foundation and the Fund for the City of New York. The chapter was written in two parts. The beginning section was coauthored by Altman, Nawrocki, and Potter in the spring of 1973. At that time Project Scorecard was just getting started, and those of us involved were groping to figure out how to create an independent agency dedicated to the concept of public accountability of government services while at the same time creating an opportunity for ex-addicts on drug-free programs or methadone maintenance programs to find their way back into the mainstream of society. Since the original version was written, Altman has had the opportunity to update this progress report on Project Scorecard. The section entitled Project Scorecard—One Year Later, written only by Altman, tells what has happened since this chapter was originally presented at the WORC-Urban Institute Symposium.

Rather than dealing directly with the quality of services provided, the focus has been on improving the efficiency of various subsystems of the process through which the service is provided.

Traditionally the department has given its highest priority to household refuse collection. With the restructuring of its manpower work schedules in 1971, attention was turned to improving street cleaning operations. Since the cleanliness of the streets is one measure of the quality of service provided by the Department of Sanitation, we have been able to trace from 1971 through 1974 a number of changes that have been made to improve the delivery of this service.

Commissioner Elish recognized that maintaining improvements over a sustained period required an information system to provide feedback about the department's efforts to keep New York City's streets clean. In addition he recognized that for such information to have credibility with the public, it should be assembled by an independent organization outside of the Department of Sanitation. For these reasons he approached the Fund for the City of New York and the Program for Urban and Policy Sciences at Stony Brook and asked that they both participate in a research project to develop a capacity for citywide evaluation of street and sidewalk cleanliness. The system to be developed would draw upon experiences of both the department and The Urban Institute in measuring effectiveness of service delivery.

After some preliminary department studies during the summer of 1972 it became evident that several critical elements were required to carry out such a research project. First, there was a need to develop a framework in which data collected could be objectively interpreted. The cleanliness rating can be affected by factors such as time, location, and weather conditions. These must be incorporated in the model used to interpret the data. Second, further work on defining a relative scale for rating street cleanliness was required. Third, there was need for a full-time field survey force dedicated to the citywide rating effort. This meant designing an organization and recruiting personnel. The actual rating procedure requires training surveyors to provide consistent, reliable data. This implies that training programs had to be developed to insure the reliability of the data collected.

Because of the possibility of enlisting manpower through the Vera Institute of Justice and Wildcat Services Corporation's supportive services program, it was agreed that the field survey staff would be drawn from the programs for ex-drug addicts operated by Wildcat Services Corporation. Initially the salaries of the field staff were paid for from Wildcat Services funds, with project funds provided by the Fund for the City of New York used to supplement the existing Wildcat Services salary structure. It was also agreed that this project could serve the added purpose of providing employment for a number of ex-addicts, with the possibility of opening up more jobs in service evaluation as the project developed.

In proposing this project Commissioner Elish saw the Street Cleaning Evaluation Project (more popularly known as Project Scorecard) as a possible feedback mechanism for achieving accountability of the Department of Sanitation staff in achieving improved operation. While he recognized the importance of making information public, and, in fact, initially proposed Scorecard as an organization outside of the department, his position dictated that he view this information in the more classical framework of an improved management information system; he saw Scorecard as a service organization for the Department of Sanitation.

On the other hand, as the executive director of an independent foundation, Gregory Farrell saw the need for an informed public to play an increasing role if government is to become more responsive. A necessary first step is to establish feedback paths through which the public can hold government accountable for the services provided. As such, Scorecard is seen as an experimental project for testing the feasibility of creating new institutional forms outside of, but working cooperatively with, government to improve the quality of services provided. While these two views are not necessarily incompatible, they do suggest a different set of priorities. It is too early to say what the consequences of this difference may be.

In considering the major viewpoints of the participants in this project, let us continue by completing the discussion for the remaining two parties. Wildcat Service Corporation was established to provide a supported environment for ex-addicts by creating new jobs in the public services field. Scorecard is seen in this light. With the increasing concern about productivity in provision of public services, undertakings such as Scorecard offer the promise of providing jobs analogous to those service functions in light manufacturing and industry through which those in low economic classes achieved upward mobility. Scorecard may be the prototype for stimulating such a new job market (although not on the same scale).

Initially, Stony Brook saw Scorecard as a mixture of the three views mentioned above. However, we at Stony Brook became victims of our own mixed set of objectives. There are times when the interests of the field observers as expressed by Wildcat have been at odds with the objective of collecting field data for evaluation of sanitation services. In examining our own goals and objectives we concluded that Scorecard is first an experimental project to test the feasibility of evaluating public services, with a strong commitment to provide a supportive work environment for the individuals provided by Wildcat Service Corporation.

EARLY RESULTS

Our initial efforts were directed at collecting field data to determine the effects that time of day, day of week, land use patterns, individual raters, and other factors had on the street and sidewalk rating. In addition we were interested in testing the hypothesis that within a census tract the variation among the ratings would be small enough to consider census tracts homogenous for the purpose of developing a stratified sampling strategy. To gain experience over a cross-section of census tracts and at the same time to keep the data collection effort manageable, we selected a single sanitation district (on the east side of Manhattan) and selected six census tracts with different land use and socioeconomic characteristics. For each tract we tried to collect complete data for each day. The experimental design called for this phase of our data collection efforts to cover four weeks, using two three-person teams, a driver and two raters. Because of problems of weather during February and March, and difficulties encountered in getting Scorecard operational, we did not accomplish this objective for all the tracts. Instead we were forced to revise our initial design and decided to concentrate our efforts in the tracts where we expected to find the dirtiest streets and sidewalks.

Some of the findings from this effort are interesting but not surprising. First, litter levels were found highest on Monday and Tuesday. This results from no cleaning services being performed on Sunday. Second, we grouped all of our street and sidewalk ratings into one of four classes depending on the absence of a litter basket, the presence of an empty, a half-full, or a full litter basket. We found that the cumulative distribution of percentage of block faces with ratings below a given cleanliness rating for each class formed four nonintersecting curves, a greater percentage of streets or sidewalks having a lower cleanliness rating if there was a litter basket than if there was no basket. For block faces with litter baskets the greater the percentage of clean streets and sidewalks, the emptier the litter basket. This finding led the Environmental Protection Administration to experiment with additional litter baskets.

We adopted the view initially that raters could be trained to rate against a standard set of pictures (similar to those used by The Urban Institute and New York City Department of Sanitation). [1] Each picture represents one of four different levels of cleanliness. Level 1 depicts no street or sidewalk litter, with each successive level depicting more litter. To give the reader some physical feeling for how much street (sidewalk) litter corresponds to each level we have drawn a hypothesized idealized curve in Figure 5.1. While we do know

FIGURE 5.1

Hypothesised and Idealized Relationship between
the Rating Scale and the Amount of Street (Sidewalk) Litter

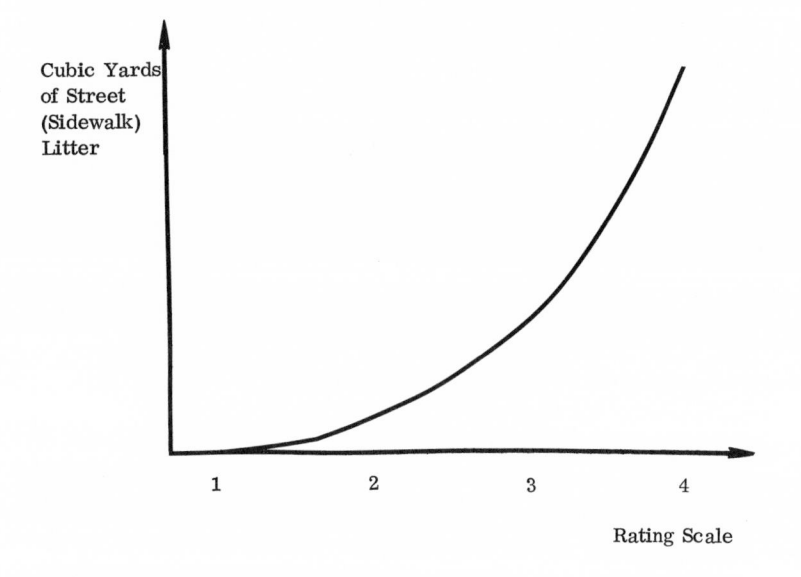

Source: Compiled by the authors.

that such a nonlinear relationship exists, we as yet do not know what
the actual curve is. It is important to note the relatively slow rate
of increase that occurs between 1 and 2, and the rapid rise that occurs
beginning around 2.5.

In addition to the data collected to determine the effect of different factors on the ratings, we conducted a pilot project to determine
the potential impact of providing data on the conditions of streets and
neighborhoods that have low cleanliness ratings on a routine basis to
sanitation districts' supervisory personnel, and we began a pilot
project of reporting the location of abandoned cars and bulk refuse
(such as sofas, refrigerators) within a six-block area on the lower
East Side of Manhattan.

Over a six-week period we provided reports on the supervisory
personnel of Sanitation District 4. Daily reports were given for the
first two weeks, then no reports for two weeks, then we began our
daily reports again. As shown in Figure 5.2, there was a continual
improvement in the overall cleanliness rating of the area. Even more
dramatic is the fact that on May 5, the day we began our second set

FIGURE 5.2

Street Ratings for Census Tract 26.02

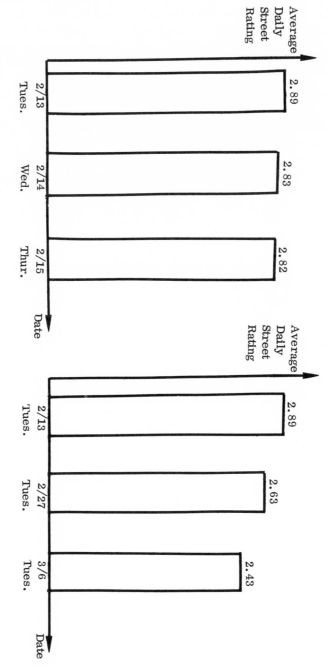

Source: Compiled by the authors.

of reports, the cleanliness rating had returned to the level initially observed. Since it takes one day before any action can be taken, the dramatic change from the 5th to the 6th of May indicates that the reports had some effect. While we are unable to present a hard and fast case because we did not collect baseline data initially, both the improvement in ratings and our staff's subjective opinion that more resources have been assigned to this area indicate that such information has the potential of creating change.

The third project that Scorecard has been involved in to date has been the evaluation of New York City's Department of Sanitation Intensive Cleaning Program directed at 42 business areas spread throughout the Bronx, Brooklyn, Manhattan, and Queens.[2]

THE INSTITUTIONAL SETTING

One issue that is critical to the long-term effectiveness of organizations such as Scorecard is how are they institutionalized. Should Scorecard be absorbed by the department and become an evaluation project office in the commissioner's office, or should it become an independent organization? Experience of the Vera Institute of Justice on the Bail Reform Project[3] in the 1960s with New York City Department of Corrections and The Urban Institute's experience in Washington seem to indicate that Project Scorecard should be institutionalized as a separate, independent organization.

In the case of the Vera Institute of Justice, when the Bail Reform project was turned over to the Department of Corrections it became just one more program that the department administered. It no longer received the same attention or commitment from those involved as it did under Vera's direction. This experience has led the Vera Institute to adopt the philosophy that it will institutionalize its projects as independent organizations whose primary priority is providing the service they were established for. In addition, because of the belief that bail reform is important, Vera has recently taken the program back from the Department of Corrections.

The experiences we relate about the impact of evaluation on agency performance are the same as those encountered by The Urban Institute during its involvement with the Department of Sanitation in Washington, D.C. It is our understanding that once the evaluation system was developed and turned over to the department, the effectiveness of this program decreased, for reasons similar to those encountered by Vera.

In addition to our concern that, once institutionalized inside the agency it is designed to evaluate, such a program may become ineffective, we are concerned about maintaining a continuity in the pressure that program evaluation can apply. As long as Herb Elish remains as commissioner of Sanitation we are convinced that such an effort will have his support. But once he leaves in January 1974 and the new administration appoints its choice for commissioner, what about the future of such an effort? The gamble is not worth taking.

PROJECT SCORECARD—ONE YEAR LATER

Since the preceding section of this chapter was written, in the spring of 1973 when Scorecard was just beginning to define its own identity and to gain experience, a great deal has happened.

The most important event so far is that Scorecard still exists as an independent organization. In July 1973 a proposal was submitted to the Board of Directors of the Fund for the City of New York requesting $85,000 for the continuation of Project Scorecard for another year. If the board approved this proposal, Stony Brook, through its National Science Foundation grant, agreed to provide $50,000 and the Sanitation Department $68,000 to cover the remaining cost of operating Scorecard. Wildcat Service Corporation agreed to continue to supply personnel. Based on three months of experience monitoring the Department of Sanitation's intensive cleaning campaign, the board approved Scorecard's continuation. *

One difference in the organization of Scorecard since July 1973 is the creation of full-time staff positions, exclusive of the project manager, which were paid for from Project Scorecard's budget. Of the seven staff members employed by Scorecard at this time, five were being supported by Wildcat Service Corporation while two others were working part-time supported by funds from our original Fund grant. With the approval of Scorecard's new budget, all seven became permanent Scorecard employees. Since July the staff of eight has grown to a full-time staff of 28. Eleven are paid directly from Scorecard's budget and the remaining 17 by Wildcat Service Corporation.

---

*At the same meeting the Fund's board approved the creation of the Project on Improving Government Productivity. Project Scorecard is one of three monitoring projects that are under this umbrella organization within the Fund. The other two are concerned with the quality of ambulatory care provided by outpatient clinics and parks maintenance.

An evaluation of the impact of Scorecard's monitoring of the intensive cleaning program from April 1973 to February 1974 is presently being completed. Preliminary results showed that the cleanliness of streets and sidewalks in the business areas included in this program have improved. Part of the success of this program can be attributed to Scorecard's efforts.

During the month of April 1973 field personnel were not aware that Scorecard was collecting data that the department planned to use to evaluate the effectiveness of this intensive cleaning program. Therefore, as was typical with intensive cleaning programs run during previous years, the initial improvement in street cleanliness (which coincided with department efforts in launching the program) began to deteriorate once the program was running several weeks. May 1973 ratings showed a decrease in program performance.

On May 9, 1973, the department issued its first field report, announcing the use of Scorecard to evaluate the intensive cleaning program. Table 5.1 shows the ratings on street cleanliness and sidewalk cleanliness contained in the report. Indicated in this table are ratings from the baseline period, ratings for April 1973, the percent improvement, and the relative rankings by magnitude of improvement. Scorecard's ratings were not only used to rank sanitation boroughs* in terms of their improvement but were also used to direct Bureau of Industrial Engineers (BIE) staff to specific business areas that have shown little or no improvement. For example, during May 1973, Jim Moar, the director of BIE, visited the borough superintendent of Manhattan West to discuss the lack of improvement in street cleanliness in that sanitation borough. As a result of this meeting and the ability to document program performance, Manhattan West showed a steady improvement in its cleanliness ratings. Its street ranking went from 7th in May to 2nd in June. A similar result was seen after a meeting with the borough superintendent of Queens West in June. An interesting anecdote from the competition that resulted from comparing the performance of each sanitation borough involves the borough superintendent of Brooklyn North. Brooklyn North ranked first for the month of April. After receiving Jim Moar's memorandum announcing this, that borough superintendent wrote across the top of it: "We are number 1, we will stay number 1" and circulated copies to all of his field personnel.

---

*The Department of Sanitation divides the five boroughs of New York City into 11 "sanitation boroughs." Each sanitation borough coordinates the field operation of five or six "sanitation districts."

TABLE 5.1

Project Scorecard Initial Ratings, May 1973

Street Cleanliness

Zone		Baseline Period Rating	April 1973 Rating	Percent Improvement	Rank
Manhattan	West	1.90	1.72	9.5	9
	East	2.28	2.04	10.5	8
Bronx	West	2.20	1.55	29.5	3
	East	1.95	1.58	19.0	6
Brooklyn	West	2.21	1.63	26.5	4
	North	2.61	1.53	41.5	1
Queens	East	2.37	1.60	32.5	2
	West	1.70	1.42	16.5	7
	North	1.69	1.32	22.0	5
	South	no data			

Sidewalk Cleanliness

Zone		Baseline Period Rating	April 1973 Rating	Percent Improvement	Rank
Manhattan	West	1.89	1.79	5.5	8
	East	2.46	2.09	15.0	3
Bronx	West	1.94	1.65	15.0	3
	East	1.65	1.49	10.0	5
Brooklyn	West	2.01	1.96	2.5	9
	North	2.32	1.66	28.5	1
Queens	East	2.22	1.84	17.0	2
	West	1.67	1.51	9.5	6
	North	1.46	1.33	9.0	7
	South	no data			

Source: Compiled by the authors.

When the intensive cleaning program began in April 1973 there appears to have been a clear pattern of sidewalks being cleaner than the streets. As the Department of Sanitation continued its efforts during the earlier months of the program, both street and sidewalk ratings began to approach the same level of cleanliness. It is interesting to note that sidewalks, which are the responsibility of merchants and the public, have followed the same trend in improved cleanliness from April 1973 through November 1974. For whatever reason, the impact of the department's street cleaning program has affected both streets and sidewalks. It is only after the department curtails its efforts because of the snow-season alert it goes on after Thanksgiving that sidewalks begin to rate consistently cleaner than streets.

To get a feeling for the usefulness of Scorecard's monitoring efforts from the department's perspective a meeting was held on May 1, 1974, with Walter Bridgewood, assistant chief of staff for Street Cleaning Operations, and other members of the Department of Sanitation's Bureau of Cleaning and Collection. Bridgewood reiterated the usefulness of Scorecard's efforts because it provided him data on cleaning operations that are not available from other sources. He stressed the importance of receiving Scorecard's data by business areas in addition to the aggregated averages by sanitation borough because it would allow him to compare the performance of department personnel working in similar business areas throughout the city as well as to pinpoint for borough superintendents business areas that are trouble spots.

Starting in April 1974 Scorecard began to monitor the Department of Sanitation's routine street cleaning services. We have begun to collect cleanliness reports on all 254 sanitation sections in the city. For the purposes of monitoring, every sanitation section was assigned to one of three classes: (1) heavily traveled streets that are cleaned by sanitation up to six times weekly; (2) streets cleaned two or three times weekly; and (3) those city streets that tend to be cleaner and are not scheduled for sweeping on a regular basis. Scorecard will evaluate the cleanliness of each class of streets as follows:

> Class I   - twice a week once every two weeks
> Class II   - twice a week once a month
> Class III - once every three months.

For each sanitation section the sample of block faces to be rated were selected by stratifying all block faces in five distinct groups and randomly selecting from each group a starting block face. The next three contiguous blocks are then selected to form a sample of 20 block faces consisting of five clusters of four. Each cluster has an

TABLE 5.2

Project Scorecard Morning Printout

```
MORNING    24 SEP 74   11:43

GOOD MORNING. . . . .IT IS SEPTEMBER 24 1974.

THIS IS THE 7 TH DAY OF THE 10 DAY CLASS 1 CYCLE.
THIS IS THE 16 TH DAY OF THE 22 DAY CLASS 2 CYCLE.
THIS IS THE 59 TH DAY OF THE 63 DAY CLASS 3 CYCLE.

THE FOLLOWING IS THE STATUS OF SCORECARD RATINGS AS OF
THIS MORNING PRIOR TO THE ASSIGNMENT OF TEAM ROUTES.
```

	CLASS			
	I	II	III	TOTAL
TOTAL NUMBER OF SECTIONS	89	105	80	274
NUMBER COMPLETELY RATED	25	76	80	181
PERCENTAGE OF TOTAL	28.1	72.4	100	66.1
NUMBER RATED BUT NOT RERATED	22	12	0	34
SECTIONS WHICH CAN BE RERATED TODAY	0	0	0	0
SECTIONS WHICH MUST BE RERATED TODAY	0	0	0	0

```
WOULD YOU LIKE TO SEE THE SECTIONS WHICH ARE IN ANY OF
THESE CATEGORIES? NO

INDICATE NEXT TO EACH OF THE FOLLOWING CATEGORIES WHAT PRIORITY YOU
PLACE ON IT TODAY. (1 IS THE HIGHEST PRIORITY; 6 IS THE LOWEST).

PREVIOUSLY UNRATED CLASS I SECTIONS? 1
PREVIOUSLY UNRATED CLASS II SECTIONS? 1

ARE THERE ANY PARTICULAR SECTIONS TO WHICH YOU WISH TO GIVE ANY
SPECIAL PRIORITIES (EITHER TO DESIGNATE THEM AS NOT TO BE RATED
OR TO GIVE THEM A HIGH PRIORITY)? NO

WHAT IS THE MAXIMUM TIME YOU WISH TO HAVE TEAMS IN THE FIELD?
(EXPRESS IN MINUTES; FOR EXAMPLE '300' AS A RESPONSE TO THIS
QUESTION WOULD EQUAL FIVE HOURS).?   360

HOW MANY TEAMS ARE AVAILABLE TODAY? 3

ROUTE # 1
 394      25        41        24
 7         7         7         7
TOTAL ESTIMATED TIME: 316.87

ROUTE # 2
 305      302       21        22
 7         7         7         7
TOTAL ESTIMATED TIME: 309.77

ROUTE # 3
 513 B    81        82        83
 7         7         7         7
TOTAL ESTIMATED TIME: 327.508
```

<u>Source:</u> Compiled by the authors.

equal probability of being selected. At least one but no more than three days will elapse between ratings.

To assist in managing data collection and reporting, a management information system is under development. The first operational version of this system allows Project Scorecard's manager to obtain a daily status report of work completed against monthly targets. It also prints daily work assignments and sanitation sections to be rated, using a version of the Clarke and Wright algorithm for efficiency routing. At the end of the day the work completed is entered. Any sanitation sections that are scheduled to be rated but were not are automatically reconsidered the next day for reassignment. These programs provide the tools for more effectively managing the day-to-day operations of Scorecard but can also be used as a planning tool for determining staff requirements over long periods of time once monthly or long-term targets are set. A typical morning print-out is shown in Table 5.2.

In addition to the work assignment features of this system, there is a separate system to aggregate and summarize data at different management levels. For New York City data is aggregated first by sanitation section, then all sections in sanitation districts are combined, then all districts in a sanitation borough are combined, then all sanitation boroughs in a geographic borough are combined, and finally all data are aggregated to give citywide statistics.

Plans call for the interfacing of the assignment programs and reporting programs to permit more effective validation of data and the addition of the capacity to automatically generate special routes that overlap work routes being run that day to permit a standard team to periodically check the consistency of the field teams ratings.

The question raised a year ago about the potential conflict between providing a supportive work environment and carrying out ongoing evaluations seems to have disappeared. During the summer of 1973 Scorecard began to experiment with a program of supportive services designed to help individual employees improve their lives. Individuals were helped in locating better housing. Those with pressing financial problems were helped in securing bank loans. In addition Scorecard created opportunities for educational advancement for these men. Also during the summer of 1973 a special program was offered in cooperation with Staten Island Community College that made it possible for all those participating to gain admission to the City University and earn credits toward both high school equivalency and college degrees. This program is now a permanent feature of the benefits Scorecard makes available for all of its employees, regardless of who pays their salary. Scorecard pays all course costs, while each individual pays the student fees.

In a recent set of interviews conducted with Scorecard employees it became clear that Scorecard was beginning to achieve some small degree of success in providing a supportive work environment. There is a general feeling that the individuals responsible for managing Scorecard care about what happens to the workers.

NOTES

1. The New York City Department of Sanitation, through its Bureau of Industrial Engineering, used such a technique to evaluate the Midtown Manhattan cleaning campaign, and The Urban Institute, the originator of this system, developed the evaluation system in cooperation with the Washington, D.C., Department of Sanitation. The results are reported in Lewis, Blair, and Alfred Schwartz, How Clean is Our City? (Washington, D.C.: The Urban Institute, 1972).

2. Three additional business areas located in the Borough of Richmond in the Intensive Cleaning Program are not being evaluated at this time.

3. Programs in Criminal Justice Reform, Vera Institute of Justice Ten-Year Report 1961-1971.

6

THE USE OF EX-ADDICTS TO DELIVER LOCAL SERVICES: THE SUPPORTED WORK EXPERIMENT
Lee S. Friedman

When an innovative social program is launched the questions of the social scientist interested in the study of policy usually fall into one of two areas. The first area is a consideration of whether the new program makes sense in principle: that is, the extent to which the underlying rationale for the program has been carefully examined. The second area concerns evaluation: that is, how can we measure the successes and failures of the program.

In this chapter I would like to describe an innovative program affecting the area of criminal justice. In addition to providing some information along the lines suggested above, I will argue that a broad perspective concerning the development of social programs can lead to more useful evaluations. In particular, an evolutionary understanding of the way programs develop and change over time leads the analyst to confront squarely the problem of organizational design.

Public policies and programs evolve in response to both perceived demands of society and to adaptational pressures from organizations in the supply channels. The attempt by one group or agency to implement a new program or policy should be viewed as an attempt to solve or ameliorate a particular problem. However, among the

---

I would like to thank David Seidman and Robert Yin for their thoughtful comments. In revising this chapter from its preliminary version, I have responded to their remarks where I thought it appropriate. The opinions expressed herein are my own, and do not necessarily reflect the views of the institutions with which I am or have been affiliated.

different groups of society, conceptions of the problem are often different. These different conceptions may lead to different avenues in the search for solutions and may lead to demand pressures to change, modify, or eliminate solutions offered by the original group or agency. Similarly, organizations providing other services may be affected by the new program, and the resulting supply adaptations may serve to frustrate the intended goals of the new program or create new problems elsewhere.

When one is evaluating a new policy or program it is important to keep this evolutionary struggle in mind. Not only does this framework alter perspectives on the significance of the research, but it also affects the choice of questions to be analyzed.

The phenomenon of the evolutionary struggle seems particularly true in the polarized field of criminal justice, and the problem of drug addiction provides an illustrative example. One view of the drug problem concentrates on the crime believed to be associated with addiction. Such a view can be based on more or less rational grounds, involving society's right to protect itself and the freedom of an individual to choose his own state of well-being. Another view is more insistent that the wasted individual lives are the major problem. That is, an alternate view is that society is responsible for the waste in human potential. [1]

This chapter will report on the development of Supported Work programs, which use ex-addicts in the delivery of a variety of local services. The following section briefly presents an overview of the drug addiction problem and some of the alternative approaches to it. In the next section the role of employment as part of the solution is discussed and the idea of Supported Work is introduced. In the third section the role of rational systematic analysis in answering important questions about Supported Work is discussed. The final section returns to the importance of an evolutionary framework in the choice of questions to be tackled by analysts.

AN OVERVIEW OF THE PROBLEM OF DRUG ADDICTION

Because of the nature of the problem, the extent of addiction in the United States is not known. However, it is believed to be concentrated in the poorest areas of our largest cities. The Ford Foundation report concluded that the best estimate of the addict population was between 250,000 and 300,000 (in December 1971). [2] The addicts referred to in this estimate are those who use heroin daily, "shooting up" on a regular basis as the high from the last injection wears off.

It is also not clear to what extent the addicts are responsible for property crime in the United States, though most estimates suggest a surprisingly high fraction. The Ford Foundation report suggested that up to 50 percent of property crimes in major metropolitan areas are committed by addicts.[3] J. Wilson, M. Moore, and I. Wheat say the estimates range from 25 to 67 percent of all property crime.[4] Both of these studies are quick to add that there is no clear causation between addiction and crime; that is, it may be that criminals tend to become addicts.

Starting with a philosophy that emphasizes crime as the primary social cost to society from addiction, a variety of policy options have been suggested or tried to reduce crime. In general, these can be referred to as "law enforcement" strategies. These options usually involve stiff penalties for the use or sale of narcotics and high enforcement levels to provide a high degree of deterrence. The strategy of civil commitment of addicts is one such policy.[5] A more dramatic example is the recent proposal by former Governor Rockefeller of New York, stressing life-term lock-ups.[6] In general the law enforcement approach has been the primary policy mechanism utilized by society. Heroin addicts, on the average, get arrested at least once during every two years of addiction and spend approximately 15 percent of their addicted life in jail.[7] This approach is commonly described as the "revolving door" approach, and as indicated by the term, has not been noted for its success.

Other strategies, involving treatment programs, have been devised by groups favoring efforts to rehabilitate the addict. These programs may involve abstinence combined with an intense experience in a therapeutic community, such as Synanon or Daytop. They may involve drug maintenance programs, such as methadone maintenance. All of these programs focus on improving the use the addict makes of his life. The therapeutic communities concentrate intensively on changing the motivations of the addict and tend to be more expensive than the more common methadone maintenance programs.[8] The methadone programs, while they may offer some counseling, rely more heavily on simply relieving the addict of the burden of supporting an expensive habit and removing the euphoric effects of heroin. This gives him the chance to find a more stable, rewarding, and productive lifestyle.

There are two important facts to note about the treatment programs. The first is that only between 15 and 20 percent of all addicts are in treatment.[9] That leaves 80 to 85 percent in the "revolving door." The second fact is that the treatment programs, while only working with a minority of the addict population, have been successful to some extent. For example, the retention rate in New York's

Methadone Maintenance Treatment Program is approximately 80 percent.[10] Out of 100 entrants to the program, 26 were employed when they entered and 45 were both employed and still in the program four years later.[11] It is not known how many total individuals of the original 100 were employed at this time since some had dropped out of the program. Also, there are some indications that criminal activity has decreased. James DeLong, in describing the program, reports:

> For the group that stayed in the program criminal activity apparently decreased. In the three years before admission to the program, the methadone patients had 120 arrests and 48 incarcerations for every 100 man-years. In the four years after admission, they had 4.5 arrests and 1.0 incarcerations.[12]

It is important to recognize, of course, that to the extent these programs reduce addict-related crime, they are compatible with the crime-reduction strategies. I would speculate that the viability of the methadone programs particularly is a result of both their success at reducing criminal activity of the participants and the relatively low cost of the program. That is, the groups stressing rehabilitation have found financial support and met with some success, and the groups stressing crime control find the program in their interest as well.

THE EMPLOYMENT PROBLEM

Let us now turn from the overview with two points in mind: (1) that there are real tensions among different groups of society in the process of seeking solutions to the drug addiction problem; and (2) that the efforts to date have largely been unsuccessful (that is, the problem, however defined, still exists).

It has been suggested that one of the problems in achieving successful rehabilitation is the limitation on alternative opportunities. The existence of a criminal record is a long-recognized barrier to decent employment. Many addicts and ex-addicts can find nothing but jobs that fall into the secondary labor market; that is, the only job opportunities are part-time or temporary and pay low wages with little or no chance for advancement.[13] The effects of these constraints on the individual's behavior may be severely debilitating.

Many of us have recognized that the barriers to decent employment are unjust as well as self-defeating, particularly to those individuals who have "paid their debt to society." To some addicts and ex-addicts the whole process is not unlike a huge loan-sharking operation, where the payments never end. Yet efforts to convince employers to give ex-addicts or ex-offenders a chance have not met with very much success (as, for example, indicated by the statistics for New York's methadone program cited previously).

The reasons for this behavior are economic and not simple prejudice. We must explicitly recognize that the employer's reluctance is based on powerful economic reality. For the private firm it is, in fact, riskier to hire individuals who have been involved in criminal activities and who have no job references rather than those fresh from school or with prior steady employment. Given that firms are interested in expected profits and avoid unnecessary risk, it is more efficient for them to exclude risky individuals from hiring consideration. No amount of moral suasion can make this reality disappear. We must fact this reality and ask what can be done about it.

One can argue that the labor markets for risky individuals operate inefficiently. While each employer may be making a decision that is economically rational, society in the aggregate may be absorbing unnecessary losses. Let us assume there are $\underline{m}$ risky individuals, of whom $\underline{sm}$ would prove to be reliable and valuable employees and $\underline{(1-s)m}$ would not. Then we could represent the social loss to society of not hiring these individuals as $\underline{smL}$, where $\underline{L}$ is the value to society of an additional productive member. (This assumes that the private employer finds the expected benefits of hiring outweighed by the expected costs.)

Suppose a screening procedure could be devised so that of the $\underline{m}$ risky individuals, $\underline{r}$ could be convincingly identified as very good risks ($r \approx \underline{sm}$ with low Type I and Type II errors, and employers are willing to hire the $\underline{r}$ individuals). If the cost of that screening procedure, $\underline{cm}$, where $\underline{c}$ is the cost of screening a risky individual, is less than $\underline{smL}$, then the social benefits outweigh the social costs and the screening procedure should be undertaken.

It is partially in this belief that the Vera Institute of Justice proposed and received funding for an experimental program in New York City called Supported Work. The Vera program is not simply a screening procedure; it also encourages the development of job skills. The idea behind the Supported Work experiment is to create useful employment opportunities for ex-addicts, but in a low-stress environment. The ex-addicts work in groups of their peers and thus know their coworkers share similar backgrounds of addiction. It is not expected that the Supported Work employee will initially be as productive as a nonsupported employee performing the same task in the regular market. Graduated performance demands are established by management. However, the normal market wages are paid for his employment. Stress is reduced in a number of other ways. Time is allowed for the employee to continue attending his drug treatment program. The ex-addict knows the employer is aware of his criminal history, and thus he is relieved of the anxiety that his past will be discovered.

Thus the Supported Work program is "supported" in two important senses. First, looked at as a delivery system for goods and services, there are structural inefficiencies purposely permitted in the system. Second, there is the peer group support of coworkers.

The kinds of employment situations created varies tremendously. As of January 1973, 58 employees were staffing the Pioneer Messenger Service. Pioneer was created by Vera in July 1971 and derives its revenues by selling message delivery service on the open market. It is subsidized by the Department of Labor. Two branches of New York's Off-Track Betting Corporation are staffed by 41 Supported Work employees. Forty-nine other ex-addicts are in three Supported Work programs operating under city auspices: a pest control unit in Bedford-Stuyvesant under the Health Service Administration, a newspaper recycling program under the Environmental Protection Administration, and a Department of Public Works project involving water blasting techniques to clean the exteriors of public buildings. The most ambitious Supported Work project is the Wildcat Service Corporation, a nonprofit service organization created to contract and deliver public services. Wildcat currently employs 179 ex-addicts and delivers services to the Parks Department (involving painting and maintenance work in the parks), to the Health Service Administration, to the Department of Public Works, to the Police Department, to the New York Public Library, and to Stony Brook's Project Scorecard. * One of the more interesting aspects of Wildcat is that it is partially funded through the diversion of welfare payments into a salary pool (that is, the welfare that the average Supported Work employee would receive if he were not in the program).

It is expected that most of the Supported Work employees will increase their productivity over time and move into nonsupported employment. Presumably they will have demonstrated by their success in Supported Work the capability of maintaining steady and productive employment and earned job references so indicating. It should also be pointed out that the exceptions may still be leading far more

---

*Project Scorecard involves rating the cleanliness of city streets and is discussed in Chapter 5.

productive and successful lives and commiting fewer crimes than if Supported Work did not exist.

THE USE OF RATIONAL OR SYSTEMATIC ANALYSIS TO EVALUATE AND GUIDE THE SUPPORTED WORK PROGRAM

What Are the Major Questions?

The broadest and most important question that rational, systematic analysis can attempt to answer is whether or not the program is worth doing. To answer this question one must measure as accurately as possible the benefits and the costs. In a pluralistic society it also seems important to be able to state who bears the costs, how much they bear, who gets the benefits, and how much they benefit. These questions are all of an evaluative nature.

A second broad area for rational, systematic research is of a guiding nature. What is the best organizational structure for the program? What kinds of services should Supported Work employees deliver? Should Supported Work be limited to ex-addicts, or should it be extended to other groups trapped in the secondary labor market, like ex-offenders, the handicapped, or welfare recipients?

Even within the context of the existing program the measurement of costs and benefits depends on the objective function. Yet there are different objectives that the program may serve, and one cannot aggregate the costs and benefits unless it is with respect to a well-specified objective function. Consider the following five conceptually distinct objectives that may be served by Supported Work:

1. Supported Work is an alternative to the current welfare system. It may be that from the non-Supported society's point of view the difference between the cost of Supported Work and the value to them of the output is less than the cost of the existing welfare system. This could conceivably be true with no crime reduction benefits and no future earnings gains to Supported Work employees.

2. Supported Work may be an efficient way of delivering public goods and services. It is conceivable that the value of the work done exceeds the cost of doing it.

3. Supported Work is a manpower program designed to improve the efficiency of the labor market. It may be that individuals considered risky investments for the primary labor market can be screened

successfully by creating job opportunities and observing their performance. If the cost of the screening procedure is less than the
value of the expansion of the primary labor market, then Supported
Work is an improvement in the efficiency of the labor market.

4. Supported Work is a manpower training program designed to
develop and increase job skills of its participants. The costs of the
program may be justified in terms of the future earnings increases of
the participants.

5. Supported Work is a crime prevention program. It may be
that the reduction in crime and criminal justice system costs more
than offsets the expenditures for Supported Work.

It should be clear that Supported Work may rate high with
respect to some objectives and low with respect to others. The problem is how to evaluate the results to indicate how the program fares
with respect to different objectives while at the same time recognizing
the importance of presenting aggregate measures with respect to
mixed objective functions.

For example, suppose for some hypothetical program there
is a $50 benefit in raised job skills for the employee and a $50 benefit
in crime reduction. The former is relevant to objective 4 but not
objective 5, while the latter is relevant to 5 but not 4. However, the
measured benefits do not always fall into just one objective function.
Both might be relevant to objective 1, and neither be relevant to 2.
To come to a social decision, where different groups are concerned
with different objectives, some aggregation is necessary. If society
is composed of only two groups, one concerned solely with crime
reduction and the other solely with increased job skills, and the total
program costs less than $100, then they may be willing to share the
costs of the program. If one aggregated these benefits, taking the
"one big family" view of society as a whole, then the program would
seem efficient (that is, assuming constant marginal utility of income,
the gainers could compensate the losers and still be better off than
without the program.[14] Whether or not one believes in the "final
reckoning," it is important to calculate the transfer payments from
different groups. Though the "one big family" approach ignores
changes in transfer payments, it seems to me that any decision
maker would be interested in this question and that the analyst is
best qualified to answer it. In sum, the analyst should try to direct
and present his research from at least several points of view.

From the list of objectives and the above remarks one recog-
nizes that the productivity of the employee (defined as the value of
labor's share of the output) is a critical factor in determining the
value of the program. For example, suppose the typical individual

is supported in a $5,000 job and has a productivity worth $3,000 (that is, the output is of genuine value to the community, and the labor share of its value is $3,000). It is quite possible that without Supported Work this typical individual would have received $2,100 in welfare payments. * The community and the Supported Work employee are both gaining, without consideration of crime reduction benefits or future earnings increases.

The reason I mentioned this example is because I think it illustrates the real difficulties of the evaluation: The benefits are highly sensitive to the value of the work being accomplished. In the case of the Pioneer Messenger Service, which operates in a competitive market, one can be fairly confident that total revenue less managerial costs, support costs, and the market return to capital, leaves as a residual the real returns to Supported Work labor. Then the difference between the salaries paid and the labor value tells us what the true subsidy is. If that true subsidy is less than what welfare payments would have been, then the taxpayer is saving money and getting an investment besides (if future crime is reduced and earnings are increased). However, in Supported Work projects like pest control or parks maintenance, the real value of the work accomplished is far more difficult to quantify.

Therefore, it may pay to evaluate the program in pieces as well as the whole. If, despite the best efforts, no reliable measures can be constructed for some projects, it may be more meaningful to offer a calculation where the data are restricted to those programs where there is confidence in the results. This should not prevent the analyst from performing the overall calculation in addition.

I should also add that evaluating the different pieces can serve a useful function in guiding the expansion or contraction of the overall program by helping to weed out the unsuccessful projects and encouraging the growth of the better ones.

What Information Is Needed To Answer the Questions?

In order to assess correctly the effects of Supported Work on an individual, one must know what would have happened to him without the

---

*A preliminary investigation of a small part of the control group (described later) indicated that the average member received $680 in welfare during a four-month period.

program. For this reason the program is being run as a controlled social experiment (starting with spring 1972 applicants). All applicants must be in a drug treatment program successfully for at least three months to be considered for Supported Work. For every job vacancy, candidates are screened until two are found acceptable. Then by means of a random lottery one is assigned to the control group and the other is offered the job. In order to assess both the short- and long-term effects of the program, a control group of 300 individuals will be followed-up for a period of three to five years.

The expected reductions in crime and criminal justice system costs can be measured by gathering data on arrests, incarcerations, convictions, and sentences for both the experimentals and controls. Similarly, future legitimate earnings increases as a result of the program can be estimated by comparing the two groups. Benefits in terms of health differences can be assessed. There may be important changes in family stability. One of the interesting differences that may be observed concerns educational investments—it is possible that the control group will show a greater investment in education than the experimentals. The foregone earnings of Supported Work employees can be measured precisely by looking at the earnings of the control group. This figure is important because it represents a part of the true opportunity cost to society of operating Supported Work programs (the real costs to society of Supported Work are the opportunity costs of the production factors used to operate the program).

Of course the program has not been operating long enough to allow any reliable estimates of the benefits and costs at this time. However, there is information on the typical background of a Supported Work employee. The majority are black, under 30, single, and on methadone; 44 percent have been convicted of three or more crimes; 61 percent have never worked more than 18 months on one job; 74 percent were receiving public assistance prior to the program (in New York addicts qualify for assistance under the Aid to Disabled program); 57 percent have not attained a high school diploma. Given this population it is reassuring to know that of the 401 Supported Work employees hired by January 1973, approximately 70 percent are still with the program and 10 percent have successfully moved into non-supported employment (the average time since hiring is approximately six months). In a follow-up of the control group two months after their initial interview, 87 percent were unemployed.

Though it is clear that having a randomly selected control group goes a long way toward providing the data base necessary to make an effective evaluation, it does not by itself provide sufficient information. The critical role of productivity information, for example, is still present. Perhaps some of the experiences with a preliminary study (underway) of the Bedford-Stuyvesant Pest Control project will prove illuminating.

After the first four months of the project (August–November 1972) it was decided to begin testing our evaluative power—the ability to come up with a reliable indicator of what promise, if any, this project was showing. We were surprised to learn that the control group for this project (only 13 individuals) was unemployed for 95 percent of the time and estimated their average public assistance payments to be $679.44 per control individual for the period. The average labor value of the work produced by the control individual was only $90. By contrast, the Supported Work employee had earned $1,326 during the period. This last figure includes the subsidy, and the true economic value of the services performed still has to be calculated. There were no differences between the groups in education or arrest.

At first it seemed that a reasonable productivity estimate could be made. The city has many non-Supported Pest Control crews, and it did not seem bad to assume that the true economic value of the work performed by an average city crew member was equal to his wage. The city keeps records on the number of tons of rubbish collected per man-day by the different Pest Control units. One could then adjust the wages of the Supported Work employee by the ratio:

$$\frac{\text{tons/Supported man-day}}{\text{tons/Regular crew man-day}}$$

From the city data the ratio was estimated to be 77 percent. This implied that the true subsidy was $305, far less than the subsidy received by the control group. In fact it does seem safe to conclude tentatively that the city is saving money through this program, since any productivity ratio higher than 50 percent would demonstrate that. However, that tentative conclusion is about all that can be said.

We soon discovered that the city data was not reliable enough for our purposes. The rubbish is weighed when it is dumped, but not all of the dumps have scales and the figures are often arbitrarily recorded. The different crews may share the same truck, and there is no way to tell how much each crew collected. Different kinds of trucks are used by different crews, and the time spent loading may vary significantly because of the truck type. Crews complained that garbage bagged the day before and left to be collected the next day would often be stolen. To some extent adjustments could be made on the data (the ratio quoted above is the "adjusted" estimate). However, too much uncertainty remained to be confident about a "point" estimate.

Plans are now being made to conduct a short (two-week) field experiment to observe city and Supported Work crews in order to derive a better estimate of the value of Supported Work labor. However, this still finesses the question of measuring the value of pest control itself.

The point of this example is that despite the best efforts at measuring productivity in this project other projects allow estimates with a good deal more confidence (though no studies have been completed). Thus if I were asked to give my impressions on how productive Supported Work employees are, I would refer to the Off-Track Betting project where daily shortages of each office in the corporation are accurately reported and thus are a good measure of productivity. During the first year of operation of the two Supported Work offices, they have shown no significant differences in shortages relative to the corporation average.

WHAT EFFECT WILL THE ANSWERS HAVE?

Too often the analyst undertakes his study with the implicit assumption that a benevolent dictator will read and observe his findings and respond by making appropriate changes in the program. Researchers have long ignored dealing with the organizational realities of the operation of public programs, when it may be that changes in the organizational design hold the most promise for more effective public policy.

Perhaps an analogy with the operation of private markets will be revealing. Economists have long recognized that profits and prices can be a very powerful control mechanism over the behavior of both individuals and firms. Sometimes we observe attempts at using moral suasion to change their behavior when it is clear that the market will not support the change. The attempt to reduce automobile pollution by convincing people not to drive automobiles is a good example. Though there may be a few cases where some success was achieved, the reality is that consumers demand the transportation freedom offered by their automobiles and will not substitute to any great degree more limiting alternatives (like the bus). In an important sense the cost-benefit analyst must recognize that he is trying to be the voice of persuasion in a different kind of market structure, where the organizations comprising the sector are controlled by a variety of powerful forces and may not be able to heed his word. The cost-benefit analyst must recognize that he is working in an evolutionary environment.

A very real example of the importance of this phenomenon is contained in an earlier study of mine on bail reform.[15] In that study I argued that a cost-benefit analysis of the 1961 Release on Recognizance experiment in New York City would have agreed with the favorable judgments of those experiencing the operation of the reform. In fact the same technique could be used effectively today. However, the cost-benefit study would not have predicted the actual deterioration of the reform after it was institutionalized. Yet that deterioration was predictable based on an evolutionary view of organizational motivations, search activity to maintain or improve the output, and survival conditions. A different organizational structure was far more successful in Washington, D. C. It was not simply a question of the people involved but a meta-question of the structure to attract and guide its workers by continually generating appropriate incentives. It seems to me that the highest payoffs for rational, systematic research on policy issues is to work out a theory of organizational structure that allows these predictions to be made with some confidence. That is, I think, the major lesson of the evolutionary perspective.

Of course I raise these issues here with the Supported Work experiment in mind. It seems likely to me that an important new way of delivering services has been found, with promise of substantial rehabilitative benefit to the employees as well as external economies in crime reduction to the community. If the studies bear out these speculations, much thought will have to be given to the design of institutions that can successfully build from the experimental program.

It will be important to build in incentives for the institution to maintain a high quality of their graduates as well as efficient turnover. The Vera Institute has these incentives because the survival of the program at this stage depends upon its quality and cost. The typical entrenched public bureaucracy does not have these incentives. Perhaps a number of federally funded independent Supported Work agencies within a given area will prove most efficient. Each will be competing with the others to get the best placements for their graduates, and the funding could be allocated to the region as a whole on demographic characteristics and to each agency by its turnover rate (this would have the effect of making the agencies compete for the most likely candidates to succeed, performing the market sorting function.)

Of course the above is only a first speculation, and a better understanding of the expected evolutionary forces must be achieved before a more serious proposal can be made. However, I hope the main point is clear. The best use of cost-benefit analysis of experimental programs is achieved in conjunction with a serious effort at understanding how the programs will evolve under alternative organizational structures. With careful thought we may be able to learn enough about the determinants of organizational behavior in public sectors to use the controlling forces to our advantage.

NOTES

1. For an interesting discussion of this, see J. Wilson, M. Moore, and I. Wheat, Jr. "The Problem of Heroin," The Public Interest 29 (Fall 1972): 3-28. A more general discussion of polarization in criminal justice is found in H. Packer, The Limits of the Criminal Sanction (Stanford, Calif.: Stanford University Press, 1968), Part II.

2. Dealing With Drug Abuse, A Report to the Ford Foundation (New York: Praeger Publishers, 1972), p. 61.

3. Ibid., p. 6.

4. Wilson, Moore, and Wheat, op. cit., p. 12.

5. The Ford Report states (p. 29): "The law-enforcement approach to drug-abuse problems has been ameliorated by legislation permitting civil commitment in lieu of criminal punishment. Under present legislation, however, such treatment is largely illusory, since it is almost wholly institutionalized and often results in greater punishment than would be imposed by a criminal sentence."

6. New York Times, January 4, 1973, pp. 1, 28. The proposal, with some modification, has become law in New York state since the writing of this article.

7. Dealing With Drug Abuse, op. cit., p. 27.

8. Ibid., p. 25.

9. Ibid., pp. 22, 61.

10. Ibid., p. 207.

11. Ibid., p. 207. There were 13 people unemployed but still in the program after four years.

12. Ibid., p. 207.

13. P. Doeringer and M. Piore, Internal Labor Markets & Manpower Analysis (Lexington, Mass.: D.C. Heath, 1971), pp. 165-67.

14. For an excellent discussion of the cost-benefit methodology applied to manpower programs, see G. Cain and R. Hollister, "Evaluating Manpower Programs for the Disadvantaged," in Cost-Benefit Analysis of Manpower Policies, ed. G. Somers and W. Wood (Kingston, Ontario: Industrial Relations Centre at Queen's University, 1969), pp. 119-51, particularly pp. 138-39.

15. L. Friedman, "Innovation and Diffusion in Non-Markets: Case Studies in Criminal Justice," Ph.D. dissertation, Yale University, 1973, Chapter II.

David R. Seidman

The three chapters concerned with delivery of public services
deal with three very different services, in different stages of development. Refuse collection, discussed by Stanley Altman, is one of the
earlier services provided by local government. The supported work
program for former drug addicts, addressed by Lee Friedman, began
in 1972. The Impairment Payment Program proposed by William
Pollak does not yet exist in a coherent form. Understandably then,
Altman's paper is mostly concerned with program evaluation issues,
Pollak's with program development issues, and Friedman's with
some of each.

Because of the different kinds of issues raised by each author,
I have chosen to address each chapter individually, rather than seeking
to discuss them jointly.

I am concerned that William Pollak does not discuss whether
the services to be provided under his proposed Impairment Payment
Program should be provided by the government in the first place.
Certainly the services are desirable, but they are as close to consumption goods as we can get in social programs. Many underfunded
education and training programs, for example, can be justified as
investments that can benefit all of society; programs for the impaired
elderly benefit mainly the recipients and their immediate families
and are justifiable primarily on ethical or political grounds. These
are valid grounds, to be sure, but the analyst should discuss the
existence or lack thereof of economic justifications for the program
he is analyzing.

The Impairment Payment Program has interesting similarities
to the various third-party medical payment programs. Pollak discussed many aspects of the supply issue, including diseconomies of
of small-scale operation caused by inadequate demand. But he did
not discuss high costs caused by large and unsatisfied demands, the
problem in medical care. I hope that in the future policy makers
will concentrate on increasing the supply of services in proportion
to increased demand. There needs to be more thought on providing
"front-end" money to get new service providers started. Permitting
payment only to approved service providers with reasonable cost as
a criterion for approval is another possible way of controlling cost.

Evidently we are making the same mistake in these services that the medical insurance companies made for years: We pay more for institutional care than for home care, just as we paid for inpatient but not outpatient care. Pollak states that home care may not be much more economical as currently provided, but there should be ways of improving its efficiency. One might take advantage of and further encourage clusterings of the impaired elderly into communities of the elderly, or centralize provision of services, rather than just information on services. If several services could be provided in one home visit, the cost might be sharply reduced.

Finally, we should provide an incentive for the consumer to seek economical services, if a voucher system is used, by paying only a fixed amount for various services, or only a percentage over the fixed amount. It might turn out that certain services should be paid by voucher and others by cash, depending on the ability of the consumer to assess the quality of the given service.

I remain skeptical of the private coordinator concept. The incentive for this person would be to select the cheapest services that he can get away with, and pocket the difference. It would be very difficult to monitor and evaluate his actions.

Evaluations of services should not be only for internal use, but should be provided freely to the public, as Commissioner Herbert Denenberg has done in Pennsylvania for a variety of consumer goods and services. Service providers who wish to be eligible to receive payments from the Impairment Payment Program should be required to submit to such periodic evaluations.

Stanley Altman notes that The Urban Institute's development of a street cleanliness measure was done in cooperation with the District of Columbia government, where I have been employed. We have had some experience using the measure, and I will mention a few similarities and dissimilarities in our approach and experience. I believe our joint experiences emphasize the critical importance of executive leadership in introducing an innovation of this type. Herbert Elish, then head of New York City's Department of Sanitation, was regarded by many as one of Mayor Lindsay's greatest finds, combining both analytical and managerial acumen.

In Washington we began more shakily. At that time the Sanitary Engineering Department and the Sanitation Bureau were both headed by old-line engineers, and when I proposed the contract with The Urban Institute, implementation seemed chancy. However, just after the work was completed, a major reorganization occurred that brought two very energetic new managers to head the new Department of Environmental Services and the new Solid Waste Administration (SWA). Both men had experience in the use of evaluation techniques; neither had any experience in sanitary engineering.

They immediately launched Operation Clean Sweep to get rid of accumulated trash in yards, dwellings, vacant lots, streets, and alleys. We came forward with the new methodology and said we could provide a quantitative measure of street and alley cleanliness—extending it to back yards and lots if desired—before, immediately after, and perhaps three months after Clean Sweep. This offer was immediately accepted and the evaluation was done. The results showed that there were statistically significant improvements in nearly all of the city's nine service areas, but of a rather short duration, perhaps on the order of one to three months.

The utility of the measure in Clean Sweep convinced the new administrators to install it as a permanent activity, which they are in the process of doing now, using some EPA money to begin. The SWA head has estimated that the measure has allowed him to reallocate his resources between and within service areas and to achieve an increase in effectiveness—as determined by the cleanliness measure—that would have taken a 30 percent increase in his street cleaning staff, at a cost of nearly $1 million if he had just added staff.

The measure not only showed him what reallocation was needed but helped him to justify it to anyone complaining about the changes. It allowed a new definition of equitable distribution of street cleaning services based on effectiveness rather than either input or output.

Despite Altman's belief that the evaluation activity should be performed outside the government to be credible, I consider it possible to have measurement systems reporting at the levels of the mayor and the department heads which would develop data for public dissemination as well. However, if the collusion problem Altman mentioned, where the evaluation tipped off the sanitation crews on where they would be observing conditions, should exist in the District of Columbia, I would certainly be in favor of removing the evaluation activity as far as necessary to avert that.

Our technique for collecting data in Washington differs from that in New York in that we have only one person in a car, rather than three, and he looks only at the right side of the street. Thus only one side of a street is judged, a random systematic sample we believe is justified. To me either a three-man car or a foot patrol seems unnecessarily expensive. Perhaps rather than a full-sized auto, one of the little enclosed three-wheel scooters such as the Post Office uses would be most appropriate, providing better visibility and easier handling than a car.

Some of the data in Altman's tables appears to be compressed, that is, to leave too small a range. The observers may be uncertain of themselves, and therefore tend to choose the same moderate value unless conditions are quite extreme. The only sound way of checking this is by replication by a judge whose ratings serve as the "standard."

Lee Friedman's statement that only 15 or 20 percent of the addicts are in treatment leads me to wonder why the rest are not. Is it primarily that there are insufficient funds to serve all who wish to be in the methadone program, or do most of the remainder not wish to join? Are there not usually requirements that addicts on parole must join a treatment program of some kind, and if so would that not mean just one swing through the revolving door if the dropout figures are as good as reported? If only volunteers are now in a methadone program, then one is "creaming" your addict population, that is, obtaining the most easily helped, just as many poverty programs did, and the resulting dropout rates have no implications as to the success of the program if it is expanded.

There were some discrepancies between the general concepts Friedman espouses for the Supported Work Program and what he describes as actually being done. He writes of the need to provide the employer with financial incentives to hire ex-addicts and implies heavy use of private employers, but the examples he provides are of public or quasi-public organizations. Was Vera not successful in finding interested firms, or does it simply want to develop some successful examples before it pursues this?

I was also curious about the relationship between the screening process and the financial incentives. If you screen very carefully, perhaps no incentives are needed; if your incentives are high enough, you might not need to screen. In particular, you might vary the incentive in accordance with the estimated risk. Again, if you "cream" your population too carefully, you may not have a program that can be replicated with a larger percentage of the addict population.

There have been some interesting uses of discriminant analysis to predict parole performance, and I wondered if any thought had been given to using this technique to assess the risks of employing addicts.

It was never specified either conceptually or in the actual examples how long the subsidization would continue. Would the employees be moved to other jobs, or would their subsidization simply cease in the ones they have? Also, is there any relation between parole time, if the addict is on parole, and the subsidization time?

My understanding is that most addicts are male and not married and therefore presumably not eligible for welfare unless they are minors living at home. The welfare cost in the cost-benefit analysis is thus not applicable, unless you wish to use it as a surrogate for the cost to society of somehow supporting the addict, whether by crime, other kinds of hustling, or what have you. If so, the case for using welfare costs rather than some other proxy is not made.

Finally, I am not entirely sure what point Friedman is making concerning evolutionary organizations. If he fears that the quality of his supported work program will suffer as it expands, I would say that was made inevitable by the creaming process I have described. Other theorists of bureaucracy, such as Anthony Downs, have made the more general point about the deterioration of organizations over time. Certainly my own experience with the District of Columbia government confirms this theory. I view the process as one of exponential decay; a drastic reorganization infuses the organization with new vigor and purpose, then the new people leave or get discouraged, and the organization gradually goes to sleep again. The trick for the analyst is to introduce his new methods during the period of vigor, and to see that they are institutionalized by the time the organization again slumbers, so that it at least snuggles up to the improved methods, as to a new teddy bear, as it drops off to sleep.

Robert K. Yin

The three chapters in Part II present a variety of experiences in applying research and analysis to urban service delivery systems. Each experience tends to focus on the initial stages of analysis. For example, Pollak distinguishes among major strategies in planning new services. Altman is concerned with research design and research-agency relationships. Friedman is concerned with planning for evaluation. In spite of this focus on the initial stages of analysis, the reader should nevertheless rest assured that there has been an increasing amount of research in public services that has in fact been drawn to completion, and that municipal officials are now able to tap a diverse pool of analytic talent. Obvious examples include:

1. The Urban Institute's extensive work on program and service evaluation, with resulting handbooks;
2. the New York City-Rand Institute's continued work with the fire, police, and welfare departments in New York City;
3. State University of New York at Stony Brook's work on sanitation services; and
4. considerable work in many quarters on such new topics as cable television, where municipal officials can obtain direct assistance on a full range of issues, including franchising and regulations, engineering and hardware questions, and service applications for telecommunications systems.

Remarkably, the bulk of this urban analysis enterprise has emerged in the last five to ten years. While the scale of effort and the typical breakthroughs may not have yet fulfilled the more ambitious hopes of the technology-transfer proponents of the mid-1960s, [1] the research community has at least achieved one landmark: that of putting urban policy analysis on the map. All this is not meant to suggest that urban policy analysts now have reason to be smug or overly self-laudatory. Rather, and on the contrary, it suggests that we are ready to begin meeting a broader challenge and to ask more penetrating questions of our own work. We are ready, in short, to begin setting the ground rules for evaluating ourselves and for determining the impact that the research and analysis of the last few years has had on urban management and urban life.

Interestingly, some of the criteria for this evaluation are suggested by the preceding chapters. If, for instance, one is deeply concerned with sanitation, drug addiction, or the care of the elderly, the work reported in these three chapters may be welcomed and viewed attentively. If, however, one is not directly concerned at the moment with any of these three problems, one begins to review these three chapters somewhat more critically, and the questions raised can provide the foundation for our broader self-evaluation.

The first question that comes to mind is simply: What difference does analysis make? Or, what impact has research and analysis made on the urban scene? For instance, even if, as Altman suggests, improved feedback on street cleanliness really affects street cleaning, will improved street cleaning affect the major sanitation function, which is garbage collection, much less affect the major environmental problems of a city? In short, in assessing any research effort, we need to have some sense of the order of magnitude of the stakes involved, that is, the potential gains and losses, to interpret the full value of the research effort.

The second question that arises is whether research has acted on the critical points in the delivery system. In other words, even if we have been satisfied on the first question that the stakes are sufficiently high, have our research tools and opportunities been applied to the jugular vein of a system, or have we merely toyed with the peripheral arteries? A recent newspaper article, for instance, noted that proposed federal fire regulations could result in the closing of the vast majority of the nation's nursing homes. [2] The impact of this type of change might warrant much more research and analysis than, say, the mechanics of any specific nursing home program.

Friedman's chapter on the supported-work programs for ex-drug addicts raises similar issues. He notes in particular that a delivery system has a peculiar history and evolution. This being so, we should focus our analysis on the most critical parts of the system. In drug addiction we still do not know why addiction rates rose so sharply toward the end of the 1960s, nor why they appear to have leveled off in the last few years. Perhaps this basic supply and demand nature of the addiction market will have a greater effect on supported-work programs than any piece of research will.

A third question concerns the inevitable feedback loop: Are we learning from our past experiences, and is there an appropriate institutional framework for this feedback? Without such a feedback loop, researchers in the urban arena tend to approach each new topic from scratch. The most obvious need is to avoid having a researcher in one city duplicate unknowingly that which has already been studied in another city. Less obvious, and thus worth amplifying here, the feedback loop is often faulty because the intellectual organization of our analysis unfortunately tends to accept the social problem boundaries created by society. For example, research on alternative delivery systems for the aged (such as Pollak's) should be well-informed by previous experiences not only in dealing with the aged, but also in dealing with the poor, the inform, and the medically needy. In these cases the major strategies, such as the direct provision of services, payments to beneficiaries, payments to providers, or some voucher system, tend to be alike, and the consequences may be similar regardless of the target population differences.

Just these three questions, then, can form the basis for beginning an evaluation of the overall impact of urban analysis. The evaluation could begin by creating a catalog of the major analytic accomplishments during the last few years and arriving at a preliminary judgment as to the value of the urban analysis effort.

In terms of assessing the stakes, we may judge the merits of urban analysis, perhaps, in relation either to increases in the productivity of urban systems or to improvements in the quality of urban life. On productivity increases in state and local governments, some observers have suggested that analysis is now playing a widespread role.[3] Yet no one has assessed the actual order of magnitude of the savings, and we do not have a clear picture of whether urban analysis has had a significant or only slight impact on municipal management.

For other urban research the stakes may involve improvements in the quality of urban life, rather than productivity gains. Here science and technology have already made impressive marks, if we count communications developments such as the telephone, radio, television, and even the automobile; or public health advances such as vaccines, innoculations, and medical care; or environmental gains, such as substitute fuels for soft coal. However, many of the gains have resulted from the new technology of years ago, raising a familiar question: What has research done lately? In one notable field—urban transportation—there is doubt, with the exception of air conditioning, if many of us travel to work in a much different fashion than we did 10 or even 20 years ago in spite of the considerable investment in urban transportation research.

The evaluative catalog also ought to cover the typical analytic strategies for influencing service delivery systems. In some cases government regulatory activity may be more important, and thus worthy of more research, than the direct provision of specific services. Other critical points in the system may be the availability of manpower, the implementation phase of research findings, and that all-encompassing attribute that so many analysts recognize, but so few study or try to create, the "proper political climate." One wonders which analytic strategies have been tried most, which appear to be most effective, and whether the greatest impact often occurs as a result of very unobtrusive and indirect means.

Finally, the catalog may reveal important findings about the institutional framework, and whether the framework makes a difference. Numerous studies and conferences over the last few years, for instance, have recommended that the federal government support new types of research institutes or public technology corporations to bridge the gap between the producers and users of urban research. [4] We have now had some experience with these institutions, including the urban observatory program sponsored by the Department of Housing and Urban Development, The Urban Institute, the New York City-RAND Institute, university-based groups such as the Harvard-M.I.T. Joint Center for Urban Studies and the SUNY Stony Brook program, and service-oriented organizations such as Public Technology, Inc. [5] We ought to begin to study the advantages and disadvantages of such institutional arrangements and to determine which features, if any, make a difference in the ultimate research quality and impact.

In summary, we are in a good position to begin a serious self-evaluation. The results may be disappointing. For instance, in a recent study of the role of science and technology in the administration of state governments, two years of interviews and field research revealed only some three dozen research projects worth of mention; none of the projects had led to major changes in the way state governments do their business or in the quality of life. [6] On the other hand, there may be some pleasant surprises. Whichever the case, the evaluation could serve historical purposes, that is, to provide a comparison between the actual results and some of the grander schemes proposed in the past. The evaluation could certainly serve immediate budgetary purposes, that is, to provide a guide in determining what type of work should be supported. I choose, however, to view the evaluation as serving heuristic purposes, that is, it can help to identify the ways in which urban policy analysts can effectively increase the impact of their work. And for this reason I am anxious that we begin such a self-appraisal.

NOTES

1. For example, see M. Rogers and A.M. Carton, "Aerospace Technology: Possible Applications to our Cities," paper presented at the Fifth Annual Meeting of the American Institute of Aeronautics and Astronautics, Philadelphia, 1968.

2. Boston Globe, April 12, 1973, p. 25.

3. For example, see Edward K. Hamilton, "Productivity: The New York City Approach," Public Administration Review 32 (November-December 1972): 784-95.

4. For example, see Mason Haire, "Industrial Technology and Urban Affairs," Technology Review 71 (February 1969): 22-27; Knowledge into Action: Improving the Use of the Social Sciences (Washington, D.C.: National Science Foundation, 1969); The Struggle To Bring Technology to Cities (Washington, D.C.: The Urban Institute, 1971); and Science and Technology Report, Power to the States (Lexington, Ky.: Council of State Governments, May 1972, RM-485).

5. For preliminary discussions of some of these institutions, see Lawrence A. Williams, "The Urban Observatory Approach," Urban Affairs Quarterly 8 (September 1972): 5-20; "Urban Problems," special issue of Operations Research, May-June 1972, 20(3); Stanley M. Altman and Robert Nathans, "The University and Approaches to Problems of State and Local Governments," Policy Sciences 3 (September 1972): 339-47; and Frederick O'R. Hayes and John E. Rasmussen, eds., Centers for Innovation in the Cities and States (San Francisco, Calif.: San Francisco Press, 1972).

6. Power to the States, op. cit. For a more general but journalistic critique of urban analysis, see James A. Kalish, "The Urban Problems Industry," Washington Monthly, November 1969.

III

SOCIAL AND POLITICAL URBAN PROCESS MODELS

INTRODUCTION
TO PART III
Frank L. Adelman

In Part III we have three very different essays united by one common characteristic: They all attempt to model important social processes that are usually considered to be immune to quantitative analysis. The first chapter treats social phenomena by mathematical analogy to gain insight into their fundamental character. The second attempts a detailed and relatively faithful mathematical representation of a social process. And the third chapter describes the incorporation of a set of supposedly nonquantifiable criteria into a broader resource framework.

Our objective is to discuss mathematical modeling of social phenomena in the hope of stimulating more work in this important direction. The chapters and the discussion sections that follow them were chosen to this end, as it is my firm belief that the rigor and the discipline imposed by mathematical approaches to these very difficult problems can contribute significantly to our understanding of social phenomena.

SEGREGATION ON A CONTINUOUS VARIABLE
Thomas C. Schelling

Consider an organization whose members are of varying ages and care about the ages of their associates. To fix ideas suppose the age distribution is horizontal from 20 to 70, with a 50-year spread, and suppose that nobody is willing to remain in a group whose average age exceeds his own by more than 10 years or whose average age is less than his own by more than 20 years. Initially, with an even spread of ages from 20 to 70, the mean age is 45 and everybody under 35 will depart, as will everybody over 65. What happens to the group— the size of its membership and its age distribution?

What we have is a population in which individuals are responding to an "environment" that consists of other individuals who are responding to that same environment of responding individuals. As individuals respond they change the environments of the people they associate with and cause further responses and adaptations. Everybody's presence affects, if only slightly, the environment of everybody else. "Respond" in these cases involves departure or, if we permit it, joining or rejoining. The ultimate outcome is the result of individual decisions; but the outcomes are described in terms of aggregates, averages, or frequency distributions.

This chapter is about abstract and idealized models of sorting and mixing, of segregating and integrating. We postulate a population consisting of individuals who respond to certain parameters of the population itself, those parameters depending on the particular collections of individuals that constitute the "initial conditions," on the dynamics of response, and on the particular set of preferences regarding those parameters that we impute to the individuals. And in this chapter the population variable to which people respond is a continuous variable.

Discrete variables would be things like "color," religion, language, sex, nationality, and the dichotomous divisions between officers and enlisted men, faculty and students, doctors and nurses, and so forth. The continuous variables are things like age, income, IQ, height, and skill or proficiency at tennis or chess or even argument. Some variables, like age, are well defined and in principle measurable and cardinal; some, like income, can be crudely and approximately defined. Some, like IQ or skill at tennis, are susceptible only of ordinal measurement and may or may not have been calibrated on some kind of scale. Some, like "status," may involve too many dimensions to be treated as a single variable even in an abstract model.

In addition to the basis for discriminating among people, the model has to identify the action that is involved. If we talk about racial segregation or age segregation in residential neighborhoods, we need definitions not only of "race" and "age" but also of "residence" and "neighborhood." If we talk about racial discrimination by job, or age discrimination by job, we need definitions of "job." We may work with a model in which my neighbor's neighborhood is the same as mine, a "bounded neighborhood" model, or one in which my neighbor's neighborhood extends a little further in his direction and is different from mine but spatially continuous with it. Thus the "environment" can also be continuous or variable. And the activity—association, contact, or even residence—can be an on-off variable or a continuous variable measured in proportions or frequencies.

It may take more than a single statistic to describe a person's preferred age distribution for his colleagues or neighbors. With language or sex or religion we usually don't have to describe a "threshold of difference," but with age or income or IQ or tennis skill it takes at least one parameter to describe the range or bracket with which one identifies himself or with which one identifies his preferred neighbor or associate. If you ask a person what racial mix he prefers in his apartment building or his work place, the answer may be a single number; if you ask him what age mix he likes, it is unlikely that a single number will suffice.

A Simple Example

For the very simplest example of what I have in mind, consider a residential home and the age distribution of its residents. Suppose nobody is willing to live in a place where on the average people are older than he is. The people who are below average will move out;

in doing so, they raise the average age; somebody else is now below average and moves out; the average goes up and somebody else moves out. Eventually only those who are tied for oldest, within whatever threshold people recognize, remain behind. The same would be true of a tennis club in which the 10 percent poorest tennis players find membership intolerable, or a college in which the bottom 10 percent in grade average are uncomfortable and leave.

The question of whether groupings can occur in which everybody is satisfied is especially pertinent to "open-ended" models—models in which people depart if their absolute requirements are not met. In a "closed model," people move only if things are better in the place they move to. We rank people according to some variable, like age, and ask how they will distribute themselves among two or more compartments—neighborhoods, organizations, or just "compartments" abstractly. Suppose everybody wants to be in the room in which the average age is nearest his own. We ask whether or not there is an equilibrium; if there is, whether it is stable; and what the process is by which a stable equilibrium may be arrived at, and how it will be affected by rules of movement, errors and accuracies of perception, the order in which different people make their choices and the speeds with which they act, and whether they are allowed a limited number of attempts or can make continuous adjustment.

Evidently if we have two rooms, and everybody wants to be in the room in which the age group is nearest his own age, we can find an "equilibrium." Spread everybody out in a line according to age and make a partition somewhere. The marginal individual, the one located at the partition, prefers the left group or the right group or is indifferent. If he prefers the left group, put him into it by moving the partition to the right, and keep doing that until the marginal individual no longer prefers the left group. At that first partition there was some number of people, say to the right of it, who preferred to be to the left; as we move individuals from the right group to the left group, we raise the averages in both groups. Some people who were content to be in the right group will prefer to move into the left group as the lower average approaches their own age and the higher average moves away. But it can easily be determined that we reach an equilibrium, even if it contains only the oldest person in the right-hand room. With a few plausible assumptions about the speed with which they can estimate that parameter in which they are interested, we can generate a damped adjustment that will converge on a division of people into the two rooms. But there are other preferences to consider.

There is the extreme case in which everybody wants to be in the room with the highest average. A possible equilibrium is that

everybody ends up in one room. (Whether or not this is actually an
"equilibrium" depends on whether we let the oldest person move into
an empty room, attracted by the potential average age of that room
when he alone is in it.) Another possibility is that people who are
above average want to be in the room with the lower average, and
vice versa. There are more complicated preferences.

Consider now the question posed at the beginning of this chapter.
Initially there is an even distribution of ages from 20 to 70, with a
mean of 45. Everybody whose age is below 35 is dissatisfied and will
leave, as will everybody whose age is above 65. The outcome may
depand on the dynamics, so we have to specify whether or not everybody who is dissatisfied makes a stimultaneous decision to move on
the same day and does move, or if they do not move simultaneously,
whether the young move out faster than the old do, and whether the
20-year-olds who are "more discontent" move out faster than the
30-year-olds, who are discontent by only 5 years rather than 15.
Let all the discontent move out at once. We are left with an age spread
from 35 to 65, and a mean age of 50. Now everybody under 40 wants
to move, because the departure of more young people than old people
has raised the average age. What about the people over 65: Do we
let them back in? If we don't, the ultimate outcome will be a residual
population consisting of everybody in the age range from 45 to 65.
If we let back in the people who left before the average age rose, and
who would not have left if they had waited, we shall end up with the
age range from 50 to 70.

Two Analytic Problems

There are two kinds of problems here. One is analyzing the
consequences of a certain set of preferences. The other, a prior
problem, is arriving at some plausible system of preferences. An
interesting family of preferences is one that might be described as
"monotonic single-peaked." This is one in which everybody's preference regarding the mean value of the variable in question—age or
whatever it is—has a preferred value and slopes away monotonically
in both directions, and in which the preferred value is a monotonic
function of age. If we draw, as a function of age, a graph of the
"preferred age" of every age group, it is a single-peaked function;
and at every age mean ages are more preferred, the closer they are
to the preferred age. This is a simplified family of preferences
because it focuses only on the arithmetic mean, and it is by no means
self-evident that a single statistic, like a population mean, is all

that people would care about. But as a warming-up exercise it is instructive.

Let me illustrate, with about as simple an example as can be created, the kinds of questions that can arise and some of the kinds of results that one can get. I shall refer to "age," but at this level of abstraction any other measure will do. (Because the example uses the arithmetic mean as the motivating statistic, a cardinal measure is implied, or at least a measure that can be cardinalized in some arbitrary way. And I shall suppose that, if perceptions are inaccurate, perceptions of mean values and preferences about mean values are subsumed together in a single-peaked preference system.)

Imagine a population horizontally distributed between the ages of zero and 100. Suppose there are two rooms or compartments available, and every individual is free to enter the room of his choice and to change to the other room if that other room has an age distribution that he prefers. Nobody cares about the rooms themselves; everybody cares about the ages of the people he is with. And what he cares about is simply the mean age of the people in the two rooms. We can try some alternative preference structures, each of which will be single-peaked for the individual.

First, each may choose to be in the room in which the average age is closest to his own age. Second, everybody may prefer a room in which the average age is a little higher than his own; specifically, everybody prefers an average age that exceeds his own by a fraction of the difference between his own age and the highest age, 100; and the fraction is the same for everybody, whatever his age. (If the fraction is one-fifth, a 40-year-old prefers the room whose average age is nearest to 52.) Third, everybody may prefer to be in a group whose average age is a little closer than his own age to the population average of 50; specifically, everybody prefers a mean age closer to 50 than his own age by some standard fraction of the distance. (If the fraction is one-fifth, a 30-year-old wants the room whose mean age is closest to 34.) A little reflection suggests that any stable partition of the population has to be strictly by age, everybody above a certain age in one room and everybody below that age in the other. Then the first system of preferences is easily handled: if everybody wants to be in the room whose mean age is nearest his own, there is a stable equilibrium at a 50-50 split between the two rooms. Everybody above 50 is in one room, everybody below 50 in the other. With a split at year 40 the mean age in one room is 20 and in the other 70; everybody aged 40 to 45 would move into the younger group, raising the average in both rooms— to 22.5 and 72.5—so that now everybody between 45 and 47.5 wants to move into the younger group, and so on until the division is at 50 years.

The second set of preferences is a little more complicated. Everyone wants to be in the room whose mean age is nearest to an age that is higher than his own by a fraction of the difference between his own and 100. For example, if everyone wants to be with a group whose mean age is older than himself by one-third of that difference, the 25-year-old will want to be in the room whose mean age is nearest 50. With a split at age 50, the means in the two rooms will be 25 and 75, and the 25-year-old, who prefers a mean age of 50, is indifferent. But the 30-year-old is not. He prefers the room whose mean age is closer to 53, so he and everybody else over 25 move into the older room, leaving a mean age of 12.5 in the younger room and a mean age of 62.5 in the older room. Now everybody 7 years and older prefers the older room, and the process unravels until everybody is in the same room.

A little algebra shows that, unless that fraction—the parameter in our preference formula—is less than .25, there is no sustainable division into two rooms. If that fraction is less than .25, there is a stable division at the age given by $(1-4a)/(2-4a)$, where a is that fraction. If the fraction is .2, the stable division occurs at age 16.7. If the fraction is .1, the stable division occurs at age 37.5. And of course if the fraction is 0, the formula gives us our 50-50 split corresponding to the first preference system.

The third preference, in which everybody prefers a group that is a little closer toward the population mean, allows three possibilities. If the fraction of the distance from his own age to the population mean that denotes an individual's preferred mean age is greater than .5, no split will be sustained. Everybody will be in the same room. If the fraction is less than .5, an even split is stable. And if the fraction exactly equals .5, any division by age is in neutral equilibrium.

Look again at the second case, in which everybody wants to be with a group a little older than himself, except for the 100-year-old, who is content with a group his own age. With that fraction less than .25, we had a stable division and nobody in the older room would want to go in the younger room. When the fraction reached or exceeded .25, no split was stable because the younger people preferred the older room. We neglected to look at what happens when they vacate the "younger" room altogether.

The mean age in the older room is now 50. Anybody who moves to the empty room enjoys a mean age equal to his own, if we so interpret his preferences. If everybody wants company, an older person who wanders at random into the empty room will immediately attract elderly followers. The 80-year-olds prefer an average age in excess of 85; they prefer their own age to the prevailing mean age

of 50. If they move into the empty room they will be followed by every
one who is more attracted to age 80 than to age 50. This surely
includes everybody over 53, since the 53-year-olds prefer a mean
age of at least 65, and anything over 65 is closer to 80 than to 50.
So nearly half the people leave—the older half—generating a mean
age in the formerly vacant room that is slightly over 75 and leaving
behind the younger half, who together constitute a mean of slightly
over 25. Now everybody about age 35 and above moves to the older
room, lowering the mean in both rooms, and the process we analyzed
above is now in motion again. The "tipping" process will empty the
younger room, and the vacant room is now available for reoccupancy
by the older ones. If nothing confines the elderly to the room toward
which they attracted the entire population, endless migratory alterna-
tion will occur.

With three or more rooms the maximum value that that fraction
can have and lead to a stable division rather than to endless migration
gets smaller and smaller. To put it differently, the smaller that
fraction the more available rooms there can be without the elderly
leading the entire population through an endless circuit of the available
rooms. And with the fraction in excess of . 25, as we saw, no plural
number of rooms can lead to stability.

It is easy to show that the stable divisions need not represent
Pareto-optimal outcomes and typically will not. Nobody pays any
heed to what he does to the average age of the group that he joins,
so we should not expect optimization except in special cases.

Occurrence of Segregation on Continuous Variables

I turn now to the question of where these processes may occur
and why it may be worthwhile to examine them in some detail.

With respect to age, these processes certainly do occur in
residential patterns and social groupings.

In addition to the cases in which people may genuinely care
about their associates, in terms of variable like age or income or IQ,
there are some interesting market phenomena that have many of the
characteristics of these segregation and separation models. Consider
an insurance scheme, according to which everybody pays the same
premium and those who die or have accidents are compensated. Those
who are least likely to die or to have accidents get the poorest bar-
gain; if they know it, and if the organization cannot discriminate,
they leave and form an association of their own, one that charges
lower premiums. As they leave they raise the mortality rate and the

accident rate in the organization that they leave; the premiums go up, and some more people leave. If everybody whose expected value is negative departs the organization, there will be nobody left in the end; if everybody is willing to pay a certain fee for insurance, the scheme will unravel until what remains is the high-mortality, high-accident group that is small enough to have a mean rate of compensation that is within the fee limit of the least benefited member. If institutionally the groups cannot discriminate among members, members will get sorted out into different groups according to their mortality and accident classes. In this case it is not the people themselves that one cares about, but the costs they inflict by merely being added into the numerator of the group that one belongs to.

Another interesting question is what happens to the value of the variable associated with an individual with the passage of time. Age is a very special variable. One's age goes up by a year every year. And it does so independently of the ages of the people who surround one. Probably the age spread that one can tolerate widens with the passage of time so that, if an age distribution is unstably incohesive but it can be made to wait awhile, it may grow into mutual compatibility. An interesting question is what happens to one's income over time and whether the surrounding income affects it.

Consider skills: A person who plays bridge or tennis probably improves at a rate that depends on the average skill level of the people in his group or club. Very likely there is some optimum positive differential between the mean skill that surrounds him and his own skill. Thus a fixed contingent of people may display a reduced dispersion of skill over time, the better tennis players not improving so much for lack of competition, the poorest dropping out because they can't stand the competition, and the rest showing improvement in proportion perhaps to the difference between one's own skill and the mean skill (or some other statistic) of the group.

Status may be somewhat the same: In academic or other life one acquires status from associating with people of high status; and, just as this may be part of the motive that people have for wanting to associate with high status, it may be a mechanism whereby the dispersion of status within a group diminishes over time as the individual members gradually become assimilated to the status of the group.

I have been supposing, for convenience, that people of different ages, incomes, or IQs care about the ages, incomes, or IQs of the people they associate with or live near or otherwise participate with. The models can usually be interpreted as involving preferences regarding something that is a function of age, income, IQ, or skill. Among children, size and strength and age and skill are so closely associated that, when children are perceived to sort themselves into age groupings, as in baseball or soccer for example, the relevant variables may be strength and skill. The school system sorts people substantially by age, but it can do so successfully partly because age is associated with size, strength, skill, experience, knowledge, and training. Adults may sort themselves by age partly because of family status, partly because of life-style. Just as orthodox Jews may prefer to live near a synagogue and a delicatessen, people of an age to have small children may want to live where life is adapted to small children, that is, to families in which the parents are of a comparable age. People who like privacy may tend to associate with people who like privacy, not because they like the people but because they like the privacy. People who dislike dogs may be happier among people who also dislike dogs, not because they like the people better but because they like the absence of dogs. People who like crowds will tend to associate with people who like crowds, without necessarily liking to associate with the kind of people who like crowds. People who want to participate in a life-annuity scheme may want to participate with short-lived people, without particularly caring to be close to people who are not long for this world.

In closing I emphasize two circumstances in which models of these processes may be useful. First, they must be models of something that matters, residence or membership or participation that involves segregation and integration that is of some social significance. And second, the systemic and aggregate consequences of individual decisions must be not so transparent that one can treat the aggregate results as merely the individual preferences writ large. What I have tried to suggest is that the expectable outcomes, in terms of residence or membership or participation, may not be immediately and intuitively transparent once the individual motivations are postulated, and that the subject is worth the effort at analysis. If the second of these conditions is true, empirical studies of aggregates will not permit valid inferences about individual motives except when there is a mediating model of this sort. And knowledge of individual behavior patterns will lead neither to correct predictions of aggregate outcomes nor to policies for affecting those outcomes without careful attention to these intervening models that attempt to relate the micromotives of individuals to the macrophenomena that are the object of public policy.

8

A MODEL OF
ATTITUDE CHANGE

Frank L. Adelman
Irma Adelman

One of the crucial and least-well-understood aspects of urban politics is the operation of the forces that try to influence public opinion. It is therefore a matter of considerable urgency to try to develop some insight into the phenomena underlying the answers to the following questions:

1. How do people form their initial opinions on a controversial topic?
2. What forces induce them to modify these opinions?
3. By what mechanisms do the news media and other influence groups affect attitudes and beliefs?
4. What is the relative importance, in this context, of newspapers, television, radio, and other sources of information and opinion?
5. How do information and opinion differ in their impact upon beliefs and attitudes?
6. How do the media, in particular, choose their public positions on a controversial issue?

All of these questions should be analyzed with explicit recognition of socioeconomic differences among the various groups of voters and

---

This work was initiated at the Center for Advanced Study in the Behavioral Sciences during 1970-71. The authors are greatly indebted to Elliot Aronson, Leonard Berkowitz, and Nathan Maccoby for their invaluable insights that were so helpful in the formulation of this model.

with attention to the variation of the several effects with time during the controversy.

Unfortunately, there appears to be no generally accepted theory or set of theories that predicts the degree of influence of the mass media on voting decisions or describes the way in which people's voting decisions are formed and modified. For example, politicians ascribe to the press a significant impact on the outcome of elections; empirical studies on voting behavior, on the other hand, suggest that relatively few people are persuaded to change their voting intentions during the very intense political activity of a presidential campaign.[1] Further, it is not clear, either from these studies or from other analyses, how much of the observed change is a result of the opinions expressed and how much to the simple fact of exposure. In other words, it is not obvious to what extent the small effects actually observed reflect genuine change of underlying views and to what extent they represent the reinforcement and surfacing of intentions temporarily suppressed. A complete understanding of the processes involved is further inhibited by the general tendency of people to pay attention to sources of information and opinion that they expect will reinforce their existing ideas (selective exposure), and to notice and remember only those bits of data that support those ideas (selective perception and selective retention).[2]

While a general theory of attitude formation and change does not exist, a survey of the pertinent literature in political science, communications, and social psychology does suggest a certain amount of agreement on two of the underlying concepts. One of these is that the communication of ideas, opinions, and information from the media to the population at large takes place in two (or perhaps more) steps. The messages are picked up from the media or other sources by a relatively small subset of the population (the "opinion leaders") in each socioeconomic group and are retransmitted to the rest of the people through discussions and conversations.[3] There is, of course, some crossing of socioeconomic boundaries in this process, generally by the "opinion leaders," but most of the communications travel within socioeconomic groups.

Empirical evidence on this theory is not yet conclusive, particularly with respect to whether the process generally takes place in two steps or more and with respect to the identification of the opinion leaders, but the basic principle appears to have general acceptance.

A second fundamental concept that seems to be reasonably well established (with considerable controversy, however, concerning what are, for our purposes, the details) is "cognitive consistency." The hypothesis is that the attitudes and beliefs of an individual tend to be organized into an internally consistent system, and that the recognition of inconsistencies (or "dissonance") leads to behavior or attitude changes aimed at reconciling the inconsistencies that have been exposed. The most fruitful theory of this genre, which has produced many experiments, much controversy, and some consensus, is known as the "cognitive dissonance" theory, [4] in which, among other features, the motivation for reconciliation is proportional to the magnitude of the inconsistency.

The empirical evidence regarding the validity of this theory, while suggestive, is not definitive. In the studies we have seen, the effect of performing the experiment is often larger than the effect under study. Further, one criticism of the cognitive dissonance experiments so far reported, that almost any outcome of the experiment can be explained as confirmation of the cognitive dissonance hypothesis, [5] appears to have considerable validity.

Regardless of these criticisms of cognitive dissonance and the two-step theory of communication, there appears to be no evidence that these theses are fundamentally wrong. We have, therefore, constructed a model of the influence—attitude formation process (for inclusion in a comprehensive simulation model of urban politics[6]) based explicitly upon cognitive dissonance theory and implicitly upon a multistage theory of communication. We have done this primarily because, in the absence of definitive theories of the pertinent processes, the inherent reasonableness of these hypotheses dominantes alternative considerations. We recognize, of course, that on the frontiers of knowledge reasonableness (logic and/or common sense) is not necessarily a reliable guide.

THE POLITICAL SIMULATION MODEL

To put our attitude-influence submodel into proper perspective it is necessary to provide some background on the basic construction of the model of city politics of which the present work is part.

The approach we have adopted for the study of the political aspects of an urban community and the decision-making process within the City Council is that of simulation. The model constitutes an attempt to portray what might be termed the "reconstructed logic" of the operation of the political system and indicates how the political system might operate if decisions on all aspects of political behavior had to be made consciously.

The simulation (see Figure 8.1) describes a city of 1 million voters, divided into 20 wards, each with a total vote of 50,000 per election. Each ward chooses its own alderman on a de facto partisan

FIGURE 8.1

General Structure of Political Model

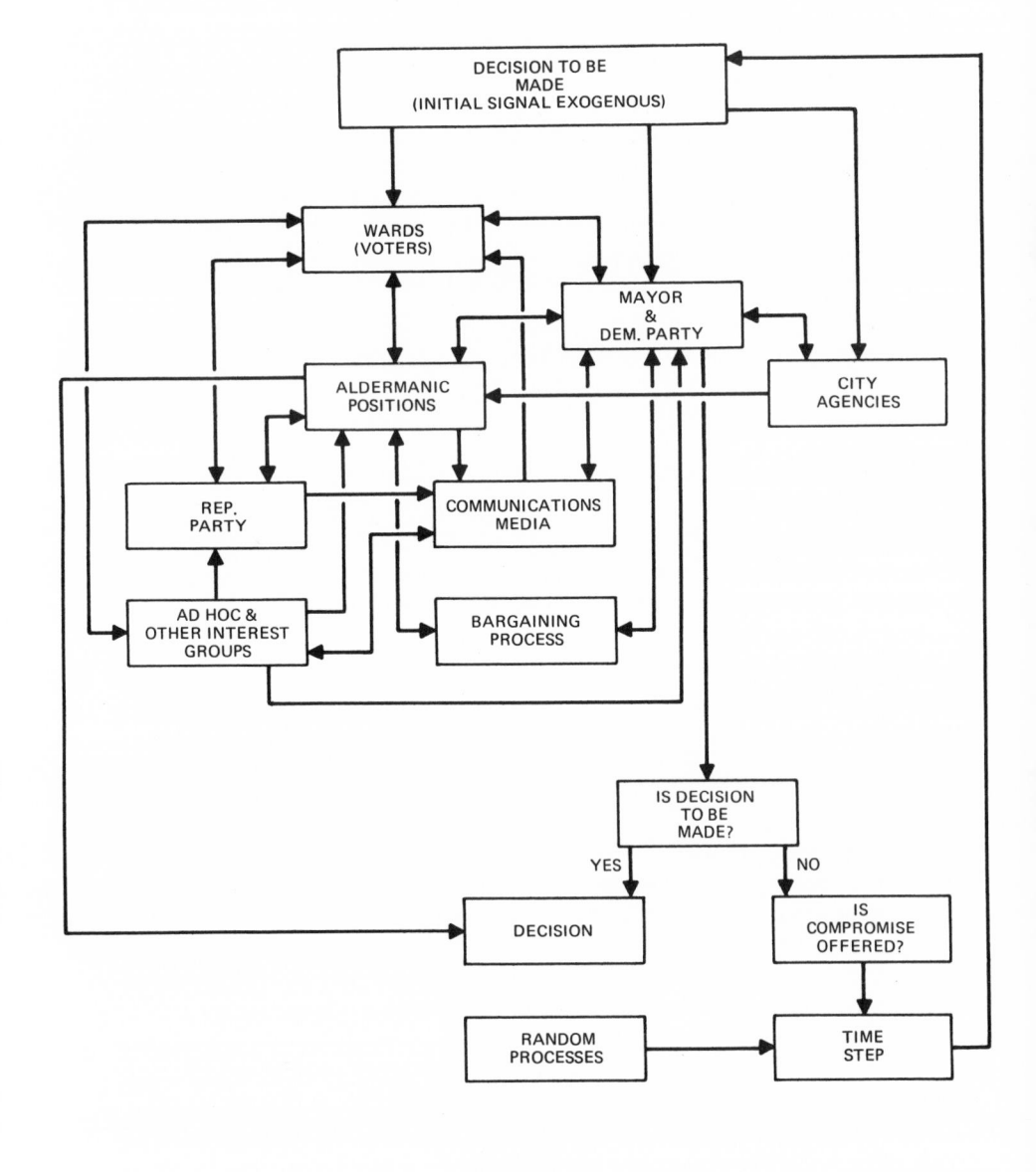

Source: Compiled by the authors.

basis. Some of the wards are ethnically and socioeconomically homogeneous, others are split, and several are transitional in character.

The city has a strong Democratic machine and small group of
aldermen who are relatively influential in running the City Council.
The mayor is elected by a partisan citywide election, and he is a
Democrat and the leader of the Democratic machine of the city. He
interacts with the aldermen in various ways to influence the outcome
of a controversy, with his power resulting from his control of both
party and city bureaucracy.

A number of special-interest groups are concerned with politics
in the city, besides the political parties. These include business and
industrial interests, industrial and craft unions, churches, various
civic organizations, and even organized crime, along with ad hoc
organizations that emerge under the pressures of specific controversies. City and county bureaucracies also may have a large stake in
the outcome of the legislative process in the City Council. In addition
the newspapers and other mass media play an important role in influencing both voters and aldermen, particularly with regard to issues
that are of special public interest.

Each of the 20 aldermen is assumed to be in perfect accord with
his ward committeeman (regardless of whether or not they are actually
the same person) and in close contact with the voters in his ward. He
therefore has a very good idea of the stance those voters want him to
take on any particular issue. He is also highly aware of the payoffs
and penalties he can expect for any combination of stance and outcome
of the issue.

Every alderman is assumed to have a certain amount of political
capital at the start of the period. One component of this capital is the
excess number of votes, over the minimum required for election,
that the alderman can expect to get at the next election. The second
component is the stock of jobs and favors that he can dispense. The
alderman is also characterized by the estimated maximum number
of votes (V) he can expect to gain in the next election and by a parameter representing his relative strength and influence in the City
Council. All these parameters are initially exogenous, but the vote
parameters are modified endogenously as time goes on.

To see how an alderman defines his position, an examination
of Figure 8.2 will be helpful. Whenever a decision to be modeled is
brought before the City Council, each ward is assigned two indices.
One of these we call E, a measure of the impact of the proposed
decision upon the welfare of the voters in the ward, as they themselves perceive it.* This perceived welfare index is a measure of

---

*Facts have very little to do with the value of E; if the people
in the ward think that a particular act will cause property values to

FIGURE 8.2

Aldermanic Position Calculation

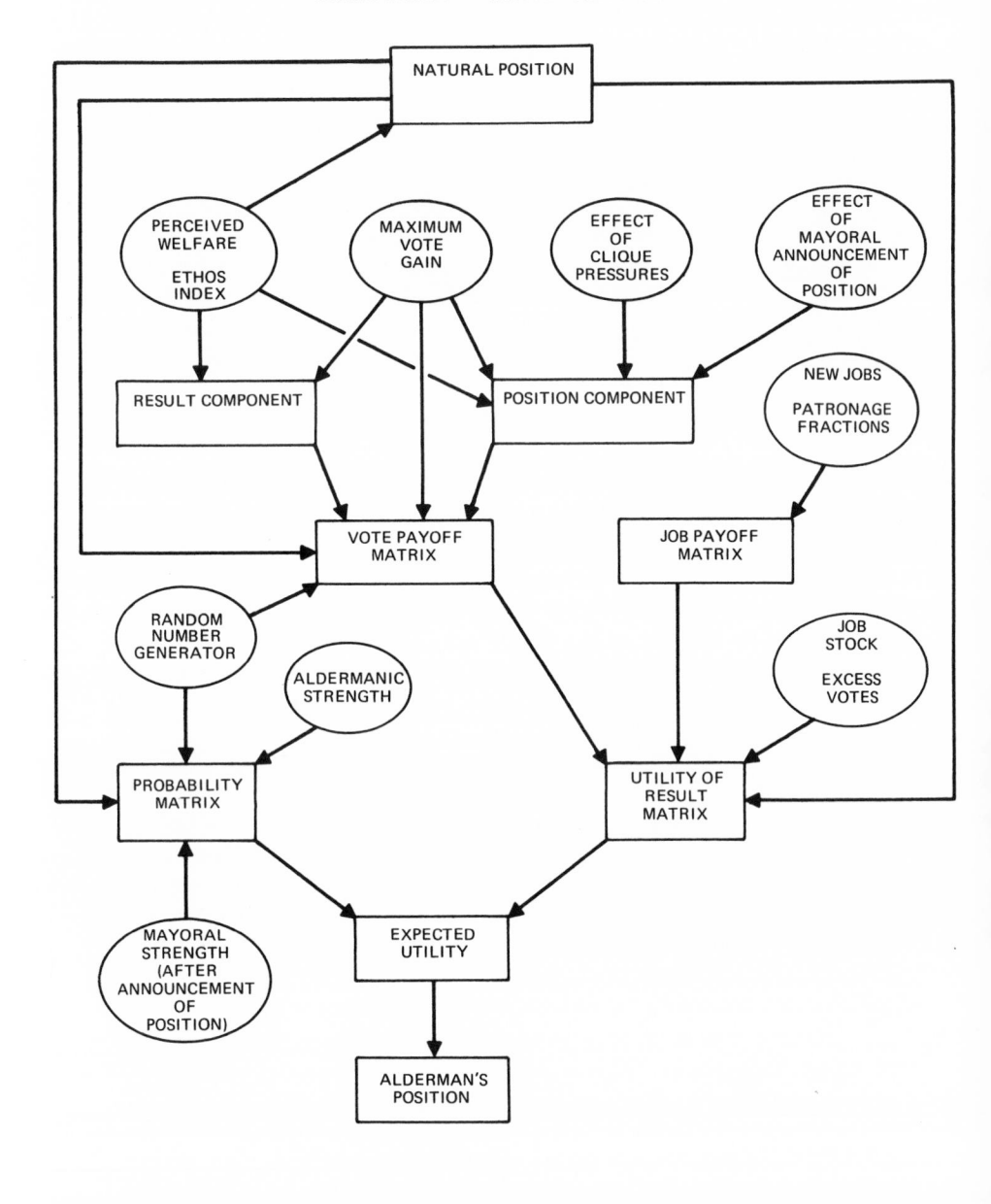

the anticipated economic, social, and psychological impact on the life-style of the voters. It can range from -3, a very strong anticipated negative impact on welfare, to +3, an equally strong positive impact. The other index, I, represents what we choose to call the "ethos effect." It represents a measure of the extent to which the voters in the ward, in choosing their positions on an issue, tend to take into account the welfare of people in other wards. Typically, wards composed primarily of the middle and wealthier classes, particularly if highly educated, tend to have values of I approaching the maximum (I = 2), while the poorer wards with a poorly educated populace tend to have I = 0, or even negative.

It is ultimately on the basis of these indices that the alderman chooses his position. He may adopt any of five positions (-2, -1, 0, +1, +2), representing the range from strong opposition to strong support of the proposition. We assume that the alderman has a utility function that permits him to aggregate the individual components of his political capital into a single index, and that he will choose a posture that will maximize the expected value of his utility function. (Other decision rules can be assumed, if desired, for some or all of the aldermen.) By hypothesis, his utility function reflects the observation that he is generally reluctant to adopt a nonneutral position unless he expects strong backing for this position by his supporters.

The alderman estimates his vote payoffs from a specified function of E, I, and V. His vote payoff matrix consists of two components, one of which depends solely on which of the possible outcomes of the proposition in question will take place, the other depending only on the position adopted by the politician. His job payoff matrix is a function of outcome alone. It is constructed from exogenous parameters representing the number of new patronage jobs that will become available, the fraction he would normally get, and the additional jobs (if any) he may be awarded to compensate him for whatever damage the proposition or compromise may cause him with the voters in his ward.

The alderman estimates the probabilities associated with the passage or failure of the proposition and with the acceptance of the two compromise positions on the basis of his personal knowledge of the postures of the other aldermen. (We assume that information is generally imperfect among the aldermen, with periodic updating.)

---

decline or "undesirable people" to move into the neighborhood, then no number of studies which indicate that these effects will not occur will affect the value of E.

In the course of the controversy, bargaining can take place when an alderman holding a strong position on the issue can profitably offer a less committed alderman an incremental amount of patronage in exchange for a position switch. [7]

Before the alderman enters the bargaining process, however, his vote and job payoff matrices are modified by several factors intended to reflect additional aspects of reality. One of these represents the fact that a person's perception of his environment depends in part on the perceptions of the people with whom he interacts. For this reason each alderman perceives his payoff function to be somewhat improved as his position approaches the mean position of the aldermen in the clique to which he belongs. (We have divided aldermen into members of either of two rival cliques and nonclique members. Nonclique members have no such payoff modification.)

Secondly, when the mayor announces his stand on the issue in question the aldermen's vote payoff functions are modified to reflect the mayor's influence. A similar effect is included in Republican wards when the Republican party announces its position.

While these effects are in a real sense part of the attitude-influence sector, they are conceptually much simpler and have been treated separately in our model.

The time steps for the model are months, and the model is run until the proposition in question has been decided or until it is determined that a compromise is necessary. At the end of each month the situation is evaluated, bargains are made or not made, and other changes associated with the movement of time are taken into account at one instant. If no decision is made at the end of a time step, we adjust stochastically the stock in trade of the aldermen to represent the many political activities that are of far greater interest to the daily life of the individual politician than to our model. We then proceed to the next time step.

THE ATTITUDE-INFLUENCE MODEL—
BASIC CONSTRUCTION

In view of the considerations discussed in the beginning of this chapter, our approach to the attitude-influence sector of our political simulation model is based on the following view of the real-life basic processes. The media exercise their influence both by supplying information and by expressing their views explicitly through editorials, "news analysis," and commentators and columnists. But they inevitably express editorial opinions implicitly as well, by the choice of (in the case of newspapers) headline, lead paragraph, pictures, extent and location of coverage, amount and nature of background information, etc.* These communications, both information and opinion, may be received directly or may reach a recipient indirectly through discussions with family, friends, or coworkers. Through time there is generally a sequence of acts of reception, evaluation, modification, and perhaps retransmission that takes place between initial transmission of a message and its incorporation into the beliefs and attitudes of each exposed individual. The frequency and intensity of these processes, and therefore the rate at which the input is assimilated, depend not only upon exposure, but also on the pertinence and urgency of the issue ("salience") at the time to the people involved.

We describe the net impact of these processes on attitudes in terms of three effects. First, the selective exposure and retention of facts and opinions conducive to one's deeply held beliefs leads to a surfacing of one's underlying attitudes, which may have been previously suppressed for one reason or another. This constitutes an intensification or "hardening" of existing attitudes. Second, some communications will persuade some recipients to change their views ("conversion"), perhaps later to return toward their earlier ideas ("reversion"). Third, some people may be forced to recognize that their attitudes are to some extent inconsistent with their more or less deeply held beliefs. The exposure of such dissonant elements will trigger changes in beliefs or attitudes so as to reduce the internal conflict. This we call "resolution of dissonance."

These processes may be visualized more clearly by reference to Figure 8.3. We shall discuss both this figure and the next in terms of the mass communications media, but the considerations apply equally well to interest groups (which, after all, communicate both information and opinion to their members and to the public at large).

In our model the media transmit pertinent information and opinion to the general public. The messages are received most sensitively by the opinion leaders and are retransmitted, with varying degrees of interpretation, evaluation, and modification, within the

---

*For example, three newly elected councilmen (1971) refused to salute the flag in Berkeley, California. The San Francisco Examiner headlined the story under an 8-column, 4-inch photograph on the first page, with a follow-up article the next day. By contrast, The San Francisco Chronicle ran the story well down in column 3 of page 1, with no reference on that page to the incident. Both papers were expressing editorial opinions by their treatment.

FIGURE 8.3

Overview of Attitude Formation Processes

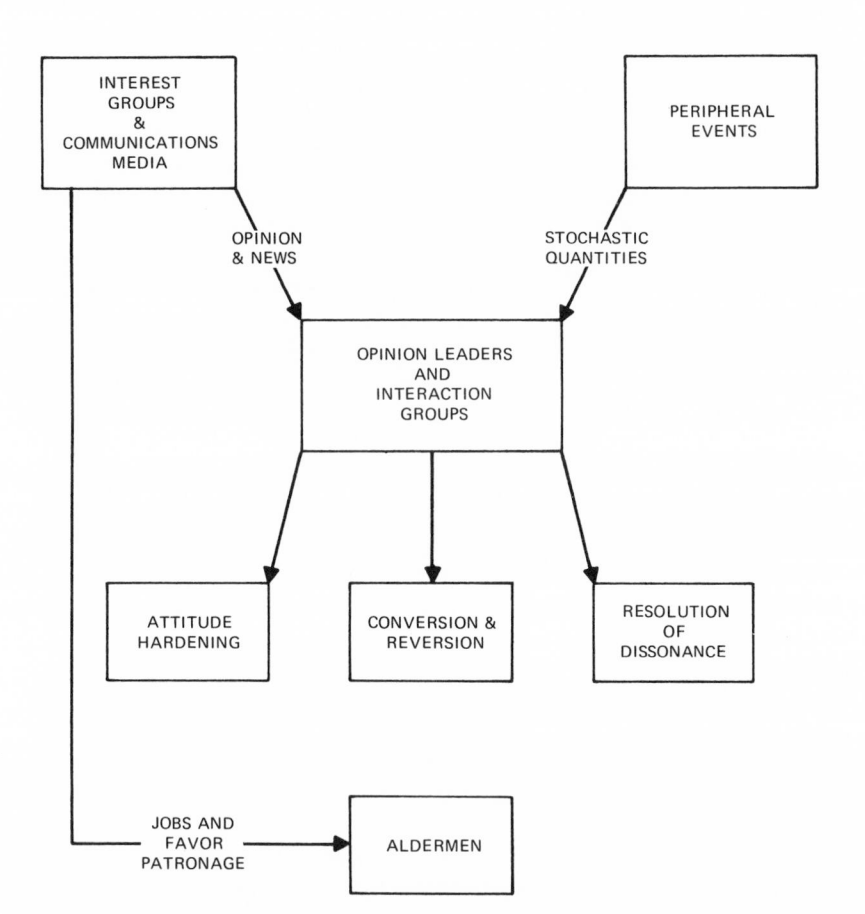

many sets of overlapping interaction groups. Meanwhile, messages regarding other events (which we must treat stochastically) may amplify, modify, or even destroy current interest in the issue under consideration in the model. The outputs of the interaction groups are changes in attitudes because of hardening, conversion and reversion, and resolution of dissonance, as described above.

THE ATTITUDE-INFLUENCE MODEL—IMPLEMENTATION

The media and interest groups represented in our model at present are two mass-circulation newspapers (one liberal, one conservative), television, four churches (white Catholic and fundamentalist, other white Protestant and Jewish, black fundamentalist, black middle-class), existing militant neighborhood and civic organizations (pro and con), their moderate analogues, ad hoc organizations (pro and con), the vitally interested bureaucracies (pro and con), that bureaucracy responsive to the mayor, and, finally, labor, business, and organized crime (!).

To translate our description of attitude change into a model, we assume that information and opinion are received in each ward from some or all of these basic sources. These sources are weighted (which will be discussed below) by the people in the ward in accordance with exposure, perceived source credibility, intensity of coverage, and, for the opinion level, the position adopted by the source on the issue. The outcome, which is intended to reflect the mediating influence of opinion leaders and of groups within which the voters interact, is an effective level of information coverage and an effective level of opinion exposure.

In our model, as in real life, these effective levels of coverage vary by socioeconomic group and therefore by ward. They must be further modified, however, by the salience of the issue to the people in the ward, a factor that tends to make the impact of events more significant for those who have stronger opinions on the issue but that reflects also the effect of competing news events and controversies on the amount of exposure and discussion (and therefore on the rate of attitude change) within the ward. (The specification of salience will be given below.)

In the discussions that follow, it may be helpful occasionally to refer to Figure 8.4.

We implement our earlier description of attitude change by introducing a new index, ETRUE, which represents the welfare of the voters in the ward as they would perceive it were they to be willing

FIGURE 8.4

Attitude Sector—Influence on E and I

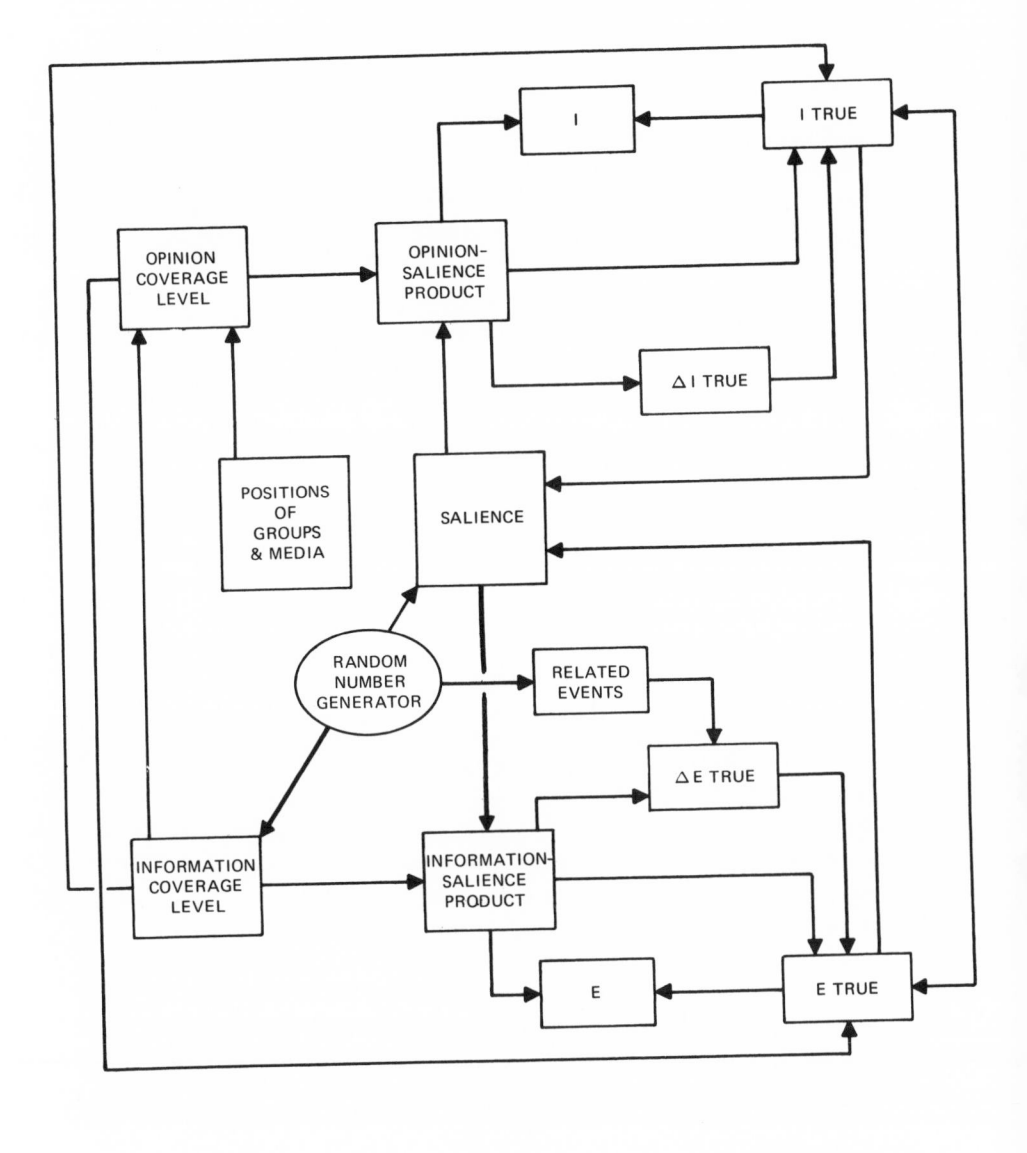

and able to analyze deeply their entire belief-attitude structure. Clearly, ETRUE is not accessible a priori by any direct measurement, as the very process of attempting to measure it would alter the belief-attitude structure. Yet, the reasonable assumption that, for a group, ETRUE is socioeconomically determined would permit estimates to be made on the basis of post hoc inference of effect discussed in the preceding section. "Reversion" appears as a negative term that is proportional, with a coefficient of 0.2, to the coverage level in the preceding period. Since information sometimes makes people change their views, rather than intensify them, we introduce a stochastic element for this component, which takes on the values 1, 0, and -1 with probabilities .5, .3, and .2, respectively. This stochastic element is the same for all wards with the same true position on the issue.

The index ITRUE, similarly, is changed by $\triangle$ ITRUE, which depends only on the ward characteristics and the level of opinion coverage. This represents conversion and reversion of the ethos index.

A third effect of the media and interest groups, the resolution of cognitive dissonance, is handled in our model by forcing ETRUE and ITRUE to converge whenever these quantities have opposite signs. The rate of convergence is proportional to their difference and to the sum of the effective levels of opinion and information coverage (multiplied by salience). We hypothesize that, on the average, ethical considerations will be subordinated to welfare perceptions in resolving dissonance, and therefore, in our model, ITRUE moves twice as fast as ETRUE in this convergence process.

To complete our description of the way the media and influence groups effect changes in voter attitudes we need to indicate how salience and the effective coverage levels are determined.

The salience factor is a function of the alderman's position, the position the voters in the ward would have him choose if they knew their own values of ETRUE and ITRUE, and a stochastic variable representing the impact of extraneous events on the attention given to the issue by the voters in the ward. It is designed to reflect three characteristics of a reasonable formulation of the concept of salience: (1) The more strongly the voters feel on the issue the greater its salience; (2) If an alderman is not in perfect accord with the underlying position in his ward, the salience is increased; and (3) The salience is always nonzero if the voters do not have an underlying neutral position.

To determine the level of news coverage we assign to various events that occur during the operation of the program values ranging from 1 to 3. The sum of the squares of these weights is a measure of the level of coverage. Only major events, such as the announcement of a strong mayoral position or the rejection of a crucial compromise, are assigned a coverage of 3. Coverage of 2 might be associated with significant protest demonstrations, announcement of the formation of a pertinent ad hoc group, * announcement of the position of a militant group, * or a news leak concerning a deal made by a strong alderman. The announcement of a newspaper's strong editorial position would receive a general coverage of 1, but in that newspaper alone an additional coverage of 2. †

A number of stochastic elements contribute to the level of coverage. For example, at each time step there is a 5 percent chance that an alderman with a strong (±2) position will do something newsworthy. If so, the coverage is 2 for a strong alderman and 1.4 ($\sqrt{2}$) if he is not. Second, at those times when information on current aldermanic positoins becomes general knowldege (except when due to mayoral announcement), the contribution to the level of news coverage is taken as either 1 or 2 (stochastically); however, whenever a strong alderman has changed positions since the previous exposure of aldermanic positions, the coverage is strictly 2. We also include a general stochastic contribution to represent the effect of pertinent events not related to specific actions of the participants. This term has a modified Poisson distribution with a mean of 1 and an 8 percent chance of 3.

Whenever the level of conflict in the city is excessive an additional increment is added to the level of coverage to reflect the fact that conflict and controversy make news.

The impact of news (information) upon the welfare and ethos indices of a single ward is determined by taking a weighted average of the level of coverage associated with each medium or interest group. ‡ The weights represent the relative attention given to that group or medium by the people in the ward. We modify this result to reflect both a sensitization of the public (low coverage level in one period followed by high coverage in the next) and a saturation effect (high level of coverage in one period lessening the impact of equal or lower coverage in the next). In addition, the level of coverage during

---

*Half the time (stochastically) the coverage is 2 and half the time, 1.

†Recall that it is the square of the coverage that is added.

‡The media and churches are always included, but are weighed more heavily (except for TV) if their positions are announced; other groups are included only if their positions have been announced.

one period will have a residual effect in the next. At present, we are using a "carry-over" factor of one-third.

To estimate the effective level of opinion coverage we start from the news coverage level by medium or group and weigh each contribution not only by relative attention (as before), but also by the position taken by the group and by a factor that reduces the weight of the source the more its position differs from that of the natural position of the ward. (This is intended to reflect selective exposure, selective perception, and selective retention.) As with the news coverage, one-third of the level of opinion coverage of the previous period is added to the current level to arrive at the effective value of this quantity.

The positions of all the interest groups are determined from their assigned values of E and I. For the mass communications media, however, the adopted position reflects both internal values and the pressures exerted upon them by the interest groups. The weighting of the internal values decreases with time, so that the external pressures, which are initially less important than internal values, gradually tend to dominate.

There is one additional effect that the media and the interest groups have on the behavior of the aldermen that has not been discussed so far. Since politicians believe that media and interest group endorsements have an impact on voter opinion over and above what they personally may have observed to that time, the aldermen include in their perceived vote payoff matrices contributions from whatever media and interest groups may have announced their positions. These contributions are weighted by the attention given to the groups by the voters in the ward and operate in the same manner as the clique and mayoral effects mentioned in the description of the general model to reinforce (additively) the positions adopted by the several groups.

It is important to recognize that the effect just discussed is a perceptual artifact of the politician. The real effects on voters are taken into account through the changes in E and I described earlier.

This completes our description of the way in which the media and interest groups influence public opinion.

THE INTEREST GROUPS AND THE ALDERMAN

In addition to influencing public opinion, some interest groups can influence the political process more directly, as indicated in Figure 8.3. Those groups that can command some form of patronage or favors can offer aldermen a number of new jobs or favors if they vote "right." Therefore, in the present model we allow business, labor, organized crime, and the affected bureaucracies to offer job payoffs to specific aldermen with whom they are used to cooperating. These payoffs go into effect only if the interest group has announced a strong ($^+_-$2) position on the issue, in the form of a modification of the job payoffs as a function of aldermanic position. The payoffs vary with the strength of the alderman and with the closeness of the relationship between interest group and alderman.

A second, smaller set of job and favor payoffs accrues in a similar manner to all aldermen who vote "right" from the strongly interested bureaucracies and from the bureaucracy directly responsive to the mayor. The vested bureaucracies pay off from the beginning of the controversy, but the mayor's bureaucracy pays off only after a mayoral announcement of a position of $^+_-$2.

In this way we believe we can represent, at least to some extent, varying levels of interdependence between some aldermen and the vested interests with which they are associated.

SOME FINAL COMMENTS

In conclusion it should be noted that this model, which is based on established theory in the fields of political science, sociology, social psychology, and communications, addresses all but the first of the questions raised at the beginning of this chapter. While the model assumes that people hold, in some sense, preformed opinions on any controversial topic (question 1) and parametrizes the relative importance of the several sources of information and opinion (question 4), it treats explicitly the forces that tend to modify public opinion (question 2), the mechanisms by which influence is exerted (question 3), the relative impact of influence and opinion (question 5), and the way in which media positions are chosen and changed with time (question 6). The model also offers a resolution of the apparent paradox that politicians believe in the power and importance of media support while, at the same time, empirical studies offer little support for major political influence by the media in presidential election campaigns.

Since the model described in this chapter appears to be in accord with theory, empirical evidence, and common sense, it would seem to be a satisfactory starting point for a more detailed and more complete analysis of political attitude formation.

NOTES

1. See, for example, B. Berelson, P. F. Lazarsfeld, and W. N. McPhee, Voting: A Study of Opinion Formation in a Presidential Campaign (Chicago: University of Chicago Press, 1954).

2. For a discussion of these phenomena see, for example, Joseph T. Klapper, The Effects of Mass Communication (Glencoe, Ill.: The Free Press, 1960), pp. 19ff.

3. E. Katz, "The Two-Step Flow of Communication; An Up-to-date Report on a Hypothesis," Public Opinion Quarterly 21 (1957): 61-78.

4. L. Festinger, A Theory of Cognitive Dissonance (Evanston, Ill.: Row, Peterson, 1957).

5. See, for example, P. Zimbardo and E. B. Ebbesen, Influencing Attitudes and Changing Behavior, Rev. ed. (Reading, Mass.: Addison-Wesley, 1970), p. 83.

6. F. Adelman and I. Adelman, "A Simulation Model of Urban Politics," 1971 Winter Simulation Conference (New York: ACM/ AIEE/IEEE/SHARE/SCi/TIMS, 1971).

7. The bargaining process is described in Adelman and Adelman, op. cit., and in F. Adelman, "A Dynamic Multi-Person Political Bargaining Model," submitted to Operations Research.

9

MEASURING THE QUALITY OF URBAN GROWTH— TOWARD A MODEL USING SOCIAL PERFORMANCE CRITERIA

Martin W. Brossman
Martin J. Redding

The growing concern for achieving a balanced combination of social, economic, and environmental well-being in our pursuit for an improved "quality of life" has not—to date—led to effective procedures and quantitative measures that permit reduction of concept to practice. Perhaps nowhere else is the potential for achieving this so great and the need so urgent than in the regional and urban development process. Here there is a rapidly evolving awareness of problems associated with overcrowding, high-density development, and intensity of human activities—in a limited space. Concommitant with these problems is the overtaxing and draining of natural resources, including potable water, open space, and clean air.

Clearly there is a need for a rational, balanced, and comprehensive means to plan and guide urban growth in a manner that considers the total environment of an area including the life-style desired.[1]

A methodology including an expanded view of the environment and society and incorporating the concept of carrying capacity* appears promising. Such a model might assist in achieving quality growth through a balanced combination of factors contributing to the quality of life of a region.

---

*Carrying capacity refers to the ability of an ecosystem to support a given number of consumers and remain healthy and productive. Although not precisely defined, the same biological principle applies to human population in terms of balancing land use needs with the ability of the resources to support those needs.

OVERVIEW OF PROPOSED MODEL

The Regional Quality Growth Model is intended initially to be a research model that would eventually be useful at the regional level for planning, decision making, and for setting policy. The objective of the model is to assess the quality of the growth of the region as measured by quality of life (social, economic, and environmental) indicators and system resource capacities.

Conceptually, the model, whose elements are shown in Figure 9.1, would consist of the following packages:

1. Regional System Description. This package would describe the characteristics of the region or system in terms of its physical and functional attributes. That is, the physical (man-made and natural) dimensions in terms of its density, configuration, dissociations, and connectivity would be described as well as the functional aspects of habitation, distribution, work, services, and recreation. In addition the resources capable of being supplied by the urban area as well as those supplied from without the area would be delineated.

2. Activity (Growth) System Description. This package describes the activities imposed on the regional system. It is actually the growth portion of the model in that the rate or quantity of growth in the region will be expressed in terms of the increase in number and intensity of these activities. Activities can be entered into the system or allowed to grow by either the private or public sector. This package should provide the alternatives for the activities to grow, to be maintained, or to be cut back (decay).

The public activities to be included in this package are education, transportation, health, safety, welfare, utilities, and administration. The private activities include heavy industry, light industry, commercial, recreational, agricultural, and personal services.

It should be noted here that the quality aspect of growth is not handled in this package. Quality will be assessed in the System Quality Assessment.

3. System Impact Description. This package will take the activities imposed on the regional system and describe the consequences that the activities have on the characteristics, attributes, or resources of the region. This is essentially the output of the activity system and regional system interaction. The major output categories are physical products, quality of life factors, and resource depletion. The physical output category includes industrial output, service output, and agricultural output. The quality of life factors include recreation, food and fiber, safety, health, education, welfare, living conditions, and economic security.

FIGURE 9.1

Elements of Regional Quality Growth Model

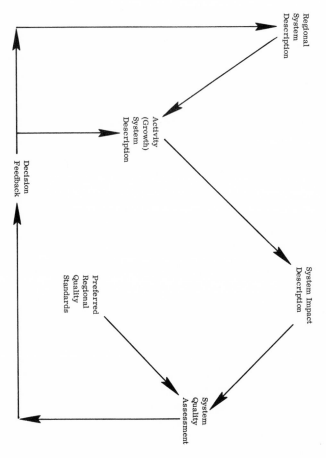

Regional
System
Description

Activity
(Growth)
System
Description

Decision
Feedback

System Impact
Description

Preferred
Regional
Quality
Standards

System
Quality
Assessment

Source: Compiled by the authors.

The resource depletion category reflects the amount of specific resources being consumed to sustain activities in the activity system as well as being consumed by the adverse impact on air, water, and other resources caused by pollutants.

4. Preferred Regional Quality Standards. This package would provide the indicators or standards for social, economic, and environmental quality assessment of the system and thus establish an acceptable range of the quality of life for the region. These indicators would be a preferred or satisfying acceptable level of measurement for the factors in each of the three areas. The impacts of the activities on the system would be assessed against these indicators in the System Quality Assessment package.

5. System Quality Assessment. This package takes the system impacts and compares them against the indicators or standards (social, economic, and environmental) that reflect the acceptable quality of life for the region. After the comparison is made those factors that are significantly affected (favorably or adversely) will be identified and the degree to which they are impacted will be displayed.

This package will also compare the resources available to resources depleted, rate of depletion, resources remaining, etc., and display these results.

The model is intended to assist the decision maker to do one of three things, depending on the level and degree of impact: (1) to allow growth to continue; (2) to maintain existing levels of activities; (3) to take corrective action to assure overall acceptable quality of life for the region. For each of the three alternatives he could then trace the effect of his action through the model to give an assessment of his decision on the system impacts and thus on the quality of life of the area. This begins to allow him to guide a quality growth for his region.

KEY AREAS FOR DEVELOPMENT

Figure 9.2 shows additional subelements of the concept discussed. Key to the detailed development of the concept is a valid and acceptable means for defining quality of life and an equally effective means for allocating resources to achieve the desired state. The Environmental Studies Division (ESD) of EPA has undertaken exploratory work in both these areas. Some of the work on quality of life indicators is described in the EPA/ESD publication, "Quality of Life Indicators," December 1972. Part of this report includes a

FIGURE 9.2

Substructure of Regional Quality Growth Model

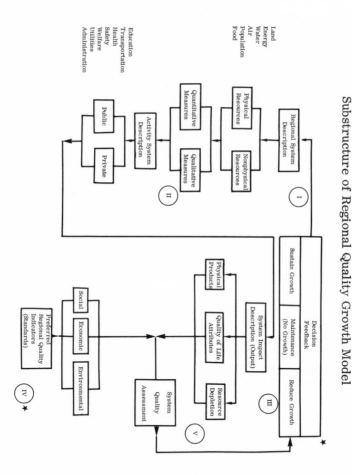

Land
Energy
Water
Air
Population
Food

Education
Transportation
Health
Safety
Welfare
Utilities
Administration

Source: Compiled by the authors.

survey of applicable work. The quality of life elements described in the "Report of the White House Conference on Youth of 1971" are typical. They are:

1. Natural Environment. Preservation of natural beauty and wildlife and opportunity to regularly experience unspoiled wilderness and water. Tabulation on the use of reserves of natural resources.

2. Living Environment. Overall maintenance of urban, suburban, and rural living and working areas. Maintenance of minimal conditions for clean air and water, available space, general sanitation and health, housing and structural safety, and building and street aesthetics.

3. General Health. Basic sanitation and safety maintenance, ample available health care, and intensive medical services for the young and elderly.

4. Income and Basic Economic Security. Minimization of individual economic deprivation, minimum guaranteed living standard, equitable distribution of wealth, and continual opportunity to pursue improved economic conditions.

5. Employment and Productivity. General provision for productive opportunity which provides equitable distribution of wealth and continual opportunity to pursue improved economic conditions.

6. Productive Employment Areas. Study of the variations from the mean that exist within minority groups regarding educational attainment in relation to earning power.

7. Aggregate Economic Advancement. Overall economic production of society, which takes into consideration negative and preventive production (such as smog control devices) and environmental deterioration costs.

8. Training, Education, and Culture. Opportunity to learn usable skills, problem-solving abilities, and the value of the world.

9. Justice and Freedom Concerning Threat and Coercion. Minimum threat of harm or loss of security. Extent of positive as opposed to negative sanctions used in social and individual interaction.

10. Individualism. Opportunity for free expression and selection of "life-style," and levels of social tolerance and alienation.

An alternate approach to structuring the elements of quality of life is shown in Table 9.1. Whatever the quality of life structure chosen, however, the elements must ultimately be reduced to some measurable form such as indicators to be useful in the model concept we are proposing.

Development of a technique for allocation of resources to achieve a system quality is another key development area. One initial approach of promise is that suggested by Peter House.[2]

TABLE 9.1

Quality of Life Factors

ENVIRONMENT
Air
Water
Noise
Radiation
Solid waste
Hazardous substances (pesticide/chemical)
Aesthetics
Land use
Natural resources
Housing
Transportation
Utilities
Material quality
Communication and media

SOCIOPOLITICAL
Education
Privacy
Safety
Personal skills
Equality
Community
Health
Choices in life
Social relationships
National security
Democratic process
Justice

ECONOMIC
Accumulated assets
Living costs
Income distribution
Economic security
Economic growth
Public spending
Discretionary income
Leisure

This list is a typical composite compiled by the Environmental Studies Division of EPA.

He describes a concept for developing a quality of life indicator from a set of subindicators and a rationale for combining such indicators into a resource allocation scheme for improvement of the quality of life. A definition of quality of life (QOL) is suggested that provides a relationship of weighted societal preferences for achievement of individual environmental, sociopolitical, and economic goals. The functional relationship is defined as

$$QOL = \sum_{i=1}^{n} w_i(I_i)$$

where w_i is a preference function derived from society for the elements of QOL expressed by the indicators I. Functional relationships are also defined between resource costs (RC_i) required to maintain and improve QOL and the indicators of status I. A numerical example is then exhibited in which an allocation of resource costs (RC_i) is made to maximize QOL.

CONCLUSION

The foregoing is suggestive of the concept of a quality growth model and some key areas for development. The concept is now at best rudimentary. However, we believe it provides a useful framework for further definition and evaluation of priority areas for more extensive development. At a minimum an expanded form of the concepts may provide useful, general guidelines and an orderly procedure to guide quality growth.

NOTES

1. Some noteworthy work has begun, including "Ecology and the Economy—A Concept for Balancing Long Range Goals—The Pacific Northwest Example," Pacific Northwest River Basins Commission, November 1973; and "Carrying Capacity in Regional Environmental Management: A Feasibility Study," Utah State University for the Washington Environmental Research Center, EPA, February 1974.

2. Peter W. House, "How Do We Know Where We Are Going," presented to a Seminar on Multiple Criteria Decision Making at the University of South Carolina, October 26-27, 1972.

Carl F. Christ

Social and political processes in urban life can be studied in
several ways, ranging from the building of explicit self-contained
models of a city as a whole, at one extreme, to concentration on a
particular aspect of urban processes, at the other. Two chapters
here provide examples of each extreme. The Adelmans describe their
work with a simulation model of urban politics and attitude formation,
while Schelling considers the consequences of individuals' choices as
to which groups they wish to associate themselves with. Both chapters
combine the approaches of operations research and economics.

The chapter by Frank and Irma Adelman begins with a verbal
description of political forces and decision making in city politics,
containing many acute observations whose broad outlines are familiar
to the alert urban citizen.

The first part of the chapter describes in verbal terms an
abstract conceptual model of city politics. The political simulation
model is not presented, but from the verbal description and two
diagrams we get some understanding of how it is supposed to work.
Each member of the city council is assumed to maximize a preference
function that depends upon the consequences of the positions he takes.
Presumably the mayor also acts to maximize a preference function.
There are other actors in the model, including influence groups who
bring pressure to bear in the hopes of influencing political decisions
and groups who stand to benefit from patronage. We are told that the
model has been used successfully to simulate the political process,
including bargaining and compromises, but we must take this on faith
because neither the simulation methods nor the results are presented.

The remainder of the chapter concentrates on a model of attitude influence. The attitude sector includes news media, interest
groups, voters, and officials. Again the technique is one of simulation,
but again the chapter does not present the model and does not give a
clear indication of how the simulation process works.

For each ward of the city there is an important pair of variables
representing the true level of welfare of the voters and the consciously
perceived level of welfare. An important part of the model is the
mechanism by which the perceived welfare level approaches the true
level through a process of information flow and evaluation. For each

118

ward there is another important pair of variables, representing respectively the true extent and the consciously perceived extent to which voters in the ward, choosing their positions on an issue, take into account the welfare of people in other wards.

The attitude model contains relationships describing the interactions of these variables with those of information and opinion and the manner in which interest groups and members of the city council and the mayor choose positions on issues. The main diagram, Figure 8.4, gives a description of the process, but the verbal description does not entirely agree with the diagram.

There is a need to clarify the nature of the model in several respects. The descriptions of the relations in the model should be made more precise, though in fairness it must be added that the model is apparently more complex than can be portrayed in detail in a short presentation. The diagram and the verbal description should be made to correspond. A few apparent contradictions need to be resolved. For example, the text says that the index ITRUE is changed by ΔITRUE, which depends only on the ward characteristics and the level of opinion coverage. However, the text also says that ITRUE moves toward ETRUE at a rate that depends upon both of their values and the levels of opinion and information coverage and a variable called salience. There appear to be two different descriptions of the manner in which ITRUE changes.

The Adelmans state that the middle and wealthier classes, particularly the highly educated, tend to pay more attention to the welfare of others, while poorer people with poor education do not. This suggests that wealthy people vote for progressive taxes and for closing tax loopholes. This is a testable proposition of which I am not convinced.

This chapter is interesting and promising. I hope the authors will pursue their research further and report more about how the model works, what behavior it generates, how it corresponds to reality, and how it might be tested.

Thomas Schelling's approach contrasts sharply with that of the Adelmans. Whereas they have built a model designed to explain in a simplified way the entire range of political forces and decision making in a city, Schelling has dealt on a much more micro level with a single aspect of urban behavior, namely, the consequences of choices by each individual concerning which groups of individuals he wishes to associate himself with. Of course, every time an individual moves from one group to another he changes the character of both groups, and this may give rise to further moves by other members of one or both groups. Schelling gives us a number of ingeniously contrived examples, sometimes explaining why a particular equilibrium is reached in this process, and sometimes explaining why no equilibrium is reached.

In many of Schelling's models it is assumed that an individual can move from one group to another without cost to himself. Informally he has mentioned cases in which some kind of price must be paid. This makes the exercise much more realistic, since individuals often do pay a substantial price to move from one group to another, either in the form of household moving expenses, the purchase price or the rental price of residential property, the time and energy required to adjust to a new group of associates, or the like. It is clear that the preferences of the people who pay such costs must be rather strong.

Schelling notes that the kind of self-segregating process he describes does not necessarily lead to a situation of the type that economists call Pareto optimal. This is defined as a situation in which it is impossible to make a change that benefits anyone without at the same time harming someone else. A Pareto optimal change is defined as a change that does benefit one or more persons without harming anyone else. If, starting from an initial situation, such a change is possible, it can be regarded as desirable, simply because it provides costless benefits to someone. The achievement of a Pareto optimum, however, does not settle the really controversial political issues, because most of those issues concern whether to make a change that will benefit some people at the expense of others. Nevertheless, it may be agreed that a self-sorting process of the type discussed by Schelling that does not lead to a Pareto optimum leaves something to be desired.

Schelling's models are highly intriguing, and I believe that the segregation of people according to race, income, and other characteristics can be better understood with the aid of such models. I hope he and others will continue such work.

Joseph F. Coates

Our society as well as its managers, governors, advisors, and savants are beleaguered by problems of unaccustomed complexity, pervasiveness, and subtlety. The management of this subtle complexity is in some sense our central problem. Operations research as one approach to that management enjoys auspicious historical antecedents in its origins as a practical tool in the analysis, guidance, and management of operating or planned systems. While operations analysis is not totally deaf to the sirens' call of empty models and vacuous subtlety, its historical lock to reality, continually reinforced by fresh challenges and success, provides partial immunization.

Schelling logically extends his premier work in bargaining its applications to strategic analysis into another problem area. The subtlety of his chapter, however, recalls feelings on first reading Ludwig Wittgenstein's Philosophical Investigations. The effects produced in each case being rapid vacillations between grasping the newly obvious and then retreating with an appreciation for the subtlety and again grasping the obvious and retreating in the face of its subtle implications. The appreciation of the joyful stimulation associated with these clever conjectures, the micro game playing, subtle play-offs of options may not be enough. One may ask a methodological question, whether this approach is likely to be fruitful in dealing with the public management of urban affairs. One of the characteristics of bargaining in national security or strategic problems is the small number of players, notwithstanding that the historical audience as well as the number affected may be quite large. In the domestic public policy process, however, as implemented through any agency of government, the actors are numerous, policies are many, and interactions are likely to be gross rather than subtle at the decision-making level. Consequently, I doubt whether the stimulation and mind-raising potential of this approach is likely to have any substantial payoffs in urban public policy process or any close connection to primary option generation. The levantine subtlety that the illustrations themselves represent would be marvelous for stimulating small group interaction or individual bargaining, but I fail to see the connection or potential extrapolation to public policy processes. On the other hand, since policy discussion generally suffers from malnutrition and anemia, one can expect as an absolute minimum that the enrichment that this bargaining analysis approach offers would ultimately have an effect in making analysts or decision makers more subtle in their general thinking and more aware of the complexities entering into and flowing out of their decisions.

The Adelmans' chapter is stimulating, provocative, and engaging, but raises several basic questions about modeling social and political processes. Assuming that one is interested in going beyond consciousness raising and the value implicit in using such a model strictly for game playing, one must raise several serious questions. What would be the data base required, its cost, availability, and generalizability to test and validate the model? The question of the validation of the model itself, as the authors imply, may be difficult insofar as it depends on cognitive dissonance theory. The latter shares some of the methodological shortcomings of psychoanalysis in that it tends to be compatible with all possible outcomes, hardly a desirable condition for model testing.

On a more positive note, the model is isomorphic or nearly isomorphic with many other systems. It might be lots of fun to attempt, by isomorphic transformation, to model middle-level bureaucracies of many sorts, as in a department store or a government agency. Perhaps because of the leanness of the presentation there is some failure to relate these submodels to the larger models in a way that is straightforward and easy to follow.

Reflecting on a pathological tendency in much recent operations research, the indifference to the needs or even the existence of the user for the model, one must raise the question to whom would such a model be useful. Presumably not to the alderman who very well understands his own behavior. Certainly not to the mayor who is likely at one time or another to have been an alderman. It would seem to be of very little value to those attempting to influence or impact the system. It seems to me that the model as it stands, even if tested and validated, would to a substantial degree be in the literal sense only of academic interest and only of incidental value to those concerned with managing, manipulating, and influencing the urban processes.

And finally, it seems to me that the model as presented is not a model of attitude change, but is rather a model of behavior change, a condition that should go a long way to facilitating the model's validation. The Martin Brossman/Martin Redding chapter seems to me to most closely approach in intent the traditional operation analyst's goals of developing a useful tool for decision making. But it raises some general issues having to do with quality of life factors in models, the use of social data. First, the notion of "quality of life," is a voguish term that seems to add little to the public policy discussion except to muddy up well-established categories. For example, little in the quality of life discussion cannot be subsumed under the classic economic concerns with identifying, quantitating, and managing externalities. Second, the notion of life-style is a tricky concept since the life-style desired now may be circumscribed by a narrowness of which one may be completely oblivious. For example, ten years ago who would have expected a Catholic college, even in California, to have sexually integrated dormitories? Who, 15 years ago, would have expected the prosperous children of middle- and upper-class families to affect the garb of poverty and economic deprivation? Most talk about desired life-styles ignores the overwhelmingly difficult problem of anticipating desirable, undesirable, and neutral social change from present perspectives and the even more difficult problem of anticipating desirable, undesirable, and neutral social change from present perspectives and the even more difficult problem of anticipating those changes from shifting future perspectives. But after all, the future is all we have, and that is what we must manage.

"Indicators" is virtually an invitation to being misled, for a variety of different reasons. First, the implications are that the indicators are surrogates for something more basic, but not as susceptible to measurement. Yet it is a rare discussion of social indicators that makes that distinction, much less comes to grips with what is to be measured and the derivative problem of what surrogate or indicator measures there are for it. Second, there is the question of subtlety again; often an apparently negative measure can be interpreted quite positively. For example, one could interpret any increase in white-collar crime committed by black citizens as a gross measure of social progress. Similarly, one could consider in view of what we already know about the dark figure of crime that an increase in reported crime, particularly in black, Chicano, and Mexican slum areas, is a positive indicator, indicating that rather than hiding or ignoring crime by failing to report it, increasing confidence in the system is leading to more crimes being reported. One must go well beyond simple statistics in order to interpret these as indicators. Third, there is a pathological aspect of indicators that one might call "the body count syndrome" in which the indicator itself can rapidly become the bureaucratic measure of success and strong action taken to maximize the indicator while suppressing the subtleties and difficulties associated with its relationship to reality.

With regard to modeling in general we are in much better shape on measures of the input components to models of almost any system. The system itself as far as modeling goes is off in a black box, relatively little understood in its ramifications and complexities. Generally on the output side we have virtually no understanding of appropriate measures. But we must therefore guard against indicator systems that indicate on the input side and ignore the output end. The latter is really the absolutely more important.

The particular system described in the chapter offers little on either the uses to which the system would be put or the needs for or capabilities of such systems in use. It seems to be a cardinal principle for helping decision makers that the helper knows who the decision makers are and what their range of responsibilities or actions might be. I did not see that here.

The future is in general so totally discounted in the material presented as well as in many discussions on the quality of life that one would hardly think that many if not most social- and political-process models are in fact oriented toward the future. Yet the future is little attended to in terms of the basic social, institutional, and technological changes, potentially influencing separately or in convergence with the various factors the area that concerns us. Finally, the model as reported seems to exist in a political limbo. The quality of life elements drawn from the Youth Conference of 1971, for example, neatly illustrate the risk that any modeler or serious student of the public policy process is likely to run up against, namely some combination of the vacuous, platitudinous, and the wrong-headed. Consider as evidence its item 4, "incumbent basic economic security, minimization of individual economic deprivation, minimum guaranteed living standard, equitable distribution of wealth, continuing opportunity to pursue improved economic conditions."

IV

THE IMPACT OF
PUBLIC POLICIES
ON URBAN MARKETS

Oftentimes distortions in the economy, imbalances between supply and demand, and what appear to be perverse forms of economic behavior on the part of the private sector are the result of policies of the government that interfere with the market mechanism. The three chapters presented in Part IV discuss examples of "market failure" in three areas of concern to urban policy makers: housing, health, and education.

Two describe theoretical models. The chapter by Frank de Leeuw presents a model explaining changes in the location, quality, and stock of housing as a result of, among other things, various housing policies initiated by federal, state, and local governments. The chapter by John Holahan and Stuart Schweitzer develops a model for estimating the impact of the Medicaid program on the market for medical services. While Medicaid reduces the barriers imposed by price for those eligible for the program, it results in increased prices and lower utilization of medical services for those not eligible for the program. Medicaid may also affect the overall quantity and quality of medical services available to the public.

The de Leeuw and Holahan and Schweitzer chapters describe what is likely to have happened because of public policy in the housing and health areas. Neither study has yet progressed to the point where it describes what has, in fact, happened.

Dennis Doyle describes OEO's experimental educational voucher program in San Jose, California, in contrast to the other two. Not only does he present some preliminary results of the voucher experiment, he also describes an effort to create a market mechanism where, by tradition,none has existed, rather than interference in existing markets by relatively recent policies intended to change, presumably for the better, urban market behavior. Local education has traditionally been a monopoly or near monopoly. Students have been required to attend public schools in their local communities, with the only element of competition provided by private schools available to the relatively few. The purpose of the voucher program is to determine whether injection of greater freedom of choice in the educational marketplace would result in better performance by the suppliers of educational services and greater satisfaction on the part of the demanders.

The three chapters are limited in their discussion of how policies have impacted on urban housing, health, and education markets. The major purpose of these chapters, however, is to outline how the analyst might undertake a study of the impact of these policies. To this end they provide the analyst with useful direction and guidance.

10

A MODEL OF HOUSING
QUALITY AND LOCATION

Frank de Leeuw
Raymond Struyk
with Sue A. Marshall

THE MODEL IN BRIEF

The Urban Institute housing model deals with ten-year changes in housing quality and household location within a metropolitan area. A capsule description of the model would contain four key phrases: "ten-year changes," "housing quality," "household location," and "within a metropolitan area." Each of them serves to distinguish the model from other models or studies—for example, from short-run explanations of housing market dynamics, from location-free theories of the filtering process, or from macroeconomic analyses with a national focus. The model emphasizes two characteristics that distinguish housing from most other goods: the durability of housing and the inescapable link between housing and neighborhood.

The model represents a metropolitan housing market by a few dozen "model" households, a few dozen "model" dwellings, a building industry, and possibilities for a variety of government restrictions or programs. The four "actors" in the model are thus households seeking a place to live, owners of existing dwellings offering housing services at various prices, a building industry meeting demands at an acceptable rate of return, and governments able to regulate the housing-location process at many different points. The model searches for a "solution"—a situation in which no one can improve his position

---

This chapter draws upon data from The Urban Institute housing market model project, sponsored by the Department of Housing and Urban Development.

according to the rules of behavior and constraints he obeys—through a matching of households with new or existing dwellings. The brief description in this section takes up each of the four actors in turn and describes the solution process. It then introduces a price-quantity diagram illustrating the interaction of the four actors. An appendix presents the behavioral rules and constraints in mathematical terms.[1]

"Model" Households

Each "model" household represents several hundred or thousand actual households, the exact number depending on the size of the metropolitan area to which the model is being applied. A household belongs to one of several household types and is characterized by two measures of its income. The household types with which we have worked in the model so far include white nonelderly families, white elderly/single-person households, black nonelderly families, black elderly/single-person households, and in the case of Austin, Texas, Chicano nonelderly families and Chicano elderly/single-person households. Some of the parameters of the model, as we shall see in the next section, differ by household type.

Characterizing each household by two income measures represents a modification of the original formulation of the model. Initially we attempted to represent each household by a single income measure, the mean "permanent" income of the hundreds or thousands of actual households that it represented. Now each model household is represented by (1) an actual income figure, the estimated mean actual income of the actual households it represents; and (2) a "model" income figure, which is a weighted average of its actual income and the median income for its household type.

There are two reasons for going to two income figures instead of one for each household. The first is that certain of the programs that the model is intended to analyze—for example, housing allowances —operate on actual income rather than any transformed version of income. The second, perhaps more important, reason is that use of a single income figure seemed to produce a systematic simulation error in the first three areas to which the model was applied—namely a considerable overstatement of the degree to which wealthy households choose new dwellings (and moderate-lower-income households choose existing dwellings). Use of the present "model" income instead of the previous "permanent" income for calculating the utility of each dwelling to each household has greatly reduced this systematic error without introducing any new errors.

The present model thus uses actual income as the variable directly affected by certain housing, tax, or transfer programs and uses "model" income in actually determining the choice of location and quality that each household makes. A change in actual income— a result of a housing allowance, for example—is of course translated into a change in "model" income but the latter change is smaller than the former.

The behavior of households in the model consists of deciding which of all possible dwellings to occupy. "All possible dwellings" includes a new dwelling of any desired level of services (subject to any government-imposed minimum standards for new construction) or any of the existing dwellings in the model. The household makes its decision on the basis of the quantity of housing services that each dwelling offers, the price per unit of housing service at which it offers those services, the household's "model" income, and three characteristics of the zone in which each dwelling is located. The three zone characteristics are (1) average travel time to and from work, (2) average net rent per dwelling, and (3) the proportion of zone residents that belong to the same racial group as the household making the choice.

All of these variables influencing household choices are combined into a utility function that the household is attempting to maximize. The utility function has four parameters whose values decisively influence what the model predicts about the effects of housing policies. One of the principal goals of the application of the model to specific metropolitan areas is to obtain estimates of these parameters.

"Model" Dwellings

Each model dwelling, like each model household, represents several hundred or thousand actual cases—in fact the number of actual cases per model unit should be the same for dwellings as it is for households. Each model dwelling belongs to one of several zones (5 or 6 zones in work so far) differing in accessibility, initial wealth, and/or initial racial composition. Each model dwelling is also characterized by the quantity of housing services that it is supplying at the beginning of the ten-year interval to which the model applies. The level of housing services of a dwelling, one of the basic concepts of the model, refers to an index of all the things of value that a physical structure provides—space, shelter, privacy, pleasing design, and a host of others. It does not refer to the neighborhood characteristics associated with each dwelling; these are measured by the various attributes of the zone in which a dwelling is located.

The behavior of the owners of existing dwellings consists of making price-quantity offers with the goal of maximizing expected profits. Each price-quantity offer consists of a quantity of housing services to be provided at the end of the decade to which the model refers and a price at which that quantity will be provided. The offers thus resemble rental advertisements appearing in newspapers. The price-quantity offers for each dwelling must lie along a supply curve whose position depends on (1) the initial quantity of housing services offered by the dwelling and (2) two parameters of the model, one related to a depreciation rate and the other related to an elasticity of supply with respect to price.

The owner of each existing dwelling seeks to locate as high up along his supply curve as he can, for his expected profits are an increasing function of his position along the supply curve. Competition among the owners of actual dwellings comprising each "model" dwelling is assumed sufficient to keep landlords from making offers above their supply curves.

The model includes a minimum price per unit of service, defined as that price which is just sufficient to cover the cost of operating a dwelling. If the owner of a dwelling is unable to find an occupant at any price above the minimum price then his dwelling is withdrawn from the stock of housing. The model does not distinguish among abandonment, conversion to nonresidential use, long-term vacancy, or other forms of withdrawing a unit from the stock.

Builders

The third actor in the model, the building industry, plays a more passive role than model households and model dwellings. The building industry is characterized by a horizontal supply curve. That is, it is prepared to offer new dwellings at a monthly total cost that is proportional to the level of services that the dwelling provides. The price per unit of service at which new dwellings are available is taken as given for each housing market. It is measured on the basis of FHA data for each metropolitan area separately.

This exogenous price tends to set a ceiling for the price structure of the existing stock, although existing dwellings with especially favorable zone characteristics can command prices moderately above the new-construction price. Newly constructed dwellings are assumed to be concentrated in a single "zone of new construction."

Governments

The final actor of the model, government, can influence the housing-location process at so many different points that it is impossible to describe its behavior succinctly. Tax charges, subsidy payments, transfer payments with or without earmarking for housing, minimum new construction requirements, and minimum quantities of housing services in a particular zone are among the ways in which government can affect housing markets in the model.

An income tax can be represented by replacing a household's actual income by income less the tax, and by making a smaller reduction in its "model" income, before it enters the housing market. The tax rate and other parameters of the tax formula—for example, an exemption level—can be set separately for each household type, or even for each model household. A transfer payment is represented using the same procedure as an income tax. A transfer earmarked for housing, or a housing allowance, can be represented by requiring an eligible household to consume at least some minimum level of housing services or spend some minimum amount on housing in order to receive the transfer; the household then determines his utility-maximizing choice without the allowance, his choice with the allowance and its requirements, and the larger of these two maxima. A restrictive zoning ordinance can be represented by setting a minimum quantity of housing services for all of the dwellings in a zone.

The Solution Process

The solution of the model, as mentioned earlier, is a situation in which none of the four actors has any incentive to change his position. Each household is occupying the dwelling that maximizes his satisfaction given all the price-quantity offers he is facing. The owner of each existing dwelling is as high up along his supply curve as he can be without finding his dwelling vacant. The building industry is supplying the maximum number of new dwellings that households are willing to purchase. Government regulations are strictly enforced.

The computer program to solve the model searches for a solution with these properties through a process of trial and error. Departures from solution conditions in one trial govern the way in which the solution is modified for the next trial. The steps in the search process have no theoretical or empirical significance; it is only the final solution of a problem that is of interest. Once the program finds a solution it tabulates results in a variety of ways. Prices, quantities, and locations are shown by household, by dwelling, by zone, by household type, and in the case of certain subsidy programs by eligible households.

Application of the model has revealed some problems with the solution process, and modifications of the basic algorithm are continuing during the third year of work on the model.

A Price-Quantity Diagram

The model in effect represents the housing market as a set of demand and supply functions for closely related submarkets. Prices per unit of housing service in all these submarkets need not be the same because housing in one submarket is not a perfect substitute (in demand or supply) for another. Prices in various submarkets can't differ too much, however, because substitution is strong enough to cause vacancies or overoccupancy if the price in any submarket is out of line with prices in closely related submarkets.

The device of a price-structure curve is a useful way to summarize outcomes under the model. Figure 10.1 illustrates two hypothetical price-structure curves. The horizontal axis measures quantities of housing services produced by individual units. The vertical axis measures price per unit of service for these same dwellings. The points on the curve represent specific dwellings (or averages of groups of dwellings) showing the quantities of service they produce per month and the price per unit of service that the occupant pays for these services. Each point on the curve can be thought of as the intersection of a demand curve and a supply curve.

The curve depicts the variation of price with level of services, but does not depict the variation of price with location. Although the latter variation is difficult to represent diagramatically, it is an important part of the underlying model.

Generally, prices per unit of service tend to lie between the two points labeled P_n and P_o on the price axes. P_n is the price per unit at which new dwellings are available. In actuality, of course, it is not a single point but a band within a metropolitan area depending on variations in neighborhood land costs and other housing costs. In most areas, however, the band is fairly narrow compared to the whole range of housing prices; and representation by a point is convenient. P_o represents the minimum costs per unit of service necessary to keep a dwelling in operation. If a unit is vacant even when it has lowered its price to P_o, then the dwelling (in the model, at any rate) will be withdrawn from the residential stock.

FIGURE 10.1

Hypothetical Price-Structure Curves

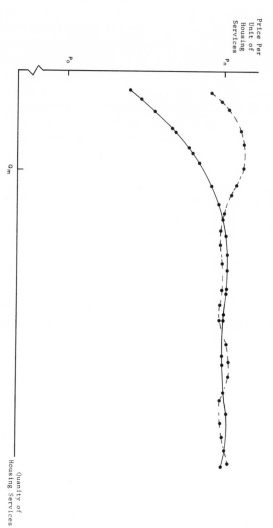

Pₙ = Price per unit of service of a new dwelling.
Pₒ = Minimum operating cost per unit of service.
Qₘ = Minimum permitted quantity of services for a new dwelling.

Source: Compiled by the authors.

The reason that P_n tends to serve as an upper limit to housing prices is that a household is very unlikely to pay more per unit of service for an existing dwelling than for a new dwelling of identical level of services. An important exception to this ceiling role of P_n arises from the fact that most metropolitan areas effectively prohibit new dwellings at a low level of services. Large parts of most metropolitan areas exclude mobile homes, for example; in addition, building and housing codes tend to set lower limits to the quantity of services provided by any newly constructed dwelling. Below this minimum level of new housing services, represented by Q_m in Figure 10.1, there is no reason why prices per unit of service cannot exceed P_n—as they do in one of the two curves depicted in the figure.

Dynamic forces within most housing markets tend to keep prices close to the P_n ceiling for moderate- and high-services dwellings. These dynamic forces are (1) growth in real income over time, (2) growth in the population of the metropolitan area, and (3) depreciation of dwellings over time. All three of these tend to create a shortage of housing at the high-service end of the range with the result that new construction tends to take place in this range of services and prices of existing dwellings in this range tend to be driven up toward the P_n ceiling.

In the low-service end of the range the three forces do not act in the same direction. Growth in real incomes and depreciation of housing services probably tend to create an excess supply of dwellings in this range and hence lower price. Metropolitan population growth, on the other hand, tends to increase the demand for services in this range, especially where there is a heavy influx of low-income households. Where the excess-supply forces dominate, the result may be a situation like the solid line in Figure 10.1 in which low-service dwellings sell at a discount per unit of service. There population growth is very rapid and where the P_n ceiling is not operative at the low-service end of the scale, the result may be a curve like the dashed line in Figure 10.1 in which housing fairly near the low-service end of the scale sells at a premium.

Perhaps the most useful way to conclude this brief description of the model is to mention some of the things that the model does not do. The model does not attempt to capture any of the short-run dynamics of the housing market; it restricts its attention to ten-year changes. The model does not analyze the markets for inputs into housing services; it simply takes construction costs, financing costs, and costs of operating inputs as given. At present the model does not separate renters from owner-occupants; owner-occupants are viewed simply as landlords who rent to themselves. A good deal of work is underway, however, to introduce tenure into the model. Finally, the model deals in only a restricted way with the market for urban land. It takes no account of nonresidential uses of land and it takes the short-cut of locating all new dwellings in a single zone rather than attempting to explain the geographic location of new construction in detail.

Mathematical Appendix

This appendix specifies in mathematical terms the utility function of households and the supply function of the owners of existing dwellings. It includes only the briefest of explanations of why particular functional forms were chosen, how the functions described relate to demand curves or production functions, and so on.[2]

1. Household utility functions. Each household evaluates each dwelling by means of a utility function. The utility of the dwelling "j" to household "i", U_{ij}, can be represented as

(1) $U_{ij} = H X Z_1 Z_2 Z_3$

H, the term representing the utility of housing services, is defined as follows:

(2) $H = (Q_j - \alpha_i \gamma_1 Y_i^m / P_n)^{\alpha_i}$

in which Q_j is the quantity of housing services offered by dwelling j, α_i is a parameter expressing the strength of housing preferences (versus preference for other goods) of households of the type of household i, γ_1 is a parameter expressing the degree to which households will alter their housing choice in response to a price discount, Y_i^m is household i's "model" income after adjustment for taxes and transfers, and P_n is the price per unit of service of newly constructed dwellings.

The term in the utility function described by equation (2) is an elaboration of the idea underlying the so-called linear expenditure system, namely that the utility of housing services is best approximated by measuring their excess over some minimum acceptable level. Unlike the linear expenditure system, however, equation (2) makes the minimum acceptable level itself a function of income. The importance of the minimum depends on the parameter γ_1, which is determined empirically. For γ_1 equal to zero, equation (2) reduces to a simple Cobb-Douglass expression for the utility of housing services.

X, the term representing the utility of nonhousing goods, is specified in a manner analogous to H. The budget constraint facing the consumer is used to define nonhousing goods as $Y_i^m - P_j Q_j$, where Y_i^m is the household's "model" income and P_j and Q_j are the price and quantity of services of dwelling j. The term defining X is as follows:

$$(3) \quad X = [(Y_i - P_j Q_j) - (1 - \alpha_i)\gamma_1 Y_i^m]^{1-\alpha_i}$$

The terms in this expression are defined following equation (2) above.

The three zone characteristics, Z_1 through Z_3, relate to accessibility, wealth, and racial composition. Z_1, the term representing accessibility, is defined as follows:

$$(4) \quad Z_1 = (200 - T_j)^{.5 + \alpha_i - \alpha_1}$$

where T_j is the average travel time (in hours per month) of the zone in which dwelling j is located, α_i is a parameter expressing the strength of housing preferences of households of the type of household i, and α_1 is the value of α_i for white nonelderly families.

The term in parentheses, $200 - T_j$, is an approximation to monthly hours of leisure time available to an average worker in the zone in which dwelling j is located. The exponent of this term is based on studies of the value households place on travel time and on analysis of how we might expect this value to vary with strength of housing demand.

The second zonal characteristic is defined as follows:

$$(5) \quad Z_2 = \left[\frac{\overline{(P_j - P_o)Q_j}}{\overline{\overline{(P_j - P_o)Q_j}}} \right]^{.01\gamma_2}$$

where P_j is price per unit of housing services, P_o is minimum operating costs per unit of housing services, Q_j is quantity of housing services, and γ_2 is a parameter expressing the strength of preferences for a wealthy zone. One line above a variable refers to a zonal average (the zone in which dwelling j is located), while two lines above a variable refers to an SMSA (Stanadard Metropolitan Statistical Area) average.

This term represents the average net rent (gross rent less operating costs) of a zone relative to the average net rent in an SMSA. It probably serves as an indicator of zonal wealth.

The third and final zonal characteristic is defined as follows:

$$(6) \quad Z_3 = R_{ij} + (1,000/[100\gamma_3 + 1])$$

where R_{ij} is the proportion of households in the zone of dwelling j belonging to the same racial group as household i, and γ_3 is a parameter expressing the strength of preferences for racial homogeneity.

The larger the parameter γ_3, the more sensitive Z_3 (and hence U_{ij}) is to variations in R_{ij}. With γ_3 equal to zero, Z_3 can vary only between 1,000 and 1,001, a range of one-tenth of a percent. With γ_3 equal to one, Z_3 can vary between approximately 10 and approximately 11, a range of 10 percent.

2. <u>Existing dwelling supply functions.</u> The supply curve for existing dwelling j is specified as follows:

$$(7) \quad Q_j = \left[\beta_1 + \beta_2 \left(\frac{2}{3} \right) \left(\frac{P_j - P_o}{P_c} \right) \right] Q_o$$

in which Q_j is the level of housing services currently provided by dwelling j, Q_o is the level of housing services provided by dwelling j ten years ago, P_j is the price per unit of service offered by dwelling j, P_o is operating costs per unit of service, and P_c is capital costs per unit of service for a new dwelling. β_1 and β_2 are parameters to be determined empirically. Prices are all on a flow basis—that is, they are costs per unit of service per month, not costs per unit of capital stock.

Equation (7) is derived from the maximization of an expression for expected profits constrained by a production function for housing services. [3]

POLICY SIMULATIONS

To conclude this chapter we present the "calculated" results of a housing allowance plan in each of the four areas to which the housing market model was applied: Durham, N.C.; Austin, Tex.; Portland, Ore.; and Pittsburgh, Pa. These results should not be taken too seriously. They refer to only one program design of one type of policy; and they do not include any systematic analysis of how results are affected by initial housing stock characteristics, household characteristics, accessibility, or other features of a housing market. Furthermore, they are based on a solution algorithm that has certain faults that may well bias the simulation outcomes. What is presented in this section is suggestive of the <u>kinds</u> of policy-relevant results that the model will be able to provide.

The simulated housing allowance plan was designed so that it would attract about 10 percent of the 1970 households in each of four areas. The proportion was kept down to the neighborhood of 10 percent by making the subsidy offer small rather than by making the minimum standards high or by arbitrarily assuming a low participation rate. Specifically, the subsidy offer was set at $65 minus 25 percent of income for all nonelderly families and at $35 minus 25 percent of income for all single/elderly households.* To receive the allowance an eligible household had to consume a minimum quantity of housing services set at 39 units per month for nonelderly families and 21 units per month for elderly/single households.

To finance the allowance payments and administrative costs of the program, a tax was imposed on all incomes above an exemption level. The exemption level was $480 for nonelderly families and $320 for elderly/single households. The tax on income minus exemptions was seven-tenths of one percent (.007).

The presentation of results below first discusses what happens to eligible households (according to the calculations of the model) with respect to participation, earmarking, and quantities and prices of housing services. It then discusses the smaller changes the program causes for ineligible households.

Results for Subsidy Recipients

Almost all of the income-eligible "model" households in the four cities accepted the housing allowance plan. Of the 16 income-eligible model households, 15 elected to participate. The low level of the required minimum quantities of housing services clearly has a crucial influence on this participation rate. By raising the minimum quantities high enough the participation rate could be lowered to zero. The high participation rate is thus a special characteristic of the particular program design selected and not in any sense a general prediction about participation in housing allowance programs.

The earmarking ratio for participating households—that is, the change in housing expense as a fraction of the subsidy payments—is well below 100 percent in all four areas. It reaches its highest level, 74 percent, in Austin. Its levels in Durham, Portland, and Pittsburgh are 55 percent, 26 percent, and 24 percent, respectively. Again,

---

*Income here refers to total household incomes as reported in the 1970 census. Since the census understates actual incomes significantly, an allowance plan intended to apply to actual incomes would have to offer a higher dollar amount or a lower percent of income to be equivalent to the one we have simulated.

these results are heavily influenced by the minimum quantities of hous-ing services required under the program. With higher minima, par-ticipating households would be compelled to spend a higher fraction of the subsidy on housing. On the other hand, with higher minima more households might be tempted to decline participation in the program.

The degree of earmarking is also influenced by the marginal cost per unit of housing services facing eligible households as they consider improving their housing conditions. As we shall see, this rise in price as quantities of housing services increase is, according to the model, much less severe in Austin than in the other cities, and this difference contributes to the relatively high earmarking ratio in Austin.

The price-quantity results for subsidy recipients in the four cities are shown in the top section of Table 10.1. They are most favorable—or least unfavorable—in Austin, with less than one-third of the expenditure increase going into price increases and more than two-thirds into improved housing services. In the other cities roughly half of the increase in expenditure goes into price increases.

The reason for this difference between Austin on the one hand and Pittsburgh, Portland, and Durham on the other is suggested by an examination of prices and quantities in the four areas in 1970 according to the calculations of the model. Figure 10.2 shows these "calculated" quantities of housing services and prices per unit of housing service for all existing "model" dwellings in the four cities. It summarizes the background price-quantity situation into which the allowance is introduced in each area.

In addition to prices and quantities for model dwellings, the figure contains three arrows for each city. The arrow along the horizontal axis shows the estimated minimum quantity of housing services required for a new dwelling in each of the four cities during 1960-70. The two arrows on the vertical scale for each city show minimum price per unit covering operating costs during 1960-70 (the lower arrow) and estimated price per unit of service for new dwell-ings during 1960-70. The lower arrow is the price per unit of services below which no existing dwelling will continue to offer housing services. The price per unit of service for new dwellings tends to serve as a ceiling for prices of existing dwellings since, apart from exceptionally favorable locational factors, a household will not pay more per unit of service for an existing dwelling than for a new dwelling. This ceil-ing effect of the new-construction price, however, can operate only above the minimum required level of services for new dwellings.

The diagrams for Durham, Portland, and Pittsburgh show price discounts at the low-quality of the range of services, a pattern prob-ably existing in a substantial number of metropolitan areas. The forces that create a price pattern of this kind are increases over time

TABLE 10.1

"Calculated" Effects of a Hypothetical Housing Allowance

	Durham	Austin	Portland	Pittsburgh
Participating Households				
1. Average subsidy per household (dollars per month)	22	24	21	22
2. Average increase in housing expense (dollars per month)	12	18	6	5
3. Earmarking ratio (2 ÷ 1, before rounding)	.55	.74	.26	.24
4. Average increase in housing expense (percent)	+37	+28	+14	+25
5. Average increase in housing services (percent)	+17	+19	+7	+10
6. Average increase in price per unit of housing service (percent)	+18	+7	+6	+13
Households Just Above Income-Eligibility				
1. Average tax per household (dollars per month)	0.0	0.0	0.0	0.0
2. Average increase in housing expense (percent)	+7.4	+1.4	+.8	+.3
3. Average increase in housing services (percent)	+3.8	+.1	+.4	-4.8
4. Average increase in price per unit of housing service (percent)	+3.5	+1.3	+.4	+5.3
All Other Households				
1. Average tax per household (dollars per month)	3.8	3.3	3.8	3.4
2. Average change in housing expense (percent)	-1.1	-.6	+1.7	+2.3
3. Average change in housing services (percent)	-.6	-.9	+1.8	-.2
4. Average change in price per unit of housing service (percent)	-.5	+.3	-.1	+2.5

Source: Compiled by the authors.

FIGURE 10.2

"Calculated" Price Structure, Four Areas, 1970

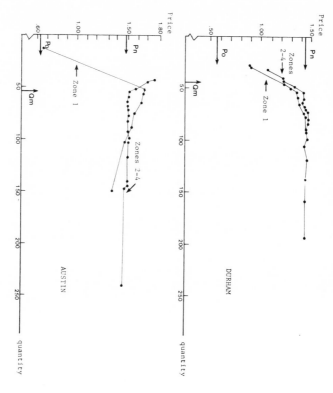

DURHAM

AUSTIN

(continued)

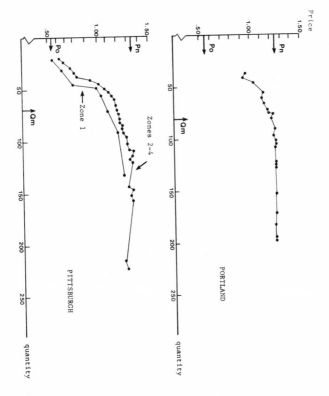

Figure 10.2 continued

Notes to Figure 10.2

The horizontal axes measure quantities of housing services for each model dwelling. The unit of measure is the housing services one dollar could buy, on the average, in 1960 <u>for each area.</u> Since housing prices are generally higher for Portland than for Austin or Durham, a unit on the horizontal axis represents less housing services for Portland than for the other areas.

The vertical axes measure estimated price per unit of housing services in 1970, in dollars per month. Again, the base is the average price per unit of housing services in 1960, since this magnitude is by definition one dollar for each area. The total monthly housing expense estimated for each model dwelling is its price multiplied by its quantity.

Q_m is the estimated minimum quantity required for each <u>new</u> dwelling in 1960–70. Its relative position for the three areas is affected not only by differences in building standards, zoning laws, etc., but also by differences in the number of housing services one dollar could buy in 1960 (see first note above).

P_n is the estimated price per unit of service for new dwelling during 1960–70.

P_o is the estimated operating cost per unit of service during 1960–70.

<u>Source:</u> Compiled by the authors.

in incomes and housing demands on the one hand and depreciation of the housing stock on the other. At the high end of the quality range these forces tend to produce increasing demands and decreasing supplies, while at the low end these same forces produce the reverse. The price pattern shown for Durham and Portland is the market response we might expect under these conditions.

The Durham and Pittsburgh diagrams indicate a discount for "zone 1" or inner-city housing apart from the low-service price discount. It is difficult to know whether this discount is at all typical. Racial discrimination can easily lead to price differences by zone; but these differences can go in either direction.

The diagram for Austin, in contrast to those for the other areas, shows a "calculated" price premium at the low end of the quality scale. Only for the very lowest "model" dwelling does a price discount emerge for Austin. The "calculated" pattern of difference between zone 1 and the other zones, furthermore, is quite different for Austin from what it is for Durham or Pittsburgh.

The Austin pattern might be expected in an area whose population growth is so rapid that there is an increase in demand for housing even toward the low end of the quality scale. Since the cost of new construction cannot serve as an upper limit for existing housing prices below the minimum-service point on the diagram, rapid growth can lead to a price premium for low-quality housing. According to the model that was the situation in Austin in 1970.

Austin's relatively rapid growth is brought out in the following tabulation of percent changes in numbers of households:

| | Percent Change in Number of Households 1960-70, Selected SMSAs | | | |
	Durham	Austin	Portland	Pittsburgh
All households	+31	+53	+27	+ 6
Households with incomes under $4,000	-19	- 9	-14	-20
Households with incomes from $4-7,000	-15	+ 2	-38	-53
Households with incomes over $7,000	+174	+223	+128	+98

The first line of figures documents Austin's rapid overall growth. The second line, focusing on poor households, shows decline in all four areas but less rapid decline in Austin than in the others.

The third line, relating to $4-7,000 incomes, shows growth in Austin and decline in the other areas. It is this contrast that lies behind the differences among areas in Figure 10.2. The final line, for households with incomes above $7,000, shows growth in all areas. Growth was more rapid in Austin than in the other areas, but differential growth in this income range probably leads to differential construction rates rather than to differences in price per unit of housing service.

To relate Figure 10.2 to the results of the housing allowance it is useful to think of two ways in which a household can improve its level of housing services. The first is by remaining in the same dwelling (and since we are talking about "model" dwellings representing several hundred or thousand actual cases, "staying in the same dwelling" means essentially staying in the same small neighborhood after receiving the allowance). Housing services in this case can improve by movements along supply curves for individual dwellings. Price increases resulting from this kind of move are about the same, according to the estimated β's of the model, in each of the four cities.

The second way of improving housing services is to move from the "model" dwelling chosen in the absence of an allowance to a "model" dwelling providing a higher level of services. Movements of this kind amount to movements along the curves depicted in Figure 10.2 (as a first approximation; the movements themselves, of course, result in some shifts of the curves). Here the price situation is evidently more favorable in Austin than in the other areas. Except for the very poorest model household, low-income households in Austin are already paying a premium for housing services. For these households, moving to a higher-service dwelling decreases this premium if it affects it at all. In Durham, Portland, and Pittsburgh, on the other hand, a move by a low-income household to a higher-service dwelling involves a substantial rise in price.

According to the model's calculation, subsidy recipients in Durham, Portland, and Pittsburgh largely occupy the same group of "model" dwellings with the subsidy as they do without the subsidy. The majority of subsidy recipients in Austin change dwellings as a result of the allowance. In Austin one additional dwelling is withdrawn from the housing stock as a result of the allowance, whereas in Durham, Portland, and Pittsburgh there is no change in withdrawals as a result of the allowance. The forces depicted in Figure 10.2 are again at work in producing these results. Low-income households in Durham and Portland have a much greater price incentive to stay in their pre-allowance neighborhoods than do low-income households in Austin.

The results for housing allowance recipients, in short, appear to depend heavily on the initial price-quantity situation. That situation, which differs between Austin on the one hand and Portland, Durham, and Pittsburgh on the other (see Figure 10.2), has clear effects on the degree of earmarking, the proportion of expenditure change that goes into higher prices, and the number of removals from the housing stock.

Effects on Ineligible Households

Ineligible households are affected by a housing allowance program from two different sources. One of them is the market changes that are caused by the behavior of the subsidy recipients. The second is the change in disposable income caused by taxes to finance the allowance payments.

In the case of three of our four cities these two sources of difference correspond pretty well to the difference between the experience of households just above the eligibility limits and the experience of all other households.

The lower portions of Table 10.1 show the price and quantity effects for these two groups of households. For households just above the eligibility limits* in Austin, Durham, and Portland prices are slightly higher as a result of the allowance, though the change is not nearly as great as the change facing subsidy recipients. In Pittsburgh, households just above eligibility do face a noticeable increase in housing price, though still far smaller than that faced by subsidy recipients.

For "all other" households—those neither eligible to receive the subsidy nor just above the income-eligible limits—price-quantity results are minor.

Nothing has been said so far about locational shifts as a result of the allowance. The reason is that such shifts as do take place do not manifest any consistent pattern. In one city there is some movement of nonwhite households away from zone 1 into zone 2, but in another city there is an increased concentration in zone 1. In one city there is a rise in the average income of households choosing new dwellings, but in a second city there is a drop, and in the other two cities there is practically no change. Results for this one housing allowance plan in these four cities, in short, do not lead to any preliminary suggestions as to locational effects.

In conclusion, it is worth recalling once more that these results refer to only one program design for only one program and make use of a solution algorithm that has faults and that has been improved since these results were generated. More analysis must precede any complete, balanced statement about the model's implications for housing allowances or for allowances in combination with supply programs or other government actions. The results presented here will

---

*These households include one "model" household directly above the income eligibility limits for each household type in each of the four areas.

have served their purpose if they suggest that after a full analysis the model may be of some use in comparing alternative programs and designing economically efficient housing policies.

NOTES

1. For some technical details, Frank de Leeuw's The Distribution of Housing Services (Washington, D.C.: The Urban Institute, 1972) remains a more complete reference than the present section. There have, however, been some minor changes in the theoretical structure of the model since completion of this earlier reference. These are noted in the paragraphs that follow this reference.

2. A more complete discussion appears in ibid., pp. 20-33.

3. The derivation is sketched out in ibid., pp. 24-28.

THE ALUM ROCK, CALIFORNIA, EDUCATION VOUCHER PROJECT

Denis P. Doyle

In December 1969 the U.S. Office of Economic Opportunity (OEO) commissioned a study to identify ways and means of making education more responsive, accountable, and effective by testing institutional changes in school financing. The completed report, prepared by the Center for the Study of Public Policy (CSPP) in Cambridge, Mass., recommended that a "regulated compensatory education voucher system" be field tested in several sites across the nation. Under this concept each child of school age is eligible for a "voucher," equal in value to the average amount being spent per student in that district; eligible schools, rather than receiving direct funding from a central source, receive vouchers from enrollees and redeem them for cash. Thus the school is held uniquely accountable to its clients; at the same time, because families chose the school of attendance, the school has a strong claim on parental support. In short, the voucher system provides tentative "operational definitions" of both school and parental accountability.

Underlying this voucher proposal is the belief that introducing certain market factors in education—"consumer" sovereignty and the notion of linking willing providers and willing clients—will produce certain beneficial effects, as follows:

1. A greater number and wider scope of education choices will appear in response to market demand.

2. Greater parental, student, and teacher satisfaction will result when these education actors are brought together in voluntary association.

3. Greater professionalism on the part of educators will appear: Not only will their clients come to them of their own volition, but also educators will be designing and delivering an educational product of their own making.

Critics of vouchers, however, raised serious questions about possible harmful effects:

1. Voucher systems could be used to promote economic segregation within schools. Wealthy parents could add money to their vouchers and be able to choose schools that charge additional fees. Vouchers also could lead to racial segregation within schools, as well as income and ability segregation.

2. The system could lead to public support of religious instruction, in violation of the Constitution.

3. A free market in education could lead to false claims by educators, which could mislead and misinform an unsophisticated public. In short, hucksterism could enter the educational market.

4. Parents—particularly low-income parents—do not have the wit, interest, or desire to make wise educational choices for their children.

5. The administration of a voucher system could be unmanageable, and a new, perhaps more unwieldy, bureaucracy could be created.

6. Finally, vouchers could jeopardize the public schools if they became schools of last resort.

Recognizing the validity of some of these criticisms, CSPP and OEO proposed that the voucher system be both "regulated" and "compensatory" and should include significant safeguards:

1. Schools must accept the voucher as full payment for educational services, minimizing socioeconomic segregation because poor parents cannot be excluded because of inability to pay.

2. Educationally disadvantaged children receive a "compensatory" voucher in addition to the basic voucher. These children become more "attractive" to schools as a source of additional discretionary income. At the same time schools are encouraged to design special programs to serve the needs of these children and become more responsive to their parents.

3. To assure meaningful choice among varied educational offerings, schools are required to provide extensive information about themselves: for example, educational philosophy, curriculum, faculty-student ratio, faculty qualifications. This information is independently verified for accuracy and completeness and broadly disseminated to parents.

4. To assure equal access by all students to all schools, non-discriminatory admissions and transfer policies are required. For example, if a school is overapplied, at least half its student body must be accepted by random selection from the pool of applicants. Invidious racial discrimination, in both hiring of staff and admissions of students, is also prohibited.

In the original voucher model proposed to OEO, private and parochial schools were eligible to participate. (In the regulated, compensatory voucher model the traditional distinction between public and nonpublic schools blurs; for example, open admission to nonpublic schools makes them "public" in terms of constituency, even though they are privately managed.) In practice, however, legal constraints make it difficult, if not impossible, for nonpublic schools to participate.

EXPERIENCE TO DATE:
ALUM ROCK UNION SCHOOL DISTRICT

OEO launched one voucher demonstration project in the Alum Rock Union School District, in San Jose, California, beginning September 1972. (In August 1973 the voucher project was transferred to the National Institute of Education [NIE], HEW's education research and development arm.) We have traveled a long road from theory to practice. But first, a brief description of Alum Rock: It is basically a quiet California suburb, less than an hour south of San Francisco, in what were until recently the verdant orchards of Santa Clara County. Although it lies within the city of San Jose, it is an independent school district with a personality of its own. The school district is run by an elected school board and has its own taxing authority. The community it serves is largely working class, with a heavy admixture of welfare recipients and a small population of middle-class residents to the east where the district rises into the foothills.

One of the most striking features of San Jose and of Alum Rock is the degree of real racial integration. San Jose proper is the most fully integrated Standard Metropolitan Statistical Area in the nation, and that residential pattern extends to Alum Rock. Although the proportion of Mexican-American families is substantially higher than the state average (48 percent), they live throughout the district. The black population (12 percent), is consistent with the overall black population of California. The balance is white, with a small Oriental population.

Because the project was limited to public schools in its first two years, it was necessary to broaden artificially the range of choice available to families. Each public school developed at least three distinctive "mini-schools," with separate faculty, curriculum, and educational philosophy. Beginning in September 1972, 3,900 elementary students, enrolled in six public schools, were given education vouchers for the 1972-73 academic year. The program was actively supported by the Alum Rock School Board, the superintendent, the teachers' association, and parents. The experiment expanded in the 1973-74 academic year to include approximately 9,000 students in 13 schools. Thus the program has met with strong community and professional support.

ANALYSIS

The analysis of the voucher demonstration is designed to accomplish three basic objectives: (1) to document the political and educational history and the consequences of the voucher demonstration; (2) to measure the progress of the program in reaching its specific objectives (to increase parental control and satisfaction with their schools, to increase the diversity of parents' educational choices, and subsequently to improve education for their children); and (3) to identify and assess other effects of the voucher plan, both positive and negative. The design is longitudinal, with observations of conditions being made before, during, and after the demonstration.

PRELIMINARY OBSERVATIONS

Although it is important to emphasize that the progress made at Alum Rock to date does not yet constitute an adequate basis for conclusions about the effectiveness of a voucher system, preliminary results are of some interest. These results are subject to change as the program evolves. Trends that have been observed may continue or may be reversed. A full understanding of the voucher system is not expected to become apparent until well into the demonstration.

As indicated earlier, the presence of "mini-schools" within a single school building allows parents a choice of education alternatives without having to move their children to a nonneighborhood school. Thus parents may exercise a voucher-related choice in their neighborhood school. Overt, measurable voucher choices can be classified into three general categories:

1. Parents who enroll their children in schools other than the ones closest to home
2. Parents who transfer their children from one program to another, either within a given building or between school buildings
3. Parents with more than one child who enroll different children in different programs.

There were 2,350 families participating in the demonstration
as of January 1973 and another 400 families had been participants at
one point but were no longer active. Among these families, approximately 100 have made Type 1 choices; 140, Type 2 choices; and 400,
Type 3 choices. (An additional 220 families used intradistrict transfer privileges to enroll their children in voucher schools.) All families
could exercise Type 1 and Type 2 choices, but Type 3 choices could be
made only by some 1,000 multiple-child families participating in the
demonstration, of whom about 40 percent made Type 3 choices.

Although these choices are not mutually exclusive, there has
been very little overlap between them. Tallies indicate that in the
first year about one-fourth of the participating families have used the
voucher to make an overt choice.

Although data on second-year choices is still not complete, a
proportionally larger number of children attended nonneighborhood
schools in 1973-74 than in 1972-73.

With 9,000 students participating this year, 5,300 were eligible
to make voucher-related changes over the summer and 1,500 students
did so. Of these, 780 students chose to move to a different school.
This represents an increase in between-year student mobility from
4 percent in the first year to 15 percent in the second year. An additional 720 students, or 30 percent of those eligible, changed programs
within their building.

Presumably parental choice is to be based on adequate and
accurate knowledge of available alternatives. Information has been
made available to parents in a variety of forms, including material
sent home from school, parent meetings, parent counseling, school
board meetings, media coverage, school bulletins and newsletters,
as well as informal personal contacts. Almost all written material
has been available in both Spanish and English.

The results of attempts at providing parents with adequate information were mixed. Few parents attended school board meetings
at which voucher program information was presented. Teachers,
principals, and school newsletters have been the most useful and
available channels of information. Because of tight schedules in the
beginning of the demonstration, and relatively high community mobility, 17 percent of voucher parents surveyed had not heard of the education voucher demonstration as of November 1972 and 23 percent did
not know the program in which their children were enrolled. These
percentages have improved as information dissemination procedures
have been institutionalized. The November 1973 parent survey indicated that only 3 percent of parents were then unaware of the demonstration and 15 percent did not know what program their children were
enrolled in.

Approximately 85 percent of all voucher parents surveyed felt that giving parents a choice between programs was a good idea, and when asked if they had sufficient information to make program choices, approximately two-thirds felt they did. Exercise of parental choice is further limited by the availability of classroom space and staff in the mini-schools. Several mini-schools have experienced some space and staff limitations that have either precluded or delayed full parental choice. This also contributed to underestimating parental choice.

No major shifts in student ethnic balance have occurred during the initial phase of the voucher demonstration. The representation of each of the three major ethnic groups (Spanish-surname, white and other nonwhite, black) in the participating schools closely paralleled the prevoucher distribution. With one exception, ethnic proportions within mini-schools mirrored the proportions within schools. There was a 7.6 percentage point increase in Spanish-surname enrollment in the school that offered a mini-school with a bilingual component.

TEACHER RESPONSES

Teachers in voucher and nonvoucher schools were given self-administered questionnaires in fall 1972 and were surveyed again in spring 1973. Personal interviews with principals, board of education members, the superintendent, community leaders, parent counselors, paraprofessionals, and other key individuals not scheduled to be surveyed are currently in process. In the spring of 1974 a sample of students were interviewed. Complete survey analyses are currently nearing completion. The results cited here are tentative and subject to revision or qualification. More complete analysis will be published periodically.

In general, teacher reactions to the voucher plan have been detailed and articulate. Although analysis of teacher questionnaires is not yet complete, their responses are mixed and complex, with teachers taking different positions on different issues. Approximately 20 percent of the voucher teachers said that their attitudes toward the demonstration had become more favorable since they first heard about it, whereas about twice as many said their attitudes had become less favorable. On the other hand, more than two-thirds of these same teachers stated that they were pleased to be participating in the demonstration. Similarly, about 55 percent felt that the voucher demonstration would increase the quality of education in Alum Rock, and only about 4 percent felt that quality would be decreased. The remaining 41 percent felt that no change in quality would occur. By spring the percentage of original voucher teachers believing vouchers would increase educational quality rose to 74 percent, with only 1 percent expecting quality to decline.

More than half of these teachers felt that the new programs represent significant departures from their school's previous educational methods. Most of the teachers (87 percent) felt they would have more freedom of decision in their classrooms: 56 percent think they will have more influence on school policy, and only 7 percent think they will not. Some three-fourths of the teachers felt that vouchers would result in decentralization, but an even larger percentage felt that decentralization was beneficial. At the same time, three-fourths observed that competition was occurring, and more than half characterized this as harmful. By the spring this concern had lessened with only one-third of the teachers of the opinion that competition would be a cause of conflict in the second year.

Most of the teachers surveyed accepted the basic theories of the voucher system. A majority of those responding to the fall survey thought that parental choice among programs was a good idea, and only a few teachers thought that parents had made poor choices. Two-thirds of the teachers felt that parents should have more to say about what their children learn in school, and a similar number believed that the voucher system would help achieve this end.

RESPONSES OF PRINCIPALS AND ADMINISTRATORS

The role of the school principal has changed significantly as a result of the voucher demonstration. Principals find that they are functioning largely as coordinators and facilitators for their mini-schools. This contrasts with prior experience; in the past, principals more often made unilateral decisions on behalf of staffs or simply implemented decisions made at the central office. The principals report that they are working harder for a variety of reasons. Their involvement in deciding the allocation of new school resources has increased dramatically. They are spending more time in meetings with parents. In previous years each school might have had one PTA or other parent group. In some cases, each mini-school now has a parent group. Broader participation by teachers in decision making has increased the time principals must spend in faculty consultation. In addition, voucher principals have been heavily involved in shaping policies that affect the demonstration as a whole, such as student transfers, evaluation, and information dissemination.

EDUCATIONAL OUTCOMES

Standardized achievement tests in reading and mathematics are being given in the fall and spring to all voucher students as well as to some nonvoucher students. Many parents and educators feel that these measures alone are not sufficient to plot a child's educational progress. An experimental battery of tests, measuring other dimensions of education, was administered in the spring of 1974. Research has shown that educational change is a long-term process, and for this reason measurements of educational change will not be interpretable for some time.

PARENTAL RESPONSES

A sample of voucher parents was surveyed in fall 1972 along with smaller samples of nonvoucher parents and other members of the Alum Rock community. Similar cross-sectional samples were administered in fall 1973 to assess parental and community attitudes toward the schools, the demonstration, and education in general. Special samples have also been drawn from selected groups of parents, particularly those who have used the voucher mechanism to affect the schooling their children receive. In addition a panel of voucher parents has been selected for several interviews during the course of the academic year. This panel will show whether smaller samples can be used without sacrificing reliability.

Three-quarters of the voucher parents think that the education their children receive in Alum Rock schools is either good or very good, with no noticable difference between voucher and nonvoucher parents.

Parents view the voucher demonstration as a minimal risk venture. When queried on the effect of vouchers on key groups—children, minorities, teachers, administrators, and parents—most parents were not sure if the result would be positive or negative, but only a handful viewed the latter as probable.

It is worth noting that levels of public satisfaction fluctuate frequently and are therefore difficult to measure with confidence. Thus high or low levels of satisfaction cannot be taken to "prove" anything about the demonstration and should not be used to draw conclusions about the impact of the voucher system so far.

CONCLUDING REMARKS

It is too early to draw firm conclusions about the impact of the voucher project itself, but we seem to be relearning a number of old lessons as vouchers move from theory to practice. Some general observations about large-scale social science research and demonstration projects are in order.

The most important lesson is that vouchers can be made to work. The project is administratively feasible. But administrative feasibility must be understood in a relatively narrow context. The initiators of the project had assumed that it would be possible to launch a major demonstration, involving nonpublic as well as public schools, with an overall enrollment of 10,000 to 12,000 students. Our scope was obviously too ambitious, our time frame too short, and our sense of the political realities of educational change too limited.

Major social change cannot be induced by simply throwing a great switch. Communities are bound by social entropy. A sudden change in social direction leaves the lucky participants reeling and the unlucky ones sprawled in the aisles. Orderly social change requires moderate and reasonable incentives and pressures, or failures are sure to result.

The original idea of a major eight-year, four-site longitudinal study of education vouchers assumed that communities, sensing the elegant interior logic of our plan, would flock to the idea. Alum Rock's most important contribution to date has been to disabuse us of that notion.

Alum Rock insisted, rightly, that the necessary first step was to educate the potential participants; not the conventional education of rules, regulation, and structure, but fundamental preparation for major social change. Alum Rock engaged a group of organizational development and management training consultants to prepare the central staff, principals, and teachers for the massive organizational and administrative reorientation that would result from a voucher system.

From the standpoint of an outside observer many of these changes seem trivial: the school secretary who must switch from handposting of student attendance registers to an automated pupil accounting system; the district business manager who must change his books of account; principals who are put on a stores-and-supplies budget instead of automatic delivery of supplies. At the higher level of both complexity and anxiety however, principals and their staff face the possibility that no one will voluntarily come to their school and that they will be subjected to public humiliation and ridicule. A principal or teacher asks, "After 15 years of hard work in a thankless job, why should I subject myself to the idle fancies of Cambridge intellectuals and Washington bureaucrats?"

That, in short, is the tough question. It is relatively easy for those of us in the ivory tower, away from the firing line, to speculate about the salutary effects of competition among schools, accountability, and parental control. But the people who bear the brunt of our planning and speculation live in tract houses in the disappearing orchards and vineyards of Santa Clara County, 3,000 miles away.

Alum Rock's prosaic insights into the practical dynamics of massive social change had other effects as well. Instead of turning the whole district into a voucher system on the first day, Alum Rock proposed a series of incremental steps: 6 schools and 4,000 students in the first year; 13 schools and 9,000 students in the second year; 14 schools and 10,000 students in the third year.

At the same time the absence of state enabling legislation necessary for private school participation permitted Alum Rock to propose an all-public-school voucher system. In retrospect the necessity of beginning with an all-public-school voucher system was fortunate—it permitted the orderly implementation of the project. Subsequently, enabling legislation was enacted, permitting privately managed schools to join the demonstration project.

The simple fact is that the public at large is, at best, ambivalent about public funds flowing to nonpublic schools, and, at worst, hostile. This is true across the board. Catholics and other religious school supporters express hesitation about supporting nonpublic schools with public funds.

From an operational as well as an ethical standpoint then, we could not superimpose nonpublic school participation on a community. We must wait and see if an organic development of constituencies for and against expanding the voucher system to nonpublic providers occurs.

Community participation in Alum Rock is a real issue. It has produced a major change in our conceptual design of the voucher project. We underestimated the holding power of the neighborhood school. Originally we had proposed that any school with more seats than students be open to all applicants; the community agreed to this. At the same time, however, we proposed that any school with more applicants than seats be allowed to select half its students and that the remaining seats be filled by random selection. This the parents—black, white, and Chicano—refused. They insisted that children currently in the system be "grandfathered-in," that to complete their term they be given "squatters rights" at their current school of enrollment. All the remaining vacant seats would be assigned by lot.

The practical effects of this approach are significant. Existing stakeholders are not dislocated—unless by choice they move to another building. As those who are "grandfathered" move on, true voucher seats open behind them.

Our major design shortfall was underestimating the intricacies of per pupil, income-outgo budgets. With the exception of single school districts, decentralized school budgeting is still in its infancy. No one that we know of has developed a system of income budgets based on the number of students enrolled and school outgo budgets based on that total income. Conceptually the program appears to be susceptible to direct solution. In practice, however, at least two serious problems arise:

1. Pupil accounting for state revenue purposes is based on average daily attendance rather than enrollment, creating the need for an elaborate proration procedure.
2. Certain schools are top-heavy with senior staff high on the salary schedule. An immediate shift to decentralized budgeting with salaries paid out of individual schools rather than central headquarters would be a rude shock to the system. Accordingly, for the initial phase of the demonstration we have averaged salaries and drawn against a central pool.

One of our major concerns at the conceptual level was that vouchers would lend themselves to the creation of highly specialized schools with homogeneous groupings; in particular, we were concerned about schools for "gifted" children that would skim off the easy to educate. A major development in Alum Rock was the emergence of a "gifted" program in which families self-selected their children for enrollment. To our knowledge, this is the only gifted program of its kind in the country, and the salient feature is that its ethnic distribution comes close to mirroring the ethnic distribution of the community at large.

Finally, NIE was accused by one set of critics of not having enough of a voucher system, and by another set of having too much. Followers of Milton Friedman see Alum Rock as a hopeless morass of rules and regulations; teacher groups see us moving perilously close to cutthroat competition among schools. There is a measure of truth in both charges. Alum Rock is not a pure voucher program. We have drifted a long way from the original design created by CSPP. But who at that time thought of "squatters rights," comprehensive pupil budgeting, and the hard realities of a massive social intervention?

It is clear, now that we have forged a partnership with Alum Rock, that the dose of reality gained there both tempers our enthusiasm about major social science demonstration projects and gives us a better sense of what is possible.

12

THE MARKET FOR MEDICAL SERVICES UNDER MEDICAID

John Holahan
Stuart O. Schweitzer

This chapter presents a model of the market for medical services under the Medicaid program. As in any model this is not an effort to accurately depict all aspects of reality, but rather to develop an abstraction that will yield useful insights into the workings of the system. The discussion focuses on the market for physician services. Medicaid reduces the price of physician services to zero for those fortunate enough to be eligible. Those not eligible continue to pay market prices unless they are insured through some other government program or privately. While services are costless to users, there is no guarantee of provision of desired services. Services are not generally provided directly but are purchased in the private sector. The willingness of private physicians to provide care to Medicaid eligibles depends on supply and demand factors in the general market for physician services and the incentives provided by the program to encourage their participation.

This model considers the impact of the program on service utilization by both eligibles and ineligibles as well as on prices of medical services. The model also suggests how both the quantity and quality of services delivered might be affected by the program. The model is in many respects applicable to other health services such as hospitals, dental care, and nursing homes, where providers are faced with similar choices between quantity and quality of service.[1] In addition to our conceptual model we present empirical evidence of the effects of alternative reimbursement arrangements on utilization of physician services in the Medicaid program. The regression model is limited in that present measures of quality are inadequate to test completely the hypotheses developed in the earlier sections. We begin by suggesting a model of the market for medical services before the introduction of the program.

SUPPLY OF MEDICAL SERVICES

The physician can be viewed as an entrepreneur combining his own labor with that of other inputs in the production of medical services. The welfare function of the physician can be written as dependent on income, leisure, and the quality of the services he renders. Quality enters as a separate argument in his utility function because it affects his professional status and prestige. As such, physicians will make trade-offs among income, leisure, and prestige in their choice of the volume and quality level of services delivered. The physician's ability to increase utility is subject to a time constraint (the number of hours available), to certain institutional and legal constraints, and to technical constraints since the quantity of his output is limited by the quality of services he provides and the quantities of labor, capital, and other inputs he chooses to employ.

The supply curve for medical services for individual firms can be derived from the shape of the utility function, the set of institutional and legal constraints, and the production function. The market supply curve is the simple aggregation of the supply curves of individual firms. The quantity of services provided will depend on the price for the service, the quality of service supplied, and other factors such as input prices, technology, etc. Thus the supply function can be written

(1) $Q_s = f[p, q, x, \mu]$

where

Q_s = the quantity of services supplied

P = the price of the service, exogenously determined

q = the quality of the service provided

x = an index of efficiency

μ = other factors such as technology and relative factor prices

The number of medical services, Q_s, is positively related to price and negatively related to quality; that is, $\partial Q_s / \partial P > 0$ and $\partial Q_s / \partial q < 0$. The number of services is negatively related to quality because increases in quality can only be achieved at higher cost. Thus the higher the quality of services provided, the fewer the number of services supplied at any given price.

Quantity and quality of service are distinguished in the following way. Quantity refers to numbers of reimbursable services such as physician visits or lab tests and is viewed as independent of the quality of the service. Services such as physician visits and lab tests might, alternatively, be viewed as inputs along with the initial visit in the provision of the ultimate output, defined, say, as restoration of health or neutralization of a health problem. The number of services would be the number of cures or health problems stabilized. This is in many ways a superior definition of output in that it allows for consideration of several important trade-offs in the delivery of care. However, the health care system, for better or worse, has traditionally involved the purchase and supply of specific health services. It is health services, not restoration of health, for which physicians are reimbursed under various public and private insurance plans and for which they are paid by uninsured individuals. Thus we consider only the demand and supply of individual health services.

Any of the reimbursable services provided can vary in quality. Quality is not necessarily associated with resource intensity of service but rather will depend on the accuracy of the diagnosis, appropriateness of treatment, and provision of information. Assume that for every type of patient contact, defined, say, by the patient's age, sex, medical history, and presenting morbidity, various levels of quality of service could be identified in terms of these criteria. By this definition an increase in inputs per unit of service would be an increase in quality only if the result was a more accurate diagnosis and/or a more appropriate treatment, and/or greater provision of information. Thus a visit of a given duration with a physician assistant rather than a physician would be a reduction in quality only if it resulted in a less accurate diagnosis, a less appropriate treatment, or less information provided. If there is no deterioration in quality so defined, the visit with a physician assistant is an increase in efficiency. The same analysis would hold for a visit to a highly skilled physician relative to a lower skilled or for a 20-minute visit rather than a 10-minute visit with the same physician.

Finally the supply of services will vary with the efficiency of the practice; the more efficient the practice, the greater the supply of services at any given price. In the typical economic market, incentives are presumed to exist that will tend to eliminate inefficiency. Thus an efficiency variable is usually excluded from economic models. However, because barriers to mobility and information limit competition in the market for physician services, physician practices are often inefficient in their use of various inputs.[2] Thus we include an inefficiency variable in the supply function.

DEMAND FOR MEDICAL SERVICES

The demand for medical services will depend on the price of services, the quality of available service, the physician's ability and willingness to influence the utilization decision, and other factors such as income, education, the distance from services, and determinants or correlates of need such as age and sex. The demand for health services will be negatively related to price and positively related to quality (the higher the available quality, the more services will be demanded, holding prices constant). (Note that if quality of care and cure rates are correlated, there may be less demand for health services at any price as available quality increases.) Feldstein has discussed the ability and willingness of the physicians to influence the demand for services in terms of availability.[3] He argues that because of the considerable consumer ignorance with respect to the appropriateness of medical services, the patient defers many utilization decisions to the physician. The physician acts as an agent for the patient in his decisions on appropriate service utilization, but because this agency relationship is incomplete (the physician's objectives do not always coincide with those of the patient) the physician's utilization recommendations will frequently result in a shift in the demand curve. Supply is typically thought of as affecting demand only through its influence on price. However, because the physician is able to shift the demand curve, the demand for services can be increased or decreased at constant prices. Feldstein argues that the propensity of physicians to shift the demand curve will depend on the relative availability of physicians. That is, an excess supply of physicians will lead to a provider-induced increase in demand rather than a fall in price. Likewise, an excess demand for physicians will call forth provider-induced reductions in demand rather than price increases. Thus this phenomenon is measured by an availability variable. We write the demand curve as follows:

$$(2) \quad Q_D = g(P, q, A, \theta)$$

where

Q_D = the quantity of services demanded

P = the price of the service

q = the quality of available service

A = physician availability

θ = other factors such as distance, health status, income, education, etc.

Suppliers will provide care at different quality levels depending on their quality preferences, market prices, and relative costs of different quality levels.* Users will also purchase care at different quality levels depending on their preferences, health status, income, as well as physician preferences and the relative prices of services at different quality levels. It follows that care will be provided along a continuum of quality levels. The equilibrium market prices for services of different quality levels will be those where the marginal rate of substitution between quality levels equals the marginal rate of transformation between quality levels.† At this point the quantities of services delivered at different quality levels will also be determined.

MEDICAID

It is unlikely, under present institutional arrangements, that Medicaid eligibles will be users of services at the highest quality levels. As long as a sufficient number of individuals are willing to pay the market price for the highest quality care, all services supplied at that price will be absorbed. All others including Medicaid eligibles will purchase services of lower quality. The quantity of relatively high quality care available to Medicaid eligibles depends on incomes, tastes, and quality preferences in each state and reimbursement rates set by the state. In some states services of almost all quality levels may be available to Medicaid eligibles. However, most states are presently fairly restrictive in their reimbursement practices, either by setting relatively low maximum fees or by using fee schedules. Therefore, we assume that when the Medicaid program is introduced, the impact on the system is directly on the market for low-quality health-care services. The impact, by altering relative prices for different quality services, ultimately affects all quality levels.

----

*We assume initially that each physician, given prices, preferences, etc., will operate on the same quality-specific supply curve for all patients. While this will not always hold, the assumption does not affect the conclusions of the analysis.

†The marginal rates of substitution between high- and low-quality care may be different for physicians and patients. An equilibrium solution might find both on lower indifference curves than if their own quality preferences were dominant. The degree of movement away from the initial equilibria will depend essentially on the degree of influence the physician has over patient decisions.

FIGURE 12.1

The Impact of Medicaid on the Market for Services

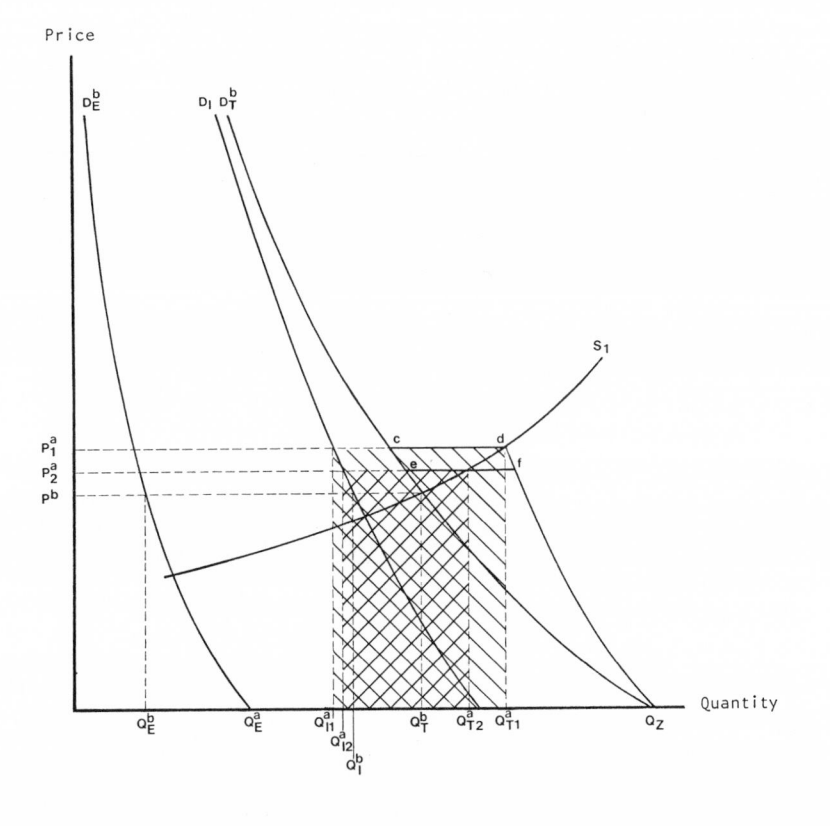

Source: Compiled by the authors.

Under Medicaid some proportion of the poor and near-poor population are declared eligible for covered services for which they pay a zero price. The rest of the population is ineligible and continues to pay the market price (unless insured). The government must enter the market offering a price sufficient to guarantee provision of services desired by the eligible population. The market for physicians' services is shown in Figure 12.1. The demand for services before the introduction of Medicaid by those later declared eligible is designated D_E^b while the demand for services by ineligibles is designated D_I^b. The eligible population is smaller and generally poorer than the ineligible group (only 8 percent of the U.S. population used services under Medicaid in 1970) and hence their demand function lies below that of the ineligibles. The demand curves D_E^b and D_I^b and their sum D_T^b are shown in Figure 12.1. In the absence of government intervention, equilibrium is established at price P^b, with utilization of services of Q_T^b. The utilization of eligibles and ineligibles is Q_E^b and Q_I^b, respectively.*

When Medicaid is introduced the demand curve of eligibles becomes perfectly inelastic at amount Q_E^a, the number of services eligibles would use at zero price. When Q_E^a is added horizontally to D_I^b, the new demand curve, $D_T^b ed Q_z$, is defined. The demand curve is determined by D_T^b above the Medicaid reimbursement level and equal to the horizontal summation of D_I^b and Q_E^a below it. The number of services actually used by Medicaid eligibles depends, therefore, on the price the government is willing to pay for the services.†

Under Medicaid physicians are reimbursed either on the basis of customary and usual fees with maximums at predetermined levels, or on the basis of fee schedules. Under the latter there is a clear set of Medicaid reimbursement rates for different medical services. Under the former physicians are free to charge what they wish as long as fees do not exceed the maximum. However, once the maximum fee is set and becomes widely known, there is no incentive for a physician to charge Medicaid patients below that level. The maximum soon becomes the normal fee. Thus we include this form of reimbursement as well when we speak of a reimbursement rate.

If the Medicaid reimbursement price is set at P_1^a, Q_{T1}^a units of service will be purchased. Of this quantity, Q_{I1}^a units will be purchased by non-Medicaid patients, and the remainder, $Q_{I1}Q_{T1}$, will be consumed by Medicaid patients, for a total Medicaid expenditure of $P_I^a \times Q_{I1}^a Q_{T1}^a$, indicated by the larger shaded rectangle. Our diagram depicts a relatively elastic supply of physician services. The lower the supply elasticity, the higher P_I^a must be set to insure that all services demanded by Medicaid eligibles at zero price will be

---

* Prior to Medicaid many physicians operated below their supply curve, providing care on a "charity" basis. Thus the quantity of care before Medicaid exceeds Q_e^b by an unknown margin. The introduction of Medicaid provided a financial transfer to such physicians.

†In this model we regard medical service prices as standardized for differentials in physician costs for claims handling. That is, if the costs of handling Medicaid claims add $1 to the cost of a service, a Medicaid reimbursement rate of $10 is equivalent to a market price of $9.

delivered.[*] In addition the lower the supply elasticity the greater the increase in physician incomes accompanying any desired increase in quantity supplied.

Low Reimbursement Rates

In the typical economic market any Medicaid reimbursement rate less than P_1^a will result in excess demand.[†] If the Medicaid reimbursement rate is set lower than P_1^a, say at P_2^a, Q_{T2}^a units of service will be consumed. As long as the elasticity of observed supply is greater than zero, Q_{T2}^a will be less than Q_{T1}^a, that quantity of care supplied at P_1^a. In Figure 12.1 Medicaid consumption falls to $Q_{T2}^a Q_{I2}^a$ which is less than desired utilization $Q_{T1}^a Q_{I11}^a$. Medicaid expenditures are now shown by the double shaded rectangle $P_2^a \cdot Q_{T2} Q_{I2}$.

When Medicaid reimbursement rates are set below that price which would assure provision of desired services, a two-price system may occur. If physicians are able and willing to discriminate among patients, they can continue to charge P_1^a to ineligibles willing to pay that price and a lower price, say P_2^a, to those willing to pay a price between P_1^a and P_2^a. If physicians are unable or unwilling to discriminate between ineligible patients, the price to ineligibles may remain at P_1^a with additional services provided to eligibles (that is, additional to services denoted by the segment ef) at P_2^a. In either case a two-price system would exist. It might also be noted that with sufficient access to information, Medicaid eligibles willing to pay a price greater than P_2^a could ensure themselves preferential treatment by choosing not to make use of Medicaid eligibility. (We assume paying supplements to Medicaid reimbursement rate is not permitted.) If, alternatively, physicians choose not to discriminate in price and quality between patients, the price to ineligibles will fall to P_2^a.

---

[*]When leisure is an argument in the utility function, at a sufficiently high price for medical services, leisure may become so attractive relative to income and quality as to cause a backward bending curve. If the elasticity of supply is greater in absolute value than the elasticity of demand of ineligibles (above the pre-Medicaid equilibrium), Medicaid eligibles will never be provided all services demanded.

[†]Medicaid reimbursement rates below P^b will result in no services provided to Medicaid eligibles. Below P^b, Medicaid eligibles willing to pay a price greater than the Medicaid reimbursement rate will consume along D_E^b.

In this chapter, we propose that there are four ways excess demand might be eliminated: (1) rationing, (2) physician-induced decreases in demand, (3) reductions in quality, and (4) increases in efficiency. We make no judgments about which reactions are most likely to occur, but suggest the trade-offs involved.

1. Services can be rationed through waiting lines, delays in appointments, and other forms of queueing. If a two-price system exists, rationing will be imposed only on Medicaid eligibles. Medicaid eligibles are less desirable in this case and are placed by providers at the end of a queue behind those willing to pay P_1^a. If physicians do not discriminate between eligibles and ineligibles and the price falls to P_2^a for both groups, eligibles and ineligibles may be treated alike and the rationing of available services imposed on both. Alternatively, if Medicaid eligibles are viewed as less desirable despite equal prices, say because of physician concern that treating them will injure their practice, rationing may be imposed only on services desired by Medicaid eligibles.

2. An alternative to rationing would be reductions in the numbers of reimbursable services prescribed by the physician. That is, the physician as an agent for the patient engineers a downward shift in the demand curve as in Figure 12.2a until it intersects S_1 at price P_2^a with utilization of Q_{T2}. As in the case of rationing discussed above, demand shifts can be applied universally, that is, on eligibles and ineligibles or on Medicaid eligibles alone. Physicians may choose to treat all patients willing to pay the new market price in a similar fashion so that all are equally affected by the reduction in services provided, as in D_0geQ_y (note that gh < ef). Alternatively, demand shifts may be imposed only on Medicaid eligibles, and the number of services used by ineligibles would not be affected, as in D_1heQ_y.

3. Equilibrium can also be reestablished if the Medicaid reimbursement rate is set below P_1^a by reductions in the quality of service provided. Referring to Figure 12.2b, we now identify supply schedule S_1 as that reflecting a hypothetical quality level, Q_{T1}, and schedule D_1 as the consumers' demand schedule for that quality service. If reimbursement price is set at P_a^a and excess demand is created, physicians may lower the quality of office visits (such as by shortening their duration), which lowers costs and shifts S_1 to S_0.* As this

---

*Note that we assume that service price under Medicaid is independent of the quality of service that is provided. Under this assumption individual physicians can always raise their income by lowering the quality of service. They nonetheless do not provide the lowest level of quality because quality enters directly into their utility function.

FIGURE 12.2

Demand Shift, Quality Reduction, and Efficiency Increase for
Low Reimbursement Rates

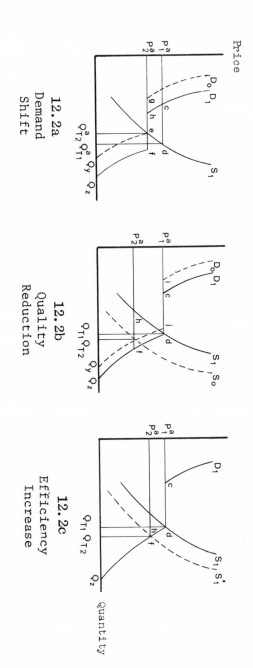

Source: Compiled by the authors.

happens, however, the demand for services shifts downward, from D_1cdQ_z to D_0ijQ_y, because demand is also a function of quality offered. This process of supply and demand shifts in response to excess demand can continue until equilibrium is reestablished at the new administered price P_2^a. In Figure 12.2b quality is reduced for all patients. However, the quality of service can be lowered for both eligibles and ineligibles or for only program eligibles. Assuming that the increase in quantity supplied that can be exchanged for a given quality reduction exceeds the reduction in demand that occurs in response to the same quality change, the number of services delivered at the lower quality will increase above Q_{T2}^a. The extent of the increase depends on the magnitude of the elasticities of demand and supply with respect to quality.

4. If the practice is inefficient it might respond to excess demand by reducing its inputs per unit of service or by using a less costly input combination without affecting the accuracy of diagnosis, the appropriateness of treatment, or the provision of information. That is, if the physician's practice is above its efficient supply curve, it can increase the number of services it provides with no reduction in quality, as shown in Figure 12.2c.

The method or mix of methods followed by the individual physician depends on his quality-leisure-income trade-off. If the practice is inefficient the physician could reduce his inputs per unit of service or change his input combination without affecting quality. This suggests that if physicians' practices are inefficiently organized, reimbursement rates below P_1^a may induce increased efficiency because given those rates the practice can increase income with no loss of quality or, perhaps, of leisure. Increased efficiency would appear to be the most desirable of the four proposed responses. However, a move to increased efficiency might be limited by fear of institutional constraints such as negative patient attitudes or of malpractice suits or by an aversion to administering a larger staff of auxiliary personnel. Of the other three alternatives, there is essentially no difference in effects on income, leisure, and quality between the first mechanism where excess demand is created and queueing develops (longer waiting time, long delays for appointments) and the second where the physician initiates a shift in the demand curve (fewer return visits, ancillary services, etc.). There is merely a difference in the method of rationing. However, a shift in the supply curve to S_0, as in Figure 12.2b, implies a decision to increase income at the cost of a reduction in quality. The impact on leisure is not clear because while there are more services delivered, there is less input per unit of service.

If the practice is efficient or limited by institutional constraints from increasing efficiency, then some combination of the first three equilibrating mechanisms is likely to be observed. The result will depend on the income-leisure-quality trade-off of physicians. Since those trade-offs are likely to vary widely among physicians, it is useless to speculate on which mechanism will dominate.

It is clear from this discussion that the observed effect of reimbursement rates lower than P_1^a on the quantity of services supplied will depend on which of the physician responses dominates. If rationing or physician-induced demand shifts are the predominant mechanisms, a decrease in services provided will be observed. If quality shifts are the most common reaction, an increase in services supplied will be observed, as long as the effect of the quality shift permits the quantity supplied to be increased by more than enough to offset the decline in demand that occurs in response to lower quality. If physicians respond by increasing efficiency, an increase in supply will be observed.

High Reimbursement Rates

A reimbursement price above P_1^a would have no effect on utilization by Medicaid eligibles. At reimbursement rates above P_1^a, suppliers are willing to provide more services than eligibles desire at zero price. The amount of excess supply generated by any given reimbursement rate above P_1^a depends on the elasticities of supply and demand with respect to price. There are also four possible reactions of physicians to excess supply: (1) reducing prices to ineligibles, (2) physician-induced increases in demand, (3) increases in quality, or (4) reductions in efficiency.

1. The excess supply of medical services at a reimbursement rate above P_1^a can be eliminated if providers reduce the price of service to ineligibles P_1^a. In this case the only effect of a reimbursement rate higher than P_1^a is to inflate Medicaid expenditures, but neither eligibles nor ineligibles consume any greater number of services. Physicians receive greater incomes for providing the same services to program eligibles than at P_1^a.

2. Equilibrium can be restored in a market with excess supply through a shift in the demand curve generated by physicians, as in Figure 12.3a. The number of reimbursable services (laboratory tests, return visits, etc.) can be increased by physicians in order to use up all or a part of the excess supply.* Demand shifts can occur

---

*Note that because quality and leisure affect the welfare of the physician, the locus of the initial demand curve, D_T^b, will not reflect his maximum capacity to influence the demand for services.

FIGURE 12.3

Demand Shift, Quality Increase, and Efficiency Reduction
for High Reimbursement Rates

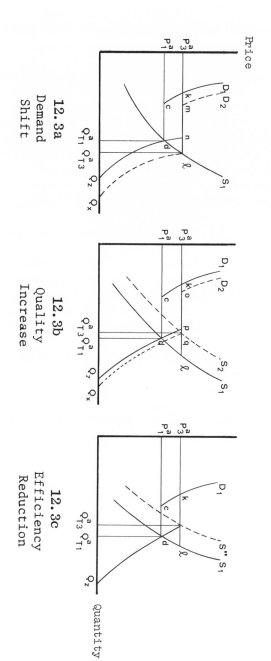

12.3a
Demand
Shift

12.3b
Quality
Increase

12.3c
Efficiency
Reduction

Source: Compiled by the authors.

for both eligibles and ineligibles, as with $D_2 m l Q_x$, or if Medicaid prices exceed market prices, for only Medicaid eligibles as with $D_1 k l Q_x$.

3. A quality adjustment model similar to that presented above is equally applicable in the case of high reimbursement rates. An excess supply of medical services may result in increases in the quality of physician services. The physician can increase the number of inputs used in the services his practice delivers with the result being greater accuracy of diagnosis and/or more appropriate treatment, and/or more provision of information. Quality increases result in a shift in the supply curve from S_1 to S_2, as in Figure 12.3b. Higher quality induces an increase in the demand for services, shifting the demand curve from $D_1 k p Q_z$ to $D_2 o q Q_z$, which clears the market at reimbursement price P_3^a. Increases in service quality may affect all patients as shown in Figure 12.3b, or perhaps be limited to services provided Medicaid eligibles.

4. Reimbursement rates above P_1^a also permit physicians to become less efficient in the management of their practices; that is, the practice may employ excessive amounts of inputs per unit of service without affecting quality. Higher prices permit cost-increasing inefficiency that a physician could not tolerate at lower prices. In this case the observed supply curve shifts from S_1 to S_1, as in Figure 12.3c.

Again, a combination of these equilibrating mechanisms is likely to be observed. Reducing efficiency would be clearly undesirable because it would yield less net income than the other alternatives with no change in quality. Increases in numbers of reimbursable services (demand shift) would involve no change in quality but would augment net income more than the other alternatives. Increasing quality would yield the highest quality practice but the least net income of the alternatives. Permitting competition among providers to bid down the price of services to ineligibles to eliminate excess supply would not involve a change in service quality while net income would be less than under the demand shift alternative. The ranking of net income between increasing quality and reducing price to ineligibles depends essentially on the elasticities of demand and supply with respect to both price and quality.

The effect on leisure is more difficult to determine. Leisure would clearly be greater if providers cleared the market by reducing the price to ineligibles than if providers increased the number of services provided via a demand shift. Under the former, fewer services are provided at the same level of quality. However, the effect on leisure from increasing quality relative to the two other alternatives is not clear. First, increasing the quality of service results in more inputs per unit of service but fewer services would be provided than if demand were shifted. Second, leisure would be greater if the price fell to clear the market than under a quality shift if the number of services provided under the latter is greater than under the former. Leisure would also be less under the quality shift if fewer services were provided as long as the additional inputs required for a higher quality of service exceed the reduction in inputs because of the lower level of output.

The effect of reimbursement rates higher than P_1^a on quantity supplied will depend again on which physician response dominates. If providers reduce prices to ineligibles in response to excess supply, no change in supply will be observed. If physician-induced demand shifts occur, the quantity supplied will increase. If quality shifts are the most common reaction, a reduction in services supplied will be observed, as long as the effect of the quality shift reduces supply enough to offset the increase in demand in response to higher available service quality. Increases in practice inefficiency would clearly reduce services supplied.

OTHER IMPLICATIONS

We have argued that the immediate effect of Medicaid is on the low-cost, low-quality market. If Medicaid causes the equilibrium price in the low-quality market to increase above P_1^a, the pre-Medicaid equilibrium price, the program will force price increases in the high-quality market as well. An increase in the relative prices of services of different qualities will result in an increase in demand for high-quality care. Prices for high-quality services will be bid up until relative prices again equal the marginal rates of substitution between high- and low-quality services.

Government policies other than setting of reimbursement rates will also influence the Medicaid program. Development of an effective system of utilization review may limit the ability of the physician to initiate shifts in the demand curve and perhaps the supply curve. Increases in medical resources, both physicians and paraprofessionals, will increase the stock of available resources. However, as we have shown, a greater supply of medical professionals may lead to physician-induced increases in demand or increases in quality or both.

The effects of government control on prices of physician services will be similar to the effects of low reimbursement rates in Medicaid. With price controls, services desired by patients will exceed the level of services physicians wish to supply. If rationing or physician-induced demand shifts are the most common reaction, the quantity of services supplied will decline. But physicians might also respond by increasing services supplied but reducing average quality. They might also respond by increasing the efficiency of their practices, which would maximize incomes given the price controls and permit maintenance of quality.

EMPIRICAL RESULTS

The Model and Variables

The model presented above is the basis for the regression equations described in this section. Unfortunately it was not feasible to test all of the hypotheses generated by that model because present measures of quality are simply not adequate for investigating the various trade-offs we have suggested. The regressions were limited to testing the effect of alternative reimbursement arrangements and physician availability on the percent of eligibles using physicians' services and expenditures per user of services.[4]

We estimated the following regression equations:

(3) $USERS = a_0 + a_1 DOCS + a_2 PRIM + a_3 R_3 + a_4 INC + a_5 SMSA$
$+ a_6 TURN + a_7 NW + a_8 ED + a_9 AGE + a_{10} TIME$

(4) $EXPENDITURES = b_0 + b_1 DOCS + b_2 PRIM + b_3 R_1 + b_4 R_2$
$+ b_5 PRICE + b_6 INC + b_7 SMSA + b_8 TURN$
$+ b_9 NW + b_{10} ED + b_{11} AGE + b_{12} TIME$

where the variables are defined as follows:

USERS	= ratio of medical users to eligibles
EXPENDITURES	= ratio of expenditures to users
DOCS	= ratio of office-based physicians to population
PRIM	= ratio of primary care specialists to all physicians
R_1	= customary and usual fees with maximum set at Medicare limits
R_2	= customary and usual fees with maximum set below Medicare limits
R_3	= customary and usual fees (of either type R_1 or R_2
INC	= income per capital of eligible population

SMSA	= percent of eligible population living in SMSAs
TURN	= ratio of part-year to full-year eligibles
NW	= percent of eligible population that is nonwhite
ED	= percent of eligible population who are high school graduates (mothers, for the AFDC population)
AGE (Disabled)	= median age of disabled population
AGE (Children)	= percent under 5 years of age
AGE (Adults)	= percent of adult population who are females under 35 years of age
SUP	= ratio of expenditures per eligible person on optional services
PRICE	= average price of physician Medicare services within states
TIME	= 0 for 1969, 1 for 1970.

The dependent variables are defined as follows: USERS is the ratio of users of physician services to eligibles, while EXPENDI-TURES is defined as expenditures per user. These two variables can be interpreted as components of a more general variable, expenditure per eligible. The former will reflect primarily patients' decisions to use services at least once in a year, while the latter will reflect the effects of prices, quality of care, composition of services, and the number of ancillary services. The components were analyzed separately because it was believed likely that each will be influenced differently by various regressors. Physician services refers to all care rendered by office-based physicians including that provided in a hospital.

Data on expenditures and users for all services for all aid categories and for all states was provided by the National Center for Social Statistics (NCSS). States are required by law to report annual totals for expenditures of users of all services. Users are an unduplicated count of persons with at least one contact for the individual service. Both expenditure and user data include persons eligible for any length of time up to one year. Regressions were estimated using pooled data from 1969 and 1970. [5] Separate regressions are shown for three categories of recipients: the disabled, AFDC (Aid to Families with Dependent Children) children, and AFDC adults.

It was necessary to make estimates of eligibles in order to develop the USER ratios. NCSS does not have estimates of eligibles, nor is it clear how eligibility should be defined. Use of all persons below the poverty index would exclude all persons receiving cash assistance who are above the poverty line and include many below the line who would not be categorically eligible. Use of the unduplicated count of all recipients of one or more services would exclude as eligibles even those receiving assistance for one or two months. This definition, by including persons regardless of length of eligibility, is consistent with the definition of users. Persons eligible for Medicaid because they were medically needy are excluded from this analysis.

The independent variables fall into four categories, each of which exerts an influence upon either the extent of Medicaid utilization (user per eligible) or the intensiveness (expenditure per user). They are provider availability, program characteristics, population characteristics, and average price of physician services.

The availability of physicians was measured by the ratios of physicians to population and primary-care physicians to all physicians within each state. This measure of availability is not wholly adequate, however, because the extent to which physicians participate in the Medicaid program is unknown. The availability of physicians to Medicaid eligibles depends upon the total supply of physicians (and especially upon the supply of primary care specialists), reimbursement arrangements that measure the inducement of physicians to participate, and other factors.

A complete model would estimate two equations recursively. First, the ratio of participating physicians to the entire supply would be estimated, using reimbursement inducements and other market characteristics (such as the characteristics of the non-Medicaid population), and then the predicted participation rate would be used in the utilization equations to adjust the observed physician supply variables. However, because of the absence of participation data, this two-stage procedure was not feasible.

Program characteristics include reimbursement arrangements, turnover rates, and a proxy variable for state support of the program. Turnover rates are the ratio of part-year to full-year eligibles. State support was measured by expenditures per eligible person on optional services, those services that states are not required to provide.

Precise data on reimbursement rates for physician services, such as the price allowed for an initial office visit, were not available. A set of dummy variables was used to represent the method of reimbursing physicians. The states were grouped into categories depending upon their method of reimbursement. There were 38 states in 1969 and 46 in 1970 that had sufficient expenditure data for our purposes. Of these, 9 states in 1969 and 12 in 1970 used customary and usual fees with maximums set by Medicare at the 75th percentile of prevailing charges in the locality for similar services. This method is generally regarded as the least restrictive of reimbursement methods. Ten states in 1969 and 13 in 1970 used fee schedules based upon the California Relative Value Schedule or other sets of feee schedules that essentially give the value of all procedures in terms of some standard procedure, such as a routine office visit. The state then determines the price for the standard procedure and consequently determines all prices. Fee schedules give the physician little flexibility in setting fees and are generally regarded as the most restrictive form of reimbursement. There were 19 states in 1969 and 21 in 1970 that used customary and usual fees with maximums set below the Medicare levels. These states frequently use relative value studies to determine if physicians' charges are excessive, but the physician is free to set charges within the imposed limits. In general this form of reimbursement is less restrictive than fee schedules but more restrictive than following Medicare guidelines.* A price variable (average Medicaid prices in each state) that was included in the regressions will capture much of the interstate variation in prices. The reimbursement variable will reflect the deviation of Medicaid reimbursement rates from these average prices. It should be noted that many of the wealthiest states employ fee schedules, the least generous form of reimbursement. Table 12.1 provides information on reimbursement methods used by each state.

A number of variables describing characteristics of the eligible population were employed. Income is defined as the mean per capita income (including cash assistance payments, earned income, and all other income) of the eligible population. SMSA is the percentage of each population group living in SMSAs within the state; NW is the percent of each population group that is nonwhite. In the disabled and AFDC adult equations, education (EDUC) is measured by the percentage in each group who are high school graduates. In the AFDC children equations the percentage of mothers who are high school graduates is used. AGE, too, is defined differently for the various population groups. In our children regressions we use the percentage of eligible children under five years of age in each state as a measure of need. In the adult regressions we use the percentage of AFDC adults who are women under 35. For the disabled we use the mean age of the cash recipients in each state. We use PRICE in the expenditure equations to control for variations in prices across states. An average of prices of services was computed using data from a U.S. Senate Committee on Finance report, <u>Medicare and Medicaid: Problems, Issues,</u>

---

*There may be occasional overlap in restrictiveness between states with fee schedules and those with low maximums on customary and usual fees. However, our results showed this variable to be consistently significant, which suggests that overlap was not a major problem. Nonetheless, estimates of effects of alternative methods are understated to the extent overlap exists.

TABLE 12.1

Methods of Physician Reimbursement, by State

Customary and Usual Fees (Maximum = Medicare)	Customary and Usual Fees (Maximum < Medicare)	Fee Schedules
Delaware	Arkansas (1970)	California
Florida (1970)	Idaho	Colorado
Georgia	Illinois	Connecticut
Indiana (1970)	Kentucky	District of Columbia
Iowa	Louisiana	Hawaii
Kansas	Maine	Maryland (1970)
Michigan	Missouri	Mississippi (1970)
Minnesota	Nebraska	New Jersey (1970)
Montana	Nevada	New York
South Dakota	New Hampshire	Oregon
Tennessee (1970)	New Mexico	Pennsylvania
Texas	North Dakota	Rhode Island
	Ohio	Utah
	Oklahoma	Washington
	South Carolina	
	Vermont	
	Virginia (1970)	
	West Virginia	
	Wisconsin	
	Wyoming	

Source: Compiled by the authors.

and Alternatives. TIME is a dummy variable taking a value of 0 for 1969 observations and 1 for 1970 observations.

It was hypothesized that the availability of office-based physicians as reflected in the number of office-based physicians per capita will affect the USER ratio in the following manner: In areas where office-based physicians are in short supply, Medicaid recipients may be denied services because of difficulty in obtaining appointments, lengthy queues, etc.; and in areas where resources are in abundant supply, Medicaid recipients may receive excessive services such as unnecessary follow-up visits, diagnostic and treatment procedures, and hospitalization. In either case one would expect a positive relationship between physician availability and utilization.

A similar relationship should be expected between physician availability and expenditures per user. More thorough care should be given eligibles who face a plentiful supply of physicians, both because greater relative supply lowers access costs (principally time costs) and because of a possible incentive of physicians to overtreat if an excess supply exists in the market.

Primary care providers, of course, are the chief entry-point for those seeking care, and so their relative abundance should be positively associated with the USER ratio. EXPENDITURES, on the other hand, result from utilization of both primary care physicians and other specialists, so the hypothesized effect PRIM on EXPENDITURES is neutral.

The three alternative reimbursement arrangements outlined above are analyzed to discern their impact on the utilization variables. In general, it was hypothesized that restrictive reimbursement arrangements will result in lower USER and EXPENDITURE ratios. The USER ratio will fall if low reimbursement rates discourage physician participation, and as a result Medicaid eligibles either go without care or receive treatment in hospital outpatient departments. The EXPENDITURE ratio will be low if those physicians who do treat Medicaid patients will limit the services they provide—for example, they will perform less complete diagnostic work and fewer follow-up visits—as well as because the actual charges for physician services will be lower. We hypothesized that the effect on the USER ratio would be stronger than on the EXPENDITURE ratio because the former reflects patients' preferences while the latter is more heavily controlled or influenced by physicians.

We hypothesized that the average income of eligibles (INC) will be positively associated with both dependent variables principally because as income increases, transportation and search costs are less of a burden. Utilization would be expected to be higher in urban areas because of lower costs of access to providers. High turnover rates (TURN) will be associated with lower utilization to the extent that health needs are distributed evenly over time, so that short-duration eligibles will be using fewer services than those continuously eligible. It was hypothesized that race (NW) would be negatively related to utilization because of inaccessibility of providers, racial discrimination, etc. Education (EDUC) can have a mixed effect. As a correlate with general health status, low educational attainment may signify increased need for health care, but the lower level of medical sophistication of the uneducated may reduce utilization. Both young children and females of child-bearing age are known to be high users of health services, and we should observe this effect in our regression coefficients. Expenditures per eligible person for optional services (SUP) is included as a proxy for the state's general attitude

TABLE 12.2

Physician Services, Regression Results

	CONSTANT	DOCS	PRIM	R1	R2	R3	PRICE	INC	SMSA	NW	ED	AGE	TURN	SUP	TIME	R̄²
								Users								
Disabled	34.38 (1.00)	-2.09 (-2.29)	47.84 (1.54)			-7.27* (-1.93)		.18** (2.64)	-.02 (-.23)	-.20** (-2.38)	-.07 (-.22)	.33 (.58)	-.58** (2.67)	.05** (2.40)	1.28 (.58)	.45
Children	-32.32 (1.31)	.07 (.07)	62.76 (1.75)			6.08* (1.65)		.47* (2.57)	.02 (.31)	-.15** (-3.16)	1.58** (3.00)		-.36* (-1.90)	.44** (2.74)	-2.49 (1.01)	.39
Adults	13.09 (.50)	-.37 (-.42)	59.04 (1.44)			.28 (.05)		.51** (2.68)	.03 (.33)	-.19* (-2.21)	-.85** (-2.87)	.26 (.98)	-.13 (.70)	.14* (2.02)	-1.81 (1.01)	.24
								Expenditures								
Disabled	-115.96 (.98)	5.34* (1.68)	52.00 (.50)	68.96** (5.30)	35.45** (2.62)		10.46** (2.46)	.03 (.14)	-.78** (3.34)	.25 (.96)	2.97** (2.74)	.44 (.24)	-.29 (-.41)	.23** (3.04)	-13.20* (-1.77)	.51
Children	7.40 (.28)	1.49 (1.59)	-9.40 (.26)	13.22** (3.33)	9.35** (2.52)		2.42* (1.94)	.07 (.37)	-.06 (-.94)	-.15 (.22)	.68** (2.84)	-.49 (-.99)	-.03 (-.18)	.11 (.71)	-.54 (-.23)	.28
Adults	-.36 (.05)	4.09* (1.72)	-78.55* (-.80)	64.81** (4.38)	44.15** (3.22)		2.07 (.53)	-.16 (.31)	-.02 (.10)	.14 (.67)	1.23 (1.52)	.08 (.12)	.30 (.63)	.22 (1.19)	-5.35 (.76)	.31

Notes: The first term on each line is the coefficient for each regressor; t-values are in parentheses.

* indicates the variable is significant at the .01 level.

** indicates the variable is significant at the .05 level (one-tail test).

Source: Compiled by the authors.

or willingness to support the program. Price should have a direct effect upon expenditures per user and is therefore included in the EXPENDITURE equation. TIME is introduced to account for the effect of increased state experience with the Medicaid program and the effect of additional states whose data is used in the analysis, principally from the South.

Results

The regression results are shown in Table 12.2. The results indicate that physician availability exerts a positive influence upon utilization, as expected, though the two availability variables operate in different ways. The physician-to-population ratio has a consistent positive effect upon the EXPENDITURE ratio, but an erratic effect upon the USER ratio. The elasticities of EXPENDITURES with respect to total physician availability (see Table 12.3) were .39 for the disabled, .33 for AFDC children, and .40 for AFDC adults. The fact that physician availability appears consistently positive in the EX-PENDITURE and not in the USER equations suggests physician-induced shifts in demand are more important than supply constraints or shortages on utilization. That is, the percent of eligibles using physician services is not apparently affected by physician availability. But the quantity and perhaps quality of services provided is increased in that component of utilization that physicians can influence. Finally, the specialty composition variable was positive and significant in the USER equations, suggesting greater access to care when primary-care physicians are relatively abundant.

There was no consistent evidence of a positive relationship between reimbursement arrangements and the USER ratio. The reimbursement variable was significant and negative in the disabled equation and significant and positive in the children equation. On the other hand, the EXPENDITURE variable was positive and significant at the .01 level for all three groups. The difference in the effect on the two utilization measures was probably because the USER ratio largely reflects patient decisions, while the EXPENDITURE ratio is controlled by physicians.

The results in the EXPENDITURE equations suggests that fee schedules reduce expenditures on physician services per user (1) by $64.96 for the disabled, $13.22 for AFDC children, and $64.81 for AFDC adults, relative to customary and usual charges with maximum charges at the 75th percentile; and (2) by $35.45 for the disabled, $9.35 for AFDC children, and $44.15 for AFDC adults relative to customerary and usual charges with lower maximums. Mean

TABLE 12.3

Physician Services, Selected Elasticity Estimates

	DOCS	INC	RACE
Users			
Disabled	-.30*	.31**	-.08**
Children	.01	.56**	.46**
Adults	-.06	.46**	-.15*
Expenditures			
Disabled	.39*	.03	.05
Children	.33	-.08	-.02
Adults	.40*	-.09	.06

* indicates the variable is significant at the .01 level.

** indicates the variable is significant at the .05 level (one-tail test).

Source: Compiled by the authors.

expenditures on physician services per user were $120.47 for the disabled, $39.59 for AFDC children, and $92.12 for AFDC adults.

A basic issue is whether the effect of the reimbursement variable on EXPENDITURES is too large to be merely a price effect, that is, to affect only a differential in fees paid physicians, or if the quantity of services delivered is affected. An estimate of the average quantity of services per user can be derived by dividing the mean expenditure by the mean price for each category of recipient. Dividing these quantity estimates into the appropriate coefficient yields estimates of the differences in fees charged, if there is no quantity effect between the alternative reimbursement arrangements. Because the Medicare price will be roughly equivalent to R_1, the quantity estimates will be minimum estimates and the fee differentials will be the maximum differentials. If the fee differences appear large relative to average prices, then there is reason to believe reimbursement procedures have, in fact, also affected the average quantity of services per user. We observed the differentials shown in Table 12.4.

In Table 12.4 the base is the average price in states utilizing the free schedule reimbursement method. The dollar values shown are the price differentials relative to fee schedules for states using customary and usual fees with maximum charges set at the 75th percentile (R_1), for states using customary and usual fees with maximum charges set below the 75th percentile (R_2), and for the mean price in all states. For example, under customary and usual fees with maximums at the 75th percentile, prices for services rendered the disabled are at the most 4.69 higher than under a fee schedule arrangement. The ratios of the price differential to mean price are also provided in Table 12.4. The differentials relative to mean prices appear moderate, suggesting that little of the differential is attributable to changes in the quantity of service delivered.

In the conceptual model developed earlier in this chapter we suggested that the effect of low reimbursement rates such as fee schedules would depend on physician responses. If rationing or physician-induced reductions in demand for services are dominant, quantity supplied would fall. If physicians increase the efficiency of their operations, quantity supplied would increase. If service quality were reduced, increases in quantity supplied would most likely be observed, but the direction of change would depend on the elasticities of both supply and demand with respect to quality. Our regression results do little to clear up this ambiguity. We observe little increase or decrease in quantity supplied and have no way of discerning changes in quality. The results do suggest that no effect is dominant, with the possible exception of the quality effect. They also strongly indicate that fee schedules have very strong effects on expenditures per user of physician services. As a result, health-care financing programs could obtain significant savings in costs under such programs as Medicare and Medicaid by employing fee schedules. However, such programs would incur the risk of adverse effects on quality of services rendered their clients. The magnitude of this risk is unknown.

TABLE 12.4

Price Differentials under Alternative Reimbursement
Arrangements, Assuming No Supply Effects

	Disabled		Children		Adults	
	Differential	Percent of Mean Price	Differential	Percent of Mean Price	Differential	Percent of Mean Price
R_1	$4.69	57.2	$2.73	33.4	$5.82	70.4
R_2	2.41	29.4	1.93	23.6	3.96	47.9
Mean Price	8.20		8.20		8.20	

Source: Compiled by the authors.

The effects of the other variables are largely as expected and will be noted only briefly here. Income appears to affect entry into the system by reducing the burden of transportation and search costs, but not the intensity of services utilized. The elasticities of the USER ratios with respect to income, as shown in Table 12.3, were .31 for the disabled, .56 for AFDC children, and .46 for AFDC adults. The percent of the eligible population living in SMSAs did not affect either dependent variable. This variable did influence the percent of eligibles using hospital outpatient services in research described elsewhere. [6]

Turnover rates are negatively related to USERS, but the effect upon EXPENDITURES is insignificant. Apparently health needs are rather uniformly distributed throughout the year, and Medicaid partic-ipation is not directly attributable to high medical needs. The propor-tion of nonwhite eligibles (RACE) is negatively related to the USER variable, though EXPENDITURES appears to not be affected. This means that despite zero price, blacks are less likely to use physicians' services than whites even when income, education, physician availa-bility, and other variables are controlled for. EDUC appears to decrease eligible participation (USER) while increasing intensity of care (EXPENDITURES). One explanation for these opposite effects could be that while the less educated seek care more often (because of poorer health) the more educated users use more services (perhaps because of higher patient compliance). The effect of AGE was not significant for either dependent variable, except for the anticipated increase in USERS in the the children equations. The state support variable (SUP) was positive and significant as expected. States that provide generous levels of optional services also institute other policies that ease access of eligibles to required services.

CONCLUSIONS

The model presented here is an effort to understand some of the many effects the Medicaid program has had on the market for medical services. Medicaid affects utilization by eligibles by reducing the price of services to them to zero and increasing the price paid to providers. Medicaid results in an increase in medical-care prices because it must bid for the services of scarce physicians in compe-tition with other users. Prices of medical services of all quality levels are increased and utilization of services by persons not eligible for Medicaid are reduced because price has increased. We argued that there exists a price at which Medicaid can reimburse providers and insure provision of all services desired by eligibles at zero prices. The lower the elasticity of supply, the greater the increase in physician incomes associated with any desired increase in services provided.

If the reimbursement rate exceeds the market clearing price, both increases in the number of services and in the average quality of care may result. Such generous reimbursement rates may also provide incentives for physicians to become or continue to remain inefficient in their delivery of care. Alternatively, if the reimbursement rate is less than the market clearing price the program will cause some increase in the total supply of services but may also reduce the average quality of service. It may also induce physicians to become more efficient in their use of various inputs to the delivery of care. Because the welfare of physicians depends, at a minimum, on income, leisure, and the quality of his practice, it is difficult to predict the effects of reimbursement rates on their behavior. The reaction to exogenous stimuli such as reimbursement rates will depend, in part, on the shape of the utility functions of physicians, and since these are likely to vary widely across physicians it is impossible to predict a priori the effect of a program parameter such as reimbursement formulae.

A preliminary effort to explore empirically the effects of alternative arrangements provided evidence that the level of expenditures per user of physician services was strongly related to the generosity of reimbursement arrangements. We could not determine which physician responses were most common or if quality of services rendered was in fact affected. It appears that Medicaid could reduce costs by employing fee schedules, but only by taking risks (which are only conceptually understood) of reducing the quality of care to its clients. More precise estimates of the various effects of the program require more detailed empirical investigations using more sophisticated data bases. The model described here will hopefully contribute to the conceptual framework required in pursuing these investigations.

NOTES

1. M. S. Feldstein, "Hospital Cost Inflation: A Study of Non-Profit Price Dynamics," American Economic Review 61 (December 1971); and J. P. Newhouse, "Toward a Theory of Non-Profit Institutions," American Economic Review 60 (1970).

2. U. E. Reinhardt, "A Production Function for Physician's Services," Review of Economics and Statistics, February 1972.

3. M. S. Feldstein, "Econometric Studies of Health Economics," Harvard Discussion Paper No. 291, April 1973.

4. This research is described more thoroughly in J. F. Holohan, Financing Health Care for the Poor: The Medicaid Experience (New York: Lexington Books, 1975).

5. Data irregularities precluded the inclusion of all Title XVIII participating states in the analysis. The following state data was included (* indicates a state was included in the study only for 1970).

1. Arkansas*	16. Louisiana	31. Ohio
2. California	17. Maine	32. Oklahoma
3. Colorado	18. Maryland*	33. Oregon
4. Connecticut	19. Michigan	34. Pennsylvania
5. Delaware	20. Minnesota	35. Rhode Island
6. District of Columbia	21. Mississippi*	36. South Carolina
7. Florida*	22. Missouri	37. South Dakota
8. Georgia	23. Montana	38. Tennessee*
9. Hawaii	24. Nebraska	39. Texas
10. Idaho	25. Nevada	40. Utah
11. Illinois	26. New Hampshire	41. Vermont
12. Indiana*	27. New Jersey*	42. Virginia*
13. Iowa	28. New Mexico	43. Washington
14. Kansas	29. New York	44. West Virginia
15. Kentucky	30. North Dakota	45. Wisconsin
		46. Wyoming

6. Holohan, op. cit.

DISCUSSION
OF PART IV
Steven J. Carroll
Robert Harris

Steven J. Carroll

Each of the chapters in Part IV attempts to assess the implications of a government intervention in a market. Despite this agreement in motivation and intent, each reflects a fundamentally different research approach. Moreover, none of them is limited in application to the analysis of a particular market. In combination these chapters illustrate the relative strengths and weaknesses of three different research methodologies.

John Holahan and Stuart Schweitzer use an analytic model to study the impact of Medicaid on the market for health services. The model is based upon a set of assumptions about the behavior of the individuals who participate in the market. (Holahan and Schweitzer embody their assumptions in families of supply and demand curves.) The analysis consists of "solving" the model for the endogenous variables—the prices, quantities, and qualities of health services. In essence they attempt to derive the functional relationships between the endogenous and the exogenous and policy variables.

The important characteristic of this approach is that the researcher's attention is concentrated on the relationships among the variables in the model with the objective of understanding how the endogenous variables are affected by the intervention. The particular values of the endogenous variables are not the primary interest. Holahan and Schweitzer, for example, attempt to identify the directions in which the endogenous variables will move if the Medicaid reimbursement rate is set above (or below) what would be the equilibrium price for health services in the lower quality market. They are not concerned with the precise amount by which the value of an endogenous variable will change as a consequence of setting the Medicaid reimbursement rate at a particular level.

The primary objective of research using the analytic approach is to develop understanding of the ways in which a market might respond to an intervention. Because our ability to analyze explicitly the interactions among complex processes is quite limited, the analysis must exclude many important aspects of the market being studied. Accordingly, studies employing the analytical approach tend to be based on models rather far removed from reality. This is not a criticism of the approach. The purpose of such analyses is not to describe reality accurately, but rather to gain insight into certain important interactions. In a sense the analytic approach is analogous to a cross-sectional drawing of a complicated piece of machinery. There is no pretense that the drawing contains sufficient information to build the machine nor even to fully understand how it works. Rather, the purpose of the drawing is to give us insight into the relationships among certain important parts.

The simulation approach that Frank de Leeuw et al. propose to use in investigating the impact of an intervention in the housing market resembles the analytic approach in many respects. Their model is also based upon a set of assumptions about the behavior of the individuals who participate in the market. (They begin with utility functions that are maximized subject to budget constraints—in the case of consumers of housing services—or production functions—in the case of providers of housing services. These yield families of demand and supply curves, respectively.) The analysis again consists of "solving" the model for the endogenous variables—the prices, quantities, and qualities of housing services. (The de Leeuw model contains an additional set of endogenous variables, the locations of the consumers of housing services.)

The major difference between the two approaches is that de Leeuw seeks a numerical solution to his model rather than an analytic solution. This difference is, however, all-important in comparing the two methods. Whereas the analytic approach focuses on the relationships among variables, the simulation approach concentrates on the determination of what the values of the endogenous variables will be in a particular situation. In general, simulations tell us almost nothing about the process by which those values were determined.

This point needs some elaboration. We do, of course, know the computer program that was used to generate the values of those variables. But we do not know why that program yielded the particular solution associated with a particular situation. Suppose, for example, that one run of the model yielded a solution characterized by a high degree of segregation. Did this outcome result from neighborhood (zone) "tipping". (For example, the model "almost" yielded an integrated housing solution at some earlier point in the iteration but the assignment of a few more black families to housing in some zone increased the proportion of blacks in that zone enough to cause some of the whites located there to move in subsequent iteration.) Or does this outcome reflect some aspect of the initial conditions, such as the assumed distribution of income by race?

I emphasize this point because there is a tendency to view simulation studies as differing from analytic studies in degree, but not in kind. Simulations, according to those who hold this view, are just complex and detailed versions of analytical studies in which the computer's vast capacity for keeping track of things is substituted for the limited capacity of pencil and paper. I would question this argument on two counts. First, as indicated above, the kind of information yielded by a simulation is substantively different from the kind of information obtained from an analytical study. Accordingly, what the researcher using one approach to study a market learns appears, to me, to be quite different from what he could have learned had he used the other approach.

The second difference between the two approaches concerns the credibility of the model. The analytic approach can be based upon a model that bears little resemblance to reality so long as it provides useful insights into the ways in which a market works. Simulation models, on the other hand, must be acceptable reality substitutes. Because the simulation approach generates numbers rather than understanding of underlying processes, it is useful only if we are prepared to believe that the numbers are reasonably accurate. This, in turn, requires that the simulation model be an acceptable substitute for reality. This is not simply a question of detail or complexity. It matters little if a simulation analysis contains a vast array of detail. If essential aspects of the market being examined are omitted, then the numbers generated by the study cannot be believed.

Denis Doyle's chapter is based on yet a third approach, the experimental. He attempts to assess the implication of an intervention by actually implementing the intervention on a test basis and evaluating its consequences. In one sense this approach avoids the issue of whether a model accurately represents reality. The intervention is, after all, being tested in the real world. However, in another sense the usefulness of an experiment hinges precisely on that issue.

In the last third of his chapter Doyle describes the many compromises that must be made if a major experiment is to be successfully implemented. It is clear that the project now under way in Alum Rock is quite different from OEO's initial conception of the voucher demonstration. An obvious question arises: What is being tested? Or, to put it another way, What are the policy questions that will be answered by the huge amount of information gathered in the course of the project? These are, of course, questions that apply to virtually every experiment that takes place outside the purity of the laboratory and they suggest the major limitation of the experimental approach. In attempting to overcome the problems of actually implementing an experimental social program the researcher may so distort that program as to preclude testing the hypotheses that motivated the experiment in the first place.

Turning to the specifics of the chapters, Holahan and Schweitzer assume that there exist two independent markets—one for high-quality care and the other for low-quality care—in the sense that price, quality, and quantity adjustments in the low-quality will not affect the market for high-quality services. This is at odds with their assumption that quality is an argument in both the supply and demand curves for health services. If quality does, in fact, enter the demand (supply) curve for health services, and if we assume for convenience that there are only two quality levels, then a different demand (supply) curve for high-quality services is associated with each price of low-quality services. If, for example, exogenous forces drive up the price of low-quality services, we would expect to see a greater quantity of high-quality services demanded at each alternative price for high-quality services. The point is that the model specified by their supply and demand curves involves the <u>simultaneous</u> determination of prices and quantities in <u>all</u> quality markets and analysis cannot neglect the interactions among markets.

A variant of this problem appears in their discussion of Figure 12.2 in which the analysis seems to embody the notion that there will be one and only one price charged and one and only one quality of service provided. I would expect to observe a solution in which multiple prices are charged for multiple qualities of service. If we simplify the analysis by assuming that only two qualities of service can be provided, I would expect to see a result in which one quality of service is provided at the Medicaid reimbursement rate and a second quality of service is provided at some different rate. (Whether this second price is above or below the reimbursement rate depends on a variety of factors and cannot, I believe, be determined short of solving the entire system.)

In addition to these analytic problems, Holahan and Schweitzer mention two ways in which equilibrium in the market might be achieved, but offer no reasons why either series of events might take place. Why should physicians lower the quality and cost of office visits or reduce the number of prescribed reimbursable services? Presumably the supply curve arises from some sort of maximizing behavior on the part of physicians. But since that behavior is unspecified, we have no way of telling how physicians will react to an excess demand situation. The omission of this aspect of the analysis is serious since it is at this point that we begin to get some insight into the way the market will respond to Medicaid. Thus Holahan and Schweitzer provide only speculation and not understanding.

De Leeuw's model is not an adequate reality substitute. The model contains neither an industrial sector nor a commercial sector. Further, the residential sector of the model does not distinguish among types of residential units (single-family dwellings, high-rise apartment complexes, and so on). Since these factors would be expected to influence the residential housing market, we cannot accept the results of a model that omits them.

I should also note that the de Leeuw intends to estimate the parameters of the model by fitting the model to data from four cities for a variety of alternative sets of parameter values and choosing that set that yields the best fit. If the two omitted sectors have an impact on the residential market, then I would expect a model that uses the "correct" parameters for the residential sector and omits the other two sectors to yield a rather poor fit. Hence the set of parameter values that yields the best fit in the incomplete model is not likely to be a very good estimate of the true parameter values.

Doyle's discussion of the voucher experiment unfortunately gives no indication of the public policy questions that will be answered once the thousands of interviews have been conducted. Hopefully, important hypotheses are being tested in Alum Rock. It would have been interesting to see them presented by Doyle.

Robert Harris

The three chapters in Part IV are basically early reports of work in progress that lay out theoretical models or designs, discuss some of their properties, discuss relevance to policy, and promise that future reports will present us with more. Little or no empirical work is presented, and actual policy applications have not yet been tried. Thus I will focus here on the potential policy usefulness of results yet to come, attempting to point out some misgivings about the credibility that a policy maker might place in predictions based on the research presented or promised.

Holahan and Schweitzer develop a theoretical model of medical services markets and use it to develop some testable hypotheses about the impact of the introduction of Medicaid in the mid-1960s. Preliminary empirical testing is also reported. The analysis is interesting for two reasons:

1. The quality of medical services is explicitly included in the supply function, allowing predictive statements to be made about the impact of policies—such as setting maximum Medicaid fees—on the quality of service rendered, as well as quantity. The quality variable is crucial in the health services market, and health providers frequently argue that economists have nothing useful to say because they ignore the importance of quality.

2. Supply considerations are included in the demand function. It is often stated in the institutional literature that medical providers can strongly influence the demand for their services independently of price effects. Incorporating this possibility in a formal model of the market is important.

These factors make the model quite complex, which is an asset compared to working with the simpler models that are frequently used. These complexities are often only taken into account nonrigorously in discussions of the impact of policies on the medical market, as an afterthought to working out simpler models. That leads to fuzziness in analysis and prediction. The authors are able to deduce some sensible conclusions rigorously from their model. For example, it follows from the model that policy makers, in setting rates at which they will reimburse providers (prices), affect both the quantity and quality of services provided. Raising reimbursement rates will increase both the quantity <u>and</u> quality of care provided. <u>Reducing</u> reimbursement rates may <u>increase quantity</u> at the expense of quality.

Whether the model is very useful for assessing policy choices will depend upon its further development and empirical testing. Unfortunately the authors implicitly assume that the introduction of Medicaid reduced the price of medical services for eligibles from the market price charged everyone else to zero. But in many urban areas—New York City, for example—the price of medical care for current Medicaid eligibles was also zero before Medicaid. The difference is that eligibles now operate the private rather than the socialized sector of the health care market. Prior to Medicaid, eligibles received much of their health care free in public hospitals, clinics, etc. It is not clear to me how this fact fits into the scheme implicit in the model—that prior to Medicaid market prices were what everyone faced, while after Medicaid some people had their prices reduced to zero.

Anyone looking at housing policies and programs in our urban areas must have grave misgivings about them—they clearly have not done much of what we wanted them to do. Housing policies—like most social policies—have frequently been based on simple, nonrigorous, and untested theories about how very complex markets will adapt to changes induced by government. Much research is fragmentary and partial and predictions are frequently made on the basis of partial analysis, while actually, ceteris paribus, other assumptions do not hold. De Leeuw has pointed out, for example, that most existing models of residential location ignore neighborhood effects and that most models of durable goods markets assume a constant depreciation rate. Clearly these assumptions are violated in the real world of housing markets.

De Leeuw and his colleagues lay out a model that is designed to predict the location of households, the quality of housing stock, new construction, and removals of stock over time. With such a model it should be possible to simulate the results of alternative policies on crucial aspects of urban life. As such it could be an invaluable tool for policy analysis and prediction. It certainly might provide an improvement over less sophisticated forms of prediction.

So far, however, only limited estimation and testing of the model have been reported on, and it is not possible to know how well the final version will work in practice. However, there are problems inherent in the construction of any model. To construct the model, for example, a set of mathematical equations is specified and estimated. The parameters to be estimated derive from the specification of the model. In this instance three sets of parameters emerge and are estimated by imaginative use of limited data.

1. Estimates of housing expense to income ratios for different demographic groups, estimated for 1960 and 1970 by regression for a particular metropolitan area.

2. Household response to real prices, neighborhood wealth, and neighborhood racial composition. These are part of a utility function specified for households. They are estimated for 1960 essentially by trial and error. The simulation is run using estimates of the other parameters, and the combination of price-response parameters giving the best fit by a reasonable set of criteria are chosen.

3. Parameters of the housing supply function derived from a specified production function, estimated by choosing values that give the best fit over the period 1960-70 using the other parameters previously estimated.

With the specified functional forms, and estimates of parameters of those functions, simulations can be run and predictions made. But how do we test the reliability of the predictions? That is a crucial test for policy purposes, and I am afraid that the answer is by leap of faith. For reasons quite common in the social sciences, no fully independent test of the model seems possible. The parameter estimates are made by maximizing goodness of fit of the model to the data for a certain time period for certain areas. The model is then tested by running simulations for that same period and same area and comparing results with similar simulations using a different model. But any prediction based on the model runs the well-known risk of extrapolating a fitted curve beyond the range of observation. I am left with a feeling that the foundation of the predictions is built on quicksand.

In spelling out a fairly complete and sophisticated model of housing markets in some detail for estimation and simulation, de Leeuw makes the necessary assumptions embarrassingly explicit. This in itself is an important contribution. It will take a good deal more empirical work and sensitivity analysis of predictions to convince users that they can take the necessary leap of faith to believe predictions. That work is underway, and I am looking forward to seeing it.

Doyle's brief chapter cannot fully reflect the complexity of the history and progress of a pathbreaking effort. He spends little time discussing the issue that I consider paramount: educational output. In my view, one major reason for trying vouchers—or other educational experiments—is that the education system seemed to be failing to educate many children in the 1960s. The remedies tried by the federal government didn't seem to do much—they generally involved putting more money into the system. When evaluated, little different seemed to be done with most of the money (more teachers, higher salaries, some aides, lots of gadgetry—usually sophisticated audio-visual equipment). No change seemed to appear in results.

The voucher idea is attractive to me for many of the reasons Doyle cites in his introduction. They boil down to introducing competition into a market long characterized by government monopoly and professional rigidities. The author notes some of the advantages of consumer sovereignty—potentially great parental, student, teacher satisfaction, and wider scope of choices. He does not note one of the most attractive features of competition: Those suppliers who do not perform will suffer—they will be forced out of business. (That will only happen with proper information available to purchasers—but the project as described is heavily regulated to insure that.) The converse is that those producers who are best will expand, and poor performers will have to copy their successful methods to survive. Thus, the key to evaluation should be (1) whether, given the freedom to use different education methods inherent in the voucher plan, different things are happening in different schools or classrooms; (2) whether children do better in some schools than others; and (3) whether patterns of transfers reflect the differences in performance of the different schools.

It is disappointing to read that we cannot expect to learn whether there are differences in education outcome for some time. What we are told is that parents', teachers', and administrators' attitudes are being measured, that many are satisfied, that principals feel they are working harder, and that parents are using vouchers to make overt choices. Perhaps that is all we should expect at this time—but the tone of the Doyle's chapter implies that we may not learn much from this demonstration about whether competition can improve the output of this government service. Much of his discussion implies that we may have to evaluate success on the basis of a sophisticated "smiles test." (A demonstration project is a success when the teachers smile, the principal smiles, the pupils smile, and the parents smile.)

On a more positive note I am glad to note that we have learned some important things from the effort:

1. The program can be administered. This is not a trivial point, because the voucher demonstration is very complex. It is common for those who propose even simple changes in the way public programs are operated to be put off with the explanation that "it is administratively impossible." The fact that a complex scheme can be successfully implemented in a large ongoing school system is heartening.

2. The researchers who designed the new system did not really know enough about the old system to anticipate some of the difficulties. The original designers apparently ignored many realities about parental attachment to schools, how little real budgeting and accounting is done at operational-unit levels in school systems. The lesson of this is that designers of such demonstrations must be forced to do more real-world homework before being let loose in the real world.

Finally, let me note speculatively that the lessons that seem to be emerging from this effort parallel those of the income maintenance experiments that OEO and HEW have been operating for a few years. In installing a new program we learn that the old program operated on the basis of inadequate management systems. The old management systems are so hopelessly antiquated and inadequate that designers of new programs, who are not deeply involved in operating the old program, are shocked when the new program confronts the old. But they are able to design systems to run the new program and in so doing facilitate improvements in the administration of the old programs (for example, sensible accounting systems and other record-keeping systems).

Thus experimental new programs may be worth trying even if we never learn that the new performs better than the old, because in trying the new we can learn how to run the old better.

INTRODUCTION
TO PART V
Robert McGillivray
Ronald Kirby

There are a multitude of subjects that can be investigated under the general headings of "Urban Land Use" and "Urban Transportation." Among them are travel demand analysis, transportation cost comparisons, modal split, the value of traveler time, transportation service characteristics, statewide and metropolitanwide land use controls, and sewer moratoria. Examination of both research and newspaper articles on these and related topics suggests two critical points. First, very few transportation analysts have ventured into analyses treating transportation and land use together, nor have many housing or firm location analysts thought about the urban transportation problem in much more than a perfunctory way. Second, the institutions in our country are set up separately for these two topics.

Since transportation and land use are intimately related to one another, it seems obvious that bodies established to plan or regulate one should be the same as or closely associated with those set up to plan or regulate the other. Further, at least some research should consider them together. Transportation is an important component of urban infrastructure, and infrastructure is a major determinant of urban growth and development. Consequently, it should be productive to investigate explicitly the relationships between land use and transportation.

The chapters in Part V represent the types of valuable analyses that can be conducted within the land use–transportation framework. The chapters by Walter Velona of the Department of Transportation and Irving Hoch of Resources for the Future are both based on the active interest the authors have maintained in this area for a number of years. Further, the National Bureau of Economic Research (NBER) has been concentrating considerable effort on a rather massive urban simulation model with transportation and other infrastructure as important components, and Royce Ginn continues to be a major participant in the development of this model. Sydney Robertson has spearheaded much work of this type with the Federal Highway Administration, is familiar with both present and past efforts, and continues to be actively interested in this area as Director of Management Systems at the Maryland Department of Transportation.

The Chapters in this section contain a fine mixture of empirical evidence and intuitive reasoning. They are complementary, proceeding from the very general work of Velona discussing the effect on service area size of travel time limits that travelers appear to set for each travel purpose, to the more detailed work of Hoch on the effect of scale economies in urban services on density and overall size of urban areas. Ginn then rounds out the section with his discussion of the NBER microanalysis of housing and infrastructure changes in a quantitative model that permits the introduction of feedbacks.

Robertson sums up well when he says that the three chapters are closely related and come to the same conclusions even though they begin with quite different conceptual approaches. He also makes an important point when he discusses the frustration of working in this field. On the one hand, research in these areas seems to have a potentially high payoff to society by increasing understanding of urban growth and its relationship to infrastructure; this is an important topic for urban communities that are becoming increasingly concerned about the effects of uncoordinated growth on the quality of their neighborhoods. On the other hand, persons allocating research funds apparently do not consider that this area serves their short-term interests, and they seem reluctant to commit funds for long-term research. The result is a dearth of support for analyzing the relationship between land use and transportation. Although the chapters that Velona, Hoch, and Ginn have prepared are stimulating and valuable, they and their kind are rare compared to short-term efforts devoted to such matters as the best location for a shopping center or the prediction of travel patterns using extremely crude models borrowed from the physical sciences. And even these are greatly outnumbered by research efforts on materials, structures, fuels, metals, and the like.

We hope that these chapters will play at least a small role in convincing the world that the area encompassed is vital to planning for even a few years ahead and that it is so neglected relative to other matters of equal or even less importance that shift of research priorities is badly needed. If continued pressure for such a shift is generated and supported by volumes such as this one, perhaps something will happen.

13

THE ROLE OF TRAVEL
TIME LIMITS IN
URBAN GROWTH
Walter D. Velona

This chapter describes the result of what began as an effort to capture an image of the process of urban change. Specifically, it was desired to identify the components of a city, their position relative to one another, and how they changed over time.

A review of the literature failed to provide the image being sought. Studies of urban characteristics fell into various categories in which the research in one area was not directly related to that in other areas. Studies by Johann Von Thunen, Lowdon Wingo, William Alonso, and Richard Muth provided equations that identified and attempted to measure economic interactions.[1] W.A. Hansen and A.M. Voorhees attempted to measure the amount of travel.[2] M.D. Cheslow, J. McLynn, and T.A. Domencick and Gerald Kraft were concerned with transportation demand.[3] August Loesch focused on location.[4] E. Weiner et al attempted to unify these diverse models.[5] Many of the thoughts in this chapter are derived from these previous studies, but no work was found to fully translate these models into a visual entity of the urban form or process, although that of Wingo provided many insights. What was missing was a link between these interactive equations and the various types and arrangements of locations within the urban area.

This chapter was originally prepared in October 1971 as background research for the 1972 National Transportation Study of the Office of Systems Analysis and Information, Office of the Assistant Secretary for Policy, Plans and International Affairs, Department of Transportation.

The urban process may be conceptualized as an engineering design problem in which a set of materials, subject to limits of stress, interact as described by a set of equations. The extant literature on urban growth provided the equations and named such "materials" as population, income, land, work sites, residential locations, and transportation networks, but revealed no limits for these "materials." It was decided that if such limits could be identified, they might provide insight to the structure of those city components being sought.

A POSTULATED URBAN AREA DEFINITION

The search for these limits quickly focused on consideration of travel time behavior and led to the decision to postulate an urban definition based on travel time limits. The gravity and demand models discussed above relied on travel time rather than distance. Research by M. Beesley, C. Lave, and T. Lisco emphasized that travel time was the more important measure in evaluating the quality of travel.[6]

This led to the conclusion that perhaps the entire population of an urban center is constrained in its daily travel behavior by the existence of the 24-hour day. If travel time limits could be found for various trip purposes, the permanence of the 24-hour day might also endow these limits with the necessary permanence to insure their use as predictive tools. Also, limits on travel times to discrete destinations would constrain the population to reside within the locus of these travel time limits, thereby producing a specific pattern of urban locations. In turn, this pattern would provide an arena within which the forces described by the interactive equations would take place.

The literature search revealed an observation by Hans Blumenfeld that the maximum growth of cities appeared to be at a one-hour travel time limit from the city center.[7] The Chicago Area Transportation Study (CATS) contained a map that showed the outward movement of residential boundaries over time.[8] Now, assuming that Chicago is a city that tends to grow quickly to its limits, these boundaries would also appear to be at a one-hour travel time limit from city center—the Loop—by the prevailing mode of the time.

Although little additional information on travel time limits was found, it was decided that perhaps a set of travel time limits should be postulated and the effects of their possible existence examined. (Although this chapter does not discuss the matter further, it does suggest that other types of limits might also be found. For example, it is probable that there exists a minimum and maximum square footage for housing.)

Consideration of various trip purposes and travel time limits that might be applicable to these purposes finally led to the following postulated definition of the urban area:

An urban area is a populated place in which residences will be found within the locus of points formed by the set of constant door-to-door travel time limits applicable to all residents for trips from a residence to the four destinations designated "local market," "general market," "city center market," and "work site."

A set of travel time values has been chosen for the four trips as shown in Table 13.1.

There is greater certainty as to the existence of these specific travel time limits than as to their values; the latter have been chosen because they appear to be reasonable and are also mathematically convenient.

The locus of points applicable to these travel time limits when velocity is uniform in all directions is shown in Figure 13.1. Under these velocity and direction specifications it can be seen that the locus of points produces seven general market areas of which only one is a central market area and six are outer general market areas. Similarly, there are seven central local market areas and 42 outer local market areas. One of the local markets and one of the general markets are placed at the same location as the city center market. Each location of a general market is also a location of a local market.

TABLE 13.1

Travel Times to Different Markets

Residential Trip to	Postulated Maximum Travel Time
Local market	7 minutes
General market	21 minutes
City center market	63 minutes
Work site	84 minutes

Source: Compiled by the author.

FIGURE 13.1

Residential Locations, Uniform Velocity in All Directions,
Based on Postulated Urban Definition

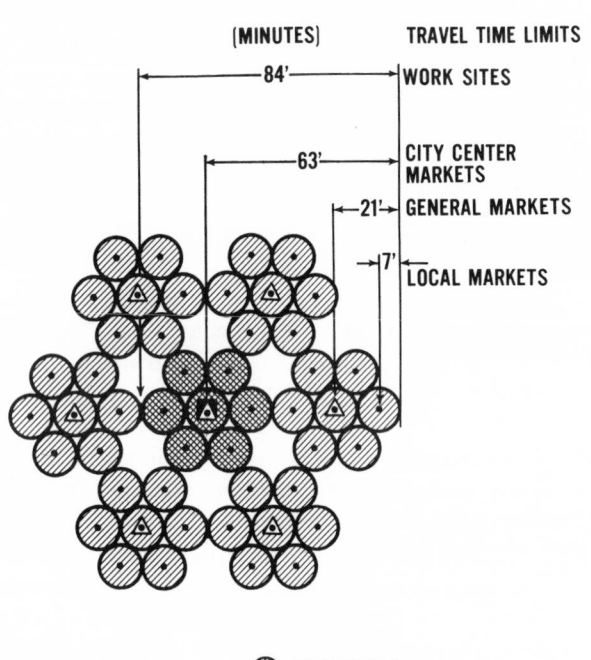

Source: Compiled by the author.

Since not all communities appear to grow to the limits of travel
time, the application of the definition requires us to distinguish between "maximum" and "dead-end" boundaries. The first condition
arises when access by the fastest travel mode is available up to the
point where the travel time limit has been reached. Movement along
this path is constrained by the travel time limit alone. The second
condition arises when motion along a path by some mode is halted at
some point by geographic features (for example, dead-end streets;
rivers) or privately owned land, and the apparent travel time to this
point is less than the postulated maximum.

The "city center market" defines those establishments generally thought to be at the urban center and unique to the urban area such as a city hall, court house, central library, museums, theaters, and specialty shops that have to rely on the entire urban population in order to generate adequate revenues. Ordinarily these are considered to be establishments, any one of which is infrequently visited by the average urban individual.

The "general market" defines a collection of establishments periodically visited by individuals for the purchase of durable goods. They may include department, furniture, hardware, and similar types of stores.

The "local market" defines one or more establishments frequently visited by individuals for the purchase of consumables and services. They may be groceries, laundries, and the like.

The effort to visualize the urban boundaries requires the conversion of travel time to distance. For this purpose it is necessary to consider the transportation characteristics that influence travel time. The first and possibly least considered characteristic is direction of travel. The travel time map in Figure 13.1 is a geographical map of the urban area only if all travel is at one velocity in any direction. Conceivably, a condition of uniform velocity might occur, but the necessity for urban structures mitigates against the possibility of travel in all directions. A more practical example is given in Figure 13.2, which assumes that the urban area consists of square blocks. The layout permits travel in only four directions (for example, east and west or north and south). It will be noted that such an arrangement produces nine general markets with one of the nine markets located at the city center market location. Similarly, each of the general market areas contains one central local market and eight outer local markets.

Obviously, velocity of travel within the urban area is never uniform. In Figure 13.3 the same square-block arrangement as in Figure 13.2 is shown, except that all travel east and west is at one half the velocity of all travel north and south. The effect is to produce an elongated urban area. All market areas are similarly elongated.

It will also be noted that in the Figure 13.2 street arrangement all of the land that falls within the city center market parameter is served by general and local markets. In this respect it differs from Figure 13.1 where much of the land is not included within the postulated city center locus.

In Figure 13.4 the street arrangement and the market locations in Figure 13.2 are retained, but the velocity of travel within the central general market area is reduced by one-half and the velocity of travel within the eight outer general market areas is increased by

FIGURE 13.2

Residential Locations, Uniform Velocity in Four Directions
Only, Based on Postulated Urban Definition

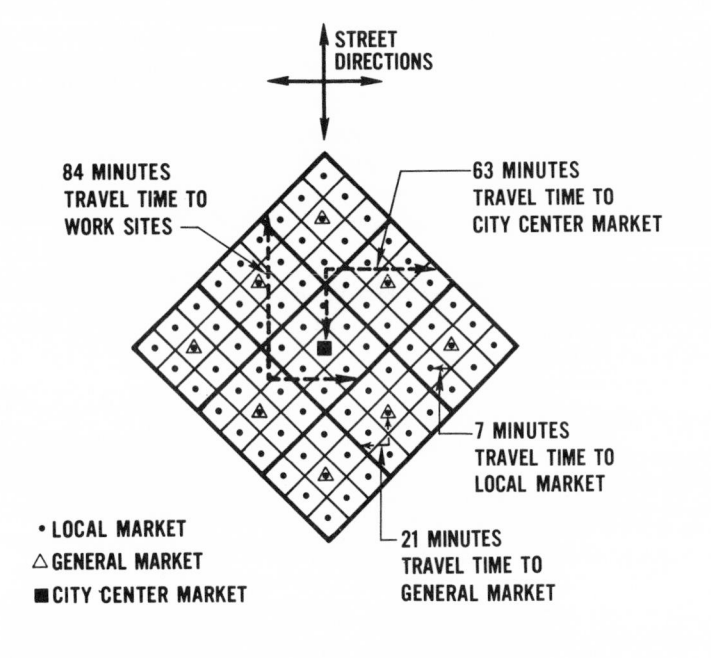

Source: Compiled by the author.

one-half. It can be seen that the central general market area is now
one-fourth its original area and that the outer market areas are over
twice as large. As a result, the central general market area has
become one-ninth the size of each of the outer market areas. The
depicted situation is akin to the introduction of the auto and its impacts.
The auto's high velocity serves to enlarge the size of the outer market
areas. On the other hand, the bulky size of the automobile overtaxes
the capacity of the streets in the central general market area. The
resultant congestion reduces automotile velocity, thereby reducing
the area of this market.

Until about 100 years ago the world's urban population had only
one mode of travel: They walked. There were those who rode horses
or carriages but they were few in number and their impact on the

FIGURE 13.3

Residential Locations, East-West Velocity
at One-Half of North-South Velocity,
Based on Postulated Urban Definition

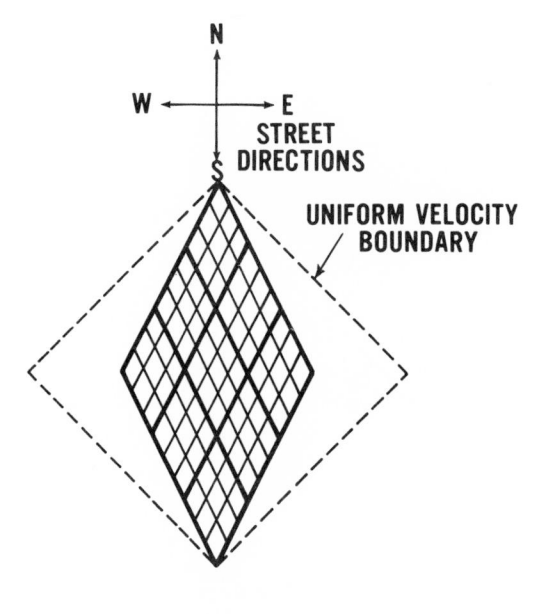

Source: Compiled by the author.

urban form was slight. The last century has seen the introduction of
the tramway and bus, the transit train, and the automobile. Fortunately, each mode has had its period of dominance at a time of rapid
changes in population and has endured for a time sufficient to influence significantly the urban form. Generally these innovations caused
an increase in the velocity of travel with a consequent increase in the
size of the area served by the urban markets.

For the most part these impacts have been beneficial. It is
only in recent years that the auto has begun to tax the capacity of
streets in the central general market area. One concomitant has
been a reduction in velocity within that zone, thereby producing the
sort of undesirable impact described in Figure 13.4. Efforts to increase street and road capacity have caused major disruptions within
these central areas and have led to the demand for alternative

FIGURE 13.4

Residential Locations, Velocity in Eight Outer Markets
Is Three Times Velocity of Center Market,
Based on Postulated Urban Definition

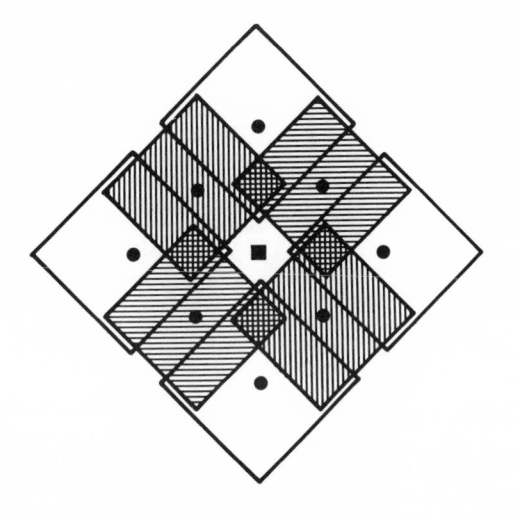

Source: Compiled by the author.

solutions. As a result it is probable that this is the first time in history that a major requirement has developed to carefully study the role of transportation in the urban scene.

Additional impacts of velocity changes can be observed when viewed in terms of the travel modes used in the past. For example, assume a period in history when the only mode is walking. Assume also that the city fathers have decided that all streets will be laid out in the form of a rectangular grid as in Figure 13.5, which describes a local market service area.

Here are laid out 12 cross streets to the mile, and 144 city blocks to the square mile. (It is further assumed that the average door-to-door velocity of walking is 2.86 miles per hour.)

Now, based on our postulated urban definition, the city produced by this "urban planning" decision will have the following characteristics, graphically demonstrated by Figure 13.6.

The city center parameter causes all residences to be located within a boundary whose points are located 63 minutes walking time (or 3 miles) from the city center. This boundary will be in the shape

FIGURE 13.5

Local Market Service Area

UNIFORM VELOCITY - 2.86 MI./HR.

BLOCKS PER MILE - 12

BLOCKS PER SQUARE MILE - 144

LOCAL MARKET CENTER — +

MAXIMUM WALKING DISTANCE - 4 BLOCKS (1/3 MILE)

LOCAL MARKET SERVICE AREA = 0.22 SQ. MILE
**   (32 CITY BLOCKS)**

MAXIMUM WALKING TIME - 7 MINUTES
**   (AT 2.86 MI./HR.)**

Source: Compiled by the author.

of a square, 4.24 miles by 4.24 miles, oriented at 45 degrees to the
street network. (It is noteworthy that these are approximately the
dimensions of the ancient wall of Peking, China.) The diagonals of
this square are streets six miles in length from corner to corner.

The general market parameter causes the city to be divided
into nine equal squares whose sides are parallel to the city boundary.
One of these is a central square and its center is also the city center.
Most towns and many smaller cities rarely exceed the size of this
central general market area.

FIGURE 13.6

Walking City Uniform 2.86 Mi./Hr.

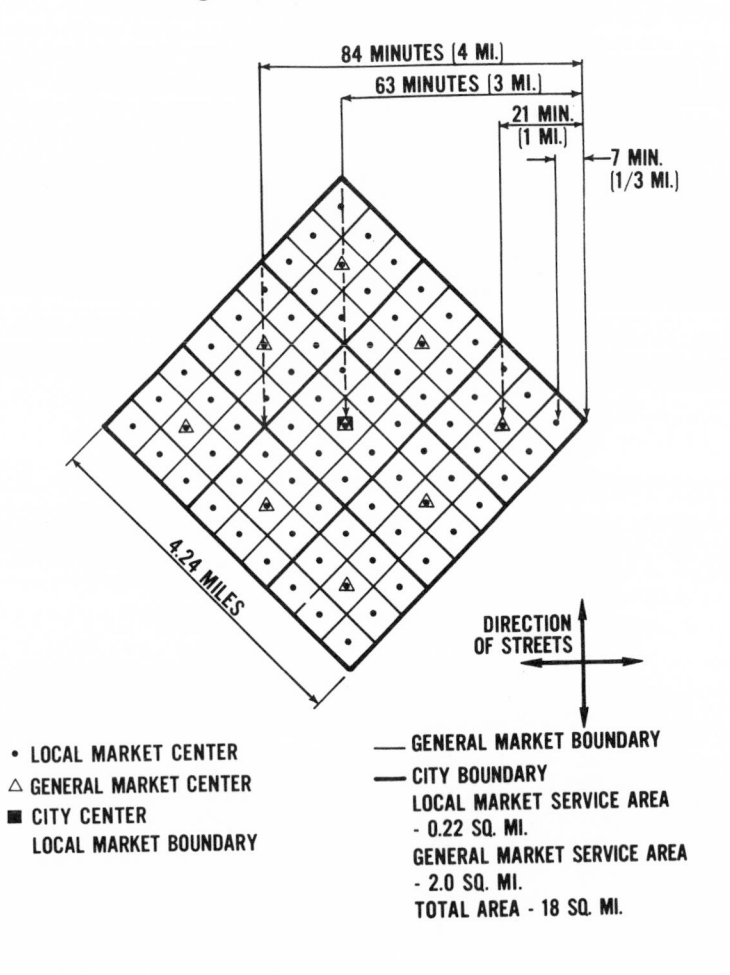

Source: Compiled by the author.

Similarly, the local market parameter causes each general market service area to be divided into nine equal squares whose boundaries are parallel to the boundary of the general market service area.

The vital statistics applicable to this walking city are described in Table 13.2.

TABLE 13.2

Travel Time Statistics for a Walking City

Residential Trip to	Maximum Travel Time Minutes	Maximum Travel Distance Blocks	Miles
Local Market	7	4	1/3
General Market	21	12	1
City Center Market	63	36	3

	Maximum Service Area Blocks	Square Miles
Local Market	32	0.22
General Market	288	2.0
City Center Market	2592	18.0

Source: Compiled by the author.

Consider next the introduction of the horse-drawn carriage. The carriage can cruise much faster than a walker. Nevertheless, only a small increase in door-to-door velocity is likely to occur. Its velocity may be reduced because of the lack of street capacity. If a street is being simultaneously used by too many carriages, it becomes more difficult to avoid obstructions. A slowing down of one carriage chain-reacts to the other carriages and all travel is slowed. Thus, the door-to-door velocity will be much less than its cruising velocity. The immediate impact of any increase, however small, in velocity of door-to-door travel is to increase the amount of land within the urban area as shown in Table 13.3. In this table the uniform velocity of walking has been multiplied by factors of 2, 3, 4, and 8. These may be considered as approximations of average door-to-door travel velocity applicable, respectively, to the carriage, bus, auto, and some new technology. In this table it is assumed that for each mode all travel is uniformly at the same travel velocity and that the city is square, as in Figure 13.6.

Although the numbers in Table 13.3 are based on uniform velocities—a condition never found in the real world—it is nevertheless apparent that increases in velocity produce exponential increases in the supply of urban land. Thus, transit, with its threefold increase

TABLE 13.3

Urban Areas as a Function of Travel Time Limits and Velocity

Service Area	Maximum Travel Time (minutes)	Door-to-Door Velocity (miles/hours)	Equivalent Mode	Maximum Travel Distance (miles)	Area within Locus (square miles)
Local market	7	2.86	Walking	1/3	0.22
		5.72	Carriage	2/3	0.89
		8.58	Transit	1	2.00
		11.44	Auto	1 1/3	3.56
		22.88	New	2 2/3	14.22
General market	21	2.86	Walking	1	2.0
		5.72	Carriage	2	8.0
		8.58	Transit	3	18.0
		11.44	Auto	4	32.0
		22.88	New	8	128.0
City center market	63	2.86	Walking	3	18.0
		5.72	Carriage	6	72.0
		8.58	Transit	9	162.0
		11.44	Auto	12	308.0
		22.88	New	24	1152.0

Source: Compiled by the author.

over the walking velocity, transforms the entire original walking city into a single general market service area. By converting to this higher speed, all of the population in the walking city originally located in the eight outer markets are added as potential customers for the transit city central general market.

It is also apparent that any new system that can cause uniform city velocities of 20 or more miles per hour will produce a central general market area (128 square miles) equal to the size of many of today's cities and thus may serve to revitalize the central business districts of these cities. Also, individuals who are constrained to use of a low-velocity mode have access to less land area than those who can use higher-velocity modes.

The size of market areas can be increased by such technological innovations as the subway and the limited-access roads. As shown in Figure 13.7, these modes serve the unique function of connecting two distant areas into one market area. They also increase city size.

In Figure 13.7 assume a subway that makes only three stops. It travels from the city center to points No. 1 and No. 2. Point No. 1 is one of the general market centers of a walking city. Point No. 2 is at a point twice this distance. By walking, Point No. 1 is 42 minutes from the city center. By subway it is 7 minutes. By walking, Point No. 2 is 84 minutes from the city center. By subway, it is 14 minutes. Assume that, except for this one subway line, all travel within the city is by walking. Figure 13.7A shows all travel time contours to the city center in increments of seven minutes. Solid contours are within the original walking city land area. Dotted contours are within the land area added by the subway. It is assumed that the capacity of the subway is adequate to handle all travel demanded.

It can be seen that the impact of this one subway line is to almost double the size of the walking city. It may also be noted that the area within the 21-minute contours at points 1 and 2 now form an additional service area served by the general market at the city center.

It can also be noted that the success of this plan hinges on the ability to produce the 7- and 14-minute travel time at points 1 and 2 including walking at the station and waiting for a train. In Figure 13.7B is shown the impact of doubling subway time to 14 and 28 minutes respectively. The added area is now reduced to close to one-half of the amount of area added by the faster time. Only a small amount of central general market service area is added at Point No. 1 and none at Point No. 2.

Figures 13.2 through 13.7 were examples of square cities formed by such modes as walking and carriages. The impact of the automobile is similar to these modes. All three are modes that permit pervasive travel wherever there are streets. Barring geographi-

FIGURE 13.7

Impact of Subway Line on City Size

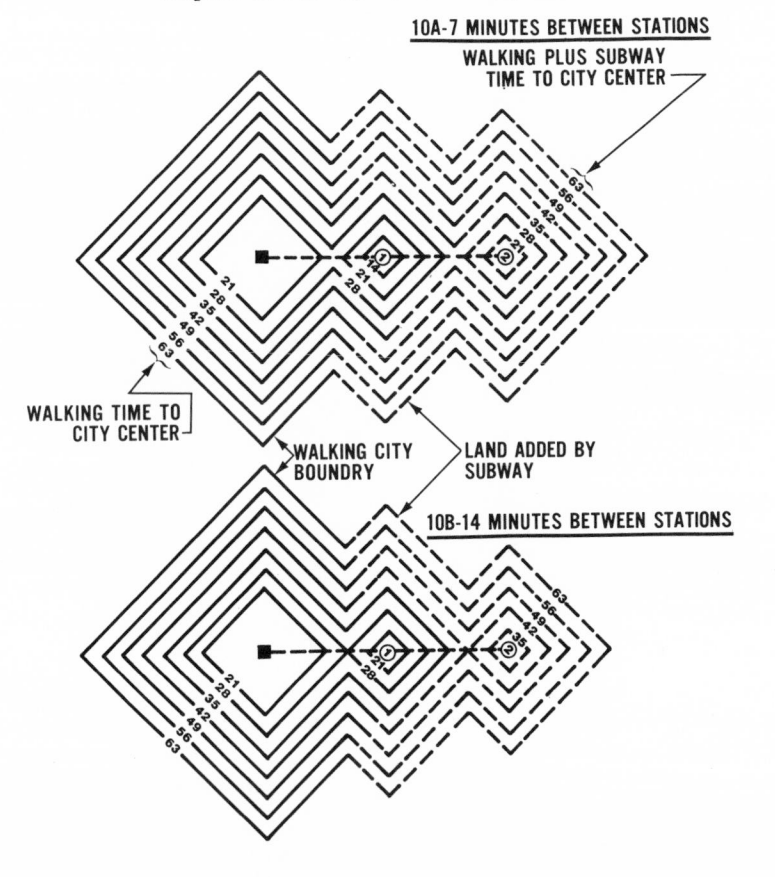

Source: Compiled by the author.

cal or nontransportation-related constraints, the urban areas can grow in all directions if the streets are provided.

As distinct from the pervasive modes of walking and automobiles, it is customary to refer to transit as a linear system. During the height of its popularity the transit system required the operation of the two modes of transit vehicles and walking. One of the phenomena described in the urban literature is that almost all transit users will walk less than seven minutes to the transit route. It is not clear whether this limit applied prior to the auto. If it did, this behavior limited transit corridors to .50 mile in width.

FIGURE 13. 8

A Walking City and a Trolley City

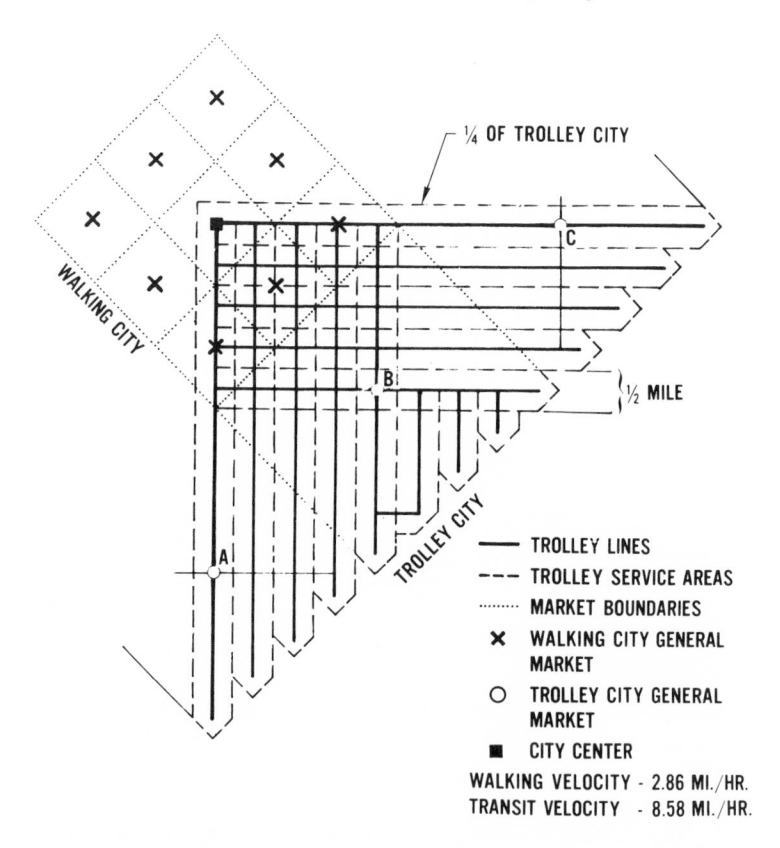

TROLLEY LINES
TROLLEY SERVICE AREAS
MARKET BOUNDARIES
✘ WALKING CITY GENERAL MARKET
○ TROLLEY CITY GENERAL MARKET
■ CITY CENTER

WALKING VELOCITY - 2.86 MI./HR.
TRANSIT VELOCITY - 8.58 MI./HR.

Source: Compiled by the author.

In Figure 13. 8 the trolley system installation forms a square city. This type of arrangment has probably never occurred, since in most cases transit routes tended to follow major paths to the city center with a few routes providing cross town service in outlying areas. Nevertheless, Figure 13. 8 does serve to introduce the walking, transfer, headway, and velocity characteristics of transit and the impact they have on the urban boundaries.

Each of the corridors in Figure 13. 8 is .50 mile wide. This imposes a maximum walking time of seven minutes to the transit line. Since seven minutes is also the postulated travel time limit of local markets, the transit route is a logical location for local markets. It also follows that in a transit city the size of a local market area is dictated by the walking mode.

Points A, B, and C in Figure 13.8 are locations for general markets and are logical points for crosstown transit route intersections. However, in the layout shown, most of the population within the area served by each market would have to use two or three vehicles and one or two transfers to reach the general market.

Transfers are part of the door-to-door trip and can cause utilization of a large portion of trip time. In actuality, layouts of transit routes tended to minimize the number of such transfers. These routes were laid out so as to radiate from market centers. As the routes extended outward they would branch out to serve additional land. The effect was to produce a radial urban form.

TRAVEL TIME QUALITY OF LAND

This discussion of the transit system also serves to introduce the subject of price and cost of travel. In turn this requires consideration of a traveler's ability to pay for travel. This ability is related to the traveler's total expenditure budget. The choices that are made are related to the "travel time quality" of land.

In choosing between two identical residences, the individual has the option of choosing the location that reduces the amount of travel. If this results in an increase in the price he pays for the residence, the increase represents a price paid for a saving in travel time. This increase may be designated as "the travel time quality" of the location and its magnitude is a measure of its "travel time quality." Since this is an actual payment, the implication of this statement is that except for its farming value, the total price of urban land is a measure of the total travel time value of its population. The price paid for "transportation technology" must be added to the travel time quality payment to arrive at the total "transportation" payment. Travel time quality is a resource that may be traded not only for travel time, but also for housing and land square footage.

It seems reasonable to assume that in general, the travel time quality payment will decrease as the transportation technology payment rises. Whether it does or not depends on the trip patterns of the eventual purchasers of the property. It can be seen that the travel time quality payment is the result of bidding which takes place among the population for that particular location. The transportation technology payment is a function of the buyer's expenditure budget and the utility he perceives for his choice of transportation technology. It is probable that for each individual there exists at least one urban location that produces a minimum transportation payment. Clearly, any effort to model urban interactions must then take into account the individual's ability to acquire both transportation technology and property.

Together with a description of transportation changes over time, it should be possible to detect the manner in which these population classes have distributed themselves over the urban area. Square footage of housing would vary with family size and income. Large families with low income would tend to walk or ride transit and occupy old low-cost rental housing within the walking city. Large families with somewhat higher income would tend to occupy residences at the extremities of the auto cities. All other groups would tend to distribute themselves between these two extremities depending on the existing stock of housing, their ability to pay, and their housing needs. Each introduction of higher-velocity technology would tend to change these distributional patterns. The land that is at the urban extremity prior to the change would be at an intermediate location and would attract a new class of population.

Since the introduction of higher velocities and the addition of route miles increase the supply of land and change travel time quality, each transportation change influences the value of every location in the urban area. Some locations will benefit and some will sustain a loss. This change depends not only on the change in travel time quality of the location but also on the changes in the transportation technology payment and travel time experienced by its occupant. A family performs many types of trips. The number and type can vary family by family. Each family is seen to measure the value of a location in terms of the total amount of time in travel to accomplish these anticipated trips by some chosen mode. The residential location is at some travel time contour with respect to some particular destination. It is another travel time contour with respect to a different destination. These contours are defined by the time for one trip. The particular set of destinations will vary for each family. The set will include not only those destinations that have been used to postulate the urban definition, but also such destinations as schools, parks, hospitals, friends, etc., depending on the particular requirements of each family. To each of these destinations a number of daily, weekly, or monthly trips will be performed. The product of trip time and trip frequency is determined for each trip and the total estimated for all trips. The calculation often includes the travel time effort of visitors or service persons to his home. A location that produces a low total has a higher travel time quality than one with a high total. This calculation is not necessarily made explicitly. It is arrived at by simply knowing the local geography. In a very real sense it is a valid intuitive practice. Its validity is testified to by the sensitivity of the land and housing markets to the change in travel time quality. Markets and industry perform similar calculations.

As the population mounts the supply of land dwindles and land prices rise. The cost of land becomes a higher proportion of the total housing cost. To restore the original ratio of housing to land costs, the amount of land per residence has to drop. In some cases the price of land rises so rapidly that the withholding of its sale represents the best use of its investment value. If such land has old housing, low rents to pay its taxes may represent its most profitable use. In most of today's cities, undeveloped land will be found in all rings of the city. In time the land value of older housing increases to the point that redevelopment to reduce the land per residence is justified. Housing with large lots disappear and new residences with smaller plots are built. The result is a reduction in the average land per house and an increase in population density.

As the population continues to mount, the number of trips on the street network rise. In time a capacity limit is reached at the city center street network. Travel time to the city center is increased. This causes the city center travel time contours for the entire city to shift toward the center. A loss in travel time quality is sustained by the entire population. The total land supply is also decreased and those who live close to the maximum boundaries sustain discomfort as the travel time quality of land drops. Pressure mounts to increase street capacity. When improvements have been made the land is once again restored to its original travel time quality.

The introduction of new and higher-velocity technology once again increases the total land supply and shifts the city center travel time contours outward. The process of selling more land per residence as an incentive to compensate for less travel time quality is once again initiated. Average densities fall. The price of older high-density housing falls as people are attracted to low-density land. The high-density housing is occupied by those who cannot afford the low-density land. The degree to which this process acts to change the character of the city depends on the sizes of the various income groups, the supply of different quality housing, and the supply of different travel time quality of land. All sorts of variations are possible and the variations produced from time to time depend on the combination of supply at that time. Almost any observed urban condition may be explained in terms of this interaction. Additional variables that affect the results are the housing technology, social segregation, which may deprive entry to those who are otherwise entitled on economic grounds, and zoning. It is surmised, however, that zoning will usually or eventually respond to the economic forces produced by this mechanism.

It is useful to cite specific applications. For example, consider how housing technology affects the units of the housing to land-cost ratio. New York is a city in which the five-story tenement walk-up predominates the landscape. During the turn of the century this was the highest-capacity low-cost dwelling structure that housing technology would permit. The size of the land area was limited to that of a transit city. The city was experiencing an extremely high rate of low-income population growth. The total supply of land, the rate of population growth, and the housing technology combined to produce many square miles of five-story tenements. In Baltimore, where population grew more slowly, the result was many square miles of two-story low-cost structures. It is possible that if the Baltimore city fathers or transit operators had prevented the rapid expansion of transit lines, it too would have a five-story tenement skyline. It is also possible that if today's high-rise low-cost housing technology had been available at the turn of the century, there would be a high-rise skyline rather than a five-story tenement skyline in New York.

Timing and income distribution are important. For example, the city of Caracas, Venezuela, is in a condition of rapidly rising population growth imposed on a young city with no old housing and a population whose income distribution results in a small high-income group and a large very low-income group. Their very large incomes permit the smaller high-income group to outbid the large low-income group for the highest travel time quality land at the city center. The large low-income group is forced to occupy land of lower travel time quality at the outer rings. The land at these outer rings has never been developed and lacks old housing. The income of this group is too low to pay the cost of new housing. The result is a squatter settlement.

Today's pattern of growth in many U.S. cities may also be explained under this mechanism. When the auto was first introduced, many U.S. cities had reached high population densities and the supply of high-density housing was large. Auto ownership grew rapidly and is still growing. The income distribution in the United States may be described as consisting of two small groups at each end of the income scale and a large group in the middle incomes. The auto increases the land supply extensively. Members of the middle group can afford to own a car and occupy new housing. Their movement to new housing on the new land of the larger auto city leaves a large supply of vacant high-density dwelling in the older transit city. Despite the high travel time quality in this inner city, its supply of old high-density housing is too large to cause its entire conversion for use by the small high-income group. The only economic use for much of this land is to attract the low-income group. In the past immigrants formed the bulk of the low-income group. The immigrants of today are the blacks and Puerto Ricans and it is these people who occupy the old housing. The black-white segregation influence attributed to the center city urbanized living pattern is displayed not by this population of black urban immigrants with low income, but rather by that portion of the black population that forms part of the urban middle-income class and that, in terms of the economic market, should be residing in suburbia and not in the center city.

One of the controversial issues in transportation planning stems from the recommendations of some economists that road users be charged a fare for the use of roads consistent with the cost of providing that increment of road capacity being used. The suggestion is here offered that perhaps a more responsive market mechanism would be one in which residential and investment land owners, entrepreneurs, and industry would be forced to bid for transportation capacity. It is the provision of this capacity that converts their otherwise inaccessible land to urban land and that dictates the travel time quality market in which it belongs. Under such a mechanism an improvement in transportation would depend on the willingness of these direct beneficiaries to pay its cost. These beneficiaries could be residents, merchants, or industrial establishments. Under this procedure a group of individuals would, in concert, contract to bear the cost of the improvement and its operating costs. Included in this cost would be a reimbursement to those whose travel time quality would be reduced by the improvement.

The previous discussion has focused on the location of residences. Work location findings may also be explained if it is recalled that they may be classified into three types. The first class has to do with the many service activities throughout the urban area. The location of work sites for these activities is contingent on the locations of the areas served by the general and local markets, and, as stated previously, they do not necessarily fall within the framework of the postulated work site travel time limit.

The second and third classes of work sites are for the most part business and industrial enterprises, whose location is seen to fit the postulated urban definition. A portion of these enterprises locate in such manner as to satisfy two conditions. First, they wish to minimize the travel time of their labor force. Second, they wish to minimize travel time to other related enterprises with whom they have a large volume of interaction. Ordinarily such enterprises will be found at the city center, although a group of strongly interacting enterprises may be found at other subcenters.

The third class of work sites is also one whose location serves to minimize labor force travel time, provides large amounts of land,

and has good access to intercity transportation. This class will locate at the perimeter of the central general market area. The influence of this parameter in real cities is often difficult to detect. Its influence can readily be seen when both past and present travel time contours are imposed on the city surface. For example, in Figure 13.7A above, location 2 qualifies as an appropriate location for the boundary industry. In this example the subway is a high-speed technology that results in placing the entire city population within 84 minutes of location 2 and qualifies it as a location for a work site. A main thoroughfare from the city center to the city boundary would serve the same function so long as its capacity limits are not exceeded and velocity is not thereby reduced.

Just as market entrepreneurs are in competition with other entrepreneurs, industry competes with itself for the labor supply. Two concerns may offer identical salaries, but the concern whose location has a higher travel time quality or a low travel time quality payment causes a reduction in transportation payments and can more easily attract employees.

To cite a typical example in today's environment, consider the problem of attracting industry to the center city. For by-pass purposes, a high-speed, high-capacity highway encircles many of today's cities at least in part. Auto travel to the center of these same cities is slow because of lack of capacity. Any point on the circumferential highway represents a very high travel time quality for residents of the outer ring. It can also be seen that the location of the intersection of the highway and the subway provides a reasonably high travel time quality for the residents of the inner city. It is very possible that within the limits of the capacity of the two modes, this outer location provides the lowest transportation cost for the income mix of employees that is usually required by business and industry. It is a location that should attract businesses and industry. To restore the attractiveness of the center city, radial subway lines that increase the travel time quality of land are proposed.

TRANSPORTATION DESIGN

The major impact of transportation systems has been described to this point in terms of travel time quality. It is next important to consider the manner in which transportation design may achieve some specified level of travel time quality.

In addition to travel time, individuals will consider such factors as cost, personal effort, safety, and pleasure. At times they will sacrifice travel time to reduce cost, to decrease personal effort, to avoid danger, or to increase pleasure.

The transportation designer must consider all these factors and one other: He must consider capacity. All transportation systems are subject to some limit of capacity, beyond which the system can no longer accept additional trips without impacting on the factors that generate demand. Travel time, cost, personal effort, safety, and pleasure are all affected. If this condition is prolonged it impacts on the travel time quality of the urban area and causes a change in its pattern of growth.

Transportation systems have been previously described as either linear or pervasive. A most difficult problem faced by such linear systems as buses and subways is not so much the lack of high-density corridors, but rather the lack of high-density corridors in which all trips start at the same point and end at the same point. Even in a high-density corridor, trip origins and destinations are dispersed up and down the corridor. The conventional linear systems must stop to pick up and discharge riders. This consumes time for all travelers, including those who remain on board. For this reason linear systems are relatively slow systems. New technology would be required to overcome this problem.

A second difficult problem for linear systems is the fact that only small urban areas can retain linear patterns of travel. The major destination points of the city are the market centers and work sites. If these could all be located at one point then a system of linear corridors could radiate to this point. But the city potentially has many important points. As new points are added, trip distribution becomes pervasive rather than linear. Trips for the majority of the origin-destination pairs in a fully developed city cannot be accomplished without travel along two or three corridors. Few, if any, of the two or more corridor combinations will have trip volumes to justify the use of the linear mode vehicle without transfers. This further reduces travel time.

Despite these disadvantages, at one time linear systems successfully served our urban areas. When the trolley was first introduced in the late 1800s, all cities were essentially walking cities. The introduction of transit opened corridors of land radiating from the city center outward to the seven- or eight-mile limit that could be traveled in one hour.

For 50 or 60 years transit systems controlled city growth. This was a period in which population grew rapidly. By the time the automobile was introduced, the old pervasive walking cities had been converted to densely populated linear (or radial) cities. During this period of transit dominance, walking continued as a major mode.

Transit had little or no impact on the size of the local market service areas. Its major impact was on the city center. The linearity of the transit system mitigated against the development of strong outlying general markets. The city center had the highest travel time quality for a general market and for work sites. Thus transit cities produced strong city centers. But even in the city center, walking was a major mode.

The introduction of the automobile changed these patterns. There is every reason to believe that a major attractive force for the automobile was its ability to reduce the necessity for walking. A second powerful force was its ability to travel pervasively. It reduced the effort of travel and its freedom of direction provided direct access to all parts of the city. The automobile might have achieved popularity even if its cruising velocity had been less than that of transit.

To an important degree the early success of the automobile can be attributed to the role played by the horse and wagon. One of the drawbacks of transit systems was its nonapplicability to the movement of goods. As transit moved the city boundaries outward, the movement of goods became heavily reliant on the use of horses and wagons. To accommodate these vehicles, reasonably wide streets were required. Thus when the automobile was introduced the street capacity to accommodate its bulk was available and in place. This street capacity also provided a place to park the auto. At first the autos were few in number and could be parked immediately in front of the origin and destination structures. When the auto was used for a trip, walking was minimal. Almost the entire trip by auto could be made in comfort, protected from the weather.

The auto provided sufficient capacity for bundles or a family. It could go wherever there were streets. It was truly an ideal mode of transportation, and one that to this day is almost universally desired by anyone able to drive. (There appears to be little question that the performance of the automobile is a standard against which all new transportation technology should be measured. It is unlikely that any new transport mode will attract significant patronage if its performance does not match this standard.)

At first the auto was used as an alternative to transit within the transit city. It availability, however, created a potential market for residences on urban land not served by transit. By 1940 about one-half of all travel in urban areas was by auto. The prosperity that followed World War II removed all constraints and since that time the market for new land has been exploited and urban boundaries have rapidly expanded. Prosperity also brought with it widespread auto ownership, including ownership among those who did not become part of the new, exclusively auto portion of the urban area.

The first impact of auto ownership on the transit system was to free the traveler from the constraint of linear travel. Travel could be performed pervasively, and transit city auto owners began to take some trips by auto. This reduced transit patronage and transit service had to be reduced.

In time some individuals moved away from the transit city to occupy the new land of the auto city. In some cases transit lines were pushed into these new areas in an effort to capture some trade or at the insistence of the political process. This only served to dilute the quality of service within the more densely populated transit city area. Each reduction in service induced further losses to the auto. A cycle was created in which patronage losses reduced service and increased fares, thereby inducing further losses in service. This cycle continues to this day.

At this time transit serves a limited use for work trips, but somewhat greater use by the residents at the city center. The growth in income should make it possible for more individuals to own cars or multiple cars and homes. A further decrease in transit would seem to be inevitable.

However, as auto ownership reached high levels of use, it soon created capacity problems at several points in the auto system. One reason is that autos occupy space. Autos may be viewed as occupying some point on a narrow travel lane. Two of them may move, one behind the other, in the same lane. If both are moving at the same speed the distance that separates them remains constant, and each may continue to move freely. If the auto in front is moving at a slower pace than the one behind, some action is required to avoid a collision. One or the other will have to change lanes, increase or decrease speed, or stop. Whatever action is taken, one or the other may experience a loss in velocity. When all lanes are occupied with many travelers, a reduction in speed by one individual cascades into a reduction in speed for an entire platoon of travelers behind him. When he once again increases his speed, those behind increase their speed. But in the meantime, because of a lag in response time, those autos back in the platoon have slowed their travel. Thus the slowing process moves in an opposite direction to the direction of travel and disappears only when the space between travelers is no longer so small as to cause anyone to slow down. At times the center of the platoon may actually come to a full stop.

A further constraint is the interference caused by cross-street traffic. In the auto city the loss in average speed is guaranteed. Auto velocity is so high that the slowing down process to avoid a collision must begin before the cross traffic is visible around a corner. For this reason all cities have a system of traffic controls including stop signs and lights, which force one or the other of the traffic flows to automatically stop to prevent collisions.

Despite the ability of the auto to travel at very high speeds, this built-in street traffic control procedure results in an average speed of door-to-door auto travel of about 12 miles per hour in an average city. The velocity is reduced drastically when traffic volumes are heavy. When traffic lights change to green, the cars in the waiting platoon of vehicles do not all start immediately. A time lag builds up as each vehicle in back waits for the vehicle in front to move. When platoons (queues) are lengthy and fill a whole block, several changes in lights may be required to negotiate one block. Under these conditions, velocity of travel sometimes becomes less than that of walking velocity.

As the city grows and more trips are added to the network, a general deterioration in network velocity occurs. Those who have settled at the perimeter of the city based on the higher velocity now find themselves outside the perimeter of the city of the new slower velocity. Everyone else in the city finds that the travel time quality of land has dropped.

The usual solution to this problem has been to increase the capacity of some of the roads by adding lanes and by allowing more traffic-light time for passage of platoons. At this point another phenomenon is observed. Each time an improvement occurs, the velocity on the improved road is initially in excess of that on any other road. Almost all travel on alternative routes is immediately attracted to this faster road. But the new road's capacity, although higher than before the improvement, is still too small to handle an almost total diversion from other roads. The addition of higher velocity, higher capacity limited access highways further aggravates this condition. Their higher velocity is a powerful magnet that trip makers cannot resist.

Clearly this must lead to the conclusion that, in providing added capacity, consideration must also be given to the trip times on those alternative routes whose capacity is also required to avoid congestion. All route alternatives should produce the same travel time qualities.

The introduction of main arterials has generated opposition not only at the "capacity constraint" boundary, but also along corridors. At grade level they inhibit cross travel. Above grade they produce a visual divider of the city. This results in a deterioration of the travel time quality of the residents on each side of the corridor. In some cases residents are displaced to provide room for additional road structure. These individuals experience a cost that is rarely compensated by those who benefit or in its full amount. The location of the improved road is a cordon through which many trips from many parts of the city take place. If the improvement reduces the velocity

of these cross trips without providing a suitable alternative, all of
these trip makers suffer a loss. These individuals are not compensated
for this loss. The result has been to produce opposition to further
city highway improvements and a demand for improved transit.

The volume of trips to a market center is a measure of the
population it serves. When capacity acts to constrain the number of
trips to the center, it also acts to reduce the number of individuals
that are served by that center. Thus the economic level of the center
is influenced not only by the population within the service area, but
also by any transportation capacity limit that deprives some of that
population of the necessary access to that center. This reiterates the
basic objective of transportation design, which is that it should provide a specified velocity and a specified capacity.

Central business districts are small in size; this is indicative
that walking remains a major mode in these areas. Neither transit
nor the auto have provided satisfactory alternatives that would serve
to increase the general velocity of travel, thereby helping to increase
the size of area this central district might occupy.

The congestion that occurs on the center city street has also
impeded passage of intercity travelers through the city. To resolve
this problem, city by-passes have been constructed. They often
encircle a city and are so designed as to provide relatively high-
volume, high-speed travel.

These highways, however, have had a significant impact on the
urban travel time quality. Any one point on this highway has a major
portion of the suburban city within a 21-minute travel time radius.
Those points along this road that are intersected by major arteries
to the city center represent a minimum travel time cost for both
suburbia and the city center. They are prime locations that will attract
a labor force, and industry will find it easier to attract its surburban
labor force by locating its plants at these locations.

Lack of transportation capacity, of course, sets a limit on the
amount of growth at these outlying points. For this reason (and because low-cost land is plentiful) industry usually disperses to several
such points. In this way no one section of the road system is over-
burdened. A pattern of growth in which industry is ringed at city
extremities is now underway in a number of cities. It is a pattern
of growth that indicates that the location of transportation capacity
favors the development of these outlying points. To a major extent,
it is indicative of the dearth of transportation capacity at the city
center. There is little reason to doubt that the continued growth of
city centers with present systems of transportation requires the installation of great amounts of highway and parking capacity in these
zones. Only in this way can a high travel time quality of suburbia to

the city center be maintained. Public opposition to this solution is so intense, however, that a search for new technology appears to be the only alternative.

That city centers have not experienced significant increases in size is an interesting historical phenomenon. As transportation technology passed through its three phases of walking, transit, and auto, the central market continued to rely heavily on walking. The linearity of transit, and the constraint on velocity and capacity imposed on the streets by the auto, have mitigated the potential of these modes to allow for full development of these areas consistent with the average velocity of these modes. Here, too, an application may be found for new technology.

The influence of intercity connecting roads on urban growth has been noted. Technological change has also occurred in intercity travel and this too has had an impact on urban growth. In many towns railroads preceded transit. Almost without exception, railroads located their terminals at city centers thereby further enhancing the value of this location. Prior to the auto, bus, and plane, rail was the major if not the only means of travel to other cities. Locating terminals at the city center provided an increase in the travel time quality of those urban rings that were close to the city center.

The introduction of the auto, bus, and plane diverted intercity travel from rail. Auto intercity travelers avoided the city center wherever possible. The need for large land areas caused airports to locate outside the city boundaries. Thus intercity travel requirements could be met without the necessity of residing close to the city center. The lack of adequate transport velocity and capacity from airports to city centers even now represents a high travel cost to center city enterprises that rely heavily on intercity travel. It represents an additional force that motivates industry to locate away from the city center.

This outward movement from the city has also been abetted by the general prosperity of the nation and the movement of income distribution toward income equality. Increases in income at low-income levels enabled a massive relocation from the old center-city housing outward to newer structures. The availability of large amounts of old housing provided low-cost dwellings for immigrants of low income. The old transit corridor neighborhoods with rich and poor living in adjacent corridors are rapidly being transformed into two large rings with the lowest incomes in the inner ring and the middle income and rich in the outer rings.

CONCLUSION

New systems should be evaluated in terms of three major objectives: they are marketable, they are a least-cost solution from a national standpoint, and they are flexible.

To be marketable, it should be a system that attracts the public away from the conventional auto usage. It should be a system that improves travel time quality.

From a national standpoint a new transportation system should provide the lowest possible consumption of resources and highest level of labor productivity.

It should have the flexibility to provide the type of urban area most desired by its population. For example, it should provide the flexibility to provide desirable density distributions, income and neighborhood mixes, and minimum disruption to previous urban investments.

The transit and auto were systems produced by private technological evolution. The economics of these systems permitted private development. There now exists a public demand to resolve the many problems that the auto has created. The conventional transit systems have shown their lack of marketability. There appears to be no new privately developed system in the offing. An effort seems required leading to invention of a new system of travel.

The important element of this discussion has been the emphasis placed on the urban area definition. This definition defines the boundaries that are included in the impacts of transportation decisions. Political city boundaries are not consistent with these boundaries; they inhibit efforts to achieve rational transportation decisions. One alternative is to produce a new mode of transportation that not only achieves desirable objectives but whose attraction is sufficiently powerful to allow the urban markets to make the desirable decisions in spite of political boundaries.

Confirmation of the urban growth process described in this chapter should provide a basis for evaluating transportation policy designed to meet specific objectives.

For example, one of today's objectives is to relieve center city congestion by the automobile. The present policy for achieving this objective is encouragement of growth in mass transit usage.

Based on the contents of this chapter, a large number of automobile travelers reside outside the transit city and could not abandon their auto mode without incurring a loss in their housing investment. On the other hand, a viable mass transit mode requires higher population densities. This too would require abandonment of low-density housing. Assuming public resistance to high-density living, a continuation should be expected in the present massive use of autos to the city center. Failure to provide improved city center highway and street flows and parking capacity would therefore represent a continuation of the present conditions of congestion.

On the other hand, the alternative of reducing congestion by prohibiting auto travel or by imposing high parking prices in city centers would eventually encourage business growth in the outer market centers to the detriment of the city center market.

It may also be concluded, however, that a general citywide increase in the velocity of travel would both increase the travel time quality of occupied land and increase the total land within the urban area. This should cause a reduction in the travel time quality payment (that is, a drop in land prices). This potential savings in land costs represents an expenditure resource that can be allocated toward possible higher costs of some new form of technology chosen to achieve these higher velocities. Obviously, the assumption that higher veolcities are produced implies that the system is a viable substitute for the automobile, that it therefore protects present investments in housing, and that it would therefore relieve city center congestion.

NOTES

1. See Carla M. Wartenberg, Von Thunen's Isolated State, ed. Peter Hall (Edinburgh: Pergamon Press, 1966); Lowdon Wingo, Transportation and Urban Land (Washington, D.C.: Resources for the Future, 1961); William Alonso, Location and Land Use (Cambridge, Mass.: Harvard University Press, 1964); Richard Muth, Cities and Housing (Chicago: University of Chicago Press, 1969).

2. W. A. Hansen, "Accessibility and Residential Growth," Master thesis, MIT, 1959; A.M. Voorhees, A General Theory of Traffic Movement (Washington, D.C.: Institute of Traffic Engineers, Special Report, 1955).

3. M.D. Cheslow, "Northeast Corridor Demand Model," in Short Haul Inter-Urban Air Systems (Washington, D.C.: Mitre Corporation, 1971); J. McLynn, et al., Analysis and Calibration of a Modal Allocation Model: Choice of the Base Mode. (Washington, D.C.: Davidson, Talbrid and McLynn, 1967). T.A. Domenich and Gerald Kraft, Free Transit Study (Lexington, Mass.: D.C. Heath, 1970).

4. August Loesch, The Economics of Location (New Haven, Conn.: Yale University Press, 1954).

5. E. Weiner, H. Kassoff, and D. S. Gendell, A Multi-modal National Urban Transportation Planning Model, prepared for presentation at the 52nd Annual Meeting, Highway Research Board, January 1973.

6. M. Beesley, "The Value of Time Spent in Traveling: Some New Evidence," Economica 32 (May 1965): 174-85; C. Lane, "The Value of Time in Urban Transportation," Ph. D. dissertation, Stanford University, 1968; T. Lisco, "The Value of Commuters' Travel Time—A Study in Urban Transportation," Ph. D. dissertation, University of Chicago, 1967.

7. Hans Blumenfeld, selected essays in The Modern Metropolis, edited by Paul D. Spreiregen. (Cambridge, Mass.: MIT Press, 1967).

8. Chicago Area Transportation Study, Volume 1, p. 15, 1959.

14

RENT,
TRANSPORTATION,
AND URBAN SCALE
Irving Hoch

Rent, transportation, and urban scale have a number of interconnections, with considerable import for both analysis and policy. This chapter develops and attempts some tests of hypotheses about those relations.[1]

Urban scale is defined as embracing both urban population size and population density (or population per unit of land). The key variable is population size, for there are both theoretical and empirical reasons to view density as a function of size. An increase in size should lead both to an increase in density and in land rent. Land rent and transportation cost, particularly in the journey to work, can be viewed as substitutes, and, in conjunction, they help determine the physical extent of an urban area. Increases in land rent and in transportation cost should have both a direct and an indirect impact on the cost of living, defined in conventional marketbasket terms. In addition, increases in population size and in density will affect nonmarket components of consumer welfare, often labeled psychic costs or psychic income and including negative things such as air pollution and positive things such as access to specialized medical services. Available evidence suggests that the negative things outweigh the positive. Hence, an overall cost-of-living index, embracing nonmarket as well as market components, will show even greater increase with urban scale than does the conventional index. However, feedback mechanisms come into play, and at equilibrium we can expect adjustments to occur in money wages and in rents, and in the distribution of population within and between urban areas. If pollution of various forms is a function of density, population will tend to shift outward from an urban center, yielding the bugbear of planners: urban sprawl. Money wages can be expected to increase with urban size and density as workers demand an increment in wages to compensate for the net negative effects of scale.

These adjustments, in turn, have further consequences, which are often only dimly perceived. Because money differs in real purchasing power between places of different size, we will often be the victims of money illusion, both in estimating such measures as national income and GNP and in applying seemingly uniform national policies in such matters as income taxes, the salaries of federal government employees, the minimum wage, and welfare payments. The framework of analysis can lead to hypotheses explaining aspects of urban behavior. For example, there is widespread belief, and even some evidence, that the bigger an urban area, the faster the tempo of life.[2] But time increases in value or in cost with population size, which should lead to some attempts to minimize its use. Put more precisely, the value of time, like the value of land, increases relative to prices of nationally traded goods, which will tend to be invariant between places. As a consequence, there should be greater intensity of use for both time and land. (High rents can impinge directly on time allocation, as in fast turnover of customers in "reasonably priced" Manhattan restaurants.) The framework of analysis can be applied to policy issues, in such uses as gauging the impact of auto emission controls on the distribution of population, or in considering proposals to divert population from large areas.

This chapter will consider some of these themes at length.

EVIDENCE

This section considers evidence bearing on the themes developed in the introductory overview, focusing first on intraurban and then on interurban relationships.

Intraurban Relationships

The intraurban distribution of land values, floor space, and population can be explained by a trade-off between space and access, or, in cost terms, by the substitution of transportation cost for rent. Consider a simple model of intraurban location. Assume that costs tend to be minimized at the urban center, so that economic activity is concentrated there, in turn making access to the center valuable. Both firms and households will bid up the value of land located near the center, with less demand as access declines. At equilibrium a firm or household will be indifferent between locales because transportation cost plus rental cost will be equivalent wherever the microunit locates. With higher land prices near the center, there will be more intense land use, with greater concentration of floor space and of population per unit of land. From the point of view of the micro-unit, at greater distances more space can be had for the same rent, at the cost of higher transportation expenditures. As J. R. Meyer, J. F. Kain, and M. Wohl note: "Many urban households . . . find it possible to get the housing and yard space they want cheaper, if they are willing to spend more on transportation and travel farther."[3]

There is good evidence that the distribution of urban population per unit of area can be well-approximated by the relation $D = Ae^{-bK}$, which, in effect, exhibits the consequences of the trade-off of space for access.[4] Here D is population density, K is distance from the center, and A and b are parameters. With $K = 0$, $D = A$ or density at the center; b is termed the density gradient, measuring the relative rate of decline from the center. A similar equation form could be used for floor space or land value. (With the use of population per unit of land, a measurement anomaly can occur in practice because nonresidential land use tends to replace residential land use near the center, despite the occurrence of some high-rise apartments near the center. The problem is often avoided by calculating net residential density, or population per unit of residential land.)

As population increases in an area, other things being equal, we can expect an increased demand for land at all points, a general bidding up of land values, and a corresponding increase in population density. The density effects eventuating are illustrated for three urban areas in Figure 14.1.

With an improvement in transportation making outer areas more accessible to the center, we can expect a shift of population outward, with corresponding declines in the values of both A and b in the density equation. The two effects are incorporated in Figure 14.2, exhibiting the log of density on distance. (The minimum level, $\log D_0$, is the density of the nonurban hinterland; the occurrence of $\log D_0$ defines the urban fringe.)

Richard Muth uses Figure 14.2 to summarize the impact of the automobile. With the introduction of the automobile, the typical urban density function shifted from T_1 to T_2. T_3 is the situation at a later point in time, given the automobile and a population increase.[5]

Several qualifications may be noted. First, the automobile has not been a once-and-for-all innovation. Over time, there are improved and increased amounts of roadway, and increases in the percentage of people owning and driving cars, so that both the shifts shown in Figure 14.2 have been occurring continuously over time. The starting point is a function of past history, with older urban areas, built up before the automobile, tending to be a good deal more densely settled than newer areas of the same population size. It is possible, of

FIGURE 14.1

Net Residential Density, by Distance from the CBD
(Chicago, Detroit, and Pittsburgh)

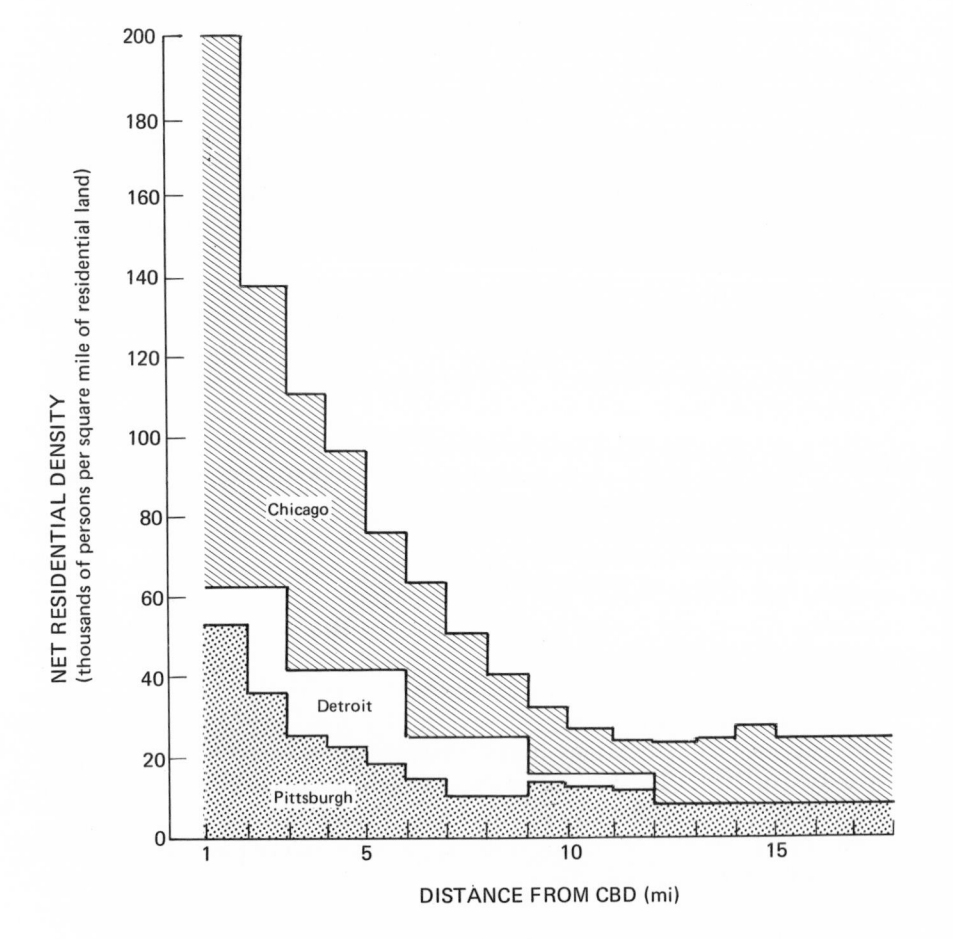

Source: J. R. Meyer, J. F. Kain, and M. Wohl, The Urban Transportation Problem (Cambridge, Mass.: Harvard University Press, 1965), Figure 33, p. 207. Their sources were: Chicago—Chicago Area Transportation Study, Final Report, Vol. 2, Data Projections, July 1960, Table 29, p. 112; Detroit—computed from Detroit Metropolitan Area Traffic Study, Report on the Detroit Area Traffic Study, part 1, Data Summary and Interpretation, Lansing, Mich., Table 8, p. 30, and Table 36, p. 123; Pittsburgh—Pittsburgh Area Transportation Study, Final Report, Vol. 2, Forecasts and Plans, Pittsburgh, February 1963. © 1965 by The Rand Corporation.

FIGURE 14.2

Relations between the Logarithm of Population Density
and Distance from Urban Center

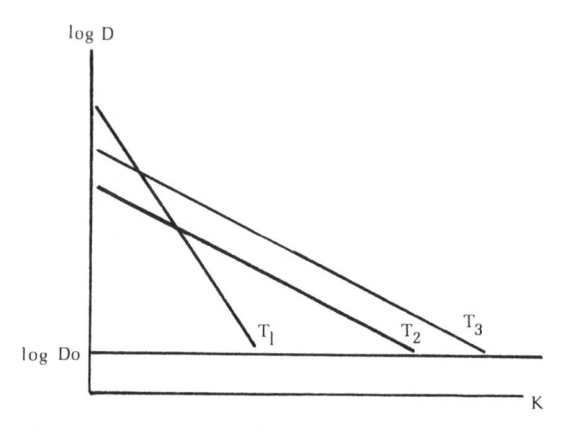

Source: Richard Muth, Cities and Housing (Chicago: University
of Chicago Press, 1969).

course, that the impact of the automobile will soon be fairly well
played out, but considerable impact might be expected in the older,
more slowly adjusting urban areas for some time to come.

Second, investment in new transportation facilities in itself is
likely to attract people into an urban area. This could be a factor in
the westward movement of the U.S. population; transportation costs
were likely to be lower, at least for automobile users, in the newer
cities of the west. Put in terms of Figure 14.2, this effect might
explain part of the movement from T_2 to T_3.

Third, investment in roads is only a quasi-market process at
best. If the efficiency of such investment decisions could be improved,
it is likely this would lead to population redistribution both within and
between urban areas. To illustrate, Edwin Mills has developed a
model in which roads compete with housing for urban land, both uses
paying the same price for land employed. Road construction is paid
for by user tolls, rather than taxes, as at present, which would considerably reduce the capitalization of access value into land values.
In Mills' solved model, there is more road construction in outlying
areas, relative to the present pattern, and a population shift along
the lines of the T_1 to T_2 shift in Figure 14.2. [6]

Finally, Figure 14.2 shows line T_3 parallel to T_2. This draws
on the implicit argument that the percentage increase in density will

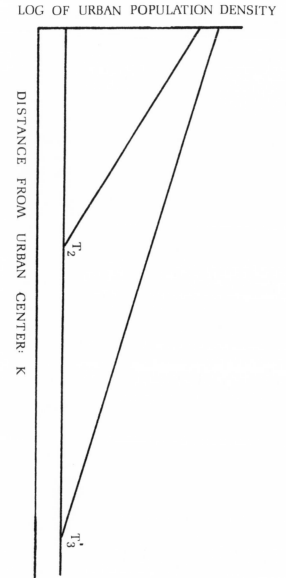

LOG OF URBAN POPULATION DENSITY

DISTANCE FROM URBAN CENTER: K

T_2

T_3'

FIGURE 14.3

Pattern over Time of Urban Population Density: Final Statement

be everywhere the same as the percentage increase in population. The T_3 density relation in effect multiplies the T_2 relation through by a scalar; in logs, this corresponds to the addition of a constant. However, it is a plausible hypothesis that the perceived disutility of air and noise pollution, and other disamenities, increases more than proportionately with density, inhibiting growth near the center and shifting it to the periphery. (Note that the hypothesis refers to the effect of population increase, per se, keeping transportation facilities constant.) The household is seen as locating such that the totality of costs due to rent, transportation, and pollution disamenity are everywhere equivalent. The modified growth pattern is shown in Figure 14.3 with T_3' replacing T_3.

Figure 14.3 can be taken as a description of urban sprawl. It is noteworthy that the automobile not only pulls people outward by virtue of improved access, but appears to push them out as well, by virtue of being a major source of air and noise pollution.

Some empirical evidence is available to support Figure 14.3. In terms of the density function, Ae^{-bK}, Figure 14.3 states that with an increase in population size, A increases less than proportionately and b decreases. (As b decreases toward zero, the density curve flattens out; this is easily seen in the log form of the function. At the limit, b equals zero.) Richard Muth has estimated the density function for each of 46 U.S. urban areas for 1950.[7] I regressed the logs of Muth's parameter estimates on log of urbanized area population and regional dummy variables and obtained results supporting Figure 14.3. Putting the equations in antilog form, these estimates were obtained:

$$A = 6.03(1.71^{*NE} 0.73^W)P^{0.208 \bullet}; R^2 = 0.26$$

$$b = 4.54(1.49^{\bullet NE} 0.90^W)P^{-0.424}; R^2 = 0.34$$

*: significant at .05 level; •: significant at .10 level. NE = 0, 1 and W = 0, 1 depending on region of observation.

The appearance of dummy variables in the logs leads to the somewhat complicated expression in the antilogs. Thus the A equation is of the form $A = CP^{0.208}$, where $C = 6.03$ times 1.71 given the Northeast region, $C = 6.03$ times 0.73 given the West, and $C = 6.03$ times 1.00 given urban areas in the remainder of the country, the north central and southern regions. P refers to urbanized area population in thousands. The hypothesis of equality to one is rejected for the P coefficient in the A equation, that is, A does <u>not</u> increase proportionately with population.

TABLE 14.1

Average Density for Urbanized Areas, Their Major Central Cities, and Their Suburban Fringe Areas, 1960 and 1970

Region and Population Size of Urbanized Areas, in Thousands[a]	Average Density: Population Per Square Mile						Number of Cases[c]
	Urbanized Areas		Major Central Cities[b]		Suburban Fringe Areas		
	1970	1960	1970	1960	1970	1960	
Regional Averages							
United States	2815.6	3306.1	4555.4	5310.8	1967.4	1963.0	206[d]
Northeast	3316.4	3620.8	7563.0	8096.0	2216.2	2212.0	44
Southeast and North Central	2722.5	3345.1	3986.3	4929.2	1786.1	1910.6	111
Southwest and West	2586.4	2949.9	3199.3	3738.3	2150.5	1860.2	51[d]
Regional and Population Size Averages							
United States							
New York City	6683.0	7512.0	26,343.0	25,966.0	3580.0	3541.0	1
2,500-<10,000	4808.5	5117.2	12,836.0	13,435.0	3514.8	3383.0	8
1,000-<2,500	3445.0	3852.1	7,045.1	7,654.5	2679.1	2660.9	18
250-<1,000	2829.1	3210.6	4,410.8	5,184.4	2263.1	1984.3	56
0-<250	2592.4	3164.7	3,689.9	4,474.7	1630.6	1756.4	125
Northeast							
New York City	6683.0	7512.0	26,343.0	25,966.0	3580.0	3541.0	1
2,500-<10,000	4670.5	5387.0	14,550.0	15,370.0	3289.0	3572.5	2
1,000-<2,500	4575.3	5425.3	11,129.0	12,063.0	3241.3	3501.0	4
250-<1,000	3412.9	3488.8	7,796.4	8,514.2	2455.9	2181.1	11
0-<250	2848.3	3113.4	5,655.8	6,062.0	1822.2	1870.9	26
Southeast and North Central							
2,500-<10,000	4905.0	5541.5	13,039.5	14,058.0	3220.5	3142.5	2
1,000-<2,500	3148.4	3592.8	7,147.5	7,956.4	2425.8	2494.8	8
250-<1,000	2705.8	3266.3	3,928.1	4,867.7	1893.7	1983.1	29
0-<250	2621.2	3288.3	3,407.0	4,364.0	1631.8	1782.3	72
Southwest and West							
2,500-<10,000	4850.0	4423.0	10,918.5	10,877.0	4035.0	3434.0	2
1,000-<2,500	3087.0	3149.0	4,185.8	4,313.0	2642.2	2322.5	6
250-<1,000	2651.3	2918.2	2,958.1	3,469.3	2800.3	1851.2	16
0-<250	2269.1	2815.3	2,551.2	3,241.1	1492.9	1637.9	27[d]

Notes and Source for Table 14.1

[a]Regions based on Department of Commerce classification. East includes New England and Mideast. West includes Rocky Mountains, Far West, and Hawaii. See Survey of Current Business, May 1971, pp. 20-24.

[b]"Major Central City" consists of one city for each urbanized area and is that city having the greatest population if more than one city appears.

[c]Cases limited to urbanized areas with observations in both 1960 and 1970 and with nonzero population in the suburban fringe.

[d]Beaumont, Texas, suburban fringe excluded because 1960 population consisted of three persons and density of one person per square mile. Hence, one less case was used in obtaining both the 1960 and the 1970 average for the suburban fringe, with 205, 50, and 26 cases, respectively, appearing for the U.S. average, regional average, and regional-population size average.

Source: Averages based on data appearing in U.S. Bureau of the Census, U.S. Census of Population: 1970, Number of Inhabitants, Final Report PC(1)-A1, United States Summary, 1971, Table 20.

The regional dummy effects square with the thesis of Figure 14.2. Northeastern urban areas are the oldest, Western the newest, and those in other regions are in-between. As noted above, we can expect the impact of the automobile to be a function of age of area, with newer urban areas much more auto-oriented than older. Investment in roads and buildings is rather long term; it is much more expensive to insert freeways in built-up than in sparsely settled areas.

James Barr obtained individual urban area estimates of A and b for 1960, using essentially the same sample of census tracts that Muth had employed for 1950, but estimates for only 30 areas were obtained, because of massive redefinition of census tracts in the remaining cases.[8] Between 1950 and 1960 there was generally substantial reduction in both A and b, presumably reflecting the growth in intraurban highways and attendant suburbanization in the period. Comparing Barr to Muth estimates, the 1960 value of A declined to .65, and that of b declined to .63 of the corresponding 1950 value, on average. These changes correspond to the T_1 to T_2 shift of Figure 14.2. Regression results using the Barr estimates as data show considerable similarity to the 1950 cases:

$$A = 2.89(1.92^{\bullet NE} 0.63^{W})P^{0.236} ; R^2 = 0.21$$

$$b = 11.80(1.41^{NE} 0.69^{W})P^{-0.616*}; R^2 = 0.34$$

The hypothesis that the elasticity of P equals one in the A equation is again rejected.

Some additional evidence on shifts in density with time and population size is shown in Table 14.1 using average densities for urbanized areas, their corresponding central cities, and their suburban fringes, by region and population size for 1960 and 1970.

Despite an occasional anomaly, the data of Table 14.1 appear to square well with the analysis. Density generally increases with population size in both 1960 and 1970; there is usually a decline in density during the decade; and density appears to be a function of age of area, with generally lowest densities in the Southwest and West, highest in the East, for given population size. Although density generally declines over time, the trend is not pronounced for the suburban fringe; the West, in fact, shows some cases with a marked increase. The general result squares with the suburban shift of Figures 14.2 and 14.3, while the Western case may involve a slowing down in impact of the automobile. Viewing central cities, the only increase over time occurs for New York City and for the West. The former probably reflects the impetus to Staten Island development given much better access to the center via a new bridge; the latter is a result of an increase in Los Angeles density, since San Francisco's

FIGURE 14.4

Estimated Carbon Monoxide Isolines, Washington, D.C., 1964

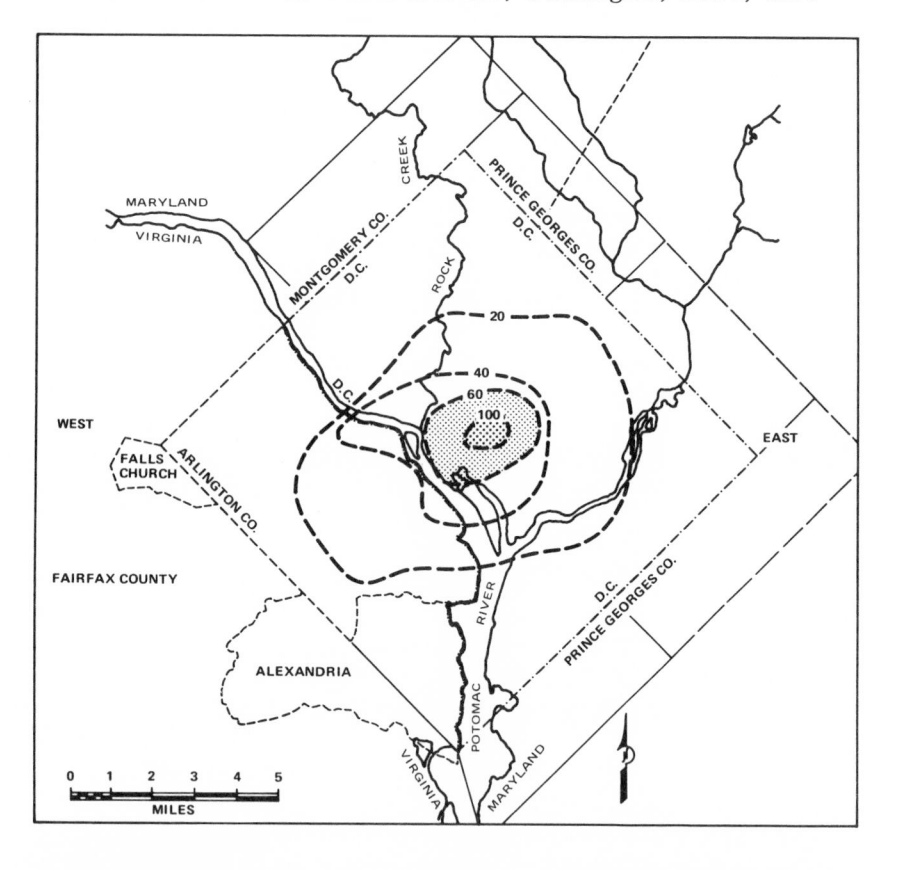

Source: Wayne Ott, John F. Clarke, and Guntis Ozolins, Calcu-
lating Future Carbon Monoxide Emissions and Concentrations from
Urban Traffic Data (Durham, N.C.: Public Health Service, 1967),
Figure 3, p. 10.

declined. This might well involve the effect of population increase
outweighing that of the automobile during the decade, suggestion some
reduction in the impact of the automobile has occurred.

Having documented the shifts in the density function, I note a
fair amount of additional evidence that can tie the shift of Figure 14.3
to the effect of pollution-disamenity. Such evidence takes the form of
(1) theoretical analyses arriving at similar conclusions on spatial
distribution using a somewhat different framework (examples include

studies by Peter Rydell and by Robert Strotz and Colin Wright);[9] (2) a number of empirical studies that exhibit a negative impact of air pollution and/or noise on property values (examples include reports by Ronald Ridker and J. A. Henning, Robert Anderson and Thomas Crocker, John Jaksch, Paul Dygert and David Sanders, and Frank Emerson);[10] (3) a number of intrametropolitan plots of air pollution showing considerable increases in levels with density and/or proximity to the urban center (an example, showing carbon monoxide concentrations for the Washington, D.C. area, appears as Figure 14.4). Though less extensive, there are similar data on noise.[11] Greenery, parks, open space, increased privacy, and less crowding are other amenities that can be involved in an outward shift, assuming such amenities have high-income elasticity and that average income increases over time. Certainly, sample surveys show a majority of respondents preferring the peace and quiet of the periphery to the hustle and bustle of the center,[12] though this is obviously a generalized preference, holding most, but not all, of the time.

Interurban Relationships

This section develops some highly simplified models of interurban population distribution through the application of the theory of the firm. Think of urban areas as analogous to firms in production theory, with a single output, produced by all areas, and only two inputs: labor and land. Urban land is employed either in production or in residential use. For this stripped-down model, the closest real-life analogue might be a situation where laborers make bricks from clay and sleep on the earth. But even in more complex and realistic cases the analogy between urban areas and firms does not seem terribly strained, given the existence of new towns as single-owner corporate enterprises, for example.

Population is assumed to be a constant multiple of the labor force; thus, say one worker corresponds to three residents. An individual area's employment of labor is determined by the intersection of its demand for labor, equal to labor's value of marginal product (VMP), and the supply of labor. Production functions vary between locales, with some places more productive than others, with the differences reflected in the VMP of labor. If labor supply were perfectly elastic, and two urban areas were being compared, we would have Figure 14.5, where N_1 and N_2 are equilibrium quantities of labor, and wages paid equals P_N times the respective quantity. Total product equals the area under the VMP curve, with the residual "profit" paid to land as the residual claimant.

FIGURE 14.5

The Labor Market for Two Urban Areas of Varying
Productivity, Assuming Constant Supply of Labor

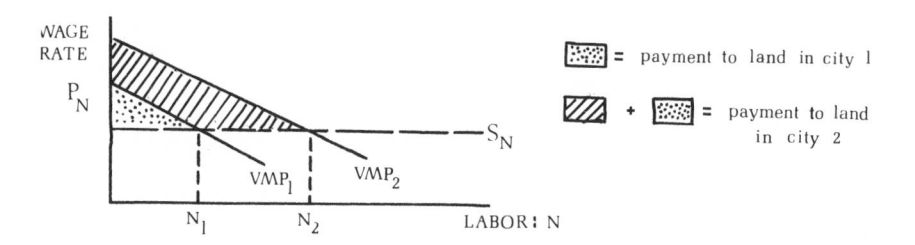

Source: Compiled by the author.

The assumption that production functions vary between places
is crucial and merits some extended reflection upon its rationale and
implications. As rationale it is argued that the natural resource base,
defined broadly, differs between locales and enters each locale's
production function. The natural resource base is seen as including
both locational characteristics and the supply of natural goods. Locational characteristics include such things as (1) the nature of production in the urban area's hinterland, and the needs of the hinterland
for services by a market cetner; (2) access to various transportation
networks and to market centers on those networks, yielding comparative advantage in regional, national, and world trade; and as general-
ization of this item, (3) "gravity" effects of the regional and national
distribution of population. The supply of natural goods includes such
things as the availability of water and its quality; soil characteristics
affecting construction: slope, drainage, rock composition; climate
characteristics; and risk of natural disasters (earthquake, flood,
hurricane, etc.). Rivers and harbors can be classified under both
headings.

As indicated in Figure 14.5, the effect of the natural resource
base will enter into total rent and should be capitalized into land
values. In this sense we can identify the fixed factor, land, with
natural resources, broadly conceived. In a more sophisticated formulation, however, the fixed factor may be yet more inclusive. In a
less than long-run context that may nevertheless last a long time, the
fixed factor will include public and private infrastructure embedded
in raw land—roads, sewers, utility lines, grading, etc. For a

somewhat shorter, but still long, period it generally will include urban structures.

Historically, major transportation networks and major cities developed in tandem. Again, older cities have an advantage, in an inflationary age, of (in effect) reaping capital gains on infrastructure laid down in earlier times. Of course times change and older infrastructure often has the disadvantage of having been put in place before the automobile. Yet it seems likely that the transportation network and infrastructure factors have given established cities some net advantage over a long period. Thus, European cities destroyed in World War II were rebuilt on the same sites. And it has been noted that very few American new towns have been developed since the time of the Civil War. [13]

Entrepreneurial capacity of various forms may be a component of the fixed factor. This could include such things as the managerial ability of the original urban land developers or later land owners, as well as the managerial abilities of local political functionaries. Wilbur Thompson identifies the service sector and universities as part of the long-term economic base. [14] Insofar as such are really fixed to a locale, they can be viewed as part of the fixed factor.

An important implication of the argument behind Figure 14.5 is that there is no one "optimal" size of city. The notion that such exists seems to draw on an even more simple-minded production model than that employed here, to wit, a production function that is the same for all firms in an industry. But there is a size distribution of firms in every industry, which is generally rationalized by arguing that production and cost functions differ between firms, perhaps because of differences in entrepreneurial capacity or in other fixed factors drawing economic rent, so that different firm sizes and the existence of nonzero profit are plausible in a long-run context.

Consider a Cobb-Douglas analogue to Figure 14.5: $X_i = K_i N_i^\gamma$ where X_i is output of urban area i, N_i is labor employed, K_i is a constant term specific to area i, and varying between areas as a function of the urban economic base, and γ is the elasticity of output with respect to labor, assumed constant and less than one. The assumption $\gamma < 1$ is necessary for profit maximization and of course tends to deny agglomeration economies. If such really exist, we can assume they have been exhausted. (It seems unlikely they exist for all areas, for then we would never see urban areas below a certain size.)

Given profit maximization, we can write

$$\frac{\partial(X_i P_X - N_i P_N)}{\partial N_i} = 0$$

yielding

$$P_X\left(\gamma \frac{X_i}{N_i}\right) = P_N$$

where P_X and P_N are price of output and labor respectively. Profit equals $(1 - \gamma)(X_i P_X)$, identified here as rent. If we solve for X_i and N_i in terms of parameters we obtain:

$$\overset{\circ}{X}_i = [K_i P_X^{\gamma} P_N^{-\gamma} \gamma^{\gamma}]^{\frac{1}{1-\gamma}} = CK_i^{\frac{1}{1-\gamma}} \qquad \overset{\circ}{N}_i = \left(\frac{P_X}{P_N}\gamma\right)\overset{\circ}{X}_i$$

where C is a constant and ∘ denotes solution value.

It is instructive to examine equilibrium levels of X_i as K_i and γ change. Defining a base output as that obtained for $K_i = 1$, relative outputs for larger values of K_i are shown in Table 14.2, which may afford insight on the distribution of urban area size. For returns to scale close to one, a small difference in K_i yields a large difference in equilibrium output. And available evidence suggests real-world returns to scale are in the .97 to .99 range. The reasoning runs this way: returns to scale equals the factor share of variable inputs at equilibrium, corresponding to γ in the two-input model, which can be estimated as one minus the factor share of rent. If buildings are included, rent comprises about 3 percent of national income, while rent for land only amounts to about 1 percent of national income. Since 90 percent of real estate value is in the nonfarm sector, this estimate is taken as applicable to the typical urban area. From Table 14.2, with $\gamma = .99$, it can be seen that an area that is 5 percent more productive than average, that is, with $K_i = 1.05$, will have an output, and population, 132 times larger than average. An urban area that is 10 percent more productive ($K_i = 1.10$), will be some 13,780 times larger, essentially the ratio of the New York City SMSA to a hamlet of 1,000 persons.

Table 14.2 suggests there may not be too much difference between countries with one primate city and countries with urban areas at a range of sizes. The pure primate city is good enough, in terms of technical efficiency, to prevent any rival from being established— but its relative efficiency may be only a bit higher than that of the largest urban area in a country with many rivals.

The analysis here might be the start of a theory of interurban size distribution.

The discussion of the interurban case to this point has concentrated on the demand side, assuming P_{Ni} constant as a first approximation. Let me now focus on the supply of labor. In Figure 14.5

TABLE 14.2

Equilibrium Output Relative to Base Output
(for $X_i = K_i N_i^\gamma$)

| K_i | γ = elasticity of output with respect to input | | | | | |
| | .75 | .90 | .95 | .98 | .99 | .995 |
	$\overset{\circ}{X}_i(K_i, \gamma)/\overset{\circ}{X}_i \;\; (K_i = 1.00, \gamma)$					
1.00	1.00	1.00	1.00	1.00	1.00	1.00
1.01	1.04	1.11	1.22	1.64	2.70	7.30
1.02	1.08	1.22	1.49	2.69	7.20	52.00
1.05	1.22	1.63	2.65	11.70	132.00	17,290.00
1.10	1.46	2.59	6.73	117.40	13,780.00	$10^{8.3}$
1.50	5.06	57.70	3,325.00	$10^{8.8}$	$10^{17.6}$	$10^{35.2}$

X_i = output of city i, N_i = labor input, $\overset{\circ}{X}$ = equilibrium output.

Source: Compiled by the author.

an increase in labor force is associated with increased total rent for land in production. We could have treated rent for residential land as a component of the rental payment in Figure 14.5 if we had defined urban output to encompass residential consumption. Alternatively, the residential land market could have been treated separately. In any event land in residential use should yield the same rent per acre as in nonresidential use, for given distance from the center. The increase in total rent can be expected to involve both more land brought into urban use from the hinterland (suburban land conversion) and an increase in price per acre, as indicated in the intraurban discussion above. (As an incidental note, the area under a rent curve as a function of distance from the center, as in Figures 14.2 and 14.3, should correspond to the area comprising rent in Figure 14.5.)

Now, an increase in rent facing workers implies the need for higher money wages to attract and keep such workers in an urban area that is moving to a higher equilibrium output. To expand on this, rent and transportation costs are substitutes, as noted earlier. At the center the totality of the two will be entirely rent; at the urban periphery the costs will be entirely transportation costs, assuming negligible opportunity costs for land in nonurban use. Hence the term

FIGURE 14.6

The Labor Market for Two Urban Areas of Varying Productivity,
with Sloping Supply Curve for Labor

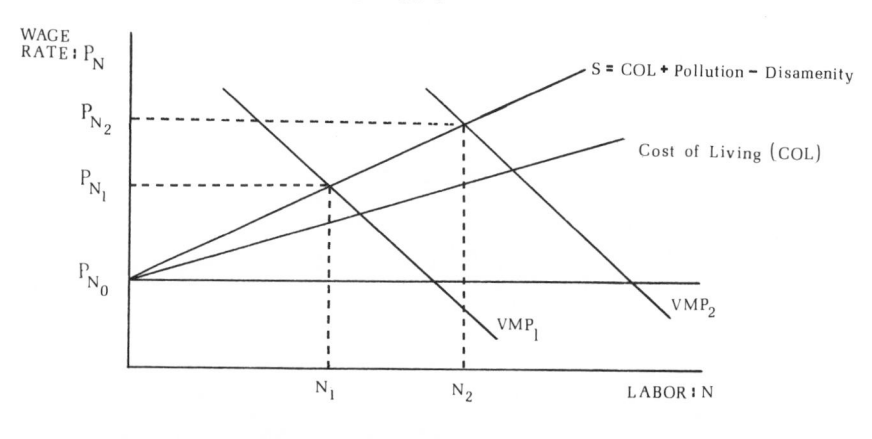

Source: Compiled by the author.

rent is shorthand for rent plus transport costs, and both will increase,
on average, given a population increase. Further, such cost increases
will tend to have multiplier effects. Food costs, for example, should
increase both because grocery store rents are higher and because
grocery store clerks' wages are higher to cover their higher residential rents. The conventional cost-of-living index will reflect the
totality of cost increases with size, for goods traded on markets, but
will neglect such items as the value of time spent in the journey to
work.

It was argued above that pollution-disamenity associated with
density would cause shifts in intraurban population distribution. However, there are some kinds and levels of pollution-disamenity that are
associated with population size, per se. As a consequence we can
expect that workers will need an additional amount of compensatory
income to cover the money and psychic costs involved. Since the compensatory income needed will increase with population size, a long-run
supply of labor in effect is generated, as shown by S in Figure 14.6.
The supply curve can be disaggregated into two basic components:
cost of living (covering market costs) and pollution-disamenity
(covering psychic costs).

Figure 14.6 shows equilibrium labor quantity and money wages
for two urban areas. Although P_{N_2} is above P_{N_1}, real wages in both
areas equal P_{N_0} in terms of workers' satisfaction. (Of course producers must pay more for their labor in city 2 than in city 1, with a

FIGURE 14.7

Estimated Rent Loss Caused by
Pollution-Disamenity

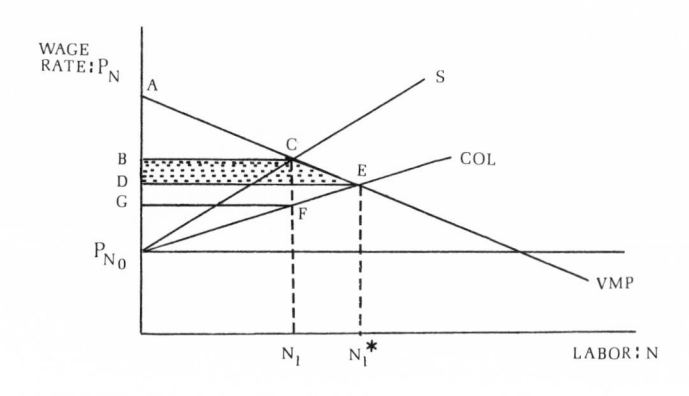

Source: Compiled by the author.

corresponding increase in labor productivity, as measured either by
VMP or average product.) In the longest run, P_{N_0} is equivalent to
the wage rate in the smallest-size settlement (presumably on the farm)
and is determined by the society's standard of living, in turn reflecting
the preference for income per capita versus children. (Standards of
living and P_{N_0} have been increasing over time in Western societies,
Japan, and perhaps some developing countries.)

The supply argument of Figure 14.6 has a number of applications.
As an example, Figure 14.7 exhibits the loss in rent caused by the
existence of pollution-disamenity, equal to BCED. A superficial estimate of rent loss might yield BCFG, rather than BCED; but area
BCED accounts for the changes induced by expansion from N_1 to N_1^*,
neglected in the BCFG accounting.

In empirical work, identification problems will be avoided under
the assumption VMP varies between areas but the supply relation is
stable. Put another way, in estimating the supply relation, urban
population size can be treated as essentially exogenous, since in- and
outmigration, as of a point in time, will be a small fraction of total
population. One can expect some short-run disequilibrium conditions
to move observed points above and below the supply curve, but this

should not affect estimates unless the direction of disequilibrium is associated with urban size, say if large SMSAs were generally expanding and small SMSAs were generally contracting. This does not appear to be the case. Finally, estimation will be improved if other factors affecting money wages are introduced. These can include region and climate, though region may be a surrogate for a number of climate effects. Good climate can be expected to shift supply down, while bad climate will shift it up, assuming workers demanded less or more money wages in the respective cases. However, some of the climate effects will likely be capitalized into land values, so there is some question of incidence. This poses a problem in estimation only if incidence varies with size. A way around the problem, in theory, is to view better climate embedded in land value as corresponding to more standardized units of average quality land, with Figures 14.6 and 14.7 drawn assuming that all places have their land measured on this common scale.

Table 14.3 exhibits some estimates of urban scale effects obtained from published estimates plus a series of regression equations using SMSA population size and region as independent variables.[15]

In Table 14.3, column (1) exhibits per capital income relative to the U.S. average by SMSA population class, while column (2) exhibits estimates of money wage relatives for a homogeneous population; that is, for the same job, this column shows the wage differential by locale. Column (3) exhibits the cost of living index for the conventional marketbasket and can be interpreted as the relative cost needed to purchase that marketbasket. Column (4) is the ratio of (1) and (2), which can be interpreted as exhibiting differences in labor quality and/or in factor mix. The latter will include any differences attributable to rent relative to other factors. Column (5) is the ratio of column (2) to (3) and in effect shows that fraction of the wage differential not accounted for by cost of living; under that interpretation, it is the net money payment for psychic costs, assuming (3) adequately covers all market costs, perhaps a somewhat strained assumption, but plausible as a first approximation.

In all of the columns the indexes increase with population size. There is a marked North-South differential in columns (1) and (2), which is pretty well accounted for by differences in cost of living.

The evidence of Table 14.3 lends considerable support to the interurban relations hypothesized here.

The distinction between market and psychic costs is often a matter of convention. Thus evidence shows that environmental quality deteriorates with size; of course, quality can be improved by environmental management, but then the costs of such management can be expected to increase with size. Again, available evidence shows that rates for major crimes generally increase with urban size, <u>after</u>

TABLE 14.3

Estimated Urban Scale Effects, 1967

SMSA Population Class and Region (population in thousands)	Magnitudes Relative to U.S. Average				
	Per Capita Money Income (1)	Money Wages for Homogeneous Population Index (2)	Cost-of-Living Index (3)	Inferred Index of Labor Quality and Factor Mix = (1)/(2) (4)	Inferred Compensatory Payment for Net Quality Decline = (2)/(3) (5)
North					
0–<250	0.977	0.975	0.983	1.002	0.992
250–<500	1.006	1.021	0.996	0.985	1.025
500–<1,000	1.059	1.051	1.005	1.008	1.046
1,000–<2,500	1.125	1.099	1.013	1.024	1.085
2,500–<9,000	1.229	1.165	1.042	1.055	1.118
9,000+	1.369	1.205	1.102	1.136	1.094
South					
0–<250	0.835	0.860	0.916	0.971	0.939
250–<500	0.879	0.910	0.929	0.966	0.980
500–<1,000	0.934	0.940	0.938	0.994	1.002
1,000–<2,500	1.026	1.000	0.945	1.026	1.058

Sources: Column (1): Data in Survey of Current Business, May 1971, Tables 1 and 2, 20–31. Column (2): V. R. Fuchs, Differentials in Hourly Earnings by Region and City Size, 1959 (New York: National Bureau of Economic Research, Occasional Paper 101, 1967), Table 8, Ratio of Actual to Expected Hourly Earnings, p. 16; and data in Bureau of Labor Statistics, Area Wage Survey, Specific Metropolitan Area, 1968–69, Bulletin 1625-1 to 1625-90, Washington, D.C., 1970. Wages deflated by Consumer Price Index, 1957–59 = 1.00. Column (3) data on Cost of Living Indexes for family of four from J. C. Brackett, "New BLS Budgets Provide Yardsticks for Measuring Family Living Costs," Monthly Labor Review, April 1969, pp. 3–16.

accounting for a number of other explanatory factors, including ethnic composition. To some extent the risks of crime can be covered by insurance, but perhaps some of the losses involved are uninsurable (pain and suffering, for example). Transportation costs include operating cost, accident cost, and time cost, all of which appear to increase with urban size. Operating cost and accident insurance should show up as market costs in the cost-of-living index, but some portion of accident cost may not be covered by insurance, and time cost is clearly a nonmarket item in conventional cost-of-living accounting. Since rent and transport cost can be viewed as a combined cost, only part is picked up in the conventional cost-of-living index.

Some evidence may be noted on time cost in transportation. A sample survey shows that daily work trips in the New York metropolitan area average about 70 minutes in total (to and from work). Within the next 12 largest SMSAs total trip time averages about one hour, and for other SMSAs the total is 40 minutes. Outside metropolitan areas the total is about 25 minutes. [16] Rough calculations yielded an estimate of the value of these time differences as about 1 percent of income for each succeeding SMSA grouping, that is, the difference between New York and nonmetropolitan areas was estimated as equivalent to 4 percent of income, assuming work trip time is valued at one-third the wage rate, on the basis of evidence developed by M. E. Beesley. [17]

There is some evidence that congestion cost, as well as length of journey to work, increases with SMSA size. A. M. Voorhees et al. present data on a sample of 23 urban areas [18] that yield these results for average journey to work by automobile:

Urban area population, in thousands	Trip length, in miles	Miles per hour
10–<100	3.0	28.6
100–<1,000	5.0	28.6
1,000+	6.2	23.1

Area wage surveys indicate that hours of work per week decline somewhat with urban size; this will cause the hourly wage to rise faster than the weekly wage. Compensatory income can thus take the form of money wages (market) or fewer hours of work (psychic) if weekly wages are the basis for comparison.

APPLICATIONS TO ANALYSIS AND POLICY

The hypotheses developed here have a number of applications to analysis and policy. Intraurban density patterns are seen as the resultant of economizing behavior in response to a variety of forces. But many advocated, and some implemented, policies on urban form appear to involve the implicit assumptions that density patterns are rather arbitrary and capricious to begin with, and that a density pattern closer to heart's desire can be imposed by fiat. The green-belt idea would cut off development beyond a certain distance from the center, or below a certain density; new towns are often planned to have densities well above the average for their population size. The two notions are combined in Figure 14.8 and compared to the standard pattern. If imposed by fiat (as in England) the policies are likely to cause a loss in real income. If there is an attempt to sell these patterns on the open market, there is liable to be either failure of an appeal to a rather specialized clientele (the new towns of Reston vs. Columbia, perhaps; initially, Reston was somewhat more unconventional than Columbia).

Turning to interurban relations, the divergence of money income from real income as a function of region and population size implies the possibility of money illusion in income comparisons and policy. For example, economic studies of migration as a function of income have often yielded mediocre or poor results, possibly because money income was improperly deflated. Measurement using rigid yardsticks will not do too well when elastic yardsticks are needed. One application of this idea is to national income accounting. Deflating U.S. personal income by size of place indexes and taking Northern nonmetropolitan areas as base, I estimated the cost of urbanization as .133 of personal income in 1969. [19]

Government policy often involves imposition of uniform dollar levels nationally, disregarding the fact that a dollar is worth more in some places than in others.

Thus the Nixon administration's Family Assistance Plan apparently came to grief because of uniform payments, which would give southern, small locality poor much greater real income than the northern, big city poor. [20]

Because the post office has a uniform national pay scale, we could expect adjustments either through upgrading in rank or lower-quality labor and service in larger cities and the North relative to smaller cities and the South. There is some evidence that squares with this prediction. For the five-week period November 25, 1972,

FIGURE 14.8

Population Density Patterns

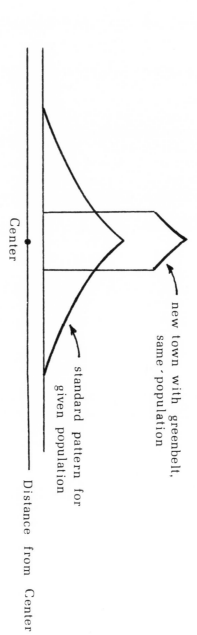

new town with greenbelt,
same population

standard pattern for
given population

Center

Distance from Center

Source: Compiled by the author.

to February 2, 1973, the percentage of next-day letter delivery by region and for New York City was as follows:[21]

National	82.6
New York City	68.6
East	84.8
Central	84.0
West	81.6
South	89.4

These percentages seem to square well with the money income differentials for the regions and for New York City.

The income tax rate is uniform nationally; hence, part of the cost-of-living differential involves an increment expressing the multiplier effect of progressive tax rates. Say disposable income in locale A had to be twice that in locale B to yield equivalent levels of welfare or real income, and assume an income tax rate of 10 percent at $5,000 of money income and of 20 percent at $10,000 of money income. Then $5,000 in locale B yields $4,500 of disposable income; to achieve $9,000 of disposable income in A, $11,250 of income is needed, so that the ratio of income between A and B will be 2.25 to yield a disposable income ratio of 2.00.

Some data is available to check this effect in practice. Using Bureau of Labor Statistics data for autumn 1971, cost of living for three income classes was regressed on region and log of SMSA population size.[22] Total budget and income tax levels were calculated from the fitted equations for three hypothetical size levels in the Western region. Results, in Table 14.4, indicate that the effect of the income tax accounts for up to 15 percent of the cost-of-living differential; that level occurs in the high-income, largest SMSA size grouping.

Some writers who dislike large cities and advocate a tax to limit entry might note that such a tax already exists.[23]

The argument that large cities impose negative effects on their inhabitants is met, I think, by the compensatory income notion embedded in Figure 14.6. The argument against large cities is that with increasing size there is a decline in the quality of life. I argue here that the decline is met by money income increases. Those who advocate limiting entry generally fall back on a "marginal social cost" idea: Entry should be limited to the point where the marginal cost of a new entrant equals his marginal product. But I see this as a form of monopoly, in effect drawing a marginal curve to the supply curve of Figure 14.6. The equating of two marginal curves is a monopolistic solution.

TABLE 14.4

Estimated Effect of SMSA Population on Budget and Income Taxes
for the Western Region, 1971

SMSA Population in thousands	Dollar Magnitudes			Calculated Indexes	
	Budget	Income Taxes	Budget Minus Taxes	Budget	Budget Minus Taxes
			Low-Income Class		
100	7,213	570	6,643	100.0	100.0
1,000	7,424	609	6,815	102.9	102.6
10,000	7,635	648	6,987	105.9	105.2
			Middle-Income Class		
100	10,294	1,135	9,159	100.0	100.0
1,000	10,784	1,243	9,541	104.8	104.2
10,000	11,275	1,350	9,925	109.5	108.4
			High-Income Class		
100	14,594	2,114	12,480	100.0	100.0
1,000	15,560	2,386	13,174	106.6	105.6
10,000	16,525	2,659	13,866	113.2	111.1

Source: Compiled by the author.

FIGURE 14.9

Result of Institutional Rearrangement
When Benefits Exceed Costs

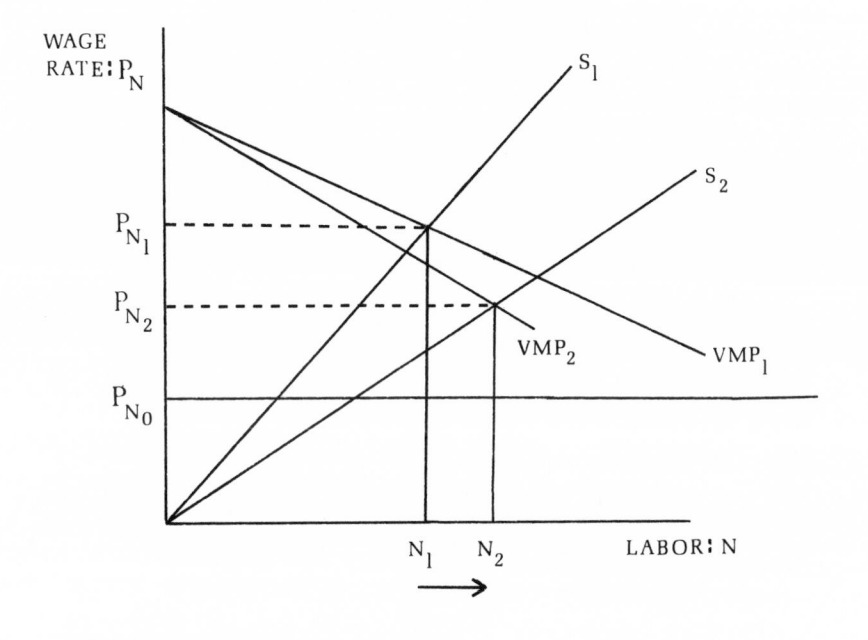

Source: Compiled by the author.

Consider the application of the marginal social cost idea to housing. If a new family comes into an area it will bid up the price of housing. The new price obtained is the marginal cost of housing to producers, but is an average cost to consumers. Because all previous consumers now pay a higher price there is a marginal social cost that is above market price. It follows the the traditional social cost argument that we ought to set a higher price than the market price to the new entrant: In effect, this will help keep the rascals out.

I see similar reasoning applying to urban transportation. Congestion tolls would make sense in situations where zero money price means fees are set wholly in terms of time; with congestion tolls, there could be a profitable-to-all exchange of time for money. However, most toll advocates seem to me to be plumping for a monopoly, rather than a competitive price.

I think the same reasoning applies in limiting entry to large cities. Monopoly is not only not very nice, in terms of distribution, but it is also wasteful, in terms of efficiency, involving the throwing away of real income. This is not to argue that the present is the best of all possible worlds. It is conceivable that institutional rearrangements, including effluent charges for pollutants and congestion tolls for highways, would yield net improvements. If benefits of such changes really exceeded costs, we could expect urban areas to become larger. Urban areas would be more attractive, both in the sense of being better places to live and in the sense of drawing people in. The situation is illustrated in Figure 14.9, which shows shifts imposed on Figure 14.6 by the presumed institutional rearrangement; VMP shifts down somewhat to express the cost of the rearrangement, but supply shifts down more, expressing the benefit: the need for compensatory income is considerably reduced. At equilibrium the city grows larger. If the institutional rearrangement reduces disamenity as a function of density, some intraurban reversal of sprawl can be expected, with the center becoming relatively more attractive.

In sum, then, proper recognition of the relations of urban scale and real income can yield a number of analytic and policy insights, with particular relevance in the domain of urban rent and transportation.

NOTES

1. This chapter draws on the author's previous reports on related topics: Irving Hoch, "Income and City Size," Urban Studies, October 1972; "Urban Scale and Environmental Quality," Commission on Population Growth and the American Future, Research Reports, Vol. III, Population, Resources and the Environment, ed. Ronald G. Ridker, 1972; and "Interurban Differences in the Quality of Life," in the book Transportation and the Quality of Life, eds. J. G. Rothenberg and Ian G. Heggie (London: Macmillan, 1974). The present chapter concentrates on and extends some of the themes in the prior reports.

2. Leo Srole, a sociologist, has been quoted on the point: "Studies have shown a direct correlation between the size of cities and the tempo at which people live. The bigger a city . . . the faster the tempo. . . . People are more in a hurry. They don't like to wait." New York Times, June 25, 1971, p. 3.

3. J. R. Meyer, J. F. Kain, M. Wohl, The Urban Transportation Problem (Cambridge, Mass.: Harvard University Press, 1965), p. 108.

4. For example, see Richard Muth, Cities and Housing (Chicago: University of Chicago Press, 1969); and Colin Clark, Population Growth and Land Use (New York: St. Martin's Press, 1968), concluding chapter.

5. Muth, op. cit., pp. 95-96; his Figure 1.

6. Edwin S. Mills, Studies in the Structure of the Urban Economy (Baltimore: Johns Hopkins University Press, 1972).

7. Muth, op. cit., Table 1, p. 142.

8. J. L. Barr, "Transportation Costs, Rent and Intra Urban Location," Department of Economics, Washington University, 1970, pp. 44-45.

9. C. Peter Rydell, Air Pollution and Urban Population Distribution (New York: Urban Research Center, Hunter College, City University of New York, 1968); Robert H. Strotz and Colin Wright, "Spatial Adaptation to Urban Air Pollution," paper presented at a meeting of Committee on Urban Economics, Chicago, 1970, pp. 2, 15.

10. Ronald G. Ridker, Economic Costs of Air Pollution (New York: Praeger, 1967), pp. 121, 137 in particular; Ronald G. Ridker with J. A. Henning, "The Determinants of Residential Property Values, with Special Reference to Air Pollution," Review of Economics and Statistics, May 1967; Robert J. Anderson, Jr. and Thomas D. Crocker, "Air Pollution and Housing," Paper No. 264 (Lafayette, Ind.: Purdue University, Institute for Research in the Behavioral, Economic and Management Sciences, January 1970), p. 12; and John Jaksch, "Air Pollution: Its Effects on Residential Property Values in Toledo, Oregon," Annals of Regional Science, December 1970, pp. 43-52, in particular, p. 46. U.S. Department of Commerce, Transportation System Noise Generation, Propagation and Alleviation, Ch. 4, by Paul K. Dygert and David L. Sanders, National Technical Information Service, Document PB 196391, 1970, pp. 4-11 to 4-36. Frank C. Emerson, "Valuation of Residential Amenities: An Econometric Approach," The Appraisal Journal, April 1972, pp. 268-78.

11. See Hoch, "Urban Scale and Environmental Quality," op. cit.

12. For example, see John B. Lansing and Gary Hendricks, Automobile Ownership and Residential Density (Ann Arbor: Survey Research Center, University of Michigan, June 1967), p. 138.

13. Carl Feiss, "America's Neglected Tradition," in The New City, ed. Donald Canty (New York: Praeger, 1969, published for Urban America, Inc.), p. 94.

14. Wilbur Thompson, "Internal and External Factors in the Development of Urban Economies," in Issues in Urban Economics ed. Harvey S. Perloff and Lowdon Wingo, Jr. (Baltimore: John Hopkins University Press, 1968), pp. 43-62.

15. Reported in detail in Hoch, "Interurban Differences in the Quality of Life," op. cit.

16. J. N. Morgan, I. A. Sirageldin, and N. Baerwaldt, Productive Americans, Survey Research Monograph 43 (Ann Arbor: University of Michigan, 1966), Table S-3, p. 80.

17. M. E. Beesley, "The Value of Time Spent in Traveling: New Evidence," Economica 32, No. 126, May 1965, pp. 174-185.

18. A. M. Voorhees et al., "Factors in Work-trip Lengths," Highway Research Record 141 (1966): 24-26.

19. Estimated in Hoch, "Interurban Differences in the Quality of Life," op. cit.

20. Daniel P. Moynihan, The Politics of a Guaranteed Income (New York: Random House, 1973), p. 354; and review of Moynihan by Peter Passell and Leonard Ross, New York Times Book Review, January 14, 1973, p. 16.

21. Peter Kihss, "A Slowing of Mail Delivery Conceded by Postal Chief," New York Times, February 18, 1973, p. 1.

22. U.S. Department of Labor, Office of Information, Autumn 1971 Urban Family Budgets, USDL-72-240, 1972.

23. For example, see Joseph Spengler, "Megalopolis: Resource Conserver or Resource Waster?" Natural Resources Journal, July 1967, pp. 376-95.

15

THE NBER PROTOTYPE URBAN SIMULATION MODEL

J. Royce Ginn

The transportation-land use study has been with us for two decades, and while many improvements have been made in the methods of analysis and the models used for projecting distributions of activities, there is still considerable room for improvement. Moving from methods that simply used "best-guess" factors and a lot of gutsy extrapolation, several successive attempts have been made to become more fundamental in this area. Transportation experts made the first steps by developing methods for estimating travel paths on the transportation system. The introduction of a new link in one location could then affect conditions in other locations. Better representations of urban activities could be obtained, but while travel-path techniques had become sophisticated, only the crudest of relations served to estimate the changes in activities that caused trips. Next, land use analysts began to insist that commercial activities responded to changes in the transportation system as well, and models began to emerge that incorporated this consideration. The state of the art has continued to change in some very important ways[1] even though the boxes drawn by early analysts before the term "systems analysis" began to be tossed about are often just as applicable to current methods.

We've a long way to go, of course, deepening our understanding and ability to reflect the conditions in urban areas. Even today trips are modeled as though they occurred spontaneously, and many discussions still begin, "Well, if you insist that transportation is a derived demand. . . . "

But there are other things happening in urban areas besides trip making. For example, growth, blight, abandonment, and new developments are all items of importance to the modern analyst of urban areas. The transportation system interacts with these other activities and is as important to them as any number of more obvious elements. It is one of many fundamental parts of the background that affects the competition for living space and the pattern of urban development.

This chapter will not succeed in tracing the full interactions of the transport system with urban growth, nor will it present the final model that will incorporate all of the relations between urban transportation and conditions in urban areas. This chapter describes a model, the NBER (National Bureau of Economic Research) Urban Simulation Model, which incorporates a number of additional factors and further advances the state of the art in land use-transportation modeling. To show the potential utility of this model for transportation analysis the chapter presents an illustrative simulation test of the effects of freeway additions in the Pittsburgh SMSA, the urban area used to calibrate the NBER model. The principal difference in the simulation portrayed in this chapter and hundreds of other such tests is, of course, in the model employed.

THE NBER MODEL AND SUPPORTING RESEARCH

The NBER model represents the housing market in an urban area as well as the interactions of this market with the distribution of employment and the transportation system of the area. The model is currently being developed as a tool for analyzing policy alternatives in the housing market, but it can also be used to study transportation alternatives. It talks about families, jobs, houses, apartment buildings, construction, moving, maintenance of housing, taxes, travel time and costs, and neighborhoods. It is, of course, simply a mathematical abstraction of these elements.

The representations of urban spatial activities in the NBER model are based on several econometric studies.[2] These studies reflected long-standing interests among members of the research team drawn from their experiences in urban studies since the early 1960s. The process has been an incremental one, building on earlier analysis,[3] and while we tend to read the critics[4] of the accepted methods a little more closely than the proponents, we would have made little progress if the accepted methods had not been available.[5]

In each investigation we attempted to reduce findings to more fundamental causal relations. We then addressed the problem of simulation by making use of the more fundamental assumptions as to the rational behavior of families, producing submodels that reflected these assumptions, and finally linking together the submodels into one overall model. Hopefully the overall model would produce results that appeared to be the outcome of fairly complex considerations by families, thus testing our basic hypothesis that it is the system that is complex, while the decisions are actually simple.

The NBER urban simulation model can be thought of as a series of submodels that take information from, and make changes in, a multidimensional matrix of states. Each dimension of this matrix is some characteristic of families relevant to their behavior or reflecting their situation in an urban area. The contents of the matrix are the number of families in each state. The matrix currently has the following dimensions: (1) family income, (2) age of the head of household, (3) family size, (4) education level of the head of household, (5) the type of dwelling unit in which the family lives, (6) the residential location of the dwelling unit with its neighborhood quality indicated, and (7) the workplace location of the head of household.

This matrix contains information that addresses a great number of urban measures. For example, it can indicate work trips if summed over all dimensions except residential and workplace locations, or the different types of occupied dwelling units in each residential area, or the distribution of dwelling unit types occupied by income groups, or even the number of jobs held by primary workers in each workplace location. We also keep four additional matrices by residence zone (the stock of dwelling units, dwelling unit prices [or rents], the property tax rate, and an index of neighborhood quality in the zone) along with the matrix of travel cost between residence zones and workplaces. Combining these matrices with the basic state matrix provides information about vacant units in each residence zone, costs of the journey to work, and many other measures of the conditions of families in the urban area being simulated.

Other matrices are required when one attempts to forecast changes in the basic matrix. For example, we made use of a matrix that represents the cost of converting any housing type to any other type, including the cost of converting raw land into a house or apartment building, and another matrix of maintenance costs for each dwelling unit type.

Even with all of this detail, there are omissions that must be handled with as-yet-undeveloped methods. Retired and unemployed household heads can be assigned to work zones $N + 1$ and $N + 2$ respectively, and special routines developed to handle them, but secondary workers pose a fundamental problem. The interaction of industry location choices with the urban land market is not clearly defined as yet, and currently we make these assignments exogenously. Renters and owners have fundamentally different moving rates, and the problem of race prejudice in the housing market is currently ignored.

We are currently engaged in further research to address these problems and to further modify methods employed in our submodels. We also wish to enrich our measure of neighborhood quality, which is currently limited to fraction of population in low-income groups and fraction of dwelling units of low quality.

In simulating changes in the basic state matrix the submodels are used once in each annual set of events. The model is then used in a recursive fashion, using outputs from the previous year's simulation as inputs for the current year's simulation. The selection of one year as a simulation period is somewhat arbitrary, but there is less latitude than one might initially expect. The "construction" concept places a lower limit on the time frame, since it is assumed that a dwelling unit can be constructed or converted from one type to another during the time specified. One constraint on an upper limit is derived from trying to select a time period during which a household will make only one move. Clearly, satisfying both constraints is impossible since a lower limit of two years might be required for the construction of some buildings, and an upper limit of one month would be required to catch the movements of young unmarrieds.

There is one fundamental concept underlying the NBER simulation model that forces us into this general recursive framework. We believe that an equilibrium condition in an urban area, if it exists at all, is inherently dynamic. We, and others, have observed only the most temporary degrees of stability in most urban measures over time as incomes rise, tastes change, the transport system is altered, and new technologies are introduced. A more appropriate characterization of urban areas would be that they are in disequilibrium and that their path of adjustment is dependent upon the particular configuration of their existing capital stocks as well as many other factors.

DESCRIPTIONS OF THE SUBMODELS

The submodels used in the NBER prototype, in the order of application, are INPUT, FILTER, INDUSTRY, MOVE, DEMAND, SUPPLY, MARKET, and PRICE FORMATION. Each of these is represented by one or more computerized subroutines, and all of them except INPUT are used in recursive steps subsequent to the first year's simulation. The PRICE FORMATION submodel serves the function of ending a year's simulation and determining "inputs" for subsequent recursions. Detailed descriptions of the submodels would take over 200 pages of typescript, but fortunately the details exist elsewhere. [6] We will quickly indicate the problems handled by the submodels after pointing out that the linkages are shown in Figure 15.1.

FIGURE 15.1

Submodel Linkages

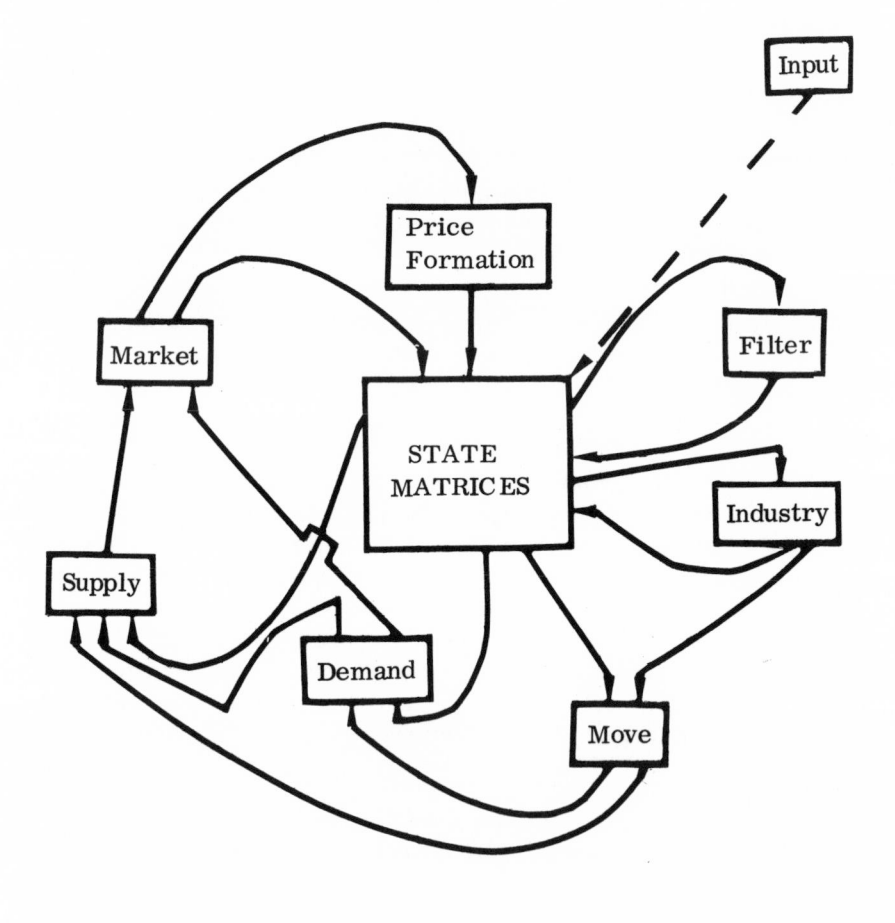

Sequence is clockwise, initialized by Input.

Exogenous changes (Zoning constraints, Transportation links, Tax rates, etc.) are signaled and enter cycle at Input position during any annual recursion.

Source: Compiled by the author.

The Filter Submodel

It is observed in urban areas that some housing, particularly near the urban center, "filters" down over time from the original owners to some economically less fortunate group. The typical example is a big single-family house, which is allowed to deteriorate, and then becomes a multifamily unit such as a boarding house or even a legitimate apartment unit. We have extracted that portion of the concept that deals with quality changes. In our model these changes are based on the differential prices for the various qualities of a structure type in a given neighborhood and the cost of maintaining a given quality level or improving its quality. It is viewed as an economic decision made for possible resale or rent adjustments. The portion of the concept of "filtering" that has to do with subsequent occupants is never explicitly addressed, but it is expected to be a natural outcome of the general problem for those structures that are lowered in quality.

The Industry Submodel

The location of industry (all types of employment) is viewed as one of the driving forces of the model. The types of jobs and their location is crucial, and in a narrow sense the existence of each job "creates" a family. The version of the model used in this chapter had no "vacant" jobs or unemployed workers (these features are incorporated in the version currently being developed), and all employment changes were exogenous.

The prototype INDUSTRY submodel accepted any exogenous change in the form of number-of-employees at a workplace by one-digit SIC (Standard Industrial Classification) group. Positive or negative changes were allowed, but it did no further simulation other than quantifying the numbers and types of households associated with the SIC categories so supplied. A transformation matrix exists for each employment category, which reflects the distribution of household types (age, family size, income, and education) typically observed. The distributions were considered to be different for three types of work zones. That is, the same SIC group is typically composed of workers with different family characteristics if the group is located in the "office section" of town, an "industrial zone, " or in intermediate areas.

The MOVE Submodel

Fundamentally the MOVE submodel determines which households will move this year, the type of household they will vacate, and where the vacated dwelling unit is located. The probability of moving is determined by the family type, and a fixed percentage of each type of family moves each year. Conceptually the MOVE submodel operates on the basic matrix introduced at the beginning of this chapter. Actually, such a matrix cannot be stored in a computer because of its enormous size (over 345 million cells in an ordinary transportation study framework with about 300 work-residence zones). Instead, marginal distributions of the basic matrix are retained (work trips by income class, households by work place by type of house occupied, and housing stock by residence zone) and the basic matrix is approximated from these marginal matrices.

This submodel also "updates" the households that are moving. That is, the head of household is "aged," family size categories are altered, old people die and are replaced by young people, etc. Since only the "movers" are updated, the types and amounts of updates are a function of the average time between moves and, therefore, a function of the annual probability of moving.

We are at this time planning to rewrite the whole routine and move to disk storage of nonempty cells of the basic matrix. We can then annually "update" all families and develop more explicit moves based on family size changes, etc. The above description applies to the Pittsburgh I version, which was used in this study.

The Demand Submodel

The function of this submodel is to match households seeking housing with types of housing. The match depends primarily on a generalized "price," which includes the purchase price or annual rent and the appropriately scaled "cost" of the work trip. The submodel is passed information as to how many of each type of household seeking housing are employed in each work zone. Prior analysis has provided equations that distribute each household type over all types of housing, given the relative price of housing. Our test model had 3,840 equations (96 x 40, one for each household type-housing type combination), each of which has parameters for 40 relative "prices." A normalizing step is made for each household type so that exactly 100 percent of them are distributed over the housing types.

To the degree that the sum over all household types seeking a particular type of housing exceeds the number of houses of that type made available by movers or vacant, an "excess demand" is created. This "excess demand" is augmented by a nominal vacancy rate and is passed to the "construction industry" in the SUPPLY submodel. The demand will not necessarily be met by the "construction industry," but it serves as an upper bound on their activities.

The Supply Submodel

An imaginary "construction industry" is viewed as operating the SUPPLY submodel. It has complete information as to the purchase-selling price of each housing type in each location. Further, it makes use of a static technology and knows the cost of converting any housing type into any other housing type, including the conversion of raw land into a dwelling unit. It is not an internally optimizing industry, however. It is assumed to be composed of small groups that are capable of handling only one construction job a year, and they actively bid for the most profitable jobs. The supply of such groups is perfectly elastic, so that there are just enough groups to perform all of the profitable jobs, but none of the unprofitable jobs are undertaken just to keep a work crew together for another year. Actually, the profitable jobs are performed only so long as there is an "excess demand" for the housing type that is to be output. Since a significant portion of the activity is the conversion of housing types, the use of housing as an input may cause a shortage where there was previously no "excess demand." In such a case the profitable list is researched to see if this newly created demand can be satisfied. Typically we observed four to eight such occurrences in each year simulated.

In the test simulations on Pittsburgh data of the roughly 82,000 conceptually possible annual conversions or creations, we observe around 2,500 that would be profitable if the inputs were available in each case, and less than a tenth of these have either the inputs available or a positive demand for the outputs so that they are simulated to actually occur. Each activity may produce from one dwelling unit to several thousand dwelling units, subject only to the limitations of inputs and "excess demands." Only vacant land and those dwelling units that are vacant or have been vacated by movers are eligible as inputs.

The Market Submodel

The operations of the previous submodels have provided the number of households desiring each housing type and the number of units of each type available at each location. The MARKET submodel matches households by income and workplace to the housing type available in each residence zone by minimizing the aggregate transportation price (different for each income group) between the workplaces and the residence locations. The "shadow prices" on each residence zone indicate the "location rent" for that house type in that zone. We are able to obtain these shadow prices for all house types in each zone whether the house type actually exists in the zone or not. (These numbers are necessary for the next annual simulation in the FILTER and SUPPLY submodels.) This same set of mathematics allows us to collapse the basic matrix for the linear programming problem, eliminating empty rows and empty columns, and optimizing over a much smaller matrix. Considerable computer time has been saved with no loss of detail.

There are two problems that arise from this method. One is the problem of disappointed expectations: A households's actual expenditure on its dwelling unit plus its expenditure on its work trip may differ from the expected total expenditure that affected its decision to choose the particular type of house in the first place. This comes about because the original choice (made in the DEMAND submodel) is based on the difference between averages, while the final solution accounts for both distributions. As everyone knows, when comparing distributions and finding that one has a lower mean than the other, there is no assurance that that distribution will also contain only values that are lower than all values in the other distribution. This problem will occur in any two-step procedure.

The second problem is one of order in the two-step procedure or whether a one-step procedure is better. There are certainly families who choose a location first and then review the housing stock available (the exact opposite of our method) and there may be those families who attempt to select both location and house type simultaneously. The one-step procedure is intellectually satisfying and conceptually simple for a mathematician. It is relatively difficult and much more expensive to actually obtain a solution from real data, and very few households have either the expertise or the data to make an optimal choice.* Naturally, anyone who critiques the method used

---

*The author moved to Boston in 1966 after having participated vigorously in the Transportation Study for that region. He had more

here and suggests the one-step method really means that he suspects that families make some rudimentary attempt to consider the prices of available housing types and the corresponding work trip while selecting both a type and a residence zone. This is exactly the phenomenon we are trying to capture since we are attempting to simulate the behavior of people and not trying to optimize some company's internal control methods.

The Price Formation Submodel

This submodel manipulates the shadow prices for each residential zone for each house type to determine the expected prices in each zone for the next simulated year. The relative height of the "rent function" is determined directly from the shadow prices, but the absolute height must be determined.

This is done by first identifying the set of residential zones that have shadow prices equal to zero for a given house type and that have at least one unit of the house type produced by construction or conversion during the simulated year. The minimum cost method for producing a unit in this set of zones is taken as the best estimate for the height of the "rent function" in that zone (and in all other zones with zero shadow prices). The addition of this minimum cost to each zone's shadow price sets a target that affects the expected price for that type of unit in that zone for the coming year.

Since house types are handled independently, there is no assurance that less-desirable structures will cost less than more desirable ones in the same zone, in fact the converse has been observed. But the occurrence is extremely rare, and so far the situation has not persisted past the next simulated year. The construction matrix and the demand equations are strong inhibitors. The reader should be aware that such an inversion is unreasonable in sample data only when zones are relatively small (a few square miles as opposed to several square miles in size), since the transportation component is not accurate within a zone and older housing frequently dominates the more

---

information available than any outsider could reasonably expect. It was all to no avail since he could not afford the computer bill to process his information, and his final decision was based on rather ordinary methods utilizing his general preference for a housing type and a real estate agent.

accessible locations within large zones. Thus the "market price" of older units may be higher than that of better units when averaged over large areas.

SIMULATION RESPONSE TO
TRANSPORTATION IMPROVEMENTS

The simulation run testing the model's response to transportation improvements is based mostly on information obtained from the Southwestern Pennsylvania Planning Commission's 1968 data. We would be more correct to state that we have simulated a region very much like Pittsburgh, rather than Pittsburgh itself. Our moving rates were determined from San Francisco data, the initial prices of vacant land were judgmental estimates by people familiar with the Pittsburgh region, and the altered travel time because of the improvements were hand calculated by the author. The altered travel times were intended to account for subsequent congestion, and speeds are therefore probably biased lower than what would be realized in the first few years after opening.

Figure 15.2 indicates the 50 residential zones used to represent the simulated area, which is roughly 40 miles wide and 50 miles tall. The central hatched area indicates the City of Pittsburgh, the broad solid lines indicate the major transportation network that existed in 1968, and the broad dashed lines indicate the transportation improvements that we are considering.

Figure 15.3 indicates the same area divided up into a core and three rings. The rings are further divided into six sectors. All subsequent data comparisons will be based on the region as indicated in Figure 15.3.

For the purpose of comparing the effects of transportation improvements, we have made two simulation runs. The first is a NULL run, which simulated the dynamically changing patterns of residential activity under the assumption that the 1968 transportation network would remain unchanged. The second run was the FWY run, in which we assumed that the two major freeways indicated in Figure 15.2 were completed in 1969. Actually they have not yet been completed.

We made no changes in the employment pattern in either run, although it is highly unlikely that employment patterns would have remained static. In fact, there is a very good chance that employment changes would have occurred even in the short period of three years that we tested since small firms frequently move in advance of anticipated improvements. They may wait for the first signs of construction

FIGURE 15.2

Residence Zones and Major Freeways

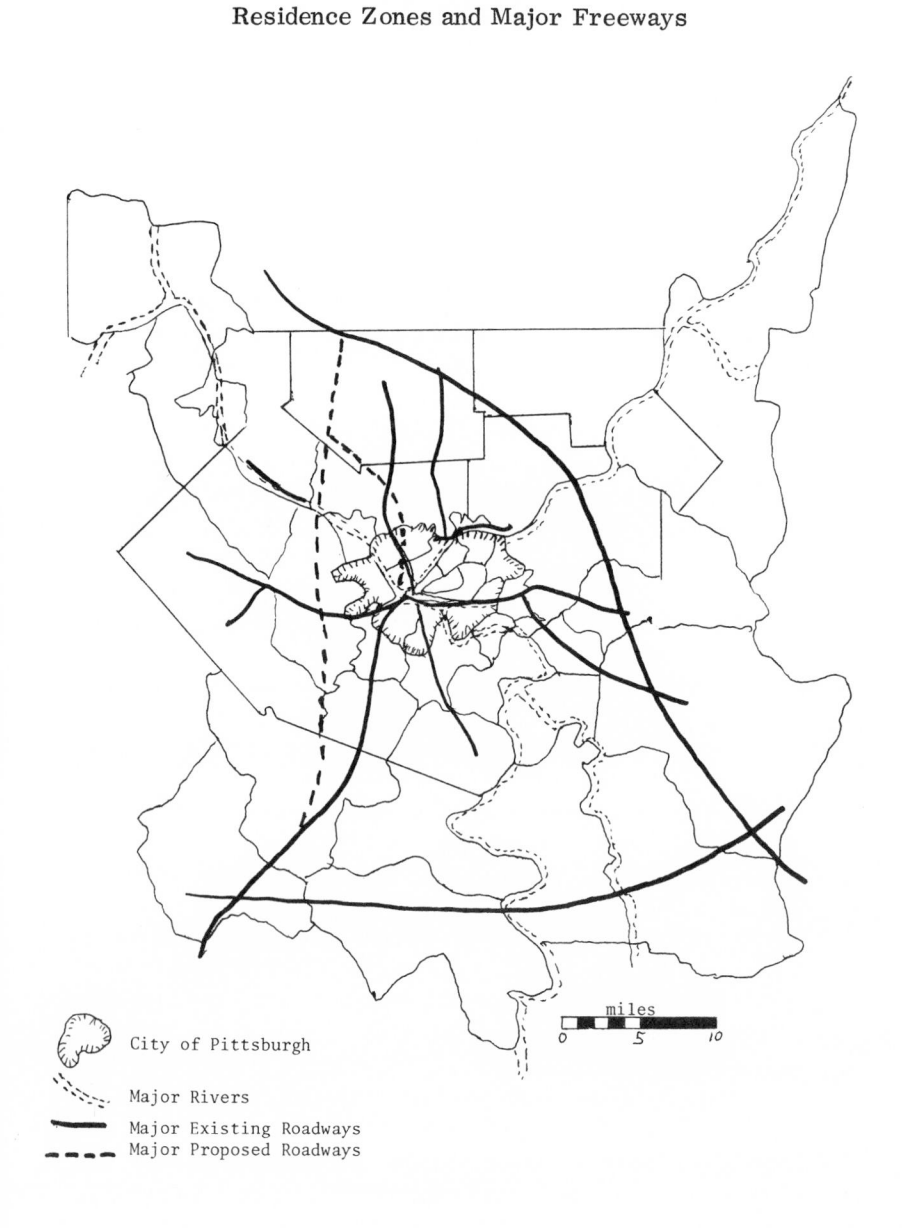

City of Pittsburgh
Major Rivers
Major Existing Roadways
Major Proposed Roadways

miles
0   5   10

Source: Compiled by the author.

FIGURE 15.3

Rings and Sectors

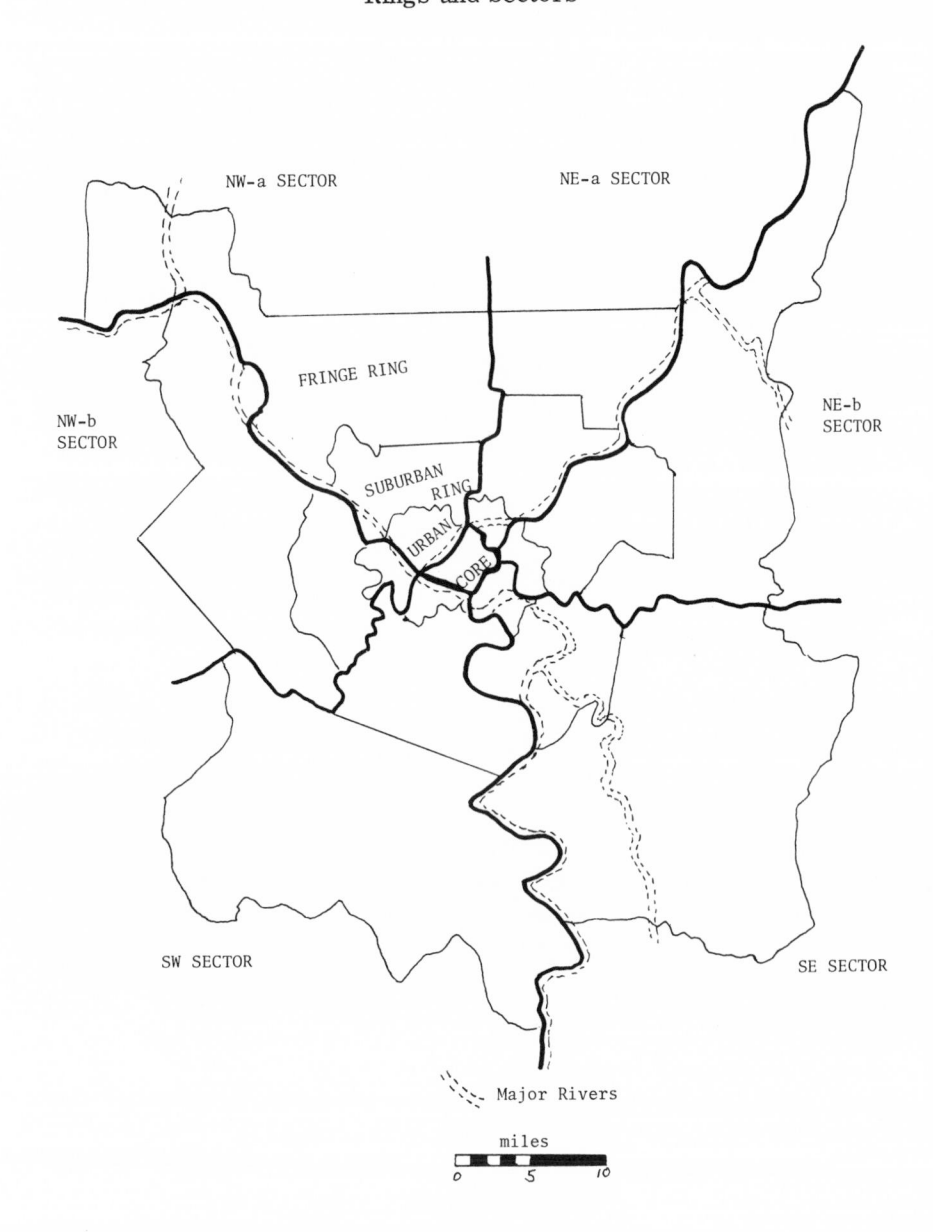

Source: Compiled by the author.

in areas where plans are frequently altered or projects are killed, but it takes a while to build a facility.

We firmly believe that changes in the employment pattern will render more dramatic changes than those we observe in these simulations; however, we feel that these simulations might be indicative of "first round" effects and are useful in their own right. A good analysis of total effects would require that both steps be performed simultaneously or with only a slight lag in employment shifts. Future versions of our model will allow the retail and service sectors to be endogenously simulated, but the user would have to specify "basic employment" changes exogenously.

In the initial sections of this chapter we stated that there were three fundamental problems in studying urban areas. We feel that we have made in-roads into the first two (defining the relevant state and simulating changes in the state) but we frankly admit that we do not have a method for evaluating the observed changes. We will therefore simply report several tables of comparative information and leave evaluation up to others.

In each table of information we will indicate the condition that existed in 1968 or early 1969, the simulated 1971 condition under the NULL assumption, and the 1971 simulated condition under the FWY assumption. The ratio of the 1971 FWY condition to the 1971 NULL condition is taken to be indicative of the effect of the transportation improvements.

POPULATION PATTERNS

The comparison shown in Table 15.1 indicates that only three subregions were significantly affected by the transportation improvements if population shifts were the only criteria. The suburban ring portion of the NW-b sector shows a rather substantial loss while the suburban and fringe rings of the NW-a sector show significant relative increases. Relative losses of 3 and 4 percent are indicated in other suburban ring subregions. These might have been much more dramatic if employment shifts had also been allowed to occur.

More detailed data about the distribution of the households over four income classes is available from the complete model printout. The only interesting observation is that of the nearly 4,000 household differential between NULL and the FWY run in the suburban ring of the NW-a sector, over 2,000 of them are in the highest income class.

TABLE 15.1

Comparison of Simulated Population Changes

	Core and Ring Summary	
Core = 11,625	(1968 Households)	
12,676 1.09	(1971 NULL ; 1971 NULL/1968)	
12,631 1.09	(1971 FWY ; 1971 FWY /1968)	
1.00	(1971 FWY /1971 NULL)	

	Urban Ring	Suburban Ring	Fringe Ring
Summed Over	65,014	143,015	92,912
All Sectors	64,711 1.00	137,516 .96	83,573 .90
	64,531 .99	136,906 .96	84,540 .91
	1.00	1.00	1.01

Sector and Ring Details

Sector			
NE-a	8,056	7,401	5,587
	8,225 1.02	6,834 .92	4,980 .89
	8,227 1.02	6,921 .92	4,981 .89
	1.00	1.00	1.00
NE-b	9,016	22,811	16,046
	10,562 1.17	20,763 .91	18,135 1.13
	10,420 1.16	20,121 .88	17,870 1.11
	.99	.97	.99
SE	16,311	29,782	29,934
	15,794 .97	27,868 .94	20,984 .70
	15,766 .97	27,833 .94	20,967 .70
	1.00	1.00	1.00
SW	14,263	49,972	12,704
	12,930 .91	49,669 .99	12,154 .96
	12,927 .91	47,791 .96	12,184 .96
	1.00	.96	1.00
NW-b	6,291	11,212	15,716
	6,621 1.05	12,717 1.13	14,938 .95
	6,589 1.05	11,100 .99	14,929 .95
	1.00	.87*	1.00
NW-a	11,077	21,837	12,925
	10,579 .96	19,665 .90	12,382 .96
	10,602 .96	23,240 1.06	13,609 1.05
	1.00	1.18*	1.10*

*values of special significance discussed in the text.
<u>Source</u>: Compiled by the author.

RESIDENTIAL PROPERTY VALUE

In this test run of the model single-family dwelling units (there were 12 basic types) were represented by "purchase prices" and multifamily dwelling units (includes row houses and there are 4 basic types) were represented by "annual rents." Both of these values are exclusive of property taxes as they are stored in the model. (Property taxes are included in the generalized prices for decision making on house types by households.) An equivalent purchase price can be estimated for rental property, and this can be added to the purchase price for single-family property, thus resulting in an estimate of total residential property values.

Table 15.2 shows the comparison of property values under the different runs. The pattern is approximately the same as that for population, but more accentuated. The indication is that the relative advantage achieved by the NW-a sector was overcompensated by reductions in other sectors. In fact there is a net loss in the region, although it is significant only in the third or fourth significant digit in the core and each ring.

It is implicit that total property values are the prices of units and the numbers of units at that price. Table 15.3 shows the average monthly rent (including property taxes passed on by the landlord) of multifamily dwelling units while Table 15.4 indicates the average purchase price of single-family units (exclusive of any property taxes). These are the values commonly examined for effects as a result of transportation improvements. Neither measure follows the patterns established by the population differences or the residential property differences. Multifamily rents seem more affected than single-family purchase prices, and in fact there is a net increase in rents because of the transportation improvement. Under the NULL condition, row houses (a rental unit in these simulations) were being converted into small multifamily walkups in the suburban ring of NW-a, resulting in a cheap cost basis. The introduction of the freeways that happen to serve that area in the FWY run cause a relative rise in prices of row houses directly in that area, and indirectly in the cost of small multifamily walkups. The latter are primarily developed from single-family units in the NW-b suburban ring in the FWY run as a net best alternative.

Strangely enough, there is also a net increase in vacancies because of the same circuitous process. The row houses that were not converted under the improved transportation condition leave an extra 900 rental units available, ultimately resulting in some 800 more vacant units. The biggest pattern change in vacancies occurs

TABLE 15.2

Simulated Residential Property Value Changes

Core and Ring Summary		
Core = 209,743		(1969 Values)
224,264	1.07	(1971 NULL; 1971 NULL/1969)
223,813	1.07	(1971 FWY ; 1971 FWY /1969)
	1.00	(1971 FWY /1971 NULL)

	Urban Ring		Suburban Ring		Fringe Ring	
Summed over	1,056,606		2,708,352		2,477,252	
All Sectors	1,115,638	1.05	2,550,689	.94	2,311,177	.93
	1,110,716	1.05	2,548,500	.94	2,309,162	.93
		1.00		1.00		1.00

Sector and Ring Details

Sector						
NE-a	126,449		191,875		109,106	
	132,872	1.05	157,039	.82	108,137	.99
	133,810	1.06	153,343	.80	109,094	.95
		1.01		.98		.96
NE-b	152,451		415,176		418,703	
	183,993	1.21	387,120	.93	396,991	.95
	181,358	1.19	379,816	.91	389,746	.93
		.99		.98		.98
SE	289,917		451,655		723,587	
	278,009	.96	464,849	1.03	733,469	1.01
	277,477	.96	464,317	1.03	728,277	1.01
		1.00		1.00		.99
SW	213,615		1,046,534		386,513	
	220,772	1.03	926,985	.89	389,065	1.01
	219,890	1.03	892,898	.85	388,818	1.01
		1.00		.96		1.00
NW-b	100,831		224,399		370,313	
	110,027	1.09	250,439	1.12	348,277	.94
	109,101	1.08	229,423	1.02	347,606	.94
		.99		.92		1.00
NW-a	173,340		378,713		469,029	
	189,263	1.10	364,255	.96	335,237	.71
	189,077	1.09	428,681	1.13	350,620	0.75
		1.00		1.18*		1.05*

*Values of special significance discussed in the text.

Source: Compiled by the author.

TABLE 15.3

Simulated Average Monthly Rental of Multifamily Dwelling Unit

	Core and Ring Summary					
Core = 93.1	(1969 Average)					
90.8 .97	(1971 NULL; 1971 NULL/1969)					
91.3 .98	(1971 FWY ; 1971 FWY /1969)					
1.01	(1971 FWY/1971 NULL)					

	Urban Ring		Suburban Ring		Fringe Ring	
Averaged over	73.9		80.9		73.4	
All Sectors	76.5	1.04	72.9	.90	67.3	.92
	77.1	1.04	73.9	.91	67.2	.92
		1.01		1.01		1.00

Sector and Ring Details

Sector						
NE-a	66.9		59.8		53.1	
	70.3	1.05	66.3	1.11	59.9	1.13
	72.0	1.08	65.5	1.10	59.4	1.12
		1.02		.99		.99
NE-b	75.2		75.9		82.2	
	79.8	1.06	71.4	.94	71.6	.87
	80.1	1.07	72.9	.96	71.6	.87
		1.00		1.02		1.00
SE	82.0		62.1		60.1	
	74.5	.91	66.2	1.07	62.5	1.04
	75.3	.92	67.7	1.09	62.7	1.04
		1.01		1.02		1.00
SW	69.5		95.1		61.1	
	76.3	1.10	79.6	.84	66.4	1.09
	77.2	1.11	80.0	.84	67.7	1.11
		1.01		1.00		1.02
NW-b	75.6		92.7		67.5	
	77.9	1.03	69.0	.74	72.7	1.08
	77.8	1.03	70.3	.76	72.6	1.08
		1.00		1.02		1.00
NW-a	69.1		75.5		87.3	
	71.0	1.14	69.2	.92	64.8	.74
	79.3	1.15	70.8	.94	64.5	.74
		1.00		1.02		1.00

Source: Compiled by the author.

TABLE 15.4

Simulated Average Purchase Price of Single-Family Dwelling Unit

Core and Ring Summary			
Core = 15,944		(1969 Average)	
17,794	1.12	(1971 NULL; 1971 NULL/1969)	
17,741	1.11	(1971 FWY ; 1971 FWY /1969)	
	1.00	(1971 FWY/1971 NULL)	

	Urban Ring		Suburban Ring		Fringe Ring	
Averaged over	16,768		19,514		19,155	
All Sectors	17,937	1.07	18,316	.94	18,997	.99
	17,848	1.06	18,354	.94	19,001	.99
		1.00		1.00		1.00

Sector and Ring Details

Sector						
NE-a	16,665		21,204		16,351	
	17,248	1.03	19,917	.94	16,401	1.00
	17,262	1.04	19,986	.94	16,409	1.00
		1.00		1.00		1.00
NE-b	16,652		19,785		19,725	
	17,626	1.06	18,232	.92	18,969	.96
	17,514	1.05	18,430	.93	18,950	.96
		.99		1.01		1.00
SE	19,205		15,370		18,138	
	18,900	.98	16,175	1.05	18,251	1.01
	18,837	.98	16,144	1.05	18,258	1.01
		1.00		1.00		1.00
SW	15,357		21,114		18,551	
	17,480	1.14	18,989	.90	18,727	1.01
	17,368	1.13	19,005	.90	18,712	1.01
		.99		1.00		1.00
NW-b	16,179		29,206		18,604	
	16,881	1.04	19,238	.95	19,793	1.06
	16,811	1.04	19,124	.95	19,831	1.06
		1.00		.99		1.00
NW-a	16,025		20,189		23,174	
	18,713	1.17	18,817	.93	20,988	.91
	18,349	1.16	18,875	.93	20,814	.90
		.99		1.00		.99

Source: Compiled by the author.

in Sectors NW-a and NW-b, with the 1971 FWY data showing almost
7,000 fewer vacancies in NW-a and almost 4,000 more vacancies in
NW-b.

LOCATION RENT PATTERNS

Since the model simulates a location rent for each type of housing
unit, and we have defined the lot sizes for all types of simulated
housing, it is a simple matter to estimate a location rent per acre of
occupied land for each housing type. It is quite another matter to estimate the "value" of unoccupied land. In previous simulations we had
tested the traditional economic principle that it should be valued
according to its best alternative use. Where zoning laws permit,
generally this would be for the larger multifamily dwelling units that
obtain location rents from several dwelling units and use very little
land in doing so. This highly efficient use of land in providing dwelling
units imputes a very high value to land. In this type of simulation the
land is held in reserve until some expected price is high enough for
land to become an economic input. Naturally it is an economic input
only for the "best" use, and since there is initially a limited demand
for large multifamily buildings, the land stays in reserve for extremely
long periods. After all upgrading of single-family units is performed,
while no new ones are constructed because of the high price of land,
the price of single-family units begins to rise due to a shortage. There
is then a shift in demand for multifamily units because of relative price
effects, and finally small amounts of land are sold for multifamily
units. Clearly we would need a more detailed simulation of the effects
of holding land for long periods of time, including property taxes to be
paid on such highly valued land.

There is, of course, a valid reason for believing that land prices
are never at the level defined by the "best alternative" use. In spite
of the increased sophistication of the real estate industry, speculation
in land is very risky and a large cushion is required. While this means
only that the "farmer" is paid less for the land while the speculator
hopes to sell for a high return, it does place the land into a true "in-
ventory" condition, where the cost of holding the investment is visible.
These speculators are well aware of the limited number of times the
"best" alternative will come by and make sales based on a "decent"
profit margin.

The developers of the NBER prototype have not reached a final
conclusion as to the way land prices should be determined, but are
experimenting with various alternatives. One of the most important

TABLE 15.5

Simulated Location Rent Per Acre of Land
(equivalent purchase price)

Core and Ring Summary

Core = 70,370		(1969 Average)	
72,150	1.03	(1971 NULL; 1971 NULL/1969)	
70,570	1.00	(1971 FWY ; 1971 FWY /1969)	
.98		(1971 FWY/1971 NULL)	

	Urban Ring		Suburban Ring		Fringe Ring	
Averaged over	24,780		11,060		7,580	
All Sectors	21,740	.88	10,870	.98	9,670	1.28
	21,280	.86	10,650	.96	9,460	1.25
		.98		.98		.98

Sector and Ring Details

Sector						
NE-a	16,940		9,710		5,670	
	17,360	1.02	10,540	1.09	8,230	1.45
	17,390	1.03	9,100	.94	7,140	1.26
		1.00		.86		.87
NE-b	24,980		8,970		6,200	
	24,910	1.00	8,060	.90	5,080	.82
	25,030	1.00	8,100	.90	4,950	.80
		1.00		1.00		.97
SE	27,210		9,740		7,690	
	19,130	.70	11,980	1.23	13,000	1.69
	18,650	.69	11,840	1.22	12,820	1.67
		.97		.99		.99
SW	25,410		11,300		7,920	
	23,060	.91	8,110	.72	10,500	1.33
	22,520	.89	7,960	.70	10,440	1.32
		.98		.98		.99
NW-b	17,360		14,770		7,410	
	14,100	.81	15,280	1.03	6,980	.94
	13,430	.77	16,040	1.09	6,940	.94
		.95		1.05		.99
NW-a	30,050		13,300		9,260	
	27,690	.92	11,190	.84	8,580	.93
	26,530	.88	11,050	.83	8,110	.88
		.96		.99		.95

Source: Compiled by the author.

benefits of the NBER model is that it provides a means of testing alternative methods of modeling debatable concepts at such a specific level. In most modeling efforts this question would be irrelevant.

In the runs used for this chapter a simple average location rent per acre was developed from the rent for each house type and the number of incidences of each occupied dwelling unit. A bias exists toward multifamily structures because of their multiple occupancy where they exist. In fringe areas the land price looks more like the average per acre price of land found under single-family units.

This averaging method cannot be justified on theoretical grounds, and under certain conditions it can be misleading. If growth in an urban area comes to a complete standstill, the price of new land may fall much below the price imputed by such a method. One might do better to hinge the price of land on the frequency of "new construction starts." Such data can be retrieved from the model.

The information displayed in Table 15.5 uses the average location rent for all types of dwelling units, making use of the incidence frequency of each type so it is a true average. There is, of course, a problem of "mix," and one cannot immediately tell whether an increase in average location rent is a result of increased competition for space or increases in the number of multifamily dwelling units.

CONCLUSIONS

Using the NBER model to estimate the "first round" effects of improvements in transportation systems produces results that are not particularly startling to one who is familiar with urban areas. That is, prices increase where you might expect them to increase, and new units are built where you might expect them to be built. Even the construction of a large number of multifamily units in suburban areas does not amaze us today, even though we would have rejected such a suggestion five or ten years ago. In fact it is only when we recall that we artificially constrained all employment to remain fixed in its location that we realize how big a 2-5 percent change is.

Assuming that we are pleased with this confirmation of common assumptions (or conversely, that the model's replication of common assumptions indicates that the model contains some elements of validity) it is interesting to observe just what levels are obtained and to see where the "negative benefits" fall and how big they are. It takes a much more detailed examination at a finer level of disaggregation to locate the real receivers of the benefits or penalties than can be presented here, but recall that the model operated at such a disaggregated level and we have simply aggregated for simplicity in presentation. In looking closer we can find that low-quality neighborhoods bear the brunt of the vacancies, even though we have a grossly inadequate representation of neighborhood quality in this version of the model.

This model is still being revised under current research grants, with the view toward making it more useful for policy analysis and toward making it more realistic with respect to neighborhood effects and the effects of racial discrimination in the housing market. We are also incorporating more modeling of industry location decisions.

NOTES

1. H. James Brown, J. Royce Ginn, John F. Kain, and Mahlon Straszheim, Empirical Models of Urban Land Use: Suggestions on Research Objectives and Organization (National Bureau of Economic Research) (New York: Columbia University Press, 1972); Frank de Leeuw, "The Distribution of Housing Services," an Urban Institute Paper, No. 208-6 (Washington, D.C.: The Urban Institute, 1972); Robert F. Engle, Franklin M. Fisher, John R. Harris, and Jerome Rothenberg, "An Econometric Simulation Model of Intra-Metropolitan Housing Location: Housing, Business, Transportation, and Local Government," American Economic Review 62, no. 2 (May 1972): 87-98; Richard Muth, in discussion of above article, in ibid., p. 98.

2. John F. Kain, ed., The NBER Urban Simulation Model, Vol. II: Supporting Empirical Studies (Springfield, Va.: National Technical Information Service, 1971), PB-198-555; John F. Kain and John M. Quigley, "Measuring the Value of Housing Quality," Journal of the American Statistical Association 65 (June 1970): 532-48; "Housing Market Discrimination, Home Ownership, and Savings Behavior," American Economic Review 62, no. 3 (June 1972): 263-77; Discrimination and A Heterogenous Housing Stock: An Economic Analysis (New York: National Bureau of Economic Research, forthcoming); Mahlon Straszheim, An Econometric Analysis of the Urban Housing Market (New York: National Bureau of Economic Research, forthcoming); Stephen K. Mayo, "An Econometric Model of Residential Location," Ph.D. dissertation, Department of Economics, Harvard University, 1971; Daniel Fredland, "Residential Mobility and the Choice of Tenure," Ph.D. dissertation, Committee on the Ph.D. in City and Regional Planning, Harvard University, 1970; John M. Quigley, "Residential Location: Multiple Workplaces and a Heterogenous Housing Stock," Ph.D. dissertation, Department of Economics, Harvard University, 1972; H. James Brown, "Changes in Workplace

and Residential Location, " Journal of the American Institute of Planners, forthcoming.

3. William Alonso, Location and Land Use (Cambridge, Mass.: Harvard University Press, 1964); Martin J. Beckman, "On the Distribution of Urban Rent and Density, " Journal of Economic Theory 1 (1969): 60-67; John F. Kain, "The Journey-to-Work as a Determinant of Residential Location, " Papers and Proceedings of the Regional Science Association, vol. 9, 1962, pp. 137-61; Edwin S. Mills, "An Aggregative Model of Resource Allocation in a Metropolitan Area, " American Economic Review (May 1967), pp. 197-211; Aldo Montesano, "A Restatement of Beckman's Model on the Distribution of Urban Rent and Residential Density, " Journal of Economic Theory 4 (1972): 329-54; Richard F. Muth, Cities and Housing (Chicago: University of Chicago Press, 1969); Robert M. Solow, "Congestion, Density and the Use of Land in Transportation, " Swedish Journal of Economics, no. 1 (1972) pp.161-73; Lowdon Wingo, Transportation and Urban Land (Washington, D.C.: Resources for the Future, 1961).

4. Douglas B. Lee, "Requiem for Large Scale Models, " Institute for Urban and Regional Development, University of California, Berkeley, April 1972 (mimeo); Ira S. Lowry, "Seven Models of Urban Development: A Structural Comparison" (Santa Monica, Calif.: The RAND Corporation, P-3673, September 1967); John F. Kain and J. R. Meyer, "Computer Simulations, Physio-Economic Systems, and Intra-Regional Models, " American Economic Review (May 1967).

5. T.C. Koopmans and M.J. Beckmann, "Assignment Problems and the Location of Economic Activities, " Econometrica (January 1957): 53-76.

6. Ingram, John F. Kain and J. Royce Ginn, The Detroit Prototype of the NBER Urban Simulation Model (National Bureau of Economic Research) (New York: Columbia University Press, 1972).

Sydney R. Robertson

The three chapters in Part V reach similar logical conclusions, though they start from substantially different premises. If I had to categorize them I would place Velona's chapter in the conceptual area, Hoch's chapter at an aggregate analytical level, and Ginn's at a very detailed analytical level. Yet when you trace the discussions through and stand back from them a bit, you see that they are very closely related and, in fact, even come to some very similar conclusions.

Walter Velona's analytical concept that people budget time within a constraint is quite reasonable. I do think it would be useful here to reference work done by Richard Worrall and Stuart Chapin in the area of activity patterns and the budgeting of time. Unfortunately, these studies tend to indicate that ther is a great deal of irrationality in this process.

Velona seeks to develop asymptotic constraints to bound the travel process. This is very reasonable and what most analysts would like to find to simplify their models. It also fits nicely with the notion of the exchange of transport costs for a housing bundle up to some limit.

The conceptual discussion of urban structure appears to closely parallel the work of the urban geographers: August Loesch, Johann von Thunen, and Walter Christaller. A simplified hypothetical construct is developed that allows, at an admittedly simple level, an understanding of the process that is operating. From this follows a series of concepts that begin to provide an understanding of the impacts that various transport policy decisions might have on the urban area. One can learn a great deal about the effect of various transport technologies on urban structure from the development of this construct by Velona. This, if nothing else, is a significant contribution and makes the chapter well worth reading. It is an excellent contribution to an understanding of the existing theory of urban structure as it might be applied to answer contemporary questions about the impact of transport technology.

Upon reading Velona's chapter I was left with the feeling that the density question was not at all adequately treated. However, this notion is not essential to the value or coherence of his chapter. In addition, Hoch contributes quite extensively in this area.

The fact that Velona contributes well to conceptual understanding is also, in a way, one of his failings. Velona deals at an aggregate level and focuses on trends and patterns rather than details. He does not provide analytical structures or information on how one would go the next step. That is, how do we actually deal with the situations he describes at a policy level in actual urban areas? These questions imply a need for a detailed analytical tool that answers, in a detailed manner, the "what if" types of questions that lead to decision making.

Irving Hoch's chapter is complementary to Velona's but from a substantially different perspective. Hoch deals directly and extensively with the issue of land use intensity in urban structure. He also addresses the classical transport/land rent trade-offs, adding new extensions. In particular, his addition of environmental costs is quite interesting. The provision of a surcharge for environmental costs is something that is needed in many more of our models. Our analytical work in the transportation/land use area does very little, in most applications, to deal with the environmental consequences of the systems that we implement. The transportation/land use tools that we are developing offer the only real capability that we would have now (or are likely to have in the near future) to assess the environmental consequences of major urban land use and transportation systems. The environmental guidelines, issued to implement the Environmental Protection Act, can only be implemented with substantial changes in urban form, structure, and infrastructure. The testing of these changes, in advance, with land use/transportation planning tools is the only way that we have to assess the steps that will be required and the consequences of those steps.

Hoch's chapter discusses a conceptual structure that is similar to the operational land use forecasting tool that was used by the Chicago Area Transportation Study. I refer to what was called the "Density Saturation Gradient Method," as used at CATS. Hoch develops results concerning urban boundaries and the impact of transport technology that are similar to those developed by Velona from a different perspective. I was also interested in the explanation of the evolution of primate cities, such as those in Southeast Asia. While I am by no means conversant in this area, I am aware that the formation of primate cities is a substantial puzzle to the community of geographers. If Hoch has solved this riddle, perhaps this information ought to be passed on to them!

Hoch's discussion of income effects is interesting. We very rarely look at the income effects of decisions that are made in urban areas. As investments are made in capital and other programs that affect city form and structure and introduce change in cities, we look very little at the downstream income effects of these actions. Also, as Hoch suggests, we cannot continue to classify all individuals or all urban areas in terms of dollar wages or average wage structures. If, instead, we classify in terms of real dollars, it is clear that we will discover differences in the impacts that result. We also need to dis-aggregate the population and look at the differential impacts on dif-ferent elements of the population, as it is likely that we will find that certain groups receive more than their fair share of the consequences of decisions that are made. Too many of our models and analyses deal with aggregates of the population and of income.

The chapter by J. Royce Ginn describes what can only be char-acterized as an extremely elaborate model. This represents one of a family of disaggregate submodel structures. The submodels are integrated by an underlying framework into an overall simulation model. These models represent the disaggregate behavioral approach to urban development modeling. The models are extremely interesting, detailed, and comprehensive. Among these, the NBER model stands alone in its comprehensiveness. It does represent a step forward in the behavioral modeling area. I do not think it represents a tool that can be considered to be operational and useful to on-line transportation and land use planning agencies. It does offer, however, the promise of developments that will extend our ability in future years.

Two key major problem areas should be considered. These problem areas are by no means unique to the NBER model. They are characteristic of all disaggregate behavioral simulation models. The first problem is that of the large number of submodels within the total model structure. In this situation, what you have is a very fragile "house of cards." The removal or failure of any element results in the collapse of the entire system. Second, as most behavioral mod-elers will admit, are the data problems. It is normally necessary to work with cross-sectional data sets, small sample sizes, a variety of data sources with varying quality, and with many parameters for which data do not exist. Perhaps the most substantial operational problem is developing the very large data set required to calibrate these models.

At this point it might be useful to step back and put land use and urban development models in some perspective. It is easy to criticize and find fault with the work of modelers in this area. The process that is being modeled is extremely complex and the elements are extensive and ill-structured. That people who have prepared these chapters have attempted to do what they do is worthy of some com-mendation. We cannot hold the constructs that are developed up to the light of reality without finding flaws, gaps, and inconsistencies. This is the nature of the process. In the development of these models many things must be left out or they become too unwieldy to be of any use. Therefore, the modeling process is a continual compromise between descriptiveness and operationality. Those models that are ultimately successful are both adequately descriptive and usable.

In the end you reach the dilemma voiced by Ira Lowry. It appears that, in modeling urban development, everything affects everything else. We must avoid the tendency to throw up our hands and say "what's the use," because it is essential that we develop tools to assess the consequences of transportation/land use decisions on urban development and structure. It is, in fact, an understanding of the processes at work in shaping urban activity patterns that is a prerequisite to the assessment of the consequences of urban programs and capital investments.

At this point it might be useful to address the question of where we have been and where we are going. Urban development models can be categorized into three generations. The first-generation models were quite simple. They dealt with aggregate relationships, were based largely on accessibility indices, and dealt primarily with the location of residential activity. Second-generation models began to pull the process apart and to introduce additional variables beyond accessibility. The models were more comprehensive, somewhat more detailed though still aggregate, dealt with more than residential activity, and were generally more comprehensive and descriptive.

It is the second-generation models and some of the first-generation models that are used as tools in operational transportation and land use planning studies. The use of these models, even today, is restricted primarily to the large sophisticated metropolitan planning agencies. In fact relatively few of the metropolitan areas in this country actually use these tools in their planning programs.

We are now in the development stages of a third generation of urban development models. They are (as is the NBER model), disaggregate, behavioral, and extremely detailed attempts at simulation.

One could question why we have not progressed any further than we have. I see two reasons. The first is what I call the on-line research problem. In a number of the major studies in this country the urban development modeling effort, while directly on-line in the production of the transportation/land use plan, was in reality a research and development effort. The staff determined that existing tools for urban development modeling were either not transferrable or inadequate. Therefore, they decided to develop their own tools. This was done in the context of tight time deadlines in developing a plan. The model development process is uncertain and unlikely to yield a product by a given deadline. This is exactly what happened in a number of the transportation/land use studies. To make it worse, policy and political people were assured that these efforts would be on time. The inability of these tools to deliver has cast a dark shadow over the entire urban development modeling profession. Today most planning policy and management people are of the opinion that urban development modeling is an endless and nonproductive activity. Therefore, relatively few studies have developed these tools. The second reason is that research monies to support the development of new models and tools are not available. Most of the federal programs have very small sums of money for these activities.

Against this unfortunately bleak background it seems clear to me that the development of usable urban activity models is essential. As noted above, these tools are key in the assessment of the environmental impact of transportation/land use decisions and in the development of environmental action programs in response to federal guidelines. It is also clear that we must do more to assess the impact and consequences of urban facility capital programs. Strong pressures are being exerted today on the planners of urban capital improvement programs to develop, during the planning process, the impacts of these programs and a range of alternatives. Urban development models that can answer a series of "what if" questions are essential for these types of assessments. This is particularly critical in the transportation area.

Therefore, we need to develop a set of usable models of urban development that can assess the broad stream of effects caused by any major facility action in an urban area. We do not fully understand the multiorder effects of these actions. We need to have the tools to describe and evaluate the reorganization effects that result from our programs. We need the tools to determine which effects are important and which are not. We need the tools to provide information on three basic aspects of any urban facility proposal: (1) the service provided by that facility, (2) the stream of costs associated with that facility, and (3) the impacts deriving from that facility. If urban development models are to be successful, then they must be able to provide these capabilities and yet be workable and usable by the variety of transportation/land use planning agencies throughout the country.

Peter W. House

Part VI was organized for the purpose of examining the inter-relationships and impact of environmental considerations on our urban development process. Within the constraints given it would have been impossible to discuss the topic in depth. Accordingly, we chose to represent a diversity of backgrounds and points of view. Our contributors were selected from the private sector, government, and the universities. Bruce Allen and Richard Mudge, on special assignment to the Department of Transportation, have written on "The Impact of Rapid Transit on Urban Development." Their chapter focuses on a specific example of environmental impact—the case of the Philadelphia-Lindenwold High-Speed Line. Robert Harmon of Development Research Associates represents the private sector. His chapter illustrates a wide range of specific examples of the impact of effective and ineffective planning on urban development. Our discussant, Joseph Bosco, was a special assistant to the secretary, U.S. Department of Transportation. This position has afforded a view of transportation/environmental impact problems at the policy-making level. It is well to note—as Bosco reminds us—that many key decisions are more influenced by exigencies of funding than merit and priority of need.

16

THE IMPACT OF RAPID TRANSIT ON URBAN DEVELOPMENT: THE CASE OF THE PHILADELPHIA-LINDENWOLD HIGH-SPEED LINE

W. Bruce Allen
Richard R. Mudge

When a transportation investment is contemplated, the important question arises of how to measure the benefits of the investment (which are needed to compare the project vis-a-vis other projects) and how to demarcate the investment's areas of impact.

This chapter attempts to develop a theory that measures the benefit area and identifies the areas of equal benefit. The model necessarily abstracts from reality. Its assumptions involve many inelasticities. However, the inelasticities make the model simple in nature—and hence simple to test. It is anticipated that others will be stimulated to increase the scope of the current research. The directions and foundations are hopefully provided herein.

The analysis is perfectly general in nature but is couched in the terms of the Lindenwold High-Speed Line (Philadelphia, Pa., to Lindenwold, N.J.)—a new radial commuter line to Philadelphia.

BACKGROUND

H. Mohring (1961), and H. Mohring and M. Harwitz (1962) have shown the impact area and zones of equal benefit for a transportation improvement entailing continous access.[1] A. A. Walters has shown a similar

Support for the research done herein was given by the Office of Policy and Plans Development, Office of the Secretary, U.S. Department of Transportation, under contract DOT-OS-10043. The views expressed do not necessarily involve those of the Department of Transportation. The authors wish to acknowledge the aid of Leon N. Moses who first presented the simple market area model developed herein in the early 1960s. The authors alone are responsible for the viewpoints and errors in this chapter.

situation in the context of economic development of the hinterlands. [2]
Both cases calculate benefits based on the change in economic rent
from before to after the transportation innovation. In the former case
the "rent" is the savings in transport cost accruing to individuals as
the result of the new investment. In the latter case the rent is the
savings in transport cost accruing to producers as increased profits.

The above analysis is expanded in this chapter to encompass the
market area of a transportation investment, which has discrete access,
to delineate the market areas of each access point and to develop
areas of equal impact concerning the effects of the line.

It is important to point out that impact will be defined in terms
of transportation savings accruing to individuals. These savings will
be dependent upon values of parameters that are chosen, for example,
values of time, automobile operating costs per mile, etc. Mohring
uses real estate transaction prices to estimate value of time. In this
chapter we will use a reverse process and use a priori estimates of
such items as value of time to delimit impact areas. Estimates of
the savings accruing to a particular area will be one of several variables used to explain the transaction price of residential real estate
in the area.

Both approaches must be pursued with care. The boundaries of
the metropolitan area are not fixed as Mohring and Harwitz assume.
Nor is the individual's demand for land constant and independent of
price and location, as those authors assume. To assume that the
transportation savings will be capitalized into the sales price of the
land ignores important supply and demand effects, such as an increase
in supply of land that is x minutes or y dollars away from a large
employment center, etc. It is not at all clear, in a micro context,
how and in what magnitude land rents will change. What is ultimately
needed to solve the problem is a model that is general equilibrium in
nature. Thus, before data on real estate transactions can be utilized
to determine parameter values, more thought about the supply and
demand for land must be forthcoming. Nevertheless, the analysis
below may provide directional guidance for future analysis.

The model presented below is simple in nature. While it is not
a mirror of reality, it is felt to be a useful construct on which to
base more sophisticated models. It also suggests some a priori
specifications for empirical tests.

THE THEORY[*]

The model presented below represents a unique application of the market area theory of F. A. Fetter and C. D. and W. P. Hyson to the problem of transportation choice and to access choice.[3] Involved is a significant departure from traditional market area theory that treats several points with fixed FOB prices and treats market boundaries as loci of equal delivered prices from the sources.

Let us suppose the following situation:

1. All economic activity occurs in the central business district (CBD). (Multicenters of activity can be handled but unnecessarily clutter the analysis.)
2. A homogeneous transportation plain, with respect to costs, exists, except for the speed line. (A grid network or a nonhomogeneous plain can be added. The nonhomogeneous plain causes considerable difficulty.)
3. The analysis is short run in nature and all locations are fixed.
4. One station exists in the CBD and one in the suburbs. (More stations are easily added.) The High-Speed Line is assumed to be a straight line system. (The model is easily generalized to allow for circuitous systems.)
5. The "cost" of transportation is different on the speed line from what it is on the rest of the plain.
6. "Cost" is considered to be monetary cost. Other costs such as time-costs, convenience, etc., can be added to the analysis if proper conversion factors (to monetary units) can be defined or the market area analysis can be done solely with one of the other variables.
7. All trips are assumed to be work trips.
8. Two modes of transportation exist: car and the speed line.

Since the origins and destinations are fixed and the trips involved are work trips, it is assumed that two trips are made per day. Thus, since the origin and destination and the number of trips are given, cost minimization is synonymous with utility maximization.

The following notation is employed:

A   Location of the Downtown station

B   Location of the Suburban station

---

[*]This section represents an elaboration of a model first introduced by Leon N. Moses in the early 1960s.

D_{AB} Distance from A to B

C   Cost by car per unit distance

F_B Fare by the speed line from station B

M   Bridge tolls

P_B Parking charges and any other charges independent of distance traveled at station B

P_A Parking charges and any other charges independent of distance traveled at the CBD

D_{BX} Distance from point of indifference X, between driving to the Downtown or driving to the station and taking the speed line Downtown and the station B

D_{AX} Distance from such a point X (as described above) and the downtown A. (Note that the Downtown is assumed to be point. Note also that an individual is assumed not to need his car during the business day.)

Given the above situation, an individual would be indifferent between driving to work or taking the speed line to work if:

(1) $2CD_{AX} + 2M + P_A = 2CD_{BX} + 2F_B + P_B$

Equation (1) can be rearranged to read:

(2) $D_{AX} - D_{BX} = \dfrac{F_B}{C} - \dfrac{M}{C} - \dfrac{1P}{2C} = \dfrac{F_B - M - \frac{1}{2}P}{C} = K$

where $P = P_A - P_B$.

All items on the right-hand side of (2) are known parameters. Hence, the right-hand side of (2) can be called K, a constant. K will be $\gtrless 0$ as $\dfrac{F_B}{C} \gtrless \dfrac{M}{C} + \dfrac{1P}{2C}$ (or as the speed line fare $\gtrless$ bridge tolls and one-half the parking fees). Note that equation (1) provides the theoretical justification for the one-half of the parking costs that often appears in modal split models.

The left-hand side of (2) is the difference between two variables. The equation form of (2) is that of a hyperbola. The exact form of the hyperbola will depend on the sign and magnitude of K. If K = 0, the hyperbola will be the perpendicular bisector of the line AB. If $K > D_{AB}$ then the hyperbola is nonexistent and everyone will drive to A. If $K = D_{AB}$ then the hyperbola is the line AB extended to the right of B.

FIGURE 16.1

Market Areas for Station B with Various Magnitudes of K

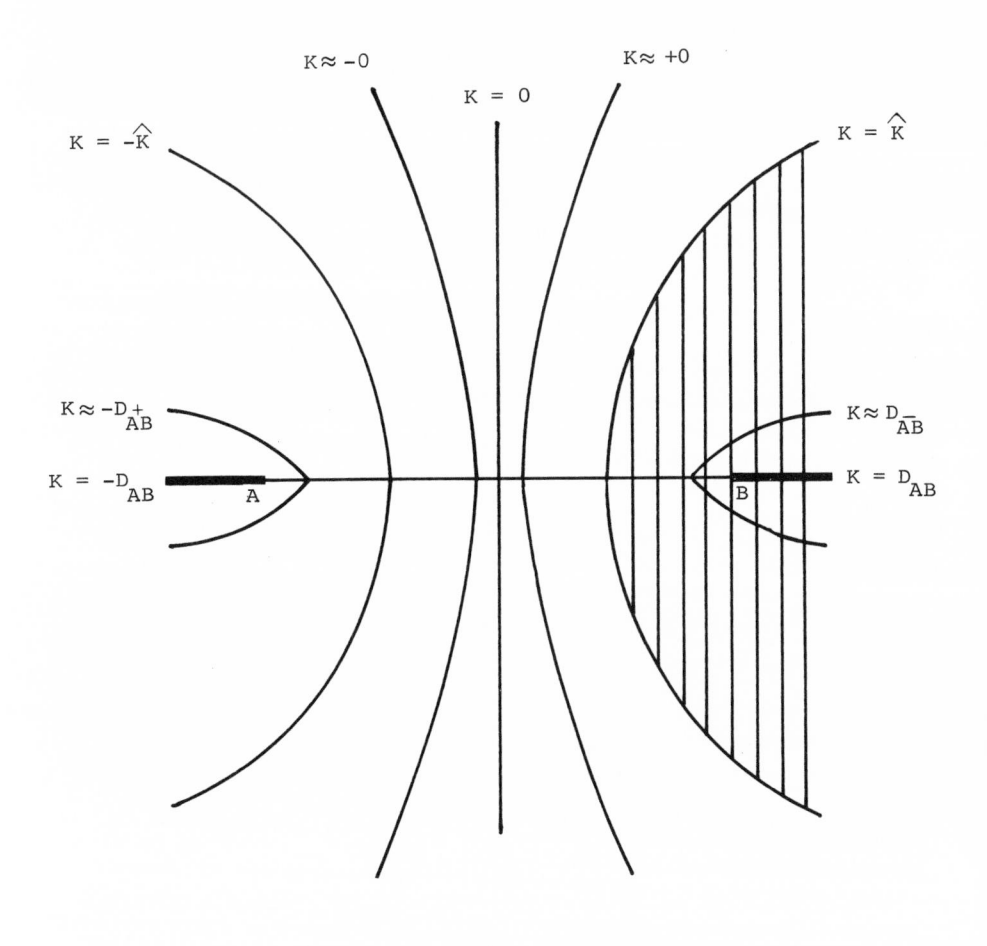

Source: Compiled by the author.

For $D_{AB} > K > 0$, the hyperbola bends around B with its vertex to the right of the midpoint of AB (at distance $K/2$ from the midpoint). The larger K becomes in this range, the closer the vertex of the hyperbola comes to B and the less "spread" the hyperbola has. Analogous types of situations occur for $-D_{AB} < K < 0$ (see Figure 16.1).

The hyperbola defines the market boundary between driving to the Downtown as opposed to taking the train to the Downtown. If $K > 0$, use of the speed line will be favored. If $K < 0$, driving will be favored. The situation is shown in Figure 16.1.

All the area contained within a hyperbola is the market area of the station around which the hyperbola bends. Thus in Figure 16.1 if $K = \hat{K}$, then all Downtown work people who live in the shaded area will use the speed line and all other people will drive Downtown.

One would certainly want to argue that not all monetary costs are perceived by the commuter. For instance, out-of-pocket driving costs are not well known.[4] In addition, time may be the crucial variable for urban commutation. Furthermore, values of time (the conversion factor to put time into monetary terms) are likely to vary with income, which, in turn, is likely to vary with distance from the Downtown (up to some finite distance). Driving costs and speeds are not likely to be uniform across the plain, nor is access to the stations or to Downtown "as the crow flies." In fact costs and time are likely to rise as the Downtown is approached, because of congestion.

All the above (and more, of course) are legitimate criticisms of the model, but all can be handled within the general framework of the model. The purpose of this first section is to establish the framework.

It is important to note both the control variables in the analysis and the influence on the market areas effected by exercising control. As shown in equation (1), $K = \frac{F_B}{C} - \frac{M}{C} - \frac{1P}{2C}$. Variables F_B, C, M, and P are in the short-run control of the authorities. Tolls may be raised or lowered, generally by direct action. Parking fees may be raised or lowered, generally by indirect action (since many parking lots are privately owned) such as tax policy changes, changes of fees in municipally run garages, or by direct action such as enforcing on-street parking ordinances, etc. Speed line fares are directly controllable, although subject to possible actions by regulatory agencies. Automobile costs are controlled through taxes on gasoline or even more directly through road user pricing. The problem with auto costs is in the perception of costs related to the specific trip that are not directly "out-of-pocket." Evidence has shown that the marginal costs (the appropriate cost if the car were retained for noncommuting uses—which would most frequently be the case) are poorly perceived by drivers.[5]

In the long run the location of stations is a control variable. Land use planning will also affect the density of population within the impacted area. Other control variables exist, of course, but not within the framework of the model as developed to this point.

By differentiating K with respect to M, P, F_B, and C, the impacts of changes in the control variables can be seen:

$$(3) \quad \frac{\partial K}{\partial M} = -\frac{1}{C} < 0$$

$$(4) \quad \frac{\partial K}{\partial P} = -\frac{1}{2C} < 0$$

$$(5) \quad \frac{\partial K}{\partial F_B} = \frac{1}{C} > 0$$

$$(6) \quad \frac{\partial K}{\partial C} = -\frac{F_B}{C^2} + \frac{M}{C^2} + \frac{P}{2C^2} = \frac{\frac{1}{2}P + M - F_B}{C^2} = -\frac{K}{C} \lessgtr 0 \text{ as } K \gtrless 0$$

As shown in Figure 16.1, as K becomes larger the market area for transit becomes smaller. Thus (3) and (4) show that increasing bridge tolls and the price for Downtown parking will increase the speed line's market area. As shown in (5), as the speed line fares increase the line will lose part of its market area.

The effect of an increase in perceived driving cost, C, depends upon the sign of K. If K exceeds zero, the market area of the speed line will decrease as auto costs increase. If K < 0, the reverse occurs. In both cases, however, an increase in C tends to make the hyperbola approach the perpendicular bisector of AB.

EXPANSIONS OF THE THEORY

Many observers of urban transportation would argue that time is a more important decision variable for suburban commuters than is cost. The time differences can be treated explicitly as follows: The average speed on area roads is assumed to be y miles per hour. Dividing y into one hour yields a result g in hours per mile. The time it takes to drive directly from location X to the center city is therefore gD_{AX} and the similar time to station B is therefore gD_{BX}. The average speed on the high-speed line is z miles per hour (z > y), which is easily converted to h hours per mile. The time from station B to center city is therefore hD_{AB}.

The above information is, in general, not sufficient to permit the drawing of market boundaries. If cost is also an important decision variable, in order to combine this analysis with the analysis of the first theory section, a value of time (V) must be found so that gD_{AX} (with a dimension of hours) can be combined with CD_{AX} (with a dimension of dollars). Obviously the measurement units of V are in dollars per hour.

Once a value of V is determined, equation (1) becomes:

$$(7) \quad 2CD_{AX} + 2VgD_{AX} + 2M + P_A = 2CD_{BX} + 2VgD_{BX}$$
$$+ 2F_B + 2VhD_{AB} + P_B$$

which can be transformed to:

$$(8) \quad D_{AX} - D_{BX} = \frac{F_B + VhD_{AB}}{C + Vg} - \frac{M}{C + Vg} - \frac{\frac{1}{2}P}{C + Vg} = K'$$

where $P = P_A - P_B$.

The right-hand side of (8) is a constant and hence (8) is the equation of a hyperbola. Other variables, such as waiting time, could be added.

One might be tempted to argue that a V could be estimated from a fit of the model to modal split. However, the model as stated above contains a variable C, which is the perceived automobile cost. One might also argue that C (or better yet W—a constant that measures perceived cost as a percentage of actual cost) can be estimated from a fit of the actual data. Unfortunately, an infinite number of combinations of V and C exist that yield exactly the same K. One cannot estimate the value of one of the desired "variables" without specifying the value of the other. Such specification may be allowable if some good a priori information exists concerning the magnitude of one of the "variables."

Analysis of cases of different value of time zones, curved speed lines, multiple stationed lines, multiple speed lines, multiple employment centers, grid network transport plains, actual highway configuration networks, etc., have been developed and are presented elsewhere.[6]

MEASUREMENT OF IMPACT

The simple model of equation (1) provides the basis of an impact theory. Prior to the existence of the speed line, all inhabitants of the plain drove down to the Center City (subject to the constraint that the wage net of commutation exceeds the return from working on the land).

After the introduction of the speed line, the market area analysis shows that some will use the line while others continue to drive. Obviously those that use the line reveal that they benefit by doing so, since their old option of driving, while still available to them, is rejected.

Savings from the use of the speed line are defined as auto cost less speed line cost. Obviously then equation (1), the market boundary equation, describes the locus of zero savings, that is, $S = 0$. In general the locus of equal savings is defined as:

$$(9) \quad 2CD_{AX} + 2M + P - 2CD_{BX} - 2F_B = S, \text{ where } P = P_A - P_B$$

Equation (9) can be rearranged to read

$$(10) \quad D_{AX} - D_{BX} = \frac{F_B}{C} - \frac{M}{C} - \frac{\frac{1}{2}P}{C} + \frac{S}{2C} = \frac{F_B - M - \frac{1}{2}P}{C} + \frac{S}{2C}$$

$$= K + \frac{S}{2C} = K''$$

Equation (10) is identical to equation (2) except for the $S/2C$. If $S = 0$, equation (10) reduces to equation (2), the market boundary equation.

For S held at a constant level of savings $S/2C$ is constant and hence the right-hand side of equation (10) is a constant K''. Therefore equation (10) is also that of a hyperbola. Since $K'' > K$, the equal savings loci will bend more around B (relatively) than will the market boundary.

In fact $\frac{\partial K''}{\partial S} = \frac{1}{2C} > 0$, demonstrating that as the savings level increases, K'' increases, thus causing the savings hyperbola to bend more and more about B. There are limits, however, to the level of savings available. The savings hyperbola will not exist if $K'' > D_{AB}$. This is easily translated into the cost formulation. Consider Figure 16.2.

FIGURE 16.2

The Speed Line with Stations at A and B
and a Commuter at Location R

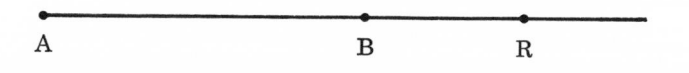

A B R

Source: Developed by the authors.

FIGURE 16.3

Equal Savings Loci for Station B

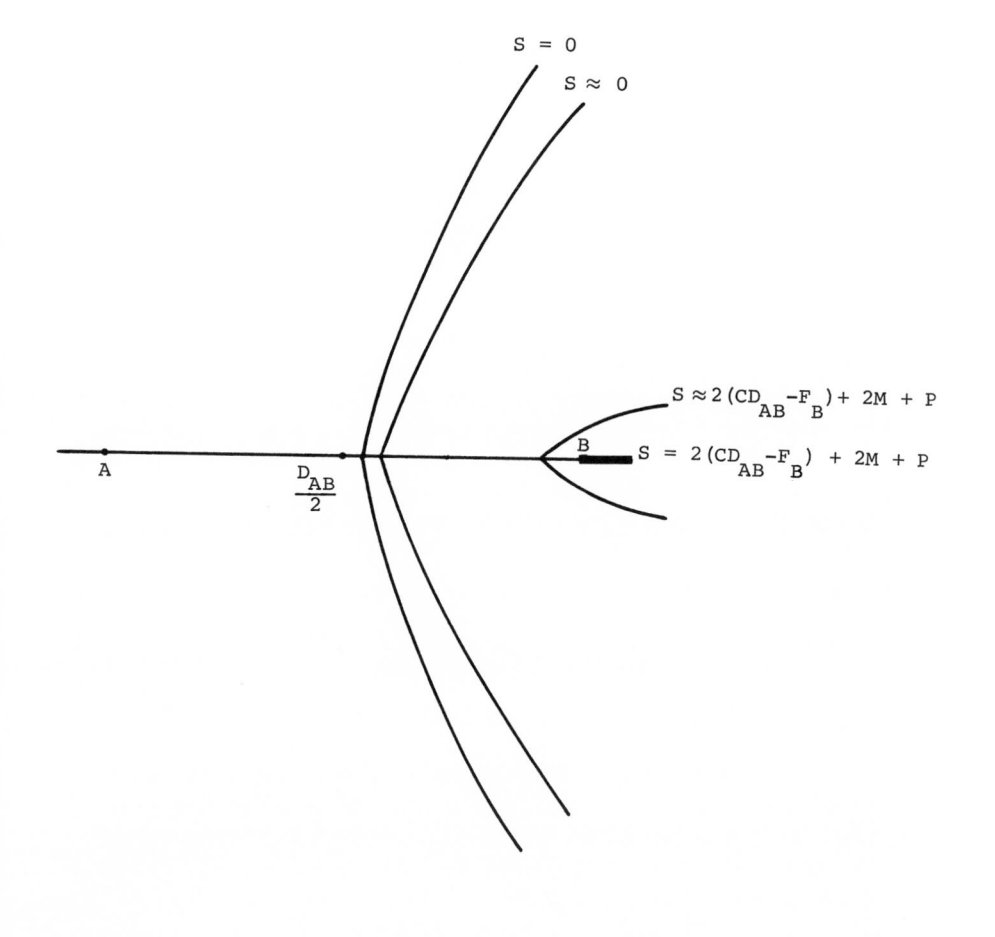

Source: Developed by the authors.

A resident at B will save:

$$(11)\qquad 2CD_{AB} + 2M + P - 2F_{B} = S'$$

Likewise a resident at R will save:

$$(12)\qquad 2CD_{AR} + 2M + P - 2F_{B} - 2CD_{BR} = S'$$

or

$$(13)\qquad 2CD_{AB} + 2M + P - 2F_{B} = 2CD_{AB} + 2M + P - 2F_{B}$$

since $D_{AR} = D_{AB} + D_{BR}$

Thus the residents cannot save any more than the bridge tolls, parking costs, and twice the fare differential from A to B between the two modes. This result is also shown from the mathematical structure of the model by setting the K" in equation (10) equal to D_{AB} (the maximum K" possible to still get a hyperbola) and equating that to the initial right-hand side of equation (10) and solving for S.

The equal saving loci for the situation depicted in equation (1) is shown in Figure 16.3, assuming that K > 0.

The equal savings loci are easily drawn for the other cases described in the preceding section.

USE OF THE IMPACT AREAS

A method has now been outlined to yield areas of equal impact of the speed line. All individuals living along a given equal savings locus benefit by the same amount. If it were desirable to tax individuals based on the benefit received, the model would be able to identify the location and degree of benefit to each location.

It might be suggested that such benefits might be capitalized into the sales prices of houses in the impact area. While this result will to a degree be true, it is very difficult to get before and after transactions on the same piece of property. (The desire to use the same property is due to the need to hold constant the structural characteristics and amenities of the particular house, although such controls can also be handled statistically, as will be shown below.) In addition, the existence of the line will increase the supply of housing with certain time and cost characteristics of getting Downtown and hence provide a possible dampening effect on the capitalization argument.

But most importantly the model dispels the claims of <u>equal</u>
bands of impact surround a facility (not necessarily a transport facility) with limited access. Clearly the areas of impact are not of equal
width about the line as has been alluded to in the literature. [7] The
impact area of the line spreads wider and wider as distance from the
center city increases.

STATISTICAL ANALYSIS OF TRANSPORTATION IMPACT ON RESIDENTIAL SALES PRICES

Residential property values are determined by many factors.
Thus even if we are interested in only a single element, such as
changes in the access to the CBD, a general model must be formulated.
One classification of the types of variables that might be included in
such a model is as follows:

1. <u>Site Elements</u>, describing the individual property, for example,
   lot size, characteristics of the structure, topography, etc.
2. <u>Neighborhood Variables</u>, describing the areas immediately
   adjacent to the property. Possible variables might include
   measures of neighborhood homogeneity, the occupational
   status of the residents, the age distribution of the residents,
   the predominant types of families (for example, retired, extended), the general physical condition of local housing, the
   degree of crowding and the degree to which other land uses
   intrude on the area.
3. <u>Regional Variables</u>, measuring such items as access to
   shopping, jobs, and schools; local tax rates, and the quality
   of local services.
4. <u>Historical or Externally Imposed Factors</u>, such as zoning
   limitations, financial markets, special prestige areas, etc.
5. <u>Impact Variables</u>, measuring the expected impact (derived
   above) of the speed line.

The basic hypothesis of this section is that property values are
a function of the five types of variables listed above. The specific
variables chosen to represent the effect of each of these factors are
limited in two general ways: (1) their accuracy as measures of the
phenomena they are intended to represent; and (2) their availability,
cost of procurement, and detail.

The data base consisted of approximately 24,000 residential
property transactions between July 1964 and June 1971 in Camden and

FIGURE 16.4

The Lindenwold and Woodbury Corridors and the High-Speed Line

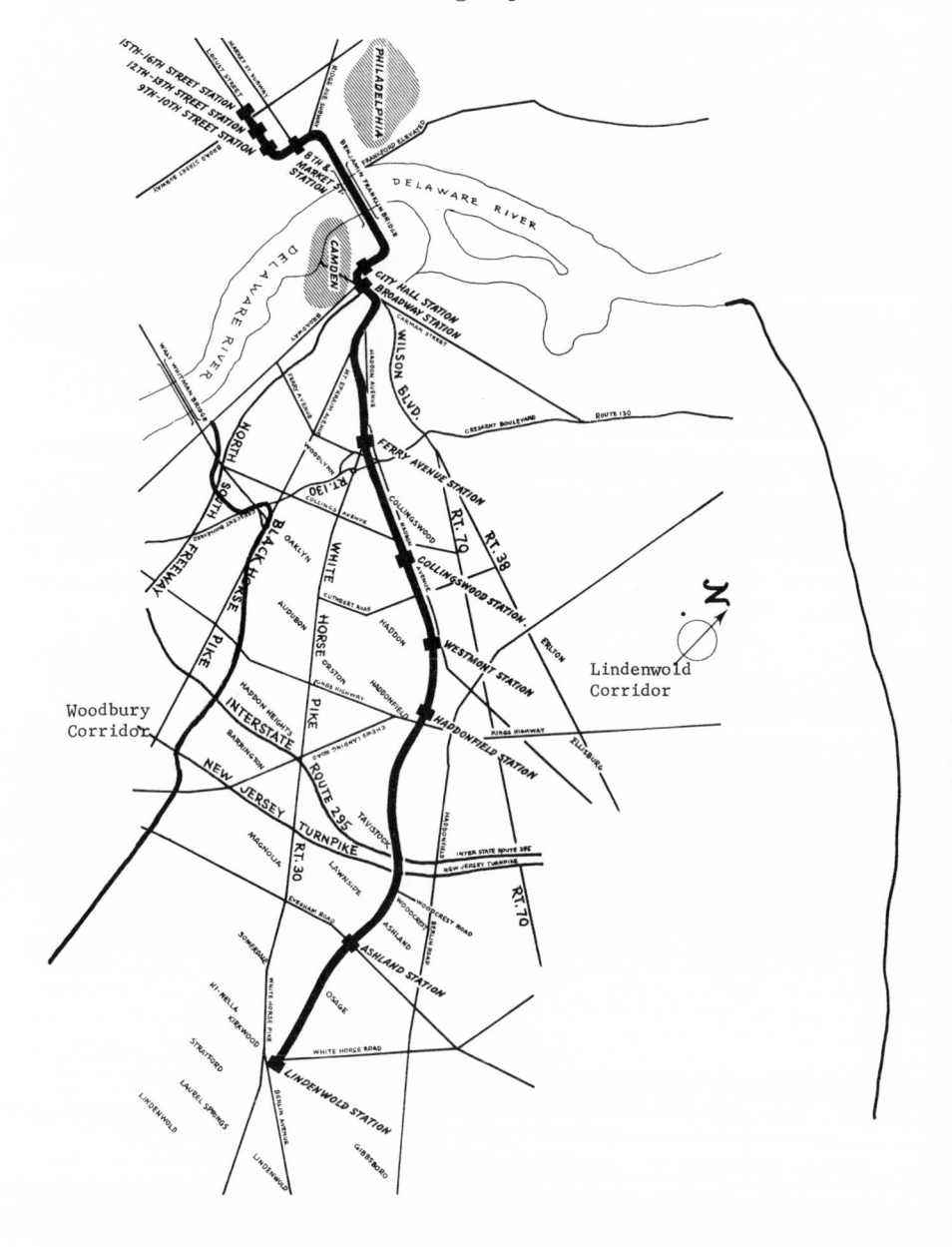

and Gloucester counties in South Jersey (exclusive of Camden City).*
These data were screened so as to include only those sales that represented valid market transactions. The analysis was restricted to
residential (at time of sale) suburban properties to ensure a large,
yet relatively homogeneous, sample. Data were also obtained from
the local county tax assessor's records and the U.S. census. Residential property values were assumed to be a function of the following
factors: individual property descriptors (site elements), a neighborhood effect, an inflation effect, a general location influence (that is,
position on urban rent gradient), and of course any influence of the
High-Speed Line.

In an attempt to parallel the approach of the more traditional
experimental sciences, a control corridor was chosen as a base for
comparison with the High-Speed Line impact corridor. The control
corridor selected was centered on an abandoned commuter rail line
passing through Woodbury, N.J. (see Figure 16.4).

The travel savings model described above predicts that the size
of the impact a property should receive is proportional to the travel
savings afforded by the transportation improvement. Thus, using the
control corridor methodology, we want to compare properties in the
impact corridor with properties in the control corridor that are similar in as many ways as possible, including the level of saving. For
example, we want to compare a house in the impact corridor with an
estimated daily travel savings of two dollars with a similar house in
the control corridor that would provide a daily travel saving of two
dollars if there were a rapid transit line there also. Because the
control corridor is also in South Jersey, it is still within the region
of positive travel savings because of the High-Speed Line. Thus, the
savings for the hypothetical rapid transit line in the control corridor
must be calculated as net of the actual savings due to the High-Speed
Line.

Estimates of travel savings were made for each of the approximately 350 census block groups in the study area. Block groups are
small enough so that any variation in savings within the block group
is substantially less than the savings at its centroid. The daily savings available to residents of block group i who travel to Center City
Philadelphia are thus:

$$S_i = 2CD_i + N - 2(CD_{ij} + F_j)$$

---

*These data were kindly provided by Robert Johnston, chief,
Sales Ratio Section of the Local Property Tax Bureau of the New
Jersey Division of Taxation.

where C is a cost per mile factor that includes vehicle maintenance costs as well as travel time costs;[*] D_i is the distance from the centroid of block group i to the bridge to Center City Philadelphia; N is bridge tolls, parking costs, and other access costs in Philadelphia; D_{ij} is the distance to the minimum cost station on the High-Speed Line; and F_j is the fare from this station to Center City.

RESULTS

One of the regression models from the impact analysis is presented in Table 16.1. The dependent variable is sales price in thousands of dollars and there are 24,082 observations. Most of the variables are entered as (0,1) dummy variables since they represent either/or conditions (a house is brick or it is not). Of course to ensure nonsingularity of the covariance matrix, one variable from each set of dummy variables has been omitted. The land use categories refer to those properties that changed land use from residential sometime after their sale. The 11 different neighborhood types were defined using AID analysis[†] with 1970 census data. Details of this process as well as complete definitions of the other variables may be found in R. R. Mudge and D. E. Boyle et al.[8]

The savings variables entered in the regression are the net daily savings for each corridor. However, both savings variables are set equal to zero for sales before July 1968 since the High-Speed Line was not in operation then. Since the time between July 1968 and the actual opening of the line in February 1969 is a time of possible anticipation of the line by the real estate market, a positive savings level is valid for this time. After July 1968 the savings value depends on which corridor the sale is in and its location within that corridor. The effect of the savings variables is entered additively to conform with the basic hypothesis that the values of residential properties near new transportation facilities increase because of the capitalization of the stream of travel savings available to them.

The regression coefficient for the impact corridor savings can be interpreted as an addition to the sales price of $149 for each dollar

---

[*] A value of travel time of $2.60 an hour was used because this value appeared to give the best fit between the observed station market areas and those predicted by the savings theory.

[†] AID (Automatic Interaction Detection) is a multivariate technique based on a sequential application of analysis of variance to divide a set of observations into mutually exclusive groups that form a hierarchial tree.

TABLE 16.1

Multiple Regression on Residential Sales Price

Independent Variable	Regression Coefficient	t-statistic	Independent Variable	Regression Coefficient	t-statistic
Log lot size	3.967	50.94	Neighborhoods (9 omitted)		
Number of stories (two-stories omitted)			11	17.129	66.63
1 story	-0.908	10.14	10	10.375	69.58
1½ stories	-0.504	3.43	13	8.248	47.56
2½ stories	-0.894	3.36	19	5.994	27.41
3 stories	0.829	1.59**	12	2.512	16.87
over 3 stories	-0.840	0.32**	18	1.545	5.90
Building description (frame omitted)			14	1.746	14.51
brick	3.190	24.06	17	-0.579	3.07
concrete block	0.209	0.81**	21	-1.811	9.09
metal	1.929	2.91	20	-3.896	21.86
reinforced concrete	-0.839	0.25**	Location and impact		
stucco	0.929	4.21	distance to City Hall	-0.280	19.60
stone	-2.380	2.09*	impact corridor savings	0.149	1.96*
number of garages	1.339	20.02	control corridor savings	-0.246	1.72**
Land use in 1971 (residential omitted)			Inflation (1968 omitted)		
public property	-2.861	2.27*	1965	-1.374	9.21
commercial	16.346	14.06	1966	-1.039	7.34
industrial	15.516	4.57	1967	-0.593	4.19
apartment	3.835	7.84	1969	1.317	6.50
vacant	0.378	1.11**	1970	2.974	14.66
			1971	5.295	25.88

*Not significant at .01 level.
**Not significant at .05 level.

Note: constant = 6.737   R square = 0.526
standard error = 5.894   F-ratio for regression = 722.15

Source: Compiled by the authors.

of savings. This is the increased value of the property as a result of
the High-Speed Line. The savings values range from about $0.50 to
over $3.00. Of course, the savings function is a relative amount and
not an attempt to measure precisely the actual travel savings.

Although the coefficient for the control corridor savings is not
significant, the negative sign is in accord with theories of transportation impact that believe the impact is really a transfer from one
part of the region to another. Such a transfer seems to be indicated
here, though whether there is a complete balance is hard to say.
Because the savings function used for the control corridor is net of
High-Speed Corridor savings, the mean level of savings in the control
corridor is significantly less than the corresponding mean for the
High-Speed Corridor. It should be noted that the basic conclusions
drawn from this regression were confirmed by more detailed analysis
of specific neighborhoods and housing types.

The travel savings model is a flexible tool. It was easily applied
to a more detailed analysis of the timing of the impact as well as to
different submarkets of the real estate market. An alternative model
based on shifts over time in rent gradients with respect to the High-
Speed Line (a linear model in contrast to the hyperbolic form of the
savings model) was also tested. The results showed that, for at least
this data set, the travel savings model performed with greater consistency.

SUMMARY

A very simple model has been developed that delineates the areas
that receive given levels of transport cost savings as a result of a
transportation improvement. It is hypothesized that a portion of these
savings will be capitalized into the value of residential property.
Statistical tests that control for other determinants of housing value,
for example, neighborhood characteristics, physical characteristics
of the property, etc., have indeed shown a positive impact on property
values, attributable to the presence of transport cost savings made
available by the High-Speed Line.

Refining and testing of the models developed herein continues.

NOTES

1. H. Mohring, "Land Values and the Measurement of Highway
Benefits," Journal of Political Economy 79 (1961): 236-49; H. Mohring

and M. Harwitz, Highway Benefits: An Analytical Framework (Evanston, Ill.: Northwestern University Press, 1962).

2. A. A. Walters, The Economics of Road User Charges (Baltimore: Johns Hopkins University Press, 1969).

3. F. A. Fetter, "The Economic Law of Market Areas," Quarterly Journal of Economics 38 (1924): 520-29; C. D. Hyson and W. P. Hyson, "The Economic Law of Market Areas," Quarterly Journal of Economics 64 (1950): 319-25.

4. See J. Lansing and G. Hendricks, "How People Perceive the Cost of the Journey to Work," paper presented at the 46th Annual Meeting of the Highway Research Board, Washington, D.C., 1967.

5. Ibid.

6. D. E. Boyce, W. B. Allen, R. R. Mudge, P. B. Slater, and A. M. Isserman, Impact of Rapid Transit on Suburban Residential Property Values and Land Development, Report to the Office of the Secretary, U.S. Department of Transportation, November 1972; D. E. Boyce, W. B. Allen, G. Desfor, and R. Zuker, Impact of Distance and Parking Availability on Suburban Rapid Transit Choice, Report to the Office of the Secretary, U.S. Department of Transportation, November 1972.

7. See the description by Mohring and Harwitz, op. cit., p. 140.

8. R. R. Mudge, The Impact of Transportation Savings on Suburban Residential Property Values, Ph.D. dissertation, University of Pennsylvania, 1972; Boyce, Allen, Mudge, Slater, and Isserman, op. cit.

URBAN ENVIRONMENTAL GOALS: HOW CAN THEY BE ACHIEVED IN RAPID TRANSIT STATION PLANNING?
Robert J. Harmon

The post-World War II era of rapid transit station planning began in the United States in the early 1960s in the San Francisco Bay Area. During this period energetic public planning efforts were undertaken to maximize the positive development influence of this type of public transportation investment. This was especially true in the designated renewal areas (for example, Market Street in San Francisco) and in the City of Berkeley. Innovative development coordination tools such as the C-5 zoning ordinance[1] were developed to guide and shape future urban development projects that would occur at or near the major transit stations. However, there are also many counter examples where relatively unplanned development has taken place.

In the decade during which the BART (Bay Area Rapid Transit) system has been under construction three other major metropolitan areas—Washington, D.C., Atlanta, and Miami—have approved major public bond issues to construct regional rapid transit systems.[2] Several other cities including Chicago, Philadelphia, Boston, and New York have undertaken significant improvements or major extensions to their present systems. Relatively little documented information was available to these cities regarding how future regional development could be coordinated with their type of major transportation system improvement.

Questions soon arose regarding the importance of the coordination of transit station development in relation to these regions' future functioning and the quality of the urban environment that would be available to future residents. Little was understood about the scale and the likely land use mix of transit station development that would be generated by the "fixed guideway" elements of the system. More was needed to be known about the development cycle that would be experienced by the region's corridor communities. The development influence of the design and scale of the public support facilities and distribution systems serving the individual stations needed to be documented. The corridor development strategies that would maximize the mobility gains and potential infrastructure cost efficiencies generated by the system needed to be identified. Some desired a determination of which public design and development controls or incentives had proven most effective in achieving high-quality cluster development. Others were concerned with the economic and social justification for this type of development. Most were interested in whether short-term urban development impact within station areas could be accurately predicated. Finally, new legislation required a closer examination of all these issues. In response to increased public concern for environmental improvement, recently enacted federal and state legislation now requires or authorizes transportation agencies to look beyond traditional engineering and cost parameters when planning transportation projects. For example, Section 102(2)(c) of the National Environmental Policy Act of 1969 (Public Law 91-190, January 1, 1970) has the effect of requiring that a transit agency developing a facility, which is financed with federal funds, prepare a statement assessing the impact of that facility on its surrounding environment. The State of New York enacted a specific, action-oriented law that expressly authorized the New York State Department of Transportation to participate in and expend funds for joint development planning beyond the immediate physical context of a given transportation facility. It authorizes "cooperative action by the New York State Department of Transportation, federal and other state governmental agencies and municipalities . . . to prepare surveys, studies and plans, including the negotiating of reservation easements, related to the development or adjustment of land uses which are affected by the construction of (transportation) facilities."[3]

These were the types of technical questions that were being raised by the regional planning and development agencies of the country. In order to provide answers to these questions and generally to create a better understanding of the station development process, the Department of Transportation and the Department of Housing and Urban Development in 1971 undertook a national case study analysis of rapid transit station development. The project was awarded to the League of Cities (Conference of Mayors). The author served as senior economist on the League of Cities project team. In this chapter I will examine several of the findings of that study. The basic purpose of the chapter is to explain what was learned about (1) the nature of the rapid transit station development cycle, (2) the role and importance of public policy, and (3) the type of planning procedure that could best achieve the urban environmental goals applicable to this type of community development project. To do this the chapter discusses the station development process in different urban settings, analyzes the fiscal tools available to influence development, and discusses various long-term impacts of station development.

THE STATION DEVELOPMENT PROCESS

To understand the transit station development process as it is occurring under existing public development policies, six transit station development sites were chosen for detailed analysis. Three of these—the 38th Street Station (Dan Ryan Line in Chicago), the Haddonfield Station (Lindenwold Line in the Philadelphia area), and the Walnut Creek Station (BART System in the San Francisco area)—represent a laissez-faire market situation. The second set—which includes the Eglinton Station (Yonge Street Line in Toronto), the Market Street Stations (BART System), and the 12th and G Street Station (the WMATA System in Washington, D.C.)—represent positive examples of public development coordination authority. Through these six cases pertinent observations will be made regarding the level and direction of influence exerted on joint-use transit station development by (1) the urban setting, (2) the system design, (3) the station design, and (4) the public implementation policy under both types of public sector involvement and coordination.

Laissez-Faire Market Situation

At first the form of transit corridor development was primarily determined by a laissez-faire market situation. An accurate or historical account of transit station development should reflect this relationship. Therefore, a major portion of the individual transit corridor and stations that were selected represent national models in a historical context of weak or poorly coordinated public sector urban development policy. The public policy program of these individual stations and the resulting urban development impact are described in Tables 17.1, 17.2, and 17.3.

TABLE 17.1

38th Street Station, Dan Ryan Line, Chicago

Type of corridor:	Fixed guideway station located in the median of the Dan Ryan Expressway
National planning parallels:	I-95, I-66, and Century Freeway Corridor
Type station design:	Above grade, pedestrian loading
Distribution service:	Feeder bus, taxi, and pedestrian escalators
Years in operation:	Five
Existing land use:	Institutional (educational), medium density residential, and commercial (stadium and related retail); no undeveloped parcels
Major system users:	Students and staff of the Illinois Institute Technology, patrons of the Comiskey baseball stadium, CBD commuters of a lower-income residential community
Coordination of public development policies:	Minimal, limited to transit station structure
Identifiable impact Land use:	1. Stimulus to expansion of Illinois Institute of Technology, especially evening class facilities and program 2. Improved employment opportunity access for major public housing potential residents 3. Increased attendance at White Sox games
Summary:	Enhancement of existing uses but no marked land use conversion
Mobility:	1. Ten minutes plus time savings to CBD commuters 2. Increased security and automobile parking operating savings for students and faculty of the Illinois Institute of Technology 3. Significant travel time, parking, and automobile operating cost saving to Comiskey park patrons
Summary:	Generated high levels of peak and off-peak users. User costs savings and mobility gains were provided for a wide variety of residents, students, and sports fans.

Source: Compiled by the authors.

TABLE 17.2

Haddonfield Station, Lindenwold Line, Lindenwold, N.J.

Type of corridor:	Fixed guideway system built in existing rail right of way, below grade operation
National planning parallels:	Livermore, Calif.; Decatur, Ga. (typical bedroom community station)
Type station design:	Grade level, park, and kiss and ride station.
Distribution service:	Limited park and ride facilities, Dial-a-bus, taxi
Years in operation:	Three
Existing land use:	Predominantly middle- to upper-income residential; limited strip commercial
Major system users:	Philadelphia commuters
Development policies:	Limited to station facility construction and distribution system planning
Identifiable impact: Land use:	1. Documented $500 net incremental increase in residential value over a three-year period attributable to the Lindenwold Line (standard based on a $30,000 valued single-family home) 2. No identifiable land use conversion 3. Increase potential for long-term growth in the downtown Philadelphia office market
Summary:	The lack of latent land use market demand and availability of undeveloped land has and will continue to restrict future land use impact
Mobility:	1. Primarily improved commuting travel option to downtown Philadelphia; travel time gains approach the ten-minute level 2. Diverted motorists save bridge toll fees, parking, and other operating costs of their automobiles

Source: Compiled by the authors.

TABLE 17.3

Walnut Creek Station, BART System, Walnut Creek, Calif.

Type of corridor:	Fixed guideway system constructed in new right of way, above grade operation
National planning parallels:	Prince George's, Fulton, Fairfax Counties
Type station design:	Elevated, suburban park, and ride station
Distribution service:	Feeder bus, taxi, and major park and ride facilities
Years in operation:	None, operation scheduled to begin in 1973
Existing land use:	Community shopping center, commercial; office and medium- to high-income residential; undeveloped property is available (30 separate owners)
Major system users:	San Francisco commuters and limited reverse commuters to Walnut Creek area
Coordination of development policies:	None, public planning limited to station facility and line-haul operation
Identifiable impact: Land use:	1. Dillingham has developed a major 10-story office complex adjacent to the 21-acre station site 2. High level of land speculation on remaining parcels but no definite development plans have been announced
Summary:	Because of excellent market image, available undeveloped land and marked access gains, high development interest is in evidence. Long-term impact will include residential gains from upper-income development in Marin County and the City of San Francisco
Mobility:	Unmeasured to date, it is expected to provide major commuter time savings, parking, bridge tolls, and operating cost savings for San Francisco commuters

Source: Compiled by the authors.

Observations of the Laissez-Faire Market Station

From the prototypical examples described above, several relevant observations can be made. These are summarized by category of development impetus below:

Urban Setting

1. In the short term, high-density redevelopment will only be undertaken by the private sector in high-prestige communities.
2. Significant land conversion normally occurs only where undeveloped land is available.
3. A significant regional shift in employment center access among competing residential markets also can be a major impetus for development, such as in Walnut Creek.

System Design

1. The highest development impact will be generated by fixed guideway systems built in new right of way, especially the first stages of a new regional system, such as in San Francisco and Washington, D.C.
2. Systems built in existing rail right of way invariably transverse established single-family communities or older industrial centers. Therefore, these systems normally generate new development only at the furthermost suburban stations where significant acreages of undeveloped land are available.
3. Elevated systems, especially those built in freeway medians, generate the least amount of short-term development impact within close proximity of the stations.

Station Design

1. Pedestrian access to ground-based transportation or to adjacent facilities is a key determinant of multiuse development potentials.
2. The design of the parking facility can be an impetus to incremental multiuse development or a major deterrent to any development.

Public Policy

1. Without major coordination of station parking, circulation, and distribution facility development, the long-term functional value of the system will be diminished.

2. Coordination of land use development within close proximity to stations will improve, not inhibit, the investment opportunities for the private sector. It is only in this manner that the true economic and social benefits of the system can be realized while ensuring that new growth will enhance the existing urban environment.

If the opportunities for joint-use transit station development are to increase, an enhanced and better understanding must be developed regarding the potential effectiveness of existing or proposed public development controls and incentives.

Consequently, the next section includes an analysis of the historical influence of varying levels of public sector coordination of the joint-use transit station development process.

Coordinated Public/Private Station Area Development

In a few isolated instances, major efforts have been successfully undertaken to coordinate public facility and private commercial development within close proximity to new transit stations. These have primarily been in prestige market areas—for example, downtown San Francisco, New York—or in urban renewal districts where adequate public planning tools and resources are available.

Certain European examples also are relevant. However, the institutional framework of North American cities obviously is more applicable to the focus of this study. Therefore, to compare the effectiveness of various levels of direct application of public development coordination authority, the following station sites have been selected as representative examples: Toronto, Canada (Eglinton Station), the Market Street Station of San Francisco (BART), and the 12th and G street station in Washington, D.C. (WMATA). These are described in Tables 17.4, 17.5, and 17.6.

Observations of Coordinated Public Development

From the prototypical examples described above, several relevant observations can be made. These are summarized by category of development impetus.

Urban Setting

1. Coordinated public/private development planning is most effective during period of major regional growth especially commercial office and retail expansion.

TABLE 17.4

Transit Authority Headquarters Station,
Yonge Street Line, Toronto

Type of corridor:	Close in subway corridor of a new fixed guideway system
National planning parallels:	San Francisco (Market Street), Washington, D.C. (Connecticut Avenue) and Peachtree Street (Atlanta)
Type station design:	Underground, urban, fixed guideway station
Distribution service:	Feeder bus, taxi
Years in operation:	Fourteen
Former land use:	Primarily single-family residential and commercial office along distribution arterial
Major users:	Downtown Toronto commuters
Coordination of public development policies:	Complete coordination of private commercial development and station design
Identifiable impact: Land use:	1. Dramatic linear city type development was induced by this type of implementation program 2. Development included several high-rise apartment towers and an air-rights development of a major office building above the station
Summary:	This is a classic example of a well-planned public transit station implementation program during a period of major commercial growth
Mobility:	Major time saving, automobile parking, and operating cost savings for downtown Toronto commuters

Source: Compiled by the authors.

TABLE 17.5

Market Street Station, BART System, San Francisco

<u>Corridor type</u>:	Downtown subway corridor of a new fixed guideway system
<u>National planning parallels</u>:	Washington, D.C. (Connecticut Avenue) and Atlanta (Peachtree Street)
<u>Type station design</u>:	Downtown, subway station
<u>Distribution service</u>:	Trolley, feeder bus, taxi, pedestrian escalators
<u>Years in operation</u>:	None; to be operational in late 1972
<u>Existing land uses</u>:	High-density office, regional and special retail, high-rise residential.
<u>Major users</u>:	Downtown San Francisco commuters, convention delegates, tourists, and shoppers
<u>Coordination of development policies</u>:	Included the development of impact zoning (C-3) and tax increment financing
<u>Identifiable impact</u>: Land use:	1. Clustering of a majority of all new office structures built in San Francisco since 1965.
	2. Dillingham building (45 stories) and the Fox Plaza Tower are closest to the station
	3. Significant increase in multiuse development project planning.
Summary:	The decision to build the BART system preceded a period of a dramatic office and hotel growth in San Francisco. The C-3 zoning code brought about a significant number of pedestrian and other public area amenities. In addition, the density bonuses provided stimulus to clustering of new construction within walking distance of new stations
Mobility:	Significant reduction in travel time, automobile parking, bridge tolls, and operating costs of San Francisco commuters

<u>Source</u>: Compiled by the authors.

TABLE 17.6

12th & G Street Station, WMATA Line, Washington, D.C.

Type of corridor:	Downtown subway corridor of a new fixed guideway system
National planning parallels:	San Francisco (Market Street) and Atlanta (Peachtree Street)
Type station design:	Downtown subway station
Distribution service:	Minibus, taxi, and feeder bus
Years in operation:	None; scheduled to be operational in 1974-75
Existing land uses:	Regional and speciality retail (older, declining operations) commercial office low- to medium-density residential (older, lower income).
Major users:	Downtown Washington commuters, tourists, and downtown Washington community to suburban job center
Coordination of development policies:	Major use of renewal redevelopment powers
Identifiable impact: Land use:	1. F Street Mall development served by minibus operation 2. Major renewal development plans now at the disposition appraisal stage of implementation 3. Major private development plans underway by Calvary Baptist Church 4. Tentative, downtown convention center development plans
Summary:	Full use of public sector renewal development authority will maximize development potential of this station site. Lack of citywide ability to fully coordinate all development complicates this current planning and implementation program
Mobility:	1. The combination of minibus service if modified to link this area to South Capital Hill area and the fixed guideway system will dramatically improve circulation in this portion of the city 2. Downtown Washington commuters and suburban commuters of the District will enjoy substantial job mobility gain and reduce automobile operating and costs

Source: Compiled by the authors.

2. Significant private speculation and early commercial development should be controlled and paced in accordance with a long-term
corridor and regional development policies that will most benefit all
sectors of the community.

3. Careful attention should be given to the induced transportation needs that will be generated by urban development located at or
near station.

Station Design

1. For those stations with high short-term urban development
potential, advanced acquisition for a people mover/minibus right of
way should be carefully considered.

2. Incremental public amenities and open space areas should
be identified during the station construction period, so the location
and size of parking facilities should be designed to optimize high
quality in short-term and long-term urban development.

Public Policy

1. Overall public policy implementation should be minimally
coordinated at the corridor level.

2. The investment planning of public floor facilities and related
parking and circulation systems should be carefully integrated into
any private incentive development program.

3. In the short term, tax abatement incentives and major density
bonuses should be strongly considered.

Coordination can make a difference. The Walnut Creek BART
station, developed in a laissez-faire environment, shows a lack of
provision for pedestrian access, and poor physical integration of a
shopping center complex, an office building complex, and the station
itself. In contrast, development around the Eglinton Station in Toronto
has been well coordinated and does not exhibit these or similar problems. Its dramatic "linear city" development is a classic urban
development event in North American urbanization. More importantly,
single-family residential neighborhoods have been kept intact. The
potential garden apartment demand was captured by high-rise development that required no commuting automobile.

FISCAL IMPLEMENTATION TOOLS

In order to address the question of how fiscal tools, such as
tax abatement, development corporations, and density bonuses can be

TABLE 17.7

Current Station Development Cycle

I. ANTICIPATED ACTIONS
  A. Final Determination of Station Location
    1. Accelerated land speculation
    2. Splintered development plans
    3. Petitions for major rezoning
  B. Planning and Development of Public Support Facilities
    1. Minimum required access roads provided or improved
    2. Parking facilities developed to meet minimum system needs
    3. Distribution system limited to feeder bus service

II. IMMEDIATE DEVELOPMENT RESPONSE
  A. Initiation of Station Construction
    1. Random construction of most feasible high density commercial facilities
    2. Construction of excessive private, commercial parking facilities
    3. Minimum allowance for pedestrian access, internal center circulation

III. LONG-TERM DEVELOPMENT RESPONSE
  A. Long-Term Corridor and Station Site Development
    1. At choice sites, continued, uncoordinated clustering of commercial development
    2. Increased circulation congestion
    3. Limited walk-and-ride patronage growth
    4. Specialized retail facility development limited to underground passenger walkways
    5. Modified linear corridor development patterns
    6. Minimal capital and maintenance cost savings in public facility and infrastructure investments

Source: Compiled by the authors.

applied effectively to improve the quality and to increase the scale
and number of joint-use transit developments, it is important to document the development cycle as it now occurs, without regular and
proper application of these implementation instruments.

In examining the transit station development process under
laissez-faire market conditions we developed a current station development cycle, presented in outline form in Table 17.7. As shown in
this table, there are several critical areas where the public planning
and implementation process needs reinforcement or modification.
Foremost among these is to have adequate preplanning for the urban
development that would occur in transit corridors. More specific
information should be developed, both prior to and during the system
construction period. This would allow the public sector to be prepared
to (1) evaluate private developer proposals, (2) develop, at least on
a corridor level, a systematic and compatible development program,
and (3) evaluate the public investment decisions for expanded or improved public support systems.

Existing Planning Procedure

Under the existing approach, available public implementation
tools are not utilized to reinforce an overall site, corridor, or regional development plan. Existing and available public tools for
carrying out planning should be evaluated to determine the appropriate
urban and sociopolitical setting and stage of development planning to
which they can be applied most effectively. In conjunction with this
effort, improvements must be made in the efficiency and predictability
of the public sector zoning, support system planning, and design control procedures. If this were done, more competent developers would
consider undertaking large-scale joint-use development projects. The
antiquated and disjointed approach now in use is one of the major
deterrents to joint-use development.

The outline in Table 17.8 represents the basic planning information that should be generated by the corridor impact and implementation evaluation effort undertaken during the final route selection
process.

If the topics listed in Table 17.8 were covered during the final
route selection process, a proper foundation would be available for
the subsequent corridor development planning. During the course
of this project—a basic transit station—corridor development planning
program was developed.

TABLE 17.8

Final Route Selection Information

Understanding of the Community
1. Describe how the dominant life-style in the corridor communities will be altered by the physical, socioeconomic, and environmental impact of the facility.
2. Show how the ethnic-cultural, family bonds of the community might be affected. Separate analysis should be made of homogeneous, transitional, and new communities.
3. Describe the nature of the urban environment now, and in 1975, 1980, and 1990. Evaluate it in terms of livability, acceptability (with or without facility).

Understanding the Nature of the Service Provided
1. List those served by the facility—by trip type, time of day, and level of improvement over present and alternate future options.
2. Discuss the alternatives to serving each of the transportation needs and indicate service levels to be provided by proposed facility.
3. Indicate whether these markets are served by new or existing facilities.
4. Describe the dominant transportation problems that cannot be resolved and indicate how critical these are relative to the negative urban environmental impacts.

Responsiveness and Acceptability of the Implementation Program
1. Show how the implementation plan responds to the Environmental Protection Act, the Federal-Aid Highway Act, and the Urban Mass Transportation Assistance Act.
   - a. Indicate whether there is minimum compliance or maximum utilization.
   - b. List the special public program packages that have been developed.
   - c. Indicate whether they include other local programs.
2. On a community basis, discuss how the local resident community needs and requirements would be met by the proposed implementation program. Indicate whether these are intended to be committed by contract or by other legal means.
3. Indicate the level of reliance or involvement required by local community and local public agencies.
4. Describe the community impact during the construction period, such as disruption costs, and show how the implementation program would compensate for the various impacts.
5. Indicate whether the same corridor communities would be affected by other public works projects in the same time period or in the near future.
6. Evaluate the importance of the unmitigated impacts in relation to the long-term gain for the affected neighborhoods, communities, or the region.
7. Indicate whether the recommended implementation program effectively integrates critical aspects of local, corridor, and regional development planning.
8. Describe the joint-use transit development opportunities that would be created by the system over the short and long term.

Source: Compiled by the authors.

Available Fiscal Implementation Tools

Prior to the formulation of an optimum station development procedure it is necessary that a more detailed examination be made of the available fiscal implementation tools. Table 17.9 shows the functional uses, national precedents, strengths, and weaknesses of the major types of fiscal implementation tools.

In the future, the public planning and implementation procedure must be capable of mitigating negative environmental impacts and overcoming obstacles to achieving a desirable scale and composition of coordinated urban development.

Initial Stage of Transit Development Planning

Intensified land speculation and inadequate development of public support systems are the major problems created during the initial stage of the transit station development process. As described in Table 17.1, the application of a freeze on rezoning and infrastructure improvement decisions for all parcels within the immediate area of an approved station site would minimize the land speculation at station sites with high short-term development potential. This could be undertaken by the local planning board.

A secondary benefit of applying a freeze would be to allow a reasonable period for the local community and regional planners to determine the short- and long-term public development goals for the area. Once the individual station area's development potential was placed in perspective with that of the overall corridor development potential, the local planning officials would be better prepared to evaluate private development plans and to decide what level of public support systems would be required.

Our basic position in this discussion is that the corridor development corporation is the ultimate and ideal implementation vehicle. Of course, if the corridor communities were to establish a corridor development corporation, these results could be achieved throughout the region. Because of parochial taxing interests and other political and legal obstacles, its use probably will be curtailed sharply during the next five years. Therefore, the implementation procedure developed in this analysis is intended to be a surrogate for a corridor development corporation, without risking the delays that appear to be inherent in its adoption.

TABLE 17.9

Public Sector Implementation Tools—A Comparative Evaluation

Fiscal/Implementation Tools	Primary Purpose	Precedent	Strengths	Weaknesses
Development Incentives				
1. Tax Abatement	Encourage development within proximity of the station.	Rosslyn, Va., Crystal City, Va., St. Louis, Mo.	Effective magnet and shaper of development	May give away excessive amounts of locally accrued tax base.
2. Density Bonus Allowances	Encourage provision for increased public amenities, especially those for the pedestrian.	C-3 zoning San Francisco, site zoning Toronto, density bonus program New York site.	Effective incentive to encourage density and open space amenities.	Effectiveness is minimized if city has weak new market demand. If market demand is weak, it can have minimal short-term attractiveness.
3. Clearinghouse	Guarantee major developments meeting guidelines as top priority - minimum red tape.	Chicago, selected large scale renewal projects.	Guarantee the large-scale project developer that he can minimize red tape delay, if he follows locally established guidelines.	Requires top executive with full authority to act.
4. Powers of Eminent Domain	Through public agency or deferred authority, complete necessary land assembly.	All renewal area station development projects, St. Louis Chapter 353.	Effective in land assembly, either by public agency or designated developer.	Must be used selectively or large portions of city remain vacant and undeveloped.
Development Controls				
1. Zoning or Utility Approval Freeze	Minimizes early land speculation.	Loudoun County, Va., Palo Alto, California, Boulder, Colorado	Minimize speculation costs to final developer. Increased potential for additional public amenities.	Must be adhered to with no exceptions. If special case rulings occur, becomes unmanageable.
2. Tax Increment Financing of Public Amenities	Guarantee availability of basic - public amenities.	Inner Loop, Chicago	Guarantee desired public amenities will be constructed.	Should only be based on small percent of incremental taxes. Fully based tax increment programs has not proved to be financially soluble.
3. Corridor Development Corporation	Guide and direct total corridor development	Legislative authority in several states -- no fully implemented example exists on a local level.	Strongest tool available to coordinate all public and private corridor development.	Lack of available qualified executive directors. Minimal track record experience in the United States.
4. Streamline Design and Development Approval Procedure	Reward quality developers who respond to design and development guidelines.	This is becoming standard practice. Must be combined with clearinghouse operations.	Organize public planning corporation for large-scale project efforts.	Weak tool without other support. At a minimum, needs to be combined with clearinghouse operation.

Source: Compiled by the authors and Development Research Associates.

Short- and Long-Term Infrastructure Requirements

Prior to the initial screening of private development plans, the public sector should establish the long-term infrastructure needs of each individual station area. Particular attention should be given to the design of the distribution transportation service and the parking facility that would be required to serve the transit patrons. Alternative design concepts should be considered to accommodate an adequate pedestrian circulation system. In addition, the public parking facility designs should offer the maximum opportunity for combined use by private or institutional activities that ultimately might be located within the station impact area. At this stage of development planning the public financing alternatives to support the total support system should be evaluated.

Public Financing Decisions

At the outset the share of the total costs expected to be financed by the public sector should be clearly established. Such decisions can be reevaluated during the detailed review of the private development projects. However, a basic policy regarding this matter should be established before that stage of decision making.

The remaining portion of the costs can be apportioned directly to the developable acreage within the project area. If any of the major incremental infrastructure requirements are an integral part of long-term regional needs, this should be taken into consideration. Depending upon the scale of short-term development activity that is expected, tax increment financing should be evaluated at least as a means to finance amenities, such as a mall or other open space areas, that the developer normally would not provide. Based on recent national experience, only a portion of the anticipated tax revenues, over and above those needed for projected basic public services, should be dedicated to revenue bond financing of these amenity facilities.

If the public sector's development implementation program successfully minimized land speculation and land assembly costs, it might be more realistic to secure these amenities through a density bonus negotiation. In either case these decisions should be considered at an early stage in the planning.

Public Sector Involvement in Land Assembly

Certainly in special instances where a station is located within a designated renewal area, full use of the public power to assemble land should be planned. This should be managed through re-use disposition and initial site planning.

In other cases, where major public interests are served by encouraging re-use development, a special application of the local eminent domain powers could be undertaken. Under current legislation in the State of Missouri, the local municipality can declare an area blighted and, after competitive bidding, transfer its power of eminent domain to a selected private developer. Other tax abatement incentives also are included in this current program. It may not be necessary to consider this type of approach, but the public development goals are almost impossible to achieve if private development plans are formulated on an individual parcel or small parcel basis. As a basic policy, direct incentives for a minimum acreage development site should be included in the master planning, zoning, and development ordinance.

Site Plan Approval Procedure and Design Control

Several major metropolitan areas have adopted a comprehensive master planning site approval procedure. Some of the most successful examples are those in use by Arlington and Rosslyn, Virginia. These programs have facilitated the implementation of adequate public support systems and design controls, while adding some measure of predictability to the project requirements and calendar time required for public sector approvals. In conjunction with the adoption of this type of program, a special executive administrator should be hired to assist in the development of major joint-use projects.

LONG-TERM REGIONAL ENVIRONMENTAL/ECONOMIC BENEFITS OF MAJOR JOINT-USE TRANSIT STATION DEVELOPMENT

One of the basic principles of urban planning is that the distribution and intensity of land use should be coordinated and balanced with a transportation system that will accommodate the movement of

people and goods within the community or region. The transportation
system can be utilized as a principal tool in developing proper land-
use patterns, thus allowing land-use planning and transportation
planning to reinforce one another. An effective regional policy to
integrate land-use development planning and transportation planning
will intensify rapid transit's catalyst effect upon the distribution of
future land-use developments.

Future policy decisions concerning land-use developments within
the major metropolitan areas will significantly affect the future role
of transit in regional and community development. If future development is encouraged in proposed transit corridors and service areas,
especially to concentrate major joint-use and to minimize strip commercial development and urban sprawl, transit will accommodate an
increasing amount of the total travel demand. In addition, the long-
term impact on regional development patterns will create the potential
for millions of dollars of savings in utilities, city services, and highways.

Utility Cost Savings

In the majority of metropolitan areas the major trunk line
utility distribution systems were designed with excess capacity. [4]
Therefore, to the degree that the coordinated development of a regional
rapid transit system encourages joint-use development in built-up
areas and activity centers within high-utility capacities, there is a
potential to reduce the incremental costs required to provide these
services for new residents and commercial development.

The public development policies that would best support transit
development also would encourage more orderly suburban growth.
This further reduces the potential need to construct additional utility
distribution systems, such as gas, water, and sewer mains, and
electric and telephone lines, to serve the region's future population
and employment.

All three of the new regional rapid transit systems—Atlanta,
Washington, D.C., and the Bay Area—are being built in metropolitan
areas that are expected to gain at least 2 million residents by the
year 1990. This represents an estimated incremental capital investment in utilities in excess of $3 billion. [5]

Based on the documented urban development impact of the
existing regional rapid transit systems in North America, it would
be reasonable to expect that a well-coordinated regional transit development program could generate 4-5 percent overall utility capital cost

savings.[6] On this basis a well-defined corridor joint-use development program could mean a minimum utility cost savings of $120 million to $150 million.[7]

City Service Cost Savings

The correlation between changes in urban density and the per capita costs of governmental services has been documented in national and regional case studies.[8] The major categories of city service influenced by density changes are public works, public safety, and general services. In the 20 largest metropolitan areas these three city service categories represented in 1970 a per capita public expenditure of about $70.[9] A basic time series regression analysis would determine the elasticity of each of these city service categories in the individual metropolitan area.

Based on the documented case studies of other operating regional transit systems and evaluations of coordinated regional urban development programs, city service cost savings should range from 1-2 percent overall.[10] In the San Francisco Bay Area, Atlanta, and Washington, D.C. this would amount to $3 million or $4 million in annual costs savings.

In the later stages of regional transit development this potential impact increases on a cumulative basis. The city service and utility cost savings potential are among the most significant regional benefits attributable to the implementation of a regional rapid transit system. Yet without major corridor scale joint-use development implementation, few of these potentials will be realized.

Short- and Long-Term Community Benefits

Within an individual community, large-scale joint-use development can (1) provide the catalyst to upgrading the overall character of urban development, (2) substantially increase the local tax base and the capture of commercial trade by existing establishments, and (3) improve the efficiency and functionability of larger facilities, such as hospitals and convention centers.

All these potential benefits are important, but the economic development benefits are of particular interest to the public transportation planners. The inherent nature of the induced development impact frequently will generate the potential for windfall profits, accruing

primarily to speculators. Thus the fiscal benefits of the public investment in the transportation system are lost from the public interest
viewpoint. These profits could be captured to offset the original system costs, to guarantee the provision for desired public amenities, or
to finance incremental public support systems.

Two approaches could be taken to capture these profits. Tax
increment financing could be utilized to pay for additional support
systems or to provide desirable public amenities. An alternative way
to recapture these benefits is to establish either a benefit district or
corridor development corporation to acquire existing station area
properties at fair market value. Under the public vehicle, lease-
back right of these properties or land sale profits could accrue to the
public sector. This general approach has been applied successfully
in the Chicago Loop, San Francisco, and Toronto. It is hoped that
with a more thorough understanding of the transit station development
process and better fiscal implementation, our nation's urban environmental goals may be achieved.

NOTES

1. See San Francisco Market Street Renewal Implementation
Plan, prepared by Development Research Associates (economic sub-
consultant), 1965.

2. Bond issues were passed in 1968, Washington, D.C.; 1971,
Atlanta; and 1972, Miami.

3. See McKinney's Consolidated Laws of New York, Annotated,
Chapter 61 (a) Section 14 (b) (1970).

4. American Gas Association Technical Regional Development
Commission, "Study of Utility Cost Savings Related to Coordinated
Regional Development," 1970.

5. Walter Isard, and Robert Coughlin, "Municipal Costs and
Revenues Resulting from Community Growth," American Institute
of Planners Journal 22 (1956): 239.

6. John Robert Meyer, John F. Kain, and Martin Wohl, The
Urban Transportation Problem (Cambridge, Mass.: Harvard University Press, 1965); Development Research Associates, Case Study of
the Urban Impact of the Operating Transit Systems of North America
(Washington: DRA, 1972).

7. See Robert J. Harmon and Michael Russell, "Historical
Case Study Applications of the Benefit Statement of the Metropolitan
Chicago Transit System," Governor's Task Force on Transportation
(Springfield, Ill.: Illinois Department of Transportation, 1973).

8. Harvey E. Brazer, "City Expenditure in the U.S.," occasional paper 66 (New York: National Bureau of Economic Research, 1959); Robert J. Harmon and Richard Recht, Open Space and the Urban Growth Process (Berkeley: University of California Institute for Real Estate and Urban Economics, 1969).

9. U.S. Bureau of the Census, City Government Finances, 1970-71 (Washington: U.S. Government Printing Office, 1972).

10. American Gas Association Technical Regional Development Commission, op. cit.

Joseph A. Bosco

Since I do not come from an urban planning background, or from
the "model building business," I will discuss the chapters in Part VI
from the perspective of the four years during which I served as special
assistant to Secretary John A. Volpe at the Department of Transportation.

Both of the chapters in Part VI involved relatively complex
analyses of the benefits resulting from a transit system in terms of
cost and time trade-offs as the individual traveler makes choices
between driving his automobile and riding the transit system. The
same kind of analysis obviously must be made for the alternative
transportation facility—the highway project—before it is constructed,
with appropriate rational comparisons made by the public officials
as to whether either or both facilities will best meet the transportation
needs of the area.

Unfortunately, state and local officials today do not have the
ability to make that kind of realistic choice under existing funding
mechanisms:

1. The source of money for highway construction is the separate
and still untouchable highway trust fund, while public transportation
projects are paid out of the general funds through the Urban Mass
Transportation Administration program.

2. The former is assured funding, while the latter must be
appropriated each year in competition with all the other demands on
the general fund.

3. The amounts of money available are disproportionately
heavy in favor of highway construction (at the federal level alone,
$5 billion to $1 billion).

4. The highway money goes to each of the states on an allocated
formula basis, while the cities or other local public authorities must
apply specifically—and found to be qualified for—UMTA grants.

So, I agree with Robert Harmon's excellent point that the single
most important change to be made in urban transportation is the
mechanism by which transportation programs are funded. This situation may be improving. The Congress is considering legislation to
permit urban areas some degree of flexibility in how they spend a
limited part of the money from the trust fund—for more highways or

possibly bus or rail transportation. The congressional decision—especially if it is in favor of increased funding flexibility—will have the most significant impact on transportation in the cities since the creation of the highway trust fund in 1956.

The relative economic costs of different transportation facilities, as examined through these models, have been discussed in terms of the "psychic" costs in terms of air pollution, congestion, noise, etc. But many of these social, esthetic, and other environmental factors also have very real economic costs, both for individuals and for society as a whole, though they may not be precisely measurable.

1. The economic costs to the individual, of course, include purchase of the automobile, insurance, registration, fuel, maintenance, repairs, parking, tolls, tickets, etc.

2. There are also economic costs to the community in the consumption of valuable urban land for the rights of way, parking lots, gasoline service stations, repair garages, etc., and in the subsidized services provided for automobile transportation and paid from general taxes—not the highway trust fund—such as the use of professional police to direct automobile traffic.

3. Then there are the real, but not really perceived, costs to both the individual and the public resulting from the energy crisis. Even under the best of circumstances, transportation consumes 25 percent of the nation's petroleum supplies each year and automobile transportation takes more than 75 percent of that share. This highly inefficient use of energy is virtually forced on commuters by the lack of efficient and reliable public transportation.

4. Urban congestion, noise, and pollution are not simply esthetic problems; there are definite economic costs involved in the deterioration of quality of urban life, including health and medical consequences of poisoned air, increased cleaning and maintenance costs for homes, clothing, and machinery, and of course the economic costs of efforts to reduce auto emissions to acceptable levels.

These are just some of the real economic as well as social, esthetic, and environmental trade-offs that federal, state, and local planners and managers will have to make in choosing their transportation systems from now on.

Finally, a comment on the value of models to the actual decision-making process in government. I agree with the view discussed by Sydney Robertson that mathematical models have gotten too complicated, too unwieldly, too unrelated to the practical problems of decision making at the state and local level to be really useful or relevant. But let me respectfully disagree with the view that models are not used enough at the local and state government levels. From my experience they are used too much at the federal level. Let me explain that statement: All the chapters in this volume that have presented models have been very carful and responsible in stating the premises, assumptions, and even biases of the authors. Thus readers can judge for themselves some of the limitations of the models.

Unfortunately, what often happens in actual practice as a model is mentioned in one report or study or briefing session after another, and gets cited by a series of officials, is that the assumptions and premises get dropped out of the conversation. Then, what started out as an artificial but useful method, a helpful tool, gets presented and becomes accepted as <u>objective fact,</u> or to use Lowdon Wingo's term, the "truth" that the social scientists have to offer the politicians. This can have a very definite impact on the kinds of decisions made by federal officials—cabinet officers and administrators—on questions of policy, program levels, legislative initiatives, etc. For example, on the question of whether flexibility in the highway trust fund ought to be pursued as a legislative program, an argument was made on the basis of some relatively narrow surveys that people won't ride transit even if it's available.

The model can be a useful and necessary tool, so long as it's honestly recognized as only that—a somewhat artificial and limited device among many other factors to be considered.

Frankly, I'd like to see the model builders come up with, either on a national or metropolitan scale, a model of a truly integrated, multimodal national transportation system. Such a system should have minimal duplication or redundancy, with each transportation mode doing the thing it does best—for example, aviation handling most transoceanic and transcontinental passenger travel; rail for long-haul freight; bus, commuter rail, and personal rapid-transit systems ("people-movers") for intraurban and suburban trips. Private automobiles could be used for recreational and other necessary noncommuter purposes, and so on. Such a model might be compared to the actual situation in this country (and increasingly elsewhere), as interstate highways are being built alongside existing railroad lines, while everyone wonders whatever happened to the railroads.

JOEL BERGSMAN was Program Chairman of the symposium of which this volume is a product. He is a member of the Senior Research Staff of The Urban Institute in Washington, D. C., where his major responsibility is research on urban economic development. His current interests are in urban and regional economics, both in the United States and in developing countries. In the past he has taught economics at Berkeley, done research in Brazil, and worked as an economist in the policy planning office of the Agency for International Development. His publications include many articles on the above topics as well as a book on industrialization and trade policy in Brazil.

HOWARD L. WIENER served as Chairman of the 1973 Washington Operations Research Council Symposium on Urban Growth and Development. He is presently employed by the Naval Research Laboratory in Washington, D. C. where he conducts analyses in support of Navy programs. Among the problem areas in which he has worked are planning within the research and development process, cost-benefit analyses of proposed Naval systems, and statistical problems related to the validation of Monte Carlo simulation of operating systems. He was previously employed by the Naval Ordnance Laboratory and by the Operations Evaluation Group of the Center for Naval Analyses. He served as a WORC Trustee during the period 1973-75.

FRANK L. ADELMAN earned his Ph. D. in Physics from the University of California, Berkeley, and has held positions as a physicist in the Lawrence Radiation Laboratory of the University of California at Berkeley and at Livermore, the Institute for Defense Analyses in Washington, D. C., and the Illinois Institute of Technology Research Institute. He is currently Senior Scientist at Systems Planning Corporation in Virginia. He has written extensively on physics and systems analysis.

IRMA ADELMAN earned her Ph. D. in Economics at the University of California, Berkeley. She has taught at Berkeley, Stanford, Johns Hopkins, and Northwestern. She is currently Professor of Economics at the University of Maryland, Consultant to the IBRD and the ILO, and member of the Social Science Assembly of the National Academy of Sciences. She has written many articles on econometrics, operations research, economic development, and economic planning, and has also written several books on the last two subjects.

W. BRUCE ALLEN is an Associate Professor of Regional
Science and Transportation at the University of Pennsylvania. He
received a Ph.D. in Economics from Northwestern University. He
has worked for the Northeast Corridor Transportation Project in the
U.S. Departments of Commerce and Transportation and for the Office
of the Secretary, U.S. Department of Transportation. He has contributed articles to such journals as Traffic Quarterly and Journal of
Transport Economics and Policy.

STANLEY M. ALTMAN received his Ph.D. in Systems Science
from the Polytechnic Institute of Brooklyn. He served as Assistant
Professor of Electrical Engineering at the City College of New York
from 1966 to 1968 and as Assistant Professor of Electrical Engineering
at Princeton University from 1968 to 1970. In 1970 he joined the
Urban Science and Engineering Program at the State University of
New York at Stony Brook as Associate Professor of Engineering. He
is presently at the Fund for the City of New York where he is serving
as the Director of the Project on Improving Government Productivity.
Project Scorecard is part of this project. He has written on transportation systems, computer-based information systems, and design of
digital systems.

JOSEPH A. BOSCO, a graduate of Harvard Law School, served
as a law clerk to the Chief Justice and Associate Justices of the
Massachusetts Superior Court until February 1967. He was then
appointed assistant legal counsel to Governor John A. Volpe of
Massachusetts. He came to Washington when Mr. Volpe was appointed
U.S. Secretary of Transportation, serving for four years as his
special assistant. He is now practicing law in Washington. In 1972
President Nixon appointed Mr. Bosco to membership on the National
Highway Safety Advisory Committee of the Department of Transpor-
tation.

MARTIN W. BROSSMAN received his B.S. in Engineering from
Lehigh University and M.S. in Engineering Physics from Penn State
University and has undertaken additional graduate work in mathematics
and operations research. He taught at Penn State, was an Engineering
Physicist for the Naval Research Laboratory, directed an Operations
Research Division at Research Analysis Corporation, and was a
principal of Planning Research Corporation (PRC) and a Vice President of PRC's management consulting subsidiary, H.B. Maynard &
Company. He is currently a Consultant to the Environmental Protection Agency on environmental management. Mr. Brossman has authored more than 40 major reports in the fields of operations

research/management science, program planning and evaluation, environmental management, etc.

STEVEN J. CARROLL received his Ph.D. degree in Economics from Johns Hopkins University. He was an Instructor at Illinois Institute of Technology during the academic years 1962 through 1964 and a research assistant at the Johns Hopkins University from 1965 to 1966. Prior to joining the RAND Corporation in 1968, where he is currently project leader of a RAND study on the demand for higher education sponsored by the National Science Foundation and co-project leader of a RAND study of school district expenditure behavior, he was employed by Jack Faucett Associates as an economist.

CARL F. CHRIST received a Ph.D. in Economics from the University of Chicago. He is presently Professor of Political Economy at the Johns Hopkins University. He has served as Chairman, Universities-National Bureau Committee for Economics Research, as a member of the Board of Editors of the American Economic Review, and as a member of the Maryland Governor's Council of Economic Advisers. He has written articles on econometrics and monetary and fiscal influences.

JOSEPH F. COATES received an M.S. in Chemistry from Pennsylvania State University. He is presently a Program Manager in the Office of Exploratory Research and Problem Assessment, National Science Foundation. His professional training is in organic chemistry, a career he pursued for ten years in the chemistry of petroleum derivatives and surface-active agents. Prior to joining NSF he was a senior staff member of the Institute of Defense Analyses. He is also an Adjunct Professor at the American University in Washington, D.C.

FRANK DE LEEUW is a senior fellow at The Urban Institute. He received a Ph.D. in Economics from Harvard University. He has contributed articles to such journals as Journal of Finance and American Economic Review.

DENIS P. DOYLE received an M.A. degree in Political Theory from the University of California at Berkeley. He has worked on Capitol Hill for a member of Congress, for several committees of the California State Legislature, for the Education Development Corporation, and for the Office of Economic Opportunity. He is currently an Assistant Director of the National Institute of Education. Mr. Doyle has published articles in Change Magazine, the Los Angeles

Times, the New Republic, and others. He is currently a contributing editor of the California Journal.

LEE S. FRIEDMAN is an Assistant Professor of Economics, Graduate School of Public Policy, University of California, Berkeley. He received his Ph.D. in Economics from Yale University. From October 1972 through June 1973 he was a Lecturer and Postdoctoral Research Fellow at the Institution for Social and Policy Studies and Department of Economics, Yale University. He serves as Special Consultant for Economic Studies to the Vera Institute of Justice and is responsible for the economic evaluation of the Supported Work experiment.

J. ROYCE GINN majored in the transportation areas of Civil Engineering at Rice and Texas A&M Universities and received his Ph.D. in the same field at Northwestern University. His experience in engineering systems includes working for the Transport Research Project, Harvard University; as an engineer with Alan M. Voorhees and Associates; as a Research Assistant, Texas Transportation Institute, Texas A&M University; and as an Engineering Assistant, Texas Highway Department. He has been with the Urban Economics Studies group at the National Bureau of Economic Research since 1968, where the major undertaking has been the creation of a large-scale urban simulation model.

CLIFFORD W. GRAVES was appointed Deputy Associate Director for Evaluation and Program Implementation in the Office of Management and Budget (OMB) in January 1974, by Director Roy Ash. He came to OMB from the Department of Housing and Urban Development, where he had been Deputy Assistant Secretary for Community Planning and Development. He received HUD's Distinguished Service Award in 1972. Mr. Graves was awarded a Master of City Planning degree from the University of California at Berkeley. He has served on the faculties of the University of California and Howard University and on the Board of Governors of the American Institute of Planners in 1971-72.

ROBERT J. HARMON is a founding principal of the Institute of Transportation and Regional Planning. He was previously responsible nationally for the coordination of fiscal legislative implementation of Development Research Associates' regional transportation and infrastructure planning programs. He is currently the senior economist on the Regional Planning Committee of the National Transportation Research Board. A graduate of the University of Southern

California, he received his bachelor's degree in Economics and completed graduate studies in Public Administration and Econometrics.

FREDERICK O'R. HAYES received an M.A. in Political Economy and Government from Harvard University. He served in the Bureau of the Budget, executive office of the president, for ten years and as Director of the Budget of the City of New York for four years. He has held a number of executive and administrative posts and is presently Visiting Professor in Urban and Policy Sciences at the State University of New York at Stony Brook. He also serves as consultant on urban and governmental problems to the Battelle Memorial Institute, the RAND Corporation, and the U.S. Office of Education. He has contributed to several books on the subjects of public systems, public workers and unions, and program budgeting.

IRVING HOCH received a Ph.D. in Economics from the University of Chicago. He served on the staff of the Chicago Area Transportation Study (CATS) from 1956 through 1959; was on the faculty of the Department of Agricultural Economics, University of California, Berkeley, from 1959 to 1967; and has been a member of the Regional and Urban Studies group at Resources for the Future since 1967. He has written an economic forecasting report for CATS and has contributed to such journals as Econometrica and Journal of Urban Economics.

JOHN HOLAHAN received his Ph.D. in Economics at Georgetown University. He is currently employed at The Urban Institute where he is engaged in analysis of the Medicaid Program and National Health Insurance Proposals. He has published a number of articles on the economics of crime, drugs, and health-care financing.

PETER W. HOUSE is the Assistant Director of the Washington Environmental Research Center in the Office of Research and Development, U.S. Environmental Protection Agency. He is the former President of the Environmetrics, Inc. He has also been associated with the Economic Research Service (ERS) of the U.S. Department of Agriculture and with the Washington Center for Metropolitan Studies. He completed his doctoral work in the field of suburban growth and development at Cornell University. Dr. House has recently published two books on urban models.

WILLIAM A. JOHNSON received a Ph.D. in Economics from Harvard University. He has served as senior economist with the RAND Corporation and with the Council of Economic Advisers. He is presently Assistant Administrator for Policy Analysis and

Evaluation, Federal Energy Office. Dr. Johnson has written several books in fields of urban problems (welfare rights, job change and mobility) and U.S. and international economic development.

RONALD KIRBY received his doctorate in applied mathematics from the University of Adelaide in South Australia. He worked briefly in Adelaide for the consulting firm of P.G. Pak-Poy and Associates, and then joined Planning Research Corporation (PRC) of McLean, Virginia. He currently works at The Urban Institute where he has been concerned with low-capital options for improving urban mobility.

SUE A. MARSHALL is a member of the housing group at The Urban Institute. She received a B.A. in Economics from Antioch College and is currently doing graduate work in Economics at the University of Maryland. She has coauthored several articles about public housing and home ownership.

ROBERT MCGILLIVRAY received his Ph.D. in Economics from the University of California at Berkeley. His experience prior to completion of that program includes two years of teaching micro-economic theory and transportation economics at Berkeley, working as a transportation analyst for a year for the Bay Area Transportation Study Commission, and several relatively shorter terms of research experience at Kaiser Engineers, the University of California, and the RAND Corporation. At the Stanford Research Institute he worked for two years as a transportation economist. In 1971 he joined The Urban Institute's Transportation Studies Program.

RICHARD R. MUDGE is a Project Leader and member of the research staff at the New York City Rand Institute. He received a Ph.D. in Regional Science from the University of Pennsylvania. He has authored or coauthored a number of articles on transportation.

DONALD G. MURRAY JR. received an M.S.W. from the Howard University School of Social Work. His present position is Community Involvement Director in the African American Studies Program at the University of Maryland, Baltimore County. In this position he set up community-based educational field work centers and has taught three community development courses. Prior to this employment he served as Associate Director of Friendship House Association, Inc., in Washington, D.C.

PAUL M. NAWROCKI was Project Manager of Project Scorecard during its first nine months of operation. Previous to that he was

343

a transportation planner for the New York City Bureau of the Budget. Mr. Nawrocki is currently with American Management Systems, Inc. of Arlington, Virginia, where he is working on a study of Environmental Costs of Energy Production for the EPA. He received both a Bachelor of Engineering and a Master of Science (Program for Urban and Policy Sciences) from the State University of New York at Stony Brook.

WILLIAM POLLAK received a Ph.D. in Economics from Princeton University. He taught courses in microeconomic theory, government regulation, and urban economics at Grinnell College before coming to The Urban Institute, where his work has involved analyses of metropolitan fiscal problems and the economics of public fire protection. More recently he has been concerned with problems of the elderly and the development of long-term health care policy. He has written articles on fire protection and care of the elderly.

FRANCIS J. POTTER received a Master of Science degree in Statistics at Florida State University. His primary work at the Program for Urban and Policy Sciences was to develop the experimental design and the data processing system and to analyze the data returning from Project Scorecard. Presently he has a position with Bristol-Myers Products in Hillside, N.J.

MARTIN J. REDDING holds a Ph.D. from Northwestern University. His employment background includes experience in industry and university training. He is currently responsible for undertaking and managing research on a wide variety of areas including quality of life, environmental planning, land use, methodology development for land use decision making and environmental management, and aesthetics.

SYDNEY R. ROBERTSON is presently Chief of the Management Systems Section, Maryland Department of Transportation, where he is responsible for the planning and management of data processing and management support resources in support of operating programs of a multimodel department of transportation. He has also worked for the Federal Highway Administration in the Urban Planning Division, where he was Chief, Land Use Planning Branch. He is author of a number of papers in the areas of transportation planning, travel demand, information systems, data base development, travel models, and land use models. He holds a B.S.C.E. from the University of California at Berkeley and has undertaken graduate studies in urban and regional planning at Northwestern University.

THOMAS C. SCHELLING received a Ph.D. from Harvard University. Since 1958 he has been Professor of Economics at Harvard and he is also a faculty member of Harvard's Center for International Affairs and the John Fitzgerald Kennedy School of Government. His professional work has ranged from economist with the U.S. government, in Copenhagen, Paris, and Washington, D.C., Associate Professor and Professor of Economics at Yale University, with the RAND Corporation in Santa Monica, California, with the Institute for Strategic Studies in London, to being a consultant to the Departments of State and Defense, to the Arms Control and Disarmament Agency, the RAND Corporation, the Institute for Defense Analyses, and other national security research organizations. He is the author or coauthor of books on arms control, international economics, and income behavior.

STUART O. SCHWEITZER received his Ph.D. in Economics from the University of California at Berkeley. From 1966 to 1969 he was Assistant Professor of Economics at Wayne State University, Detroit. Following that he joined the research staff of The Urban Institute in Washington, working principally on studies of the labor market and inflation. In 1972 he joined the School of Medicine of Georgetown University as Associate Professor, where his teaching and research activities are in the area of the economics of health. His recent publications include a jointly authored book on the unemployment inflation dilemma, and articles on preventive health care.

DAVID R. SEIDMAN received his Ph.D. in Operations Research from Case Institute in 1963. He is presently Program manager, Urban Technology Program, Division of Social Systems and Human Resources, National Science Foundation. His previous positions include Chief, Systems Analysis Group, Office of Planning and Management, District of Columbia Government; Vice-President for Research, Technical Assistance Corporation, and Research Director, Special Staff, U.S. Conference of Mayors; Senior Health Analyst, Office of Assistant Secretary for Planning and Evaluation, HEW; and Director, Research and Methods Division, Delaware Valley Regional Planning Commission.

RAYMOND STRUYK received a Ph.D. in Economics from Washington University and is presently a member of the Housing Studies Group at The Urban Institute. He has contributed articles to Review of Economics and Statistics, Urban Studies, and Journal of Human Resources.

WALTER D. VELONA received a degree in Civil Engineering from the City College of New York. He has held a number of positions with federal agencies, including the Civil Aeronautics Administration, the Office of the Chief of Engineers, the Department of Commerce, and, at present, the Department of Transportation. He has contributed to studies on transportation, technological forecasts, and airport systems capacity.

ROBERT K. YIN is a research psychologist with the RAND Corporation and Assistant Professor (part-time) at the Department of Urban Studies and Planning, M.I.T. His major research interests are the delivery of public services to urban neighborhoods and citizen feedback to urban government, including the use of new technologies such as cable television. He has published articles in urban analysis journals, edited two books, and has recently completed a comprehensive assessment of the urban decentralization experience.

DENNIS R. YOUNG is currently a member of the faculty of the Program for Urban and Policy Sciences at the State University of New York at Stony Brook. Formerly he was a member of the senior research staff of The Urban Institute, where he developed and directed a project on the economic organization of public services. His principal research interest is in this area, including work in urban sanitation, day care, criminal justice, and education. Dr. Young received his Ph.D. in the Engineering-Economic Systems Department at Stanford University.

ENVIRONMENTAL POLICY: Concepts and
International Implications

> edited by Albert E. Utton
> and Daniel H. Henning

ENVIRONMENTAL POLITICS

> edited by Stuart S. Nagel

THE POLITICAL REALITIES OF URBAN PLANNING

> Don T. Allensworth

PUBLIC HOUSING AND URBAN RENEWAL:
An Analysis of Federal-Local Relations

> Richard D. Bingham

SOCIAL SCIENCE AND PUBLIC POLICY IN THE
UNITED STATES

> Irving Louis Horowitz and
> James Everett Katz

URBAN HOUSING IN THE UNITED STATES:
A Crisis of Achievements

> Charles J. Stokes and
> Ernest M. Fisher